D1617534

Europe: a Civilian Power?

Europe: a Civilian Power?

European Union, Global Governance, World Order

Mario Telò
Brussels Free University, ULB, Belgium

First published 2006 by
PALGRAVE MACMILLAN
Houndmills, Basingstoke, Hampshire RG21 6XS and
175 Fifth Avenue, New York, N.Y. 10010
Companies and representatives throughout the world

PALGRAVE MACMILLAN is the global academic imprint of the Palgrave
Macmillan division of St. Martin's Press, LLC and of Palgrave Macmillan Ltd.
Macmillan® is a registered trademark in the United States, United Kingdom
and other countries. Palgrave is a registered trademark in the European
Union and other countries.

ISBN-13: 978–1–4039–4921–9 hardback
ISBN-10: 1–4039–4921–2 hardback

This book is printed on paper suitable for recycling and made from fully
managed and sustained forest sources.

A catalogue record for this book is available from the British Library.

Library of Congress Cataloging-in-Publication Data
Telò, Mario.
Europe, a civilian power? : European Union, global governance, world order /
    Mario Telò.
        p.   cm.
    Includes bibliographical references and index.
    ISBN 1–4039–4921–2 (cloth)
    1. European Union countries—Foreign relations—21st century.   2. European
    Union.   3. World politics—1989-   4. Globalization.   5. International
    organization. 6. Regionalism.   I. Title.
    JZ1570.A5T45 2006
    327.1'7'09409051—dc22   2005051215

10   9   8   7   6   5   4   3   2   1
15   14   13   12   11   10   09   08   07   06

Printed and bound in Great Britain by
Antony Rowe Ltd, Chippenham and Eastbourne

Contents

List of Maps	viii
Maps	ix
Foreword and Acknowledgements	xii
List of Abbreviations	xvi

1 Civilian Power and International Relations: the EU and Multilateralism from the Twentieth to the Twenty-first Century   **1**

1.1	Long-term trends and epoch-making events in the development of the international identity of the EU as a civilian power	1
1.2	The rise and fall of the myth of 'global governance without government'	10
1.3	Empire and imperialism: misleading metaphors	12
1.4	The use and abuse of the concepts of 'hegemony' and 'hegemonic stability'	18
1.5	Towards a multipolar world? The limits of American power and the emergence of China	24
1.6	The new international anarchy: informal terrorism, failed states and WMD proliferation	35
1.7	Which multilateralism? Institutions and values in a transitional phase	39
1.8	The reality of the EU as an incipient, collective civilian power	50
1.9	Europe: a civilian power at a crossroads?	58
1.10	Reforming the multilateral system	64
1.11	The EU: the engine for a subsidiary multilateral system combining force and consensus	71
1.12	A new transatlantic partnership between equals?	74
1.13	Democratic legitimacy and accountability at regional and global levels	78

2 **States, New Regionalism and Interregional
    Cooperation in the Globalized World**   **106**

    2.1 State and regional integration   106
    2.2 From regionness to new regionalism: elements for
         historical periodization at a global scale and in Europe 109
    2.3 Globalization, states and regional organizations: three
         theoretical approaches   115
    2.4 Comparative analysis of the major regional
         organizations: economic, political and cultural factors 120
    2.5 Contributing to regional cooperation and
         integration theory   125
    2.6 US-centred regionalism and interregionalism: from
         NAFTA to FTAA   129
    2.7 Latin America and MERCOSUR. American and
         European interregional projects   131
    2.8 ASEAN between Japan, China and the United States.
         Interregional dialogue with the EU   135
    2.9 The SADC, ECOWAS and African regionalism: politics
         and economics   138
    2.10 A structural and multidimensional phenomenon of
         uncertain destiny   141
    2.11 The EU, new regionalism and democratization   143

3 **The Heart of European Integration: the
    Socio-economic Model between Convergence
    and National Diversities**   **152**

    3.1 The socio-economic dimension of civilian power   152
    3.2 The concept of solidarity in the great traditions of
         European thought: Christianity, liberalism and socialism 154
    3.3 A Europe of national Welfare States   157
    3.4 The European socio-economic model and the
         challenges of the neo-conservative revolution   162
    3.5 Reforming the European social model: national and
         European solutions   169
    3.6 The question of convergence: the 'Lisbon Strategy'
         and the 'Open Method of Coordination'   171
    3.7 Modernization policies for a European model of
         a knowledge society   174
    3.8 The Lisbon agenda implementation: achievements
         and shortcomings   177

3.9 The controversy surrounding supranational European
      democracy   179
3.10 The 'mixed government' of socio-economic
      modernization   181
3.11 The impact of the 'Lisbon Strategy' on the
      international role and identity of the EU: the case
      of research policy   182
3.12 From the reform of social governance to the
      strengthening of the legal basis of economic
      government and a social Europe?   186
3.13 The socio-economic model and European identity   189

**4 The Development of the European Union as an
   International Actor   198**

4.1 The growth of the EC/EU as a global economic actor   199
4.2 A non-teleological history: the vicissitudes of the CFSP
      and CSDP   201
4.3 The roots of the ambiguity of European power   207
4.4 The widening and deepening of the EU: the
      institutional variable   210
4.5 The EU and globalization, new regionalism and
      multilateralism: three scenarios   214
4.6 A civilian and political power: the third scenario   222
4.7 A structural foreign policy   227
4.8 The challenges of the next decade: Turkish membership
      and the EU's south-eastern border   232
4.9 The challenges of the next decade: transatlantic
      partnership and new multilateralism   237

**5 The Process of Treaty Reform: the International
   Dimension   252**

5.1 The constitutional process   252
5.2 The concepts of 'civilian power' and 'shared power'   254
5.3 The EU and global governance: beyond
      cosmopolitanism   261
5.4 A 'mixed government' for the European
      Union of the twenty-first century?   266

Index   278

List of Maps

1 Main regional organizations   ix
2 European Union: main interregional arrangements
  and strategic partnerships   x
3 Main interregional arrangements including the USA   xi

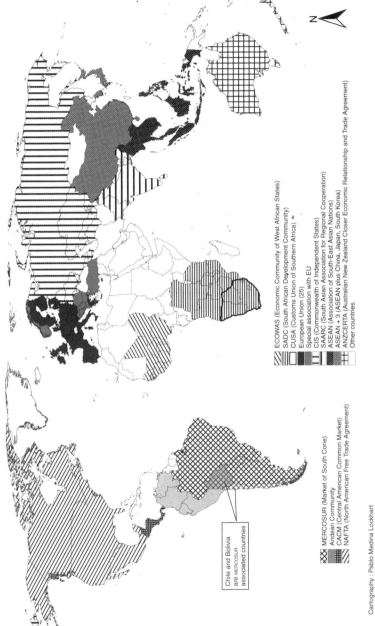

ECOWAS (Economic Community of West African States)
SADC (South African Development Community)
CUSA (Customs Union of Southern Africa)
European Union (25)
Special association with EU
CIS (Commonwealth of Independent States)
SAARC (South Asian Association for Regional Cooperation)
ASEAN (Association of South-East Asian Nations)
ASEAN + 3 (ASEAN plus China, Japan, South Korea)
ANZCERTA (Australian New Zealand Closer Economic Relationship and Trade Agreement)
Other countries

MERCOSUR (Market of South Cone)
Andean Community
CACM (Central American Common Market)
NAFTA (North American Free Trade Agreement)

Chile and Bolivia are MERCOSUR associated countries

Cartography : Pablo Medina Lockhart

Map 1   Main regional organizations

x

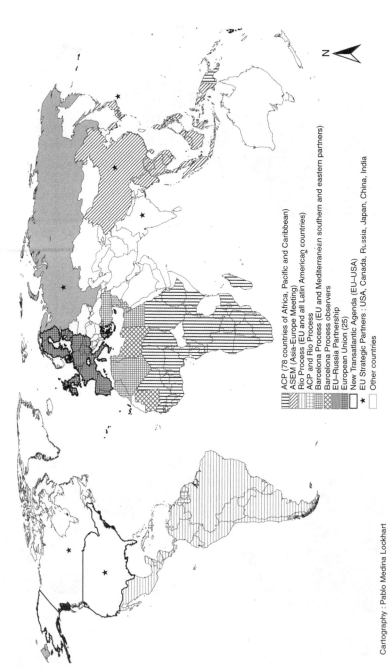

Cartography : Pablo Medina Lockhart

Map 2 European Union: main interregional arrangements and strategic partnerships

xi

APEC (Asia-Pacific Economic Cooperation)
FTAA (Free Trade Area of the Americas)
USA (New Transatlantic Agenda + FTAA + APEC)
New Transatlantic Agenda

Cartography : Pablo Medina Lockhart

Map 3 Main interregional arrangements including the USA

Foreword and Acknowledgements

This book presents the results of a long comparative research project on the EU's role in global governance and world order. My main aim is to provide a contribution to the emerging European vision of international relations which is consistent with our best traditions of political theory. By the concept of 'civilian power', contrary to normative understandings of Europe as a 'moral', 'civil' or 'fair' power, I seek to analyse the EU as it is today and as, despite its various contradictions and shortcomings, it is evolving and linking its internal and international dimensions. In 2005 the EU is a reasonably successful regional and global entity with more than 50 years' experience in fostering cooperation, democracy, prosperity and peace among an expanding number of member states. It influences its neighbours and plays an increasing interregional and global role within a multilateral framework.

When studying the place of the EU within the global system, I was convinced me that I should explore and verify a new, encompassing, appropriate concept of power. The concept of 'soft power', while providing a significant theoretical insight, is not sufficient to grasp the distinctive nature of either the EU or other emerging civilian actors within global governance. Its ambiguity is due to its structural complementarity to 'hard power', as a component of a classical state entity, of which the prime example is the US. Comparative analysis suggests that neither the EU polity nor its policies can be identified with those of a state in the making. This is even more so in the cases of other comparable regional groupings of states, in Latin America, Asia and Africa.

A book published in 2005 cannot avoid addressing the current main controversial question: is the EU civilian power emerging as a counterbalance within the 'pax americana'? This book provides a critical evaluation of the widespread description of the US as a 'hegemonic power' (or as an 'empire') and of multipolarist approaches. The epoch-making events of 1989–91 and September 11th 2001 have inevitably fostered multidisciplinary research which focuses on the distinctive regional and global roles of the EU and on its growing international identity. Beyond the short-term debate on the transatlantic rift, different geoeconomic and geopolitical interests and conflicting approaches to global governance continue to produce different views and policies regarding multilateralism and world order, on both sides of the Atlantic. Avoiding simplistic accounts, the book conducts an in-depth analysis of the current securitization of the global agenda, its impact on regional actors and the challenge it poses for the EU and civilian actors. The necessary external and internal conditions for the EU to further develop as a civilian and political actor are assessed and various scenarios are suggested.

In the five chapters which make up the book, I have combined my institutionalist approach with stimulating findings from the history of political ideas, constructivism and international political economy. I believe this methodological orientation to be the most suitable for the topics under examination, because it allows significant progress as far as two distinct, although interconnected, open research agendas are concerned.

1. It provides a solid account of the socio-economic and 'ideational' background of a new kind of power, helps us compare the EU with similar regional political groupings among neighbouring states and assess its influence within the globalized post-cold war world. We can thus analyse the dynamics of bottom-up regional co-operation in other continents and the way in which the EU supports the dissemination of its regionalist multilateral experience abroad, namely through interregional partnerships.

2. Even if not neglecting the role of states and other social actors I focus on regional and global institutions which appear to me to be the main variable, which makes the EU a distinctive actor, characterized by a political identity rich in external implications. What is interesting is that a regional entity aims at asserting universal values, precisely on the basis of its recent institutional experience: I refer to its identity marker constitutionalizing institutional framework, which balances intergovernmental coordination of national policies with supranational institutions. This framework also incorporates the memory of past tragedies, fostering human rights protection, the commitment to democratic governance and, of particular importance, the voluntary limiting of national sovereignty by member states. This leads to the question of to what extent does the EU model of governance contribute to the improvement of the efficiency and legitimacy of multilateral institutions? Which *longue durée* background could make of a regional grouping of states, due to its internal social history, international openness and democratic political culture, an actor providing not only solutions for multi-level global governance, but also ideas and policies for a multilateral world order? And, finally, is this complex political and institutional work in progress appropriate to cope with the new external threats and global challenges of the twenty-first century?

Acknowledgements

It would have been impossible to carry out for seven years the comparative and theoretical research, the first results of which are published in this book, on the EU's international role and identity without the support of several universities and research centres, the dialogue and cooperation I was fortunate enough to enjoy with EU institutions, the European Council, the EU Commission and the European Parliament, and the direct knowledge I acquired of the demands and expectations in other continents regarding the increasing role of the EU in global governance and world affairs. I would like firstly, therefore, to express my warm thanks to the various colleagues and institutes in Europe and the rest of the world for the many kind invitations I have received over the past seven years to present earlier drafts of this book and discuss its provisional findings with students and scholars.

I would like to express my deep gratitude to the following universities and centres in Europe: IEE-Free University Brussels (ULB) and EURAGG (network of studies on EU, regionalism and globalization, whose members are co-founders of the Network of Excellence GARNET, the sixth Framework Programme of the EU Commission (2005–9), coordinated by R. Higgott, University of Warwick), the Paris IEP (J.L. Quermonne), the Royal Institute of International Affairs, London (G. Joffé), the IEEI, Lisbon (A. De Vasconcelos), the CRIS, Bruges (in particular, Luk Van Langenhove and Mary Farrell), the PADRIGU, Gothenburg University (B. Hettne and F. Söderbaum), the Institute of European Studies, Geneva (N. Levrat), the Faculty of Philosophy in Zurich (F. Cheneval), the Berthelsmann, Genshagen, Ebert, and Neumann Stiftungen, the Association of International Studies (AIS, Manzanillo, Mexico, 1998), the panel members of the European Consortium for Political Research (ECPR) conferences in Canterbury (2001) and The Hague (2004). I discussed the first drafts of the book's chapters in many parts of Italy and would therefore like to thank: G. Antonelli (SDIC, University of Bologna) and C. Galli (University of Bologna and the Journal *Filosofia Politica*), S. Lucarelli, the Forum for the Problems of Peace and War and the Faculty of Political Science at the University of Florence, A.M. Lazzarino (and her colleagues at the University of Genoa), B. De Giovanni (Istituto Orientale, Naples), B. Henry and A. Loretoni (Istituto Superiore Sant'Anna, Pisa), D. Velo, M. Ferrera and L. Majocchi (University of Pavia, Centre of European Studies), the Department of History and Geography, Faculty of Education and Communication, University of Bari.

Outside Europe, I must thank the Republic Presidency and the UNDP, Brasilia, the FIESP, São Paolo; the University of Buenos Aires; the IEEM, Macau, China and the CASS, Beijing; the CES and G. Ross, Harvard, Cambridge, Boston, the Institute of Social Sciences, New Delhi (in particular G. Giri and A. Mathew), the Economic Universities of Hanoi and Ho Chi Minh in Vietnam and the following Japanese universities: Chuo (Prof. T. Furuki), Hitotsubashi (Prof. T. Kajita), Tokyo (Prof. Soiji), Shizuoka (Prof. Kokube) and International Christian (Prof. T. Ueta).

The following colleagues have been particularly helpful and generous with their support and critical insights at different times over the past decade: R. Seidelmann, F. Cerutti, J. Nagels, J. Weiler, J.L. Quermonne, M.J. Rodrigues, G. Therborn, A. Gamble, P. Magnette, E. Remacle, T. Meyer, A. Sbragia, S. Santander, J. Goetschy and G. Gozzi. I also have to mention the deep and productive dialogue I had with Norberto Bobbio in 1998 and 1999 and with Robert O. Keohane in 2004 and 2005.

I should also acknowledge the great amount I have learned in recent years as a consultant on the topics of this book to different European institutions: first the European Council Presidency in 2000, then the EU Commission (as director of the Jean Monnet Chairs Group, within the framework of the elaboration of the Commission *White Paper on EU Governance* between 2000 and 2001), the European Parliament ('Rasmussen Report', 2003) and finally, since 2002, as member of the Advisory Group for Social Sciences and Humanities in the European Research Area, EU Commission, DG Research, its workshops and international missions to China and Brazil.

This book has been possible thanks to the financial support of the ARC project 'Governance and Legitimacy in the EU' (IEE-ULB, 1998–2003) and the 'Francqui Prize', obtained by the IEE-ULB in 2000 as the top Belgian recognition of excellence for the best research on EU integration.

Naturally, I take full responsibility for the arguments presented in this book.

Even if the substantial changes provided for the English version make this a new book, a first version of this manuscript was published in Italian by Laterza in Rome in 2004. I thank them warmly. Sincere thanks are also due to the excellent maps specialist Pablo Medina Lockhart, ULB-IGEAT. Last, but not least, I would like to thank Duncan McDonnell, a PhD student in the Department of Politics at the University of York (England), for his excellent translation of the original Italian publication into English. I have since made significant additions and updates to the English text and ultimate responsibility for this final version is, of course, my own.

List of Abbreviations

ABM	Anti-Ballistic Missile Treaty
ACC	Arab Cooperation Council
ACM	Arab Common Market
ACP	Countries of Africa, Caribbean and Pacific (Convention including EU and 7 partners)
ALADI	Latin American Association for Development and Integration
AMU/UMA	Arab Maghreb Union (Libya, Tunisia, Morocco, Algeria)
Andean Community	includes Peru, Venezuela, Ecuador, Bolivia and Colombia
APEC	Asia-Pacific Economic Cooperation (including all American, Asian and Oceanian countries of the Pacific)
ARF	ASEAN Regional Forum (ASEAN plus USA, Japan, China, India, Australia and EU)
ASEAN	Association of South-East Asian Nations (including Indonesia, Philippines, Thailand, Malaysia, Singapore, Vietnam, Cambodia, Laos, Brunei, Myanmar)
ASEM	Asia Europe Meeting (including EU and East Asian countries)
AU	African Union
Barcelona Process (EMP)	Euro-Mediterranean partnership between all the countries of the South and North rims
BEPG	Broad Economic Policy Guidelines (ECT, art. 99)
CACM	Central American Common Market (including Central American countries)
CAFTA	Central America Free Trade Agreement (USA plus Central American countries)
CAO	Eastern African Community (Kenya, Tanzania and Uganda)
CAP	Common Agricultural Policy (EU)
CARICOM	Caribbean Community (including Caribbean countries)
CARIFA	Caribbean International Free Trade Association
CCASG	Council of Cooperation between Arab States of the Gulf

CEEAC	Economic Community of Central African States
CEEC	central and eastern European countries (in French: PECO)
CEPAL	UN Economic Commission for Latin America
CFSP	Common Foreign and Security Policy (EU)
CIS	Commonwealth of Independent States (Russia and former USSR member states except the Baltic States)
Coreper	Committee of Permanent Representatives (part of the EU Council of Ministers)
CSCE	Conference for Security and Cooperation in Europe (or 'Helsinki Process')
CUSA	Customs Union of Southern Africa (customs union among 5 SADC members)
DG	General Directorate (European Commission)
EC	European Community
ECFA	Economic Commission for Africa (UN)
ECHO	European Community Humanitarian Aid Office (European Commission)
ECOWAS	Economic Community of West African States (in French: CEDEAO)
ECSC	European Coal and Steel Community
EFTA	European Free Trade Association (including Norway, Switzerland, Iceland and Liechtenstein)
EMU	European Economic and Monetary Union
EP	European Parliament
EPC	European Political Cooperation
ESA	European Space Agency
ESDP	European Security and Defence Policy
ETUC	European Trade Unions Confederation
EU	European Union
FP	Framework Programme of EU Commission Research
FTA	free trade area
FTAA	Free Trade Area of the Americas (including all the American countries except Cuba)
FTCE	Free Trade Agreement of Central Europe (or Visegrad Group)
G7	Group of 7 most industrialized countries (US, UK, France, Germany, Italy, Japan and Canada)
G8	G7 and Russia
GATT	General Agreement on Tariffs and Trade
GCC	Gulf Cooperation Council

GDP	gross domestic product
ICC	International Criminal Court
ICT	information and communication technologies
IGC	Intergovernmental Conference (EU)
ILO	International Labour Office
IMF	International Monetary Fund
IPE	international political economy
IR	international relations
LAS	League of Arab States
MERCOSUR	Mercado Comùn del Sur (including Brazil, Argentina, Uruguay and Paraguay, and as associates, Bolivia and Chile)
MFN	most favoured nation
MS	member state
NAFTA	North American Free Trade Agreement (including US, Canada and Mexico)
NATO	North Atlantic Treaty Organization
NEPAD	New Partnership for Development
NGOs	non-governmental organizations
NPT	Non-Proliferation Treaty
NTBs	non-tariff barriers
OAS	Organization of American States (including all American states except Cuba)
OAU	Organization of African Unity
OECD	Organization for Economic Cooperation and Development
OEEC	Organization for European Economic Cooperation
OMC	Open Method of Coordination (EU)
OPEC	Organization of Petroleum-Exporting Countries
OSCE	Organization for Security and Cooperation in Europe
PTAs	preferential trading arrangements
Rio Process	European Partnership including all the countries of Latin America
SAARC	South Asian Association for Regional Cooperation (India, Pakistan, Nepal, Bhutan, Bangladesh, the Maldives, Sri Lanka)
SADC	South African Development Community (including 14 southern African countries)
TEC	Treaty of the European Community
TEU	Treaty of the European Union
TNC	transnational corporation

UDEAC	Customs and Economic Union of Central Africa
UN	United Nations
UNDP	United Nations Development Programme
UNICE	Union of Employers of the European Community (EU)
WEU	Western European Union
WTO	World Trade Organization

1
Civilian Power and International Relations: the EU and Multilateralism from the Twentieth to the Twenty-first Century

1.1 Long-term trends and epoch-making events in the development of the international identity of the EU as a civilian power

While not neglecting the deep historical roots of the united political entity emerging in Europe, this book looks primarily at the evolution of the EU as a civilian power since the end of the Second World War. The gradual construction of the EU contribution to global governance and of the new Europe's international identity itself owes less to controversial cultural heritage than it does to the following three factors:

1. the expansive force and attractiveness of peaceful coexistence and cooperation between neighbouring states, as confirmed by the success of the European project so far (1950–2005), its widening and deepening, and the spread of similar regional organizations in the rest of the world. As comparative research tells us, the distinctive feature of the EU is the practice of pooled and shared sovereignty among member states, i.e. the combination of cooperation and supranationality that characterizes the political and institutional structure of the EU, revising the traditional state system which traces its roots back to the Treaty of Westphalia (1648);

2. the renewed distinctiveness of the European socio-economic 'model' within the partially globalized economy, as a sophisticated example of the institutional management of global governance, inspired by a pluralistic view of globalization;
3. the network of external relations of the EU and its MS with regions and states all over the world and with international organizations. This is consistent with a worldview in which order and the spread of democracy and human rights are assured though rules, regimes, multilateral institutions and values, rather than though power relations, the balance of power and military force.

This book focuses on the external implications of this *longue durée* evolution of the EU. Despite many shortcomings, failures and internal difficulties, political scientists and historians agree that the achievements of the second half of the twentieth century make the EU the most relevant and theoretically challenging common institution ever created on the European continent.[1] This new entity, however, is currently facing the many challenges posed by the uncertainties of globalized economy and world politics in the post-cold war era.

How to understand and conceptualize the EU regional and global role and its international identity is a highly controversial research issue. While acknowledging and taking account of the achievements of multiple and parallel research agendas, we propose a new concept of 'civilian power', which differs, on the one hand, from the concept of 'soft power', developed by Joseph Nye as complementary to 'hard power', both of which were related to the international role of the US. Indeed, to an extent, the increasing civilian power of the EU reduces the soft power of the US. On the other hand, our basically realist understanding of 'civilian power' differs from the normative and idealistic notions of 'civil power' and 'civilizing power', even if its ideational factors and history of political thought are not neglected at all.[2]

How can we combine a view of this long-term process with the current acceleration of change? Epoch-making events, such as the end of the cold war and September 11th, have transformed the global system and Europe's role within it at a pace and to a degree which can be compared with the historical turning point of 1945. The origins of the current transition in world politics are to be found in the seismic events of the period from 1989 to 1991, when the fall of the Berlin wall and the subsequent implosion of the Soviet Union signalled not only the end of the bipolar world and the balance of terror, but also the end of the model of forced Western unity against the enemy which had been essential in the face of the perceived Soviet nuclear threat. As a result, western Europeans now no longer need the same degree of protection from their American ally and, similarly, Europe no longer represents a vital interest as before for the United States. This has allowed Europeans and the EU and MS to express their interests and worldviews with greater freedom and clarity than in the past.

If we look at the post-2001 period, we find that this has been symbolized not only by the fall of the Twin Towers, the new terrorist threats, and the proliferation of weapons of mass destruction (WMD), but also by the divergences between the two pillars of the West: the United States and Europe. On the one hand, we see the international policy of the Bush administration, demonstrated by the consistent body of official documentation,[3] and expressed through an upsurge in military spending and the early episodes of the 'total war on terror' and the global struggle for exporting democracy. On the other, the world witnessed the inability of the US, despite the protracted debate within the Security Council during the winter of 2002–3, to secure a majority vote in support of its 'preventive war' in Iraq. Crucially, this failure was largely due to European opposition. Indeed, for the first time in the post-war period, the core nations of the European integration process (particularly France and Germany), emboldened by political alliances and significant shows of support from public opinion, expressed their growing desire for European political autonomy.[4] Relevant European nations combined the common decision to complete the work of the European Convention, one of whose aims was the reinforcement of the EU's international political profile, with their political action in favour of the primacy of the United Nations and the Security Council.[5] The United States and its traditional European allies have thus diverged on the vital issue of war and peace. This book aims to provide key elements to help us explore and understand the origins and potential consequences of this unprecedented and serious division for the EU.

As a new evolving international actor, the EU needs to assert itself by focusing on and promoting its own particular priorities and interests. Both transatlantic partnership and discords are part of the gradual identity-building process. For the EU this requires working towards a world order that is more pluralistic, complex and variegated than one defined by a straightforward conflict between the sole superpower and the new international threats. In this book, we shall try to identify the elements and perspectives that, in a framework of contrasting unipolarist and fragmentary trends, shape the emergence of new actors, even beyond the EU. As regards the new European political entity, we shall look at it first of all in terms of its impact on the world order. In the current uncertain transitional phase, we consider a little rash the apodeictic theses of many commentators who, whatever their normative assessments of it, recognize only the peremptory establishment of a unipolar system, highlighting its 'imperial' or 'hegemonic' characteristics.

The global system is heterogeneous and includes both the evolving transatlantic partnership and the transatlantic geopolitical differences. The dawn of the new century witnessed a significant increase in serious political problems and disagreements between the transatlantic allies.[6] Their perceptions of the external threats differ considerably, as do their respective visions of the role of the United Nations and the very nature of global governance and the world order. Two new elements have come into play in moulding perceptions of the external threat. Firstly, the United States tends to view terrorism through the sole and mono-causal prism of Al-Qaeda. Europeans, while tackling the immediate threat posed by Al-Qaeda and targeting its networks and financial support system,[7] are also more sensitive to the deep roots and different national manifestations of terrorism, and to the differences between terrorist and insurrectionist movements. Secondly, unlike most of Europe, the US associates the terrorist threat directly with that posed by 'rogue states' (a category which recalls the traditional definition of 'destabilizing states' in the classic multipolar balance-of-power system). These 'rogue states' include countries like Iran, Iraq and North Korea which differ significantly in their specific histories, geopolitics, ideologies and availability of weapons of mass destruction, but are clubbed together and made to answer to the simplistic definition of the 'axis of evil'. The new secretary of state C. Rice mentioned in 2004 a longer list of tyrannies, including Cuba, Belarus, Myanmar and Zimbabwe.

The US has already come to its own clear and binding conclusions regarding what international changes are necessary and has independently developed a new approach to foreign affairs and the world order based on its 'revolutionary' conception of international relations. This can only have serious and long-term effects on transatlantic relations, global and regional multilateral organizations and the wider civilian international agenda.[8] The first G.W. Bush administration in fact embarked immediately upon an unprecedented redefinition of various elements of US political tradition already before 11 September 2001. This includes the shift in balance in favour of the national interest at the expense of international alliances: the first decisions of this new approach included implementing the anti-missile system and rejecting the Kyoto Protocol and the ICC. After September 11th, the US's broad interpretation of the right to legitimate defence fed into a growing unilateralism that objectively makes it increasingly difficult to identify US security interests with those of other states. International support decreased dramatically after the adoption of a sort of 'armoured Wilsonism',[9] i.e. a quasi-messianic mission to spread the gospels of democracy and the free-market economy throughout the world by military means, rather than by strengthening peaceful cooperation. While the aim of international democratization recalls the vision of Woodrow Wilson, it differs in that it is pursued through 'preventive' and selective wars against a long list of tyrannical regimes. These are fought not under the auspices of the UN and multilateral organizations, but with the assistance of ad hoc 'coalitions of the willing' (which between 2001 and 2004 excluded the EU and NATO as such). UN legitimization and international cooperation are sought *post festum* only to resolve post-war political complications, by providing funding, and military and civilian support.

Despite significant divisions between member states, the EU does not share the US approach. No statement or official stance of the EU institutions (European Council, Council of Ministers, European Parliament, Commission) supported this approach between 2001 and 2004.[10] It identifies with multilateralism and continues to promote its own priorities, including combating terrorism and limiting WMD proliferation through the United Nations Security Council, whose monopoly on the legal use of force it recognizes.[11] Furthermore, the EU is strengthening its multilateral commitments through the recent enlargement to the east, its even controversial Constitutional Treaty, its multiple civilian external relations and its promotion of the European socio-economic model within the context of the global network.

The third issue to split the two sides of the Atlantic is the question of whether, and to what extent, 'political' military campaigns conducted in the name of democracy against tyrannical regimes can be deemed legitimate.[12] The European Union agrees with UN Secretary-General Kofi Annan's Millennium Report (2000) on the indefensibility of the traditional principles of non-intervention and full national sovereignty in the face of human rights violations. However, in contrast to the current US administration, it distinguishes clearly between different cases of 'political' intervention.[13] For example, the EU recognized the legitimacy of the Gulf War in 1991, which aimed to redress a violation of international law and was approved 'by consensus' by the UN Security Council. It also accepted the military intervention in Kosovo of a coalition of democratic NATO member states to end the massacre of the local Albanian population at the hands of the Milošović regime. Although this action was not mandated by a UN resolution, it enjoyed both the endorsement of the secretary-general and widespread public support, at least in Western countries. The EU distanced itself, however, from the 'preventive' war against Iraq in 2003, which was waged without a supporting UN resolution. Unlike the Gulf War and Kosovo campaign, it enjoyed only minority support in the Security Council and among world public opinion. This was reflected by the limited ad hoc coalition that eventually went to war and the effect of the whole episode has been to create a serious transatlantic rift. While the joint command structure of NATO forces during the Kosovo conflict was considered to be too restrictive by the Pentagon,[14] in the aftermath of the Iraqi campaign the transatlantic debate is likely to be between, on the one hand, those who hold that a coalition of willing Western states, with the help of Japan, Australia and perhaps a few other countries, represents a sufficiently broad and legitimate basis to go to war and, on the other, those who insist on a strong UN mandate as an essential condition for any military intervention.

What then is the interplay of this triple divergence of perspectives regarding international relations and the world order with the EU's developing role as a global actor? These external challenges, combined with domestic, social, political and institutional factors, necessitate the resolution of the EU's fundamental political dilemmas. The year 2001 can be defined as epoch-making first and foremost because it marked the dramatic return of security and war to the top of the international agenda, now defined by the threat of new terrorism and arms proliferation on the one hand, and by the challenges raised by the new US international policy on the other. The first of these factors is important both because 'new terrorism' (globalized and informal violence by non-state actors) represents an unprecedented threat and because the proliferation of WMD is a reality (notwithstanding the 'state lies' and false information on Iraqi WMD revealed by the US and UK press and official committees of inquiry). The rearmament of North Korea and Iran is a fact, as are the fears and sense of uncertainty generated in the West and elsewhere by the significant increase in the number of terrorist attacks attempted or perpetrated across the world. The EU and the US agree on the dangers which 'new terrorism' and proliferation pose to the entire international community and which, following September 11th, have become (and will remain) priorities on the transatlantic cooperation agenda. The EU therefore is also trying to equip itself with new domestic and foreign policy instruments, while maintaining its focus on terrorism prevention, intelligence gathering, combating

Al-Qaeda funding, dialogue with the Muslim world, alleviating the poverty that acts as a breeding ground for terrorism and, above all, facilitating the resolution of the Israeli–Palestinian crisis.[15]

The second of the three factors is also of key importance. Since Hegel's time, Europeans have been well aware how much of world history has been determined by the dominant powers. Whatever one might think of its foreign policies, the US enjoys a qualitatively decisive influence on the globalized world, the United Nations and, indeed, on the destiny of the EU itself by exerting a certain sway over the decisions arrived at by some of the EU's member states. A new and uncertain era has begun within the evolution of the post-bipolar world order and it will condition the role and status of the EU as an actor on the international stage. It is important to stress this direct link, as no actor for at least another generation will be in the position of the EU either in terms of resources or willingness, if not to counterbalance, at least to 'civilize' (as an ally of course) the US superpower. It is thus clear that when one now speaks of the EU's political future, what is at stake is the nature of the international system and the structure of the twenty-first-century world.

In 2003, Kofi Annan decried what he termed a genuine 'crisis of the international system'. What political role do the three factors mentioned above play in this crisis and in accelerating change? Firstly, the terrorist threat has considerable implications for the interdependent global system. Commentators stress the quantitative and qualitative dimensions of a phenomenon operating through global transnational informal networks that are radical in rhetoric, rich in financial resources and Machiavellian in their manipulation of religion.[16] Moreover, on the systemic level, the world is witnessing the exposure of US vulnerability, the emergence of a new type of war which is 'global' and 'asymmetric' (of which the Afghanistan and Iraqi campaigns were the first two distinct examples) and the persistent uncertainties of post-war phases. Last but not least, the unprecedented importance assumed by the new threat in the popular imagination, albeit different on either side of the Atlantic, is nonetheless reflective of how fear has captured the public consciousness. Collective fear, whether a spontaneous generator of national solidarity or artificially manipulated, has played an important role in international politics, even in recent decades.[17] But the essential political question in the current era is whether terrorism born of Islamic fundamentalism, while constituting neither a global political actor nor a strategic alternative to the international system, can, beyond the challenge it represents to security and human rights, serve to accelerate the pre-existing trends towards the anarchic fragmentation of international relations, already visible in the failures of states in various parts of the world and the emergence of subnational and transnational criminal forces. Indeed, it is on this very dynamic that official justifications for the preventive war are grounded. These refer to the imminent dangers posed by potential aggressors (armed with WMD and coupled with the threat of terrorism), the very ambitious 'exemplary effect' of regime change in Iraq in promoting democracy in the Middle East and the strong message sent out to a lengthening list of hostile and tyrannical regimes near and far.

To view the new US international policy solely in the light of the terrorist attack on the World Trade Center would be to underestimate this second factor. President George W. Bush's 'long war on terrorism'[18] offered the US a golden opportunity to launch a (largely already planned) restructuring of the international system, i.e. a strategic redefinition of the US's place in the world, including its alliances, and the global hierarchy. Neo-conservative groups, dominant within the Bush administration, were influential well before September 11th and will probably maintain their influence through astute public relations and diplomatic restyling. As a result, the shift away from the post-1945 liberal internationalist historical phase, which the George W. Bush double term reflects, should not be underestimated in terms of its long-term impact on international relations.[19] Although we are not yet dealing with a new international order, those who see in the *Pax Americana* a possible unipolar scenario for the future raise relevant theoretical questions regarding both the structure of the world order and the evolution of the EU.[20]

Research should be increasingly looking beyond the (acknowledged) short-term transatlantic misunderstandings and the (unacknowledged) mismanagement of the transatlantic relationship. Precisely the EU resilience and autonomous stance contributed to the change of the US unprecedented preference in 2003–4 for a 'divide and rule' approach with Europeans and the repeated and explicit division in US discourse of the European continent into 'old' and 'new' Europe, based on a notion of 'wrong European integration' of the latter. That is why the central theme of this book concerns the long-term trends of the international system and the most controversial element of change within world politics, i.e. the novelty represented by the EU's increasingly autonomous stance and the potentially vast implications of its strengthened international profile, its structural roots, the great internal and external expectations it raises, and its considerable institutional and international consequences.

In order to locate the evolving transatlantic relationship and the above-mentioned epoch-making events within an appropriate long-term perspective and identify alternative scenarios, this book is structured according to two different approaches: 'bottom-up' and 'top-down'. While the next four chapters focus on the global relevance of the EU as a new civilian power in the making, this introductory chapter deals with international relations theories. This involves a critical refining of the cognitive instruments at our disposal when assessing the current transition to a new world order.

The starting point for this is the critical assessment of the theoretical fragility of the optimistic conceptual framework developed in the 1990s in order to grasp the so-called 'global governance' which came into vogue following the end of the bipolar system. After September 11th, the securitization of the global agenda made it clearer that the complexity and heterogeneity of the international system are growing due to the simultaneous strengthening of four principal conflicting tendencies:

(a) *unipolarism* is increasingly emphasized by a sizeable part of international scholarly literature, often by applying new versions of old concepts such as *hegemony* and *empire*;
(b) other commentators, with good reason, stress that multipolarism matters, both in terms of providing limits for the lone superpower and as a means for great nations and regional entities to establish a balanced inter-state system;
(c) international anarchy has taken on the new form of *fragmentation* of the international system, the breaking of nations, *terrorism* and WMD *proliferation*;
(d) finally, new *multilateralism* is not only presented as an empirical method of global governance, but is also put forward as a potential theoretical framework for a new world order based on interdependence, conflict prevention and management, and institutionalized global and regional cooperation.

Our main thesis is that the first scenario would transform the EU, by diluting it and reducing it to the level of a mere continental trading state, while the second and third scenarios would profoundly divide it according to national (or even subnational) priorities. However, since, in our view, none of the first three tendencies is likely to become paradigmatic and dominant in the international system in the near future, the fourth one merits particular attention, not only because it is the only one which allows room for the emergence of the EU as a new kind of civilian power. For this reason, the remaining six sections of this chapter will focus on the analytical and institutional, global and regional, realistic and normative sides of this scenario.

Our contribution to the ongoing shift in international political theory towards a vision of international relations which is more consistent with the history of European political thought and the political innovation represented by the very existence of the EU will be to properly evaluate the realism of this fourth scenario.

1.2 The rise and fall of the myth of 'global governance without government'

The attacks on the World Trade Center and the subsequent Afghan and Iraqi wars brought to an end the immediate post-cold-war period, marked by James Baker and Bush senior's short-lived designs for a 'new world order' and the asymmetric multilateralism of the entire Clinton era. Decreased military spending, a 50 per cent fall in international arms trading[21] and the peace dividend which flanked the reduction in inter-state violence were all accompanied not only by greatly increased interdependence, but also by the prevailing discourse of a globalization beneficial to all[22] that would provide the basis for a more democratic, peaceful, cybernetically self-governed and efficient type of global governance.[23] After the Balkan conflicts froze the rhetoric about the 'end of history', the failure witnessed at the launch of the World Trade Organization's (WTO) Millennium Round in Seattle opened the world's eyes to the democratic deficit of its multilateral organizations and to the great contradictions and difficulties of arriving at an acceptable compromise between the diverse calls and demands for a more regulated model of globalization.[24]

The 1990s represented the cradle of 'global governance' research. The concept of global governance goes beyond the mere development of a network of regimes and international organizations when set in the context of the triumph of the market economy and democracy, the growth of complex interdependence and the development of globalization and ICT which eliminate distances and facilitate the advent of the 'global village', the rise of multinational companies and transnational socio-cultural phenomena. According to Rosenau, global governance also reflects the gamut of forms of self-governance within states, fostered on the one hand by better education, a sharpening of collective democratic consciousness and civil society's ability to manage itself, and, on the other, by transnational and global regulatory processes. We stress the difference of the concepts of 'governance' from that of 'government' with the aim of underlying its greater inclusiveness. Beyond the institutionalized and formalized types of regulatory power linked to the state (and considered to be in decline), 'governance' comprises complex forms and levels of authority that can be public, private, pluralistic and informal (neither institutionalized nor hierarchical), decentralized and devolved in a polycentric, subnational and transnational system of variable geometry.[25]

Some accounts of this important trend in the social sciences emphasize the end of the state and government and go so far as to predict the demise of the state and politics itself as a consequence of globalization. These theses are proposed in particular by:

(a) 'Hyperglobalizers',[26] who foresee the complete absorption of the state and politics by a globalized economy.
(b) 'Transgovernmentalists',[27] who envisage the success of the trend towards the creation of international agencies designed to deliver technocratic solutions to common problems (such as the definition of standards by antitrust and inter-banking agencies).
(c) Neo-medievalists,[28] who borrow the pre-modern medieval metaphor to emphasize how the emergence of new technologies, transnational processes and the proliferation of non-governmental actors have given rise to partly overlapping forms of authority, postmodern politics and non-state feelings of identity within a multi-level global system that is increasingly without centre, hegemony or power.

Although they may take significant empirical elements into consideration,[29] such interpretations of the globalized international system in the post-cold war era ignore the limits of globalization, the asymmetries of power within the global system and the challenges relating to domestic and international security. They also completely marginalize the political implications of economic changes and the importance of state political power on economic issues. According to Max Weber, governments are the only institutions which may legitimately use force to uphold the law and achieve their social objectives. Finally, nor can we overlook the lack of transparency, democracy and justice in the system of global governance. When underpinned by pure economic, functionalist and postmodern illusions, theories of global governance will neither ask who governs the governance nor whether the objectives of such governance should be peace or mere efficiency.

In the 1990s the social contradictions and geopolitical limits of the globalization process were seriously underestimated. Interdependence is not always a positive-sum game and creates conflicts as well as new forms of vulnerability. Growing differences have emerged between regions of the world which react differently to the asymmetric distribution of the advantages of globalization. The aforementioned schools of thought forget that the deep roots of state durability also lie in the 'implementation deficit' of global governance, as well as in the lack of societal and economic compliance in relation to soft forms of informal governance.[30]

While useful in focusing on societal trends, these analytical approaches have been radically called into question not only by the implications of the failure to launch the Millennium Round in Seattle, the attacks in 2001, the wars in 2002 and 2003, but in general by the political conflicts and uncertainties of the world order. International hierarchies of power and the territorial dimension of authority had been forgotten in favour of the mere functional dimension of power. The political role of the US was thus inevitably overlooked, precisely when the focus was directed on economic governance alone.

On the contrary, it now seems increasingly clear that the institutionalist view of global governance has generated a more far-reaching and far-sighted interpretative strength. Its analysis of the expansion and reform of international organizations and regimes (such as the WTO, successor since 1995 to the weaker GATT) and of the strengthening of regional organizations (the EU *in primis*) does not overlook the persistent complementary role of states, which remain essential elements in global governance, both in building international regimes, in the implementation of decisions and their controversial democratic legitimization. We shall defer further discussion of this relevant approach to the section on multilateralism.

1.3   Empire and imperialism: misleading metaphors

The return of the concept of 'empire' to theoretical and media debates (in critical opposition to the optimistic world views of the 1990s) is interwoven and often confused with that of 'imperialism'. However, the latter is in no way applicable to the role of the US in so far as it is intimately associated with the global context of the interimperial conflicts of the end of the nineteenth and the beginning of the twentieth century, i.e. a particular stage of the classic multipolar world which saw the colonial expansion of a limited number of European powers and competition for access to new markets. John Hobson's economic analysis of imperialism as a solution to the domestic imbalance between supply and demand, due to the weak and pre-Keynesian nature of domestic European markets of that epoch,[31] has nothing whatsoever to do with the United States of today – a country whose domestic market is so dynamic that it has produced a huge trade deficit. As for Joseph Schumpeter's political interpretation of imperialism, this is based on the militaristic, hierarchical, pre-democratic and pre-capitalist structures of some of the powers of that era and is thus not applicable to American liberal democracy.[32] Finally, although updated by 'dependency' theorists such as Theotonio Dos Santos and Samir Amin[33] in the 1960s and 1970s, the marxist developments of imperial theory by Lenin, Luxemburg and Bukharin, based on Hobson's analysis, had already revealed their analytical flaws in the inter-war years. This can be seen in the emergence of Gramsci's alternative notion of international 'hegemony', which focused on the emerging American power and on the epochal importance of 'Americanism'.[34]

The debate about the so-called American 'empire' is more interesting, especially when viewed against a historical and sociological background. It does, however, often leave one with the impression of a somewhat generic and vague type of conceptualization, which is often more allusive than scientifically based. It is worth, therefore, reflecting for a moment on the principal versions of 'empire' proposed by international scholars.

1.   Let us first of all recall the version rooted in the post-war period, which had the advantage of referring to the massive growth in American international power. We refer particularly to Raymond Aron's and Arthur Schlesinger Jr's respective definitions of the 'imperial Republic' and the 'imperial presidency'.[35] These focus on the internal institutional developments, radically changing what Alexis de Tocqueville had admired in *Democracy in America*, that is to say the highly decentralized and polyarchic character of the polity which, according to Hegel, made the United States a pre-state. The new global leadership, however, involved strengthening the capacity of the American system to concentrate international decisions regarding the use of force at the top. A truth was thus underlined: to be able to tackle important international world challenges, the foreign policy system of a power needs to rationalize its internal polyarchy and traditional multi-level governance, to the point of achieving a real fusion of the political and economic elites in the case of a major crisis.[36] However, the current desire of the neo-conservatives to transform the US into an empire, as a political complement to globalization, has run up against high costs, both internally and externally.[37] One internal conceptual difficulty is that the US is a large liberal democracy and certain security policy choices can impose worrying limitations on the upholding of these liberal principles. Renouncing multilateralism carries very high financial and political costs. Nonetheless, the internal variables of presidential elections and the possibility of a different majority in Congress remain the decisive factors in a constitutional system that represents the archetypal federal republic, not just the archetypal republic.[38]

2. The most recent strand of the 'imperial' literature invokes metaphorical comparison of the US with classic empires. In particular, it highlights Rome as offering the only historical precedent of the type of unbridgeable gap which we see today between the US military power and its potential competitors. Alternatively, it cites the British empire as being a global, English-speaking, liberal and modern immediate predecessor of the US.[39] The debate on whether the role played by the US in the world can be classified in imperial terms remains open. However, historical literature tells us that there is insufficient evidence to fully concur with this comparison:

(a) Even if the transformation of a republic into an empire encourages parallels with the Roman case, one huge difference is the current lack of any shared imperial self-consciousness of the American elites. Important 'neo-conservative' groups openly advocate the US becoming an empire, but American political leadership (both Democratic and Republican Presidencies, including that of George W. Bush) has denied that it is pursuing this objective. Furthermore, it is disputed what is intended by the term 'empire' when used by neo-conservatives: does it mean military and economic domination or ideological hegemony symbolized by the 'wars for liberty'?

(b) The military supremacy and economic strength of the US are rightly underlined and the vast presence of the US army in 130 countries may compensate for the relatively very limited direct control of external territories (compared with the Roman and British empires). Furthermore, the ability of the US to combine hard with soft power, i.e. their role in globalization, including linguistic and media primacy, has led historians like Niall Ferguson to speak of 'the greatest empire of the modern times'. However, historical empires were able to ensure 'international public goods' such as order, peace, free trade and international development (in the case of the UK), the improvement of communications and security (at least within the borders of the empire) and respect for public and private rights (in the case of Rome). By contrast, the effectiveness of the current US military and economic/monetary supremacy in ensuring financial stability, peace and security (also against the backdrop of the informal violence typical of new forms of terrorism) is a highly controversial topic.

(c) Some empires were better able than nation states to guarantee internal pluralism and tolerance of ethnic and cultural diversity within their borders (e.g. the Austro-Hungarian and the Roman empires), to the point of making citizenship independent of ethnic or national origin. They often thus guaranteed and facilitated the flowering and coexistence of various cultures. Any similarity with the inclusiveness and appeal of the 'American dream' and the US 'melting pot' of the post-war decades is, however, less applicable today. Immigration policy has become an internal cleavage in the US and traditional tolerance and respect of human rights are being challenged. This is not, as many commentators note, solely due to the urgency of fighting terrorism.

(d) Finally, the imperial metaphor crumbles when we consider the limits of US hard power and the paradox of the most dominant force since Roman times being unable to achieve its foreign policy objectives alone. What can the US achieve without multilateral cooperation (involving the UN and the EU) as far as peacekeeping missions and post-war reconstruction are concerned? Ferguson himself refers not only to US economic utilitarianism, but also to its 'hubris' (that is, according to the Greek philosophy, the unbreakable will of overcoming its natural limits) as internal obstacles to US successful imperial ambitions.

In conclusion, the US, despite its unprecedented hard power, is not able to compel its allies and partners to do what it wants and, as P. Bender observes, it is already confronted with a problem that the Romans only faced late on (in the fifth century AD, near the end of the western empire): that of being obliged to deal with far more challenges than they are effectively able to manage.

3. In their book *Empire*, Toni Negri and Michael Hardt attempt to reconcile various metaphoric references to classic empires with a sociological analysis of the crisis of the state and contemporary politics (from Luhmann's systems theory to the many schools of postmodern thought that incorporate the idea of the decline of classic state power).[40]

To what extent does Hardt and Negri's attempt to recuperate and integrate some of the neo-medievalist and postmodern literature into their post-state concept of empire provide new theoretical insight? The decline of the modern state is interpreted as a possible end to state sovereignty *tout court*. Furthermore, such a mixture of the pre-modern and postmodern leads to the end of politics, either through the primacy of the economy and/or the competitive Foucault-style micro-powers within multi-level global governance. From this comes the functionalist and economistic and liberal idea of the radical 'deterritorialization' of power. Just as Leninism and liberalism both paradoxically underestimated the expansive nature of the new Keynesian capitalism, so too the postmodern heirs of Leninism are united with neo-liberals in refusing to acknowledge the importance of the great international political game that has been taking place, particularly since 2002. In particular, they overlook the attempt by the Bush administration not only to be at the centre of global multi-level economic governance, but also to dominate the political government of the world order. They ignore the political limits of US power and the attempts of other states and regional powers to *politically* thwart this objective along with the geopolitical conflicts of interest between the US and other major capitalist countries, including its European allies.

What renders the metaphor of empire dated and caricatured, whether it is used to demonize or in apologia,[41] is that such accounts ignore the various signs of internal fragility[42] and political contradictions that are growing with unprecedented clarity. When they limit their study of the alternatives to empire to the 'revolt of the masses', Hardt and Negri forget that, rather than the 'neo-Sorelian' myth of a 'revolt of the masses', resistance to unipolarist tendencies lies more in the emergence of a plurality of political actors and forces in the form either of single states (e.g. Brazil, China, India, Indonesia and Russia), in the new political dimension of regional groupings and in democratic public opinion. These are precisely the new political phenomena to which this book aims to draw attention, because they allow multilateral organizations to exist and act – whether in terms of opposing the imperial tendencies of the superpower or exerting their right to act more independently from its particular priorities.[43]

It is worth dwelling a moment on the central concept of the post-modern, deterritorialized, borderless, eternal and global empire that is being hypothesized.[44] Of course, the functional, transnational and deterritorialized aspect of the empire exists. However, as Robert Gilpin, for example, showed in his analysis of the relationship between the majority of multinational corporations and the US,[45] economic power is clearly anchored in territorial space and time. The strength of the leader nation lies in its ability to synthesize the functional and territorial forms of domination and hegemony. In the current historical phase, these are framed by a strategic design of a world order that reorganizes geographical spaces and technical forms of strategic and military presence.[46] These also include protectionist policies such as agricultural and steel subsidies designed to satisfy domestic electoral requirements. In addition, recent years have seen intensification in the US's policing of its Canadian and Mexican borders[47] and the national territory in general in the context of the fight against terrorism.

Although it is different from the Roman imperial concept of borders as *limes*, the new US vision includes the APEC project for the Asia-Pacific region and the progression from NAFTA to the FTAA. The latter foresees the creation of a hemispheric free-trade area, stretching from Alaska to Patagonia. The FTAA thus binds economics and politics and may be seen as a new manifestation of the classic Monroe geopolitical doctrine of 'America for the Americans'.[48]

These examples of territorial reorganization on a global level explain why Keohane, with regard to George W. Bush's United States, referred with a certain irony to classic political and territorial sovereignty, in contrast to any postmodern notion of empire. It is perhaps suprising to find a country that, unlike states in Europe, was the product of the federalist idea of shared sovereignty, but which is now relaunching important aspects of the classic image of the great power in terms of how it conceives of and manages its foreign policy and spheres of influence.[49] Messianic and territorial concepts of the war against terrorism have thus been wedded together. The preference for territorially recognizable enemies that can be occupied with troops (the purported link between Al-Qaeda and the 'rogue state' Iraq) has led to the conceptual reduction of transnational informal terrorist networks to a single, well-known code that can be interpreted according to traditional structures of territorial dimensions (e.g. Afghanistan and Iraq). This obsession for a territorial interpretation of a transnational phenomenon is so strong that it comes at the price of disastrous inefficiencies in the battle against informal terrorism. Contrary to postmodern theories, the territorial dimension matters. The shortcomings of postmodernism demonstrate the need to understand institutionalism not as simply opposed to realism but as a possible positive 'overcoming' of the best legacies of realism, while openly criticizing its updated version.

We should mention one final point on the fundamental territorial nature of global American power and the difference between the US and the Roman empire[50]: domestic representative democratic government has been an expression of the territorial nature of politics since the French and American revolutions. The United States can operate successfully abroad if there is domestic consensus. This is precisely because it is a liberal democracy and the collapse of support at home can thus lead to changes in foreign policy, as the example of Vietnam demonstrated.[51] This link between the domestic level and foreign policy shows the gulf between the US and the empires of the past, especially Rome. Rome could tolerate its renowned endemic internal disputes because, and as long as, it had no competition from rival powers.[52] While the US is the leader nation and the supreme power, it inhabits a world with pluralist tendencies, including civilian actors and democratic media that are in permanent dialogue with American public opinion within an interdependent and communicative transatlantic and global public sphere.[53]

To conclude, it is true that the US avails of deterritorialized transnational and functional tendencies. However, this is on the solid basis of a national political power that is still able, in exceptional circumstances, to reconcile the national interest with international actions through the reorganization of geopolitical spaces. The various meanings of the expression 'deterritorialized empire' therefore only highlight the difficulty in interpreting the present reality without recourse to the categories of the past. Even if refined in a syncretic sense, it remains so obsolete and imprecise a term that it does not stand up to empirical or theoretical scrutiny, or else merely refers us back to more pertinent concepts of hegemony and the hegemonic state.

1.4   The use and abuse of the concepts of 'hegemony' and 'hegemonic stability'

The term 'hegemony' is largely and improperly employed in relation to the United States. Its use in this context amounts to a rhetorical simplification reminiscent of the description of the Soviet Union's foreign policy by the Chinese leadership in the 1960s and 1970s as 'hegemonic' when, in reality, they were only referring to the USSR's aggressiveness and the threat it posed to Chinese sovereignty. This distorted version of the term continues to enjoy more journalistic success than the conceptualization developed within international relations theory by the likes of Robert Keohane, Charles Kindleberger, Robert Cox, Robert Gilpin and others. According to the Hegelian understanding of this, the dominant state not only expresses hard power, but shapes the spirit of the age, the Zeitgeist. It was Antonio Gramsci who first applied this concept to both state power and international relations in his *Prison Notebooks*. In the 1970s, Gramsci's key ideas were taken up by scholars in the English-speaking world and have greatly influenced international relations theory since. The pioneering work of Charles Kindleberger on the economic history of the inter-war period[54] examined the decline of the great hegemonic world power that was Britain in the eighteenth and nineteenth centuries and the early part of the twentieth along with the initially hesitant, but then vigorous, emergence of the new hegemony of the United States – the only country in a position to guarantee an essential international 'public good', i.e. monetary and trade stability.[55] Robert Gilpin's international political economy approach applied this notion to the study of the cycle of major powers, from their emergence, establishment and stabilization up until the appearance of a challenger and their eventual decline.[56] The neo-institutionalist Robert Keohane (the inventor, with Joseph Nye, of the 'complex interdependence theory') identified a turning point in the history of the world system in the 1970s and 1980s, with the end of the post-war hegemony established by the US.[57] In his book, *After Hegemony*, Keohane discusses how international cooperation can take place without US hegemony. Finally, the so-called 'Italian school', founded by the Canadians Robert Cox and Stephen Gill, focused on the conflictual consequences of hegemonic power in the contemporary international system and looked at the issue of possible alternatives.[58]

Whether liberal or neo-Marxist, all these scholars have found this concept to be analytically useful in relation to the British and American cases as it goes beyond simplistic accounts which attribute the roles played by these two countries to mere imperial military or economic domination. Notwithstanding its historical limits, Gramsci's concept of the 'hegemonic state' superseded theories of imperialism and paved the way for the modern concept of 'hegemonic stability'. Already Gramsci's concept is relatively clear in its study of the dominant power's world role: hegemony implies dominance plus consensus, intellectual and moral guidance plus coercion.[59] At international level, the 'hegemonic state' 'determines the options of others and is not determined by others, because its politics is based on what is permanent and not on what is casual or current, in its own interests and in those of the other forces that converge decisively to form a balanced system'. Gramsci of course was unaware of the idea of the 'international public good', but when he speaks of 'permanence' and harmony between the national interests of the great power and those of its allies, he is close to the type of concept developed by international political economy. The key theoretical element is the relationship between the particular interest of the state in question and its global ambition. When explaining the function of ideology in the emergent hegemonic state, and as an ideal introduction to his notes on *Americanism*, Gramsci cites the same example that had struck Hegel in 1806 and terrified Kant (faced some years before with the prospect of a 'universal monarchy'). He refers us to France in the period between the Revolution and the Napoleonic era when commenting that 'an "imponderable" element is the "ideological" position that a country occupies in the world at any given time insofar as it is representative of the progressive forces of history'.[60] To the territorial, military and economic criteria regarding the hegemonic state, Gramsci adds the 'ideological' criterion that exercises 'influence' on and causes 'repercussions' in other states.[61] He attributes key importance to this last criterion in the construction of the role and world image of a great power.

Although there are aspects reminiscent of the balance-of-power system, what we are dealing with here are theoretical suggestions that cannot simply be traced back to realist theory, since hegemonic stability can block and change the fragmentation and structural instability of the inter-state system,[62] unlike the Hobbesian hypostastization of anarchy developed by Hans J. Morgenthau, E. Carr and, in a systemic theory, by Kenneth Waltz.[63] The influence of the Hegelian concept of the 'absolute right' of the world power (complementary to its representation of the Zeitgeist) is clearly present in Gramsci. However, this Hegelian–Gramscian historical–dialectic conception does not correspond to the theory of hegemonic cycles as developed by contemporary international political economists like Robert Gilpin.[64]

The theory of hegemony has always involved a *pars destruens*, a critique which can be updated and adapted to current events. For instance, in examining the great force of new capitalism and modernization in the US, Gramsci's analysis of Americanism[65] represents a break not only with the Leninist theory of the imperialism, but also with the theories of collapse regarding the Second Socialist International and the interpretation of the US as a pure military and economic force, as expressed by the Comintern. Certainly, the theory of 'hegemony' should not be interpreted in angelic terms, nor should we forget that hegemony is 'armed with coercion', and with economic and military supremacy. However, the crucial point here is not the issue of hard power itself. On the contrary, the theory of hegemony is meant precisely to counteract the simple reduction of cultural power to political power and of political power to economic and military power. It is an invitation to examine the profound reasons as to why and how a world power achieves stability and achieves consensus not only with its allies, but also with those countries it dominates.

Since the authors mentioned earlier began to re-examine the question of the 'hegemonic state', the empirical reference base has consisted first and foremost of comparing the American and British experiences, while also incorporating various historical studies on hegemonies of the past. The following elements have been cited as characteristic of hegemonies:

1. The hegemonic state is not only a dominant power: it provides 'public goods' for world governance, i.e. goods of general utility, relating to the stability of the system and from which no one can be excluded.

The UK thus assumed for long time the cost of maintaining the sterling Gold Standard exchange rate. Sterling was thus the dominant world currency and served as the pillar of international free trade until August 1931 and the so-called 'great transformation' of Western capitalism.[66] Following a decade of chaos, economic nationalism and war, the United States between the years 1944 and 1971 met the cost of supporting international financial stability, especially by guaranteeing the rate of exchange between gold and the dollar.[67]

2. The policies of a hegemonic power are not defensive and inward looking. They are expansive and dynamic and spread the benefits of its model throughout the world. For example, the innovations in societal organization and modern production that originated in the US in the 1920s and with the New Deal were peacefully exported to western Europe and Japan after 1945. This encouraged the active adherence of allies and neutral countries and gradually stimulated the desire among elites in the semi-peripheral regions of the Second and Third Worlds to emulate the system. We will see in the section on multilateralism that in the three decades of 'embedded capitalism'[68] (i.e. the model of development that reconciles a Fordist model of production with commercial liberalization and public regulation of the international economy), flexible compromises were struck between national regulation traditions and the socio-economic stability of the European partners. An illustration of the willingness of the hegemonic power to pay for its position can be seen in American tolerance within GATT (art. XXIV) of the European 'entrepreneur state' and the agricultural protectionist policies of the EEC. The US as a hegemonic state has also been able to promote the modernization of social mores in public and private life, reflecting 'the American way', through such vehicles as cinema and advertisements. This has influenced the models of the family, the role of women and forms of political participation.[69]

3. The hegemonic state has great powers of persuasion and exercises influence on the cultural level as well as on the ideological education of elites in allied countries. In the case of the US, such influence is also exercised over the elites of neutral and Third World countries, through the peaceful propagation of the values of liberal democracy and welfare capitalism. Such hegemony relies on a system of spontaneous assent tied to the hegemonic power's superior productivity and the prestige associated with the wars won against militarism and Nazism. Despite McCarthyism and other deviations, it survived the disappointment of Franklin D. Roosevelt's universalism and was able to adapt to the cold war by combining with balance of terror.

4. Finally, both British and American hegemony were founded on a mix of unilateralism, bilateralism and multilateralism. In the case of the latter, this allowed the creation of multilateral institutions of political and economic international stability such as the UN and NATO, the Bretton Woods institutions and GATT.[70] Certainly, this multilateralism was not promoted everywhere (i.e. the bilateral relationship with Japan and the Far East area), but it was pursued with such vigour in the West that, from 1947, a Europe still smouldering from its 'thirty-year civil war' (1914–45) was forced down the path of intergovernmental cooperation through the 'Marshall Plan' and the OEEC, the first 'European' organization.

It is clear that American hegemony was fortified by military and economic domination. This is demonstrated as much by its eagerness to strengthen its allies as part of its containment policy towards the USSR as by its interest in spreading the neo-capitalist model to its irreplaceable trade partners in western Europe. US soft power should not be perceived as reflecting some kind of philanthropy or as a church mission, however, and nor should we forget the complementary weight of hard power and the role of force. While it cannot be seriously denied that US hegemony created public goods, it is also true that the international cooperation promoted by the US has, over the course of recent decades, potentially become the undoing of its own hegemonic power in the sense that the multilateral institutions it created have largely slipped out of its control. We need only think of the controversial, but dynamic, experiences of the EU, of the GATT-WTO or indeed of the UN Security Council.

This hegemonic stability that so characterized what E. Hobsbawm called the post-war 'golden years'[71] began to show cracks in the 1970s and 1980s as a result of the Vietnam war and its effects on the US balance of payments and the international monetary system. It is now largely over, as shown by the clear differences of geopolitical interests and political discord between the US and its allies. Nonetheless, the thesis of the 'decline of the USA' set out by Paul Kennedy, David Calleo and others was patently misleading, for they neither foresaw the eventual fall of the USSR nor the US's dynamism in being the first and most efficient adapter of the new economy, way ahead of either Japan or the EU.

All in all, the important question for us is whether the concept of 'hegemony' can still be seriously applied to the US in the twenty-first century. Does the current reassertion of US economic and military supremacy and global leadership mean that the crises of the 1970s and 1980s merely represented a temporary historical blip? None of the three elements mentioned, which marked the hegemonic stability centred on the US (as they also partly did with regard to British hegemony until 1931), can be considered to be still uncontroversial at the dawn of the twenty-first century. The US ceased to be the guarantor of international financial stability in 1971, when it decided to indefinitely suspend the system of fixed exchange rates. Since then, the dollar's devastating fluctuation has posed serious problems for the world economy and the US has paradoxically been criticized both for pursuing a 'superdollar' policy when it wants to attract international capital to finance the budget deficit, and for favouring a weak dollar and competitive devaluation when trying to rebalance its trade deficit, the latter sometimes in conjunction with recourse to protectionism.

How, therefore, should we analyse US leadership? It is true that 'American' globalization created advantages and 'inclusive' effects for various emerging countries during the 1990s. However, there are clear social, political and geographical limits (the whole of Africa for example) and dramatically increasing divisions between who is 'in' and who is 'out'. The result has been a growing demand for government of global interdependence and this has helped relaunch the autonomous role of multilateral organizations in the promotion of sustainable development, economic cooperation, protection of human rights and the fight against global pollution and infectious diseases (AIDS and SARS for example). In addition, doubts about the effectiveness of the anti-terrorism strategy adopted by the US since 2001 are being expressed with ever greater frequency in relation to the new challenges represented by the restoration of the 'common good' of international security. The more the US engages in 'preventive' warfare, whatever the brutality of the toppled despots, the weaker international consensus will be (not least because of the large number of casualties), the potentially stronger Europe is (the opposite to what Robert Kagan writes!), the freer it shall feel to express its world view. As regards the issue of consensus, concerns have also been raised within the US itself about the incomprehension of the rest of the world, the US's international isolation and so-called 'anti-Americanism'.[72] In contrast to the self-confidence and international attractiveness characteristic of Roosevelt's, Truman's, Eisenhower's and Kennedy's America, the US today presents a mixture of power and uncertainty, arrogance and doubt, cohesion and internal fragility, unilateralism and multilateralism.[73]

Finally, commentators agree that the US has not only distanced itself from new multilateral agreements and organizations (e.g. the Kyoto Protocol on emission reductions and the International Criminal Court), but also from longer-standing cooperation regimes. It has become increasingly belligerent in its relations with the very multilateral organizations in whose creation it played such a major role. For all of the above reasons, it is possible to conclude that, in contrast to the first three golden decades of the post-war period, rather than referring to US 'hegemony' today, it is conceptually more correct to speak of US 'supremacy' – economic and, increasingly, military supremacy – within an international system that is both turbulent and heterogeneous.

1.5   Towards a multipolar world? The limits of American power and the emergence of China

This criticism of the various unipolarist theses does not mean that we are seeing the emergence of a multipolar world like that envisaged by Henry Kissinger, the presidents of China and Russia and later reinterpreted by Chirac during the Iraq crisis. Within the academic community, this vision has been traditionally supported by various neo-realist scholars.[74] Certainly, no matter how one judges the events of the winter of 2002–3, the opposition presented to the US within the UN Security Council by a coalition of traditional allies (like France and Germany) and non-allies (Russia and China) was unprecedented and does not represent a one-off event. Nonetheless, the void created by the fall of the USSR and the end of the bipolar balance of terror is not going to be filled by a coalition which is willing and able to counterbalance the US in the context of a multipolar equilibrium.

In fact, the various empirical elements at our disposal do not seem to confirm the emergence of a multipolar world. It is true that the Iraqi crisis revealed the limits of US power: first, the Americans were forced to abandon hope in a second UN resolution going beyond the 1441 resolution and authorizing an attack within the context of a preventive war. Second, the unsuccessful political management of post-war Iraq is largely due to the isolation of the US from significant partners, allies and multilateral organizations. The US failure in the UN happened despite the struggle that had gone on for months within the Council and the unprecedented pressure which, in competition with the French diplomacy, the US had put on the weaker African and Latin American members of the Council. US diplomacy proved unsuccessful not only with the majority of UN member states, but also with its immediate neighbours and NAFTA co-members Canada and Mexico as the Iraqi threat was not considered imminent, nor the war necessary and legitimate. In contrast to 1991, the Arab world was united in its opposition, echoing the German foreign minister Joschka Fischer's grave reservations regarding the risk of long-term destabilization of the entire region and the superficial handling of Middle Eastern issues. Clearly, it was the decision to engage in the 'preventive war' that failed to convince public opinion across the world. While we can make a partial exception for the initial domestic support in the US and the UK, in both cases public opinion regarding the war also contained a lot of reservations and underwent important shifts over time. To recapitulate, in pursuing its policy of preventive warfare, the US can rely neither on a Security Council majority – which we cannot reduce to the mere threat of a veto exercised by China, France or Russia – nor can they force allies to change their mind.

Nonetheless, this opposition was neither able to prevent a unilateral war nor to exact a high political price, as would have been the case in the past balanced systems typical of either a multipolar or bipolar world. Indeed, in the hypothetical scenario of a neo-multipolar system, the balance of power would allow a coalition of the other powers to bring to heel that power which had violated the rules of the game. By contrast, in this case, the US's economic and military predominance allows it to act alone militarily or with an ad hoc coalition, and without bothering too much about the opposition presented to it, at least not in the purely military phase. The military asymmetry between the US and all other powers which developed after the fall of the USSR is massive, and the US is using the 'war on terrorism' to widen this gap in its favour.[75] Even the multipolarist prospect of transforming the UN Security Council into a sort of Directorate, reminiscent of the nineteenth-century European Concert, is currently extremely distant.

The post-war period in Iraq has thus not only confirmed the limits of American power, but also highlighted the absence of an effective multipolar world order. First of all, having secured control of the politics and resources of occupied Iraq, the US from May to September 2003 repeatedly requested *ex post* recognition (resolution 1483) of the military occupation of Iraq by the Security Council. The US was thus seeking a sort of 'legitimacy through efficiency', which, according to Jürgen Habermas, raises judicial and political issues.[76] In fact, notwithstanding its notable tactical and technical efficiency, serious gaps have been revealed in the ability of the US to manage the consequences of war (more than 100,000 civilian victims, humanitarian crises, various forms of opposition and an unexpected guerrilla war) and to guarantee internal security.[77] The post-war chaos and the growing costs in human and financial terms explain the efforts to secure new, unanimous resolutions in the UN and the search for EU and NATO involvement. On the other hand, the amendments proposed by France, Germany, Russia and other countries have been notably coherent in terms of requests for: (a) a change in the judicial status of the situation, from one of occupation to a political mandate for UN management, and (b) the restoration of Iraqi sovereignty through a provisional government to be legitimated by the Iraqi people.[78] All they obtained in 2004 was UN resolution 1546 which prepared the understanding of early 2005. This established a new political process which, despite problems related to the acceptability of occupying troops, is expected to be capable of easing Arab frustrations and preventing the disintegration of Iraq through more multilateral management. However, the UN does not have a magic wand and, as Afghanistan has demonstrated, it can be saddled with a situation left festering for too long, which is conditioned by the strong presence of the US army – defined for the first time as 'occupying troops' and whose withdrawal is at least announced (Resolution 1546) – and without the necessary human or financial resources to tackle it.[79] For its part, the US, despite the relatively successful elections of January 2005, still risks failing in its objectives of stabilizing democracy in the region.

In short, after the break of 2002, the US has repeatedly returned to the UN in 2003 and 2004, firstly to try to gain its endorsement for the occupation and then to secure political cooperation that would go beyond the initial merely humanitarian missions or police training outside Iraq. The Iraqi campaign is of exceptional internal and international importance and the second Bush administration, conscious of the limits of unilateralism, has, to an extent, returned *ex post* to multilateralism. The 'quartet' (UN, US, EU and Russia) formed to help resolve the tortuous Israeli–Palestinian problem and facilitate the eventual agreement of the Middle East 'road map' after years of inactivity was the first example of this. The compromises over Iraq in the UN Security Council in 2003–4 symbolize the conflictual coexistence of unipolar and multipolar tendencies within the current heterogeneous international system. It is clear, however, that when the US returns to the UN after this or future transatlantic crises in the long war against terrorism and tyranny, it is not to eat humble pie, but out of necessity and pragmatism and without any recognition of the supreme role of the UN as an expression of legitimacy and a multiplicity of forces. The world order, therefore, is out of the dynamics and rules of both a universalistic or multipolar system.[80]

The distance from a multipolar system is confirmed by the fact that the opposition coalition of France, Germany and Russia not only was unable to prevent the war, but is strategically weak due to the heterogeneity of EU and Russian interests and Russia's limited effectiveness, extremely shaky democratic credentials and internal problems with

Chechnya. Nonetheless, Putin's decision to align himself with the political nucleus of the EU on international issues such as Iraq, Palestine and North Korea deserves more attention. The tripartite convergence has partially worked in its phase of containment and in negotiating three approved UN resolutions. This marks a significant departure from the 2001 show of unity at the APEC conference in Shanghai, which saw US, Russian and Chinese leaders in agreement regarding the Afghan war and the initial marginalization of Europe and Japan, overcome to an extent in the reconstruction phase thanks to EU initiatives and the Bonn conference in 2002. In fact, the war in Iraq has facilitated renewed dialogue between the EU and Russia, Latin America, India and China. The previous three-way relationship between Russia, Europe and the US has thus become far more complex. Neither the Western anti-Russian alliance nor the EU–Russian anti-US alliance seem particularly durable and what we are witnessing now seems more a case of a multidimensional dynamic of cooperation and competition in which the EU is not necessarily the weakest link as it used to be during the cold war. The essential point, however, is that no counterbalancing alliance or coalition is emerging, despite the limits of US power.

Going by their rhetoric at least, China, France and Russia appear to be the three countries most committed to the idea of a multipolar world. Realist literature depicts China as the emerging factor behind the power shift towards a multipolar world. More worryingly, the Bush administration has declared China to be 'not a strategic partner, but a competitor', and still maintains a hard stance on the issues of Taiwan and the arms embargo, thus recalling the era of bipolar confrontation and the cold war.[81] However, China is keeping a deliberately low profile for a series of reasons: its interaction with the US within the WTO and APEC; the common fight against terrorism; the fact that China effectively finances the US's huge trade and current payments deficit, the limits of its diplomacy. China's stance also reflects a necessary prudence dictated by past and present sensitive issues such as the Korean situation and last, but not least, due to the still negative interplay (following the long Tiananmen Square crisis) between its international economic cooperation agenda and the controversy over its domestic respect for the rule of law and human rights.

Realists focus on Chinese nationalism and its internal and external dimensions. These include the attention devoted to space research (presented as a matter of national pride), the use of patriotic rhetoric aimed at managing unstable internal cohesion, the strong tones of the 'one China' principle regarding Taiwan and Tibet and the vigorous defence of the national interest over controversial issues, including tensions with Vietnam and Japan.

However, realists often tend to oversimplify modern China and the East and South Asian security complex.[82] Hu Jintao's China is already an economic giant which exerts significant influence on international markets and demands cooperation due to its consistently high GDP growth rates (9 per cent in 2004) and its needs in terms of energy, food, etc. The China economy, comparable to Italy in 2004, is expected to be double that of Germany and Japan within 15 years; however, the current economic growth is strengthening its multilateral interdependence. As a result, the new China is trying to strike a dynamic balance between the management of nationalistic tendencies and the creation of a network of peaceful, multidimensional external relations. This is in line with a distinctive 'soft power' model of its role in regional and global governance which includes:

- active membership of the global network, including the WTO and the UN and its agencies, of the World Health Organization, China's hosting of the Olympic Games in Beijing in 2008, etc. Taken together, these constitute an economic and civilian framework for confidence-building policies with global partners and the entire international community;
- China's regional multilateral relationship on the one hand with Japan (which explains the Japanese economy's recovery, i.e. more than 6 per cent GDP growth rate in 2003) and, on the other, with ASEAN states: progress has been made through 'ASEAN plus 3' and as a result of the political dialogue within the 'ASEAN Regional Forum'. This is reflected by the important 2004 decision to establish a China–ASEAN Free Trade Area before 2010;
- controversial regional/global issue and conflict prevention policy regarding the Korean peninsula: China seems more interested than the US in transforming the six-way talks, held in Beijing since 2003, into a stable multilateral regime; however, the failure of the US hard approach and the North Korean disengagement from six-part US-sponsored talks in Beijing (three meetings between August 2003 and June 2004) revealed in 2005 not only how hard the stake of setting a multilateral regime without shared values, nor hegemonic state, may be, but also how *déboutant* is the performance of Chinese diplomacy in leading international negotiation even at regional level;
- regional 'Shanghai cooperation organization' with Russia, China and Central Asian countries. This has clear relevance given the rapid increase of Chinese energy demands;

- South–South interregional dialogue with IBSA (India, Brazil and South Africa). This is not only important because it creates a counterweight to the G7 within the WTO (as it successfully did in 2003 in Cancún), but it also complements growing Chinese–South American economic and trade cooperation (reflected by Hu Jintao's visit to South America in 2004).

Within such a dynamic context, it is extremely important to note the progress made regarding bilateral and multilateral relationships with the EU. This includes the ASEM regime, bilateral relations with EU member states and, since October 2003, the milestone represented by the EU–China 'strategic partnership'. Going far beyond the annual summit mechanism which had existed since 1998, the strategic partnership establishes a regular and multi-level political dialogue and consultation. Economic and technological multidimensional cooperation is also being improved (including development aid and issues pertaining to the environment, finance, transport, science, research, ICT, education, universities and the social and tourism fields). This represents a genuine window of opportunity for the EU as a civilian power if it is able to tackle the legacy of controversial issues (first of all the arms embargo but also full recognition of China as a market economy) and can consistently and coherently combine the defence of its trade interests (such as rules implementation and intellectual property rights for example) with its democratic values and common aims regarding pluralistic globalization and a multilateral world order.[83]

To conclude, it is possible that the current shift of global economics towards the East is not only changing power relations within the region, but is also causing a shift of the centre of gravity of international politics. However, comparing it with the catastrophic emergence of Germany during the first half of the twentieth century is flawed and misleading. The Chinese have shown their commitment to establish broad international networks. This strategy may function according to a positive sum cooperation model and can hardly be interpreted as representing any kind of aggressive move towards a multipolar world. The traditional realist approach is seriously challenged by China and cannot be applied to East Asia in such a simplified form.

As far as Western policies are concerned, American oscillations between cooperation with China and containment (including Taiwanese rearmament, the tough stance of the US in relation to Korea, its long-term military presence in Central Asia, the arms embargo and so on) appear risky and could well serve merely to increase uncertainty and instability across the entire region. By contrast, a global and long-term cooperative approach looks better suited to dealing with the challenge of involving China more and more within a multidimensional bilateral and multilateral network, both at regional and global levels, as the best way to avoid the rearmament of a nationalist China. This is likely to facilitate international stability and encourage gradual internal reforms in China itself.

All of what has been said up to now, along with the unanimous international concern regarding China's internal socio-political fragilities, undermines the credibility of the multipolar rhetoric of the Chinese leadership, for example the joint declaration by the Chinese and French presidents Hu Jintao and Jacques Chirac at the Evian G8 meeting of 2003.

1.5.1   The unlikely multipolarity based on France or whomever

There are two crucial differences in this regard between Chirac's France and that of de Gaulle. The first is that the former enjoys left–right domestic consensus among the elites as regards international and EU politics, while protest of the extremes can become majoritarian as on 29 May 2005. The second is the current limits of the political cooperation between France and the pacifist and multilateralist Germany. These now irreversibly pacified former enemies have constituted the core and the motor of European integration over the past 50 years and appear to be struggling to become a new element in world politics. The events of 2002–3 are therefore better understood from the perspective of the positive outcome of Jean Monnet's historical innovation (political unity through socio-economic integration) than by quips about 'old Europe'. However, the EU crisis of 2005 shows the limits of the classical Franco-German axis and the fanciful desire of the French notion of *Europe puissance*.

If we look beyond the rhetoric of a part of the French elites, it is clear that today in France we are seeing a paradoxical reversal of roles compared to when de Gaulle in the 1960s opposed American multilateralism by defending a classic notion of national sovereignty. Notwithstanding its mistaken show of arrogance towards other EU members and the accession candidates, France took the risk of isolation by reacting with dignity and autonomy to the unprecedented diplomatic pressure put on it by the most powerful country in the world. In this, of course, France was helped by national interests and the new political convergence with German peace policy and European public opinion. In 2002–4 we were witnessing a process of Europeanization in French politics which overcomes narrow nationalism and converges with the stances of the four major EU institutions. Moreover, France seemed to be taking advantage of the strength of its African alliances (which explains Bush's swift 2003 counteroffensive in Africa) as well as the positive image consolidated by the Evian reform of the G8 in 2003, which opened that organization to the possible protagonists of a new polycentric world, including India, Brazil, China and South Africa. This represented a process of openness which coloured the next meetings of the G8 namely under British Presidency.[84] It is in line with France's multiple and controversial proposals (supported by Brazil, Spain and around 100 countries) for a kind of Tobin tax, financing the struggle against poverty and Aids and in favour of the creation of a new socio-economic Security Council of the United Nations.

How has the US administration reacted to the new direction of French foreign policy? One way has been by dropping its unprecedented threats to punish France for having 'violated the duties imposed by the alliance'. In fact, France has paid a relatively small price for having assumed the mantle of the main actor of containment in relation to American policy on Iraq. Prudence is essential, of course, as the neo-conservatives in the White House continued in 2003 and 2004 to attack France,[85] while still also hoping to win over Russia. In the short term the US have very little option but to recognize French and German autonomy. However, the central question of the next decade is whether the way out of the open discord on Iraq will be a restoration of individual and bilateral relationships on single issues (Lebanon–Syria, Iran, Africa . . .) or the settlement of a new global transatlantic partnership, strengthening EU unity.

Nevertheless the EU nucleus centred on France and Germany is not and will never become a military pole of a multipolar kind. It may represent a new political force, provided that it learns to better involve its European partners such as Spain, Italy, the Benelux, the neutral countries and of course the UK. Through its relationship with France, Germany has been able to give a political voice to the impetus provided by majority public opinion in favour of peace and multilateralism. But precisely France and Germany show the impossibility of the classical model of *puissance* within a multipolar world.

The short-sightedness that has led some commentators to view German refusal to back the 'preventive war' in simple electioneering terms – just like the myopia afflicting those who raised the opposite spectre of the neo-Bismarckian bogeyman of the 'fourth Reich' in 1990 only to then criticize 'Teutonic timidity' during the first Gulf War of 1991 – continues to blind them to the effectiveness of Berlin's 'quiet force' and its emerging leadership. Berlin is central to an eastward-expanding Europe, in which the UK remains outside the euro and France is giving up the 50-year-long equal weighting of votes in the Council of Ministers, following the move to attach more importance to population size in determining the modalities of the European decision-making process (we can see this trend already in the current Treaty of Nice and not only in the conclusions of the Convention and in the Constitutional Treaty).

The British government's greatest error as regards the Iraqi crisis was to underestimate the solidity of the Franco-German engine. This ultimately led to the Blair government's failure to achieve its fanciful aim of being in 2002–3 a bridge-builder between the US and EU, notwithstanding its break with France and Germany. However, precisely Franco-German steadfastness provided a base for a resettlement of ties with Britain (Berlin summit 2004). The UK will remain one of the key actors in EU politics because of its strength and its geography. However, inevitably, it cannot be a leader unless it changes its marginal role to all of the great innovations in the European unification process over the past 50 years. Although Tony Blair has admitted much of this negative historical legacy, he too has missed out on a unique opportunity to secure for Britain the leadership role 'at the heart of Europe' he once promised his electorate. It is sufficient to think for a moment about the Blair government's *political* choices in relation to the euro and the political dimension of the EU, including the Common Foreign and Security Policy.[86]

To sum up, therefore, we cannot speak of a 'multipolar system', but rather of genuine 'multipolar tendencies' within a heterogeneous and evolving international system. The latter are real tendencies that sometimes cause a softening of US unilateralism, but, on other occasions, provoke the US into hardening its unilateral stance. But behind the political dynamics, how many capabilities and resources can be respectively read into each of these potentially multipolar forces? In other words, how are the power relations between the nuclear powers evolving?

Even if we locate the political situation of 2002–3 in a longer-term perspective, then we can resist the temptation to resurrect realist theories of international relations. On what evidence rests the theory, suggested at least by appearances, that the world has taken steps towards political multipolarism and the logic of spheres of influence and 'security dilemmas'?[87] Even though this approach has gained renewed vigour from the double crisis of opposed ideologies that have dominated the media over the past decade – the rhetoric of 'globalization for all' and the end of history, on the one hand, and, on the other, the impressionistic prophecies regarding the clash of civilizations[88] – we should not forget that neo-realists revealed the limits of their analytical tools in two fundamental moments at the end of the twentieth century:

(a) The collapse of the Soviet system happened without war. In fact, one of the key elements in its demise was the progressive inclusion of the USSR and its allies in a system of complex interdependence, combining communication, cultural and economic cooperation, technological competition, political dialogue and international regimes and treaties (such as that of Helsinki in 1975);

(b) The theory that those international institutions born during the cold war (including the EU) would crumble following the systemic changes of the period from 1989 to 1991 and lead to anarchic disintegration and the return of historical European demons has been proved false.[89]

The multilateral system, with the EU at its heart, was in fact strengthened during the 1990s. While the attention given to European states' competition for influence during the Balkan wars or the interpretation of the eastward EU expansion and 'conditionality' in terms of hierarchical 'concentric circles' is not without interest and merit,[90] it is the very development of the vast multilateral quasi-continental network of the EU that provides confirmation of an institutionalist approach. In other words, between 1989 and 2005, in spite of several shortcomings and problems, the EU's institutional system has historically taken steps *forwards* towards broader cooperation and deeper unity and not *backwards* towards the renationalization of member states.

Certainly, coming back at the global level, G.W. Bush's first term has been a proactive factor of the return to centre stage of political competition between different world views and interests with various state entities and coalitions of nations eager to tip the balance of international power in their own favour.[91] However, before welcoming ambiguous concepts like 'multipolarism', let us briefly verify what is the real situation of power distribution among the nuclear states and look at some statistics. The empirical data of 2002 confirm the inequality and heterogeneity of military, technological and strategic resources and capabilities of the five main players in the presumed 'balance of power'[92] of the twenty-first century. The US and the EU, while on an analogous economic footing (GDP of approximately €11bn, though we must take into consideration the fact that the Union's monetary zone does not represent a true single economic unit), are poles apart when it comes to military spending. The EU15 spend a total of €130bn, the EU 25 €160bn. By contrast, the US spends €357bn. Moreover, this last figure is constantly increasing and is expected to reach €470bn by 2006. More important in explaining the transatlantic gap is the irrational distribution of European defence spending across member states than the overall quantitative differences. European nuclear power (France has 470 tactical and strategic nuclear warheads while the UK has 185) is incomparable to the US arsenal (10,656 warheads). We are thus reminded of how unrealistic the notion of the EU balancing US power in this sense really is.

The only force comparable to that of the US is Russia's (approximately 10,000 warheads), but Russia's military power exists mostly on paper now as it has been weakened by the country's poor economic situation and administrative unreliability. It is worth noting that the entire Russian GDP (€352bn), notwithstanding Putin's rhetoric, is inferior to the defence budget alone of the US and that Russia can ill afford the €72bn it spends on defence. The rising power that is China has about 400 atomic warheads at its disposal and a population of 1.25 billion compared to 450 million Europeans, 290 million Americans and 143 million Russians. China's strong point is the dynamism of its GDP, which has grown for ten years at annual rates of 5–10 per cent and, at its 2002 figure of €1315bn, allows for a military spend of €52bn. China's GDP will overcome France, UK and Germany within a few years. Finally, we should mention India, the second emerging Asian giant, which has a population similar to China's and a GDP growth rate of 6 per cent. A symbol (with Pakistan) of the ineffectiveness of the non-proliferation treaty (NPT), India possesses a nuclear arsenal consisting of approximately 60 warheads, although its limited GDP of €542bn restricts its military budget to a mere €16bn and its political role to that of a regional military power.

In conclusion, we can say that the international system is much more asymmetric and heterogeneous than a classical multipolar balance of power. It includes conspicuous, albeit different in nature, multipolar tendencies (there are nuclear powers which are weak economically and economic giants who lack nuclear and military strength) and the hierarchy of force favours the lone superpower more than ever. Empirically described by relevant scholars as the 'new world disorder',[93] this situation is certainly far removed from the model of a multipolar order. Furthermore, acting against multipolar tendencies is the inheritance left by the long season of flexible bipolarism, i.e. a vast multilateral network, both global and regional in nature, that in Europe and elsewhere has taken on a dynamic of its own and which is partly independent of the impulses that were provided at its origin by the hegemonic US. But before analysing this persistent multilateral aggregating trend, let us first discuss a partially alternative international analysis which is also a central point of the current US administration's and some EU policy makers as well, i.e. the connection between the terrorist threat, and that posed by the proliferation of WMD and failed states.

1.6   The new international anarchy: informal terrorism, failed states and WMD proliferation

We should first of all state that the 'anarchic' thesis has changed in the past ten years and become de-Europeanized. As mentioned earlier, the idea that Europe would see the return of nationalism and spheres of influence following the fall of bipolarism was put forward by neo-realists such as Timothy Garton Ash and John J. Mearsheimer.[94] It is true that nationalism, ethnonationalism and the fanaticism of small nations did return with unexpected vigour, having been artificially suppressed by authoritarian regimes and empires or mistakenly believed to have been overcome by modernization.[95] However, any possibility of the former European powers employing 'spheres of influence' politics has been largely contained by the EU and the multilateral network. Notwithstanding the tragedies of the former Yugoslavia and the western Balkans, the 1990s saw the slow imposition of a politically governed multilateral and pacific order at a continental scale through the enlargement process and the nurturing of better relations with areas bordering the enlarged EU. Fragmentation and endemic and ungovernable conflict became characteristics of more remote places such as the Caucasus (e.g. Chechnya), the Middle East and other continents. Can the internal success of EU multilateralism provide a model for tackling fragmentation and preventing conflicts? The developments of recent years are certainly rich in instructive implications.

Rather than referring to the multipolar risks associated with a strengthening Europe and an emerging China, scholars and official comments by both the US and the EU point the finger at the numerous examples of political fragmentation, failing states and proliferation. It is true that we are witnessing various forms of religious, ethnic, nationalist and subnational fragmentation. This is not only a reaction to globalization,[96] but is also the result of long-festering regional political crises such as those in the Middle East, the African Great Lakes, Somalia, western Africa (Sierra Leone, Liberia and the Ivory Coast), the Korean peninsula, Kashmir, Afghanistan, the south of the former USSR and Indonesia. This long series of crises is a structural fact of the current transitional phase within the international system. Local protagonists are not always able to integrate with the international system, nor are they just mere instruments of the great powers. In some cases, the state is strengthened as a tool of nationalistic movements. In others, it is the very weakness of the central state that is partly to blame for international crises (as occurred for example, in Somalia, Afghanistan, Lebanon, the Congo and Indonesia).[97] However, pre-2002

Afghanistan provides a clear but still rare example of a declining state becoming a safe haven for global terrorist networks.

Without falling into the trap of Samuel Huntington's *vulgata* on the clash of civilizations, we can ask: to what extent is it possible within this context to speak in terms of the specific nature of the crisis occurring within the Islamic world? Only with extreme caution. The thesis pitting Islam and the West as two rival compact blocks has been disproved by sociological research.[98] Nor does the argument supporting the structural incompatibility of Islam with globalization hold water if we think of modernizing states like Indonesia and Malaysia, even if modern regional groupings of neighbouring nations have not yet been successful in the Middle East and North Africa.[99] The Muslim world is characterized by internal divisions and rifts just like the Christian world. Muslim countries have also been the victims of terrorism and pursue anti-terrorist and democratization strategies (as within the framework of ASEAN for example). The identification of fundamentalism and terrorism with the policies of certain states is treated by the EU with more circumspection than by the US. What is certain, however, is that we are witnessing a crisis in Western manipulation of Islamic fundamentalism of the kind seen during the bipolar conflict in Afghanistan and the Iran–Iraq war.[100] We should also note that the war on terrorism has not managed to create the clear cleavage that the 'axis of evil' rhetoric required. While tragic in human terms, terrorism of itself does not yet have a direct impact on the international system except, as Kenneth Waltz says, in so far as it is used by the US to reinforce existing trends and options.[101] The question of the way, form and level of political management of the anarchic tendencies of the international system thus still remains highly controversial.

The coupling of order/disorder, with its emphasis on anarchic trends[102] and the dangers of proliferation, has been integrated with the issue of democracy/authoritarianism by the distinct visions of Blair, Wolfowitz and Rice and this has gone a long way towards legitimizing the toppling of criminal tyrannies like that in Iraq. However, though in different tone, the already quoted 'Solana paper' and the EU strategy against proliferation of WMD (both approved by the European Council in 2003) also focus attention on the threats posed by a possible conjunction of terrorist attacks and failed states. By weakening some states (moderate Islamic ones, but also others) and forging alliances with other authoritarian regimes in possession of WMD, the terrorist network could become a catalyst for change in international politics and accelerated proliferation. In other words, while terrorism itself has no direct political impact, its combination with the threat of proliferation can effectively alter high politics.

From the perspective of the international system, the incontrovertible fact is that, in part due to the demise of the USSR, we have seen a spreading of nuclear arms and technology and neither the NPT nor the UN Atomic Agency have yet been able to stop it.[103] In a context where often the very philosophy of the NPT has been put in question by neo-realist approaches, the world is faced with a highly ambiguous and variegated phenomenon, the remedies for which may prove worse than the illness itself. On the one hand, we have nuclear proliferation resulting from regional tensions, such as those between India and Pakistan, the seriousness of which is, paradoxically, being underestimated due to the imperatives of forming alliances in the 'war on terror'. Such alliances are not capable of preventing the international system from dangerously deteriorating in the long term. Following Clinton's ineffectual sanctions (1998), the US has accepted India and Pakistan's nuclear arming (as Israel's) as a fait accompli. On the other hand, some states such as North Korea and Iran use nuclear build-up not only to defend hated regimes from domestic upheaval by emphasizing the threat posed by the enemy, but also as a means of asserting their sovereignty and imposing negotiated relations on the US and, in the case of Iran, on the EU as well.

Proliferation thus poses a real challenge to the international community in so far as it represents a possible channel for anarchic fragmentation.[104] Although such a dark scenario is neither obvious nor certain, the spread of nuclear technology and chain reactions are inevitable as regards both the Iranian and North Korean nuclear cases. However, these same challenges could produce very different outcomes depending on internal and, in particular, external variables, including the nature and credibility of solutions proffered by the international community.[105] Three different developments are theoretically possible. In the absence of agreed responses from the international community, a first hypothesis is that the world can run the risk of experimenting with a complex and highly decentralized system of nuclear balance, something that Morton Kaplan (in line with Kenneth Waltz) has defined as a 'unit veto'. He makes the case for a systemic hypothesis of stabilization in the post-bipolar world through the reciprocal balancing of a certain number of small and large isolated state powers with a minimum nuclear deterrent, none of whom would strike first (hence the 'veto') for fear of a reprisal attack from a third party. However, the irrationality of domestic political actors, the possibility of a war 'by mistake' in a climate of distrust, the possibility of selling to informal terrorists, the '1914 risk' of a catalytic war and the current clear asymmetry between the powers render such a hypothesis unrealistic and dangerously destabilizing.[106] Such a scenario would only become likely if the United States, frustrated by its failure to impose its messianic world vision, retreated into a sort of neo-isolationism (however, different from its pre-1941 isolationism).

The second hypothesis reflects the current US view, i.e. the threat of 'preventive wars' in the form of political wars and military occupations, conducted in the name of democracy and international security. However, aside from the questionable effectiveness of such a strategy (as shown by Somalia, the Lebanon and Iraq) or the dangers of provoking fragmentation and civil war in the invaded state (Iraq), international legitimization of such actions would be lacking as risks and casualties would be intolerable to Western democracies. This has been confirmed in the case of North Korea by the opposition to an attack posed by Tokyo and Seoul. In short, such a strategy could produce the exact opposite to the desired effect – fragmentation, terrorism and, in certain cases, the acceleration and spread of the race to arm, exacerbated by a blurring in the distinction between nuclear and conventional weaponry.

This brings us to the third hypothesis of the evolving European approach, that is oscillating between a diplomatic stance and proactive multilateral and preventive crisis management, both at global and regional level, particularly when proliferation is caused by regional crisis. The regional dimension matters. The relationship between Brazil and Argentina is a good regional example of successful de-proliferation. Echoing Willy Brandt's Ostpolitik (also defined as *Wandeln durch Annährung*), the ideational background of a new proactive approach involves changing authoritarian regimes by engaging them in political dialogue and conditional cooperation: a strategy that led to the Helsinki pan-European Charter (1975) and the collapse of European Communism.

However, this approach is not yet shared by the US. For example it was not practised coherently during the Korean crisis in 2002–4, which allowed the North Korean dictator to withdraw from six-party talks in Beijing. While it is true that recourse to arms – especially possible Japanese moves to rearm – and an Iraq-like evolution of the situation have been avoided so far, the nuclear threat has by no means been suppressed. On the contrary, it has been enhanced. The fact that the 'tough' policy of the US had poor results may foster a change. As the EU and ASEM have indicated, a more effective and institutionalized combination of regional and global multilateral regulation of crises might allow the specific security demands of all partners to be addressed. This, however, would require combining a greater regionalization of conflict prevention (based on the special interest of China, Japan, South Korea for conflict prevention), and a radical reform of the

UN in order to reinforce its credibility and legitimacy in any eventual humanitarian and peacekeeping intervention. According to the above-mentioned 2003 strategic paper, the EU is interested in playing a leading role in strengthening multilateral regimes and agencies preventing proliferation, for example the Code of Conduct of The Hague (HCOC), the Missile Technology Control Regime (MTCR), the UN Agency AIEA and the NPT.

This approach may be worthwhile also regarding the second main risk of nuclear proliferation, Iran. Due to US failures over the last 25 years in its relationship with Iran, the key test of this distinctive 'EU approach' against proliferation concerns its ability to achieve a credible arrangement with Tehran. The EU has the motivations (e.g. geographic proximity) and the means (linking nuclear disarmament with civilian issues like trade agreement and WTO access) to create a stable regional security and economic framework in a highly sensitive area. Only if the EU multilateral and civilian approach can prove effective will it be able to halt US and Israeli readiness to use military action to try to effect dramatic regime change in Tehran.

In conclusion, therefore, it is the very international relations theory that insists on the point of the current growing anarchy and WMD proliferation which calls for a new understanding of multilateralism as a method of conflict prevention and global governance but also as a potential driver of a less unstable world order.

1.7   Which multilateralism? Institutions and values in a transitional phase

In the previous sections we sought to demonstrate that (a) the post-hegemonic international system entered a unipolar phase in 1991 that is, however, neither imperial nor neo-hegemonic; (b) the multiple limits of unipolarism do not signify the emergence of a multipolar order; (c) the variegated tendencies towards fragmentation and proliferation could evolve into different international scenarios depending on the responses of the international community. We should add that a defining feature of this heterogeneous transitional phase is the persistent complex conflictual combination of anarchy, asymmetrical balance of power, 'hierarchical system'[107] and multilateral practices, be they regional or global. The crucial question for this section is whether multilateralism is confined to low politics and socio-economic governance or the EU's experience of shared sovereignty may anticipate a new multilateral world order.

Unlike bipolarism, multipolarism and hegemonic stability (imperial or otherwise), multilateralism cannot yet be defined as an international system. However, since, as we have said, we are still in a transitional phase where none of the models previously cited can furnish a satisfactory explanation of the current system, then it is worth examining the evolution of multilateralism within global governance. Tackling this type of empirical question, which takes in the growing role of the EU, leads us to examine the explanatory force of two schools of thought underpinning research on multilateralism: institutionalism and constructivism.

The essential theoretical point we wish to stress is that multilateralism is not just one of the various means of managing intergovernmental relations. First of all, it assumes complex and different institutional forms. Secondly, multilateral institutions are shaped by the changing strategies, interests and values of the economic and political powers that have promoted them over time. the UK in the first instance, followed by the US and, in recent years, the EU. Realist approaches do not help us much here. For example, we have already noted that the American vision of multilateralism under Franklin D. Roosevelt and Harry Truman included the idea of a transnational social construct, i.e. a dynamic compromise between international liberalization and the national Welfare State. This was not the same form of multilateralism previously promoted by Britain. Nor does it correspond to that of the current globalization in terms of its shape, values and contents. In this sense, John Ruggie's social constructivist approach is more helpful than utilitarian approaches of rational choice, since it takes the ideational factors of states and powers into consideration.[108] By 'ideational factors', he means their world views, distinct identities, emotions and deep-rooted convictions, which are shared by and derived from recognized authorities that enjoy the broad consensus of states and powers.[109]

Unlike Ruggie, however, we believe that the new institutionalist approach of Keohane, Nye and others[110] has greatly helped pave the way for this new interpretative perspective, and has continued to enrich it with suggestions detailing both the relative autonomy and relevance of the institutional dimension by changing state preferences. Notwithstanding the end of American hegemony, Keohane argues[111] that international institutions perform four functions that go beyond their realist function of instruments of states: they push states to adopt negotiation rather than conflictual strategies; they replace pre-existing organizations; they facilitate exchange of information which, in turn, reduces reciprocal uncertainty and 'security dilemmas'; they specify obligations that go well beyond the level of mere 'interests'. The theory of international regimes is a first step to recognizing the binding capacity of rules and procedures laid down by intergovernmental arrangements.[112] They can also produce norms, regulations and spread principles, values and policies.[113] However, new institutionalism is the main jumping-off point for a vast body of research that, from regime theory to complex interdependence, has led to the following critical acquisitions with respect to neo-realism and which are important elements in understanding multilateralism:

- with their capacity to influence the international game by modifying the preferences of states, international organizations can contribute to a transformation of the system into a positive-sum game, and international institutionalization should also be viewed as a construction of forms of legitimate authority;
- although it remains a relevant international actor, various factors diminish the exclusive role and centrality of the state, for example the calling into question of the unitary and rational character of state behaviour by domestic political sociology through its emphasis on the increasingly complex nature of political negotiations and the growing weight of internal factors in world politics;
- the tremendous growth of transnational relations, of private networking, socio-economic links at regional and global level, along with the reinforcement of dynamics that fall outside the classic inter-state game, are increasingly creating an international environment which favours renewed understandings of multilateralism and its legitimacy;
- the paradigm of *world politics* thus goes beyond the neo-realist paradigm of *international politics*. It synthesizes the results of the theory of complex interdependence and the growing relationship between domestic and international politics, thereby changing and enhancing the space and role for international institutions.

We should also distinguish between this critique of neo-realism and those put forward by the exponents of functionalism from the 1960s.[114] Both new institutionalism and constructivism deal with the growth of cooperation and organizations involving states, but not necessarily with a kind of supranational integration that goes beyond the state. The multilateral institutional network modifies and reforms, but does not eliminate, the Westphalian world. Whereas neo-realists refuse to acknowledge the growth in importance of international institutions, especially towards the end of the twentieth century, constructivism is drawing attention to the importance of the 'normative meanings' incorporated into the increasing multilateral institutionalization of spheres of transnational relations.[115] Another contribution of constructivism to the critique of realism is that it takes into consideration the importance of ideas in the resolution of practical problems, by highlighting firstly the construction of epistemic communities and transnational networks, characterized by common convictions, and, secondly, their impact on the various levels of authority.

Without overlooking the residual importance of national sovereignty within the international system, where organizations and regimes are between states and not above them, Ruggie's constructivism tackles the fundamental reasons why and how territorial states which are legally equal in an interdependent world choose to collaborate, and what the consequences of this cooperation might be (including increased inter-dependence). The motivation changes, depending on the state and the situation. A state that is increasing its resources and national capacity might have less interest in multilateral cooperation, as is currently the case of the US. There is no functionalist process of task expansion spillover, of rapid expansion of the competencies of pyramid-type supranational institutions, as functionalists imagined. However, even if multilateral organizations initially depend on the issue they have to confront and are often internally characterized by variable geometry, they tend often to enhanced institutionalization.

Why then is international institutionalization so important? It is important because, even if it does not constitute a system of rights, obligations and sanctions, it nonetheless limits the unpredictable nature of the behaviour of states and channels them towards concerted and desired ends. The more international institutionalization there is, the less states are sovereign in the classic sense of the term and the less realism can explain why states have freely chosen to complicate their existence in this way. Ruggie discusses three levels of institutionalization:

1. the epistemic community level, purely cognitive and informative, but which can work to reform the Westphalian system;
2. the international regime of reciprocal expectations, based on rules and procedures that already imply a certain organizational effort and financial commitment;
3. formalized international organizations that institutionalize state behaviour, including that of the biggest states, and express a certain level of authority.

In our view, a fourth level should be added and verified as its extra-EU salience is concerned: a multilateral polity characterized by the primacy of supranational law over national law, consistently with the 'European Union model'.

According to Ruggie, the level of authority expressed by international organizations almost always implies a degree of *voluntary* submission. Certainly, this is different from the national level, since the transfer of authority from member states to international organizations is not definitive. We are however dealing with a concept that is more constraining, or less 'soft', than James Rosenau's concept of governance, which implies maximum consensus. Here, the concept of authority is more pertinent than that of power. Multilateral authority is only legitimized and rendered operative if there is a system of shared convictions, common interests and a common sense of duty. In our fourth level, however, the multilateral polity may evolve towards a new practice of international non-state power, as the concept of 'civilian power' is suggesting.

Multilateralism represents the most fruitful field of application for Ruggie's constructivist approach. He defines multilateralism as 'an institutional form which coordinates relations among three or more states on the basis of "generalized" principles of conduct – that is, principles which specify appropriate conduct for classes of actions with regard to the particularistic interests of the parties or the strategic exigencies that may exist in any specific occurrence'.[116] Focusing on contents and principles as an interpretative tool in understanding institutional forms opens up a new theoretical perspective and is useful as a guide to empirical research.

We come then to the example of US hegemony and the relationship of hegemonic power to multilateralism. New institutionalists and, in particular, Keohane, rightly place multilateralism at the heart of institutionalism. However, according to Ruggie, by proposing a 'nominal' definition of multilateralism as 'the practice of co-ordinating national policies in groups of three or more states', Keohane does not stress the fact that it is not the number of actors that is so important, but the type of relationship established between them.[117] This difference of approach deserves more attention. While Keohane's theory of hegemonic stability sees multilateralism as expressing the desire and capacity of the hegemonic power to create an open international economic order, constructivism places greater emphasis on the intersubjective dimension of regimes as well as on the interpretative tool of social purpose. In the case of post-war US hegemony, for example, 'embedded liberalism' goes beyond the simple distinction between an open or closed economy and stresses the dynamic equilibrium between the market and political regulation. Liberalization and the opening up of the international economy have conformed to the aim of supporting political and social stability within states.

After the Second World War, the US secured the adherence of its partner states to the principle of multilateralism. Through the Marshall Plan in Europe and bilateral aid in Japan, it fostered international growth while allowing the development of Keynesian-style, full-employment national economic policies that included collaboration with trade union organizations. National differences concerned the scope of the role of the state in the economy and not its legitimacy.[118] The case of the International Trade Organization, which was rejected by the US Senate in 1946–47 as too much of a straitjacket, shows the difficulties and limits related to the acceptance of regulation of the open economy. The birth of the GATT nonetheless represented a significant compromise between the State Department's position in favour of the application of the multilateral principle of non-discrimination (with the obligatory 'most favoured nation' clause) and that which supported granting certain exemptions and concessions to partners. These involved allowing: the preservation of Preferential Trade Agreements (PTA); the formation of regional free-trade zones (art. XXIV, organizations such as the EC, EFTA, etc.); the formation of trade and customs unions (such as the European Community in 1957); the possibility of exemptions and suspensions when justified by national policies of full employment; policies supporting agricultural prices (along the lines of the CAP); various exceptions to, and possible suspensions of, the progressive reduction of trade barriers when such moves would represent a threat to local production (art. XIX); finally the institutionalization of multilateral procedures for the resolution of trade disputes. All this serves to underline the correctness of the thesis on the flexibility of the exercise of early American hegemonic power.[119]

The 1970s and 1980s represented a turning point, however, and not only in the sense of a 'governed change', as claimed by Ruggie, but in terms of a truly significant turning point as argued by Keohane and symbolized by the unilateral decision of the US on the inconvertibility of the dollar in August 1971. The following decades were marked by instability and growing disputes in the triangular relationship between the US, Europe and Japan. This was despite the start made at the Tokyo Round (1973–79) to tackle non-tariff trade barriers (national subsidies, product standards, limits on imports, etc.) and the fact that the difficult Uruguay Round (1986–94) exceeded expectations not only in terms of tackling issues such as services and investment, but in creating GATT's successor, the more aggressive World Trade Organization, which, thanks to its dispute settlement mechanism, has made a significant contribution to the growth and development of international trade.[120]

In synthesis, the Bretton Woods institutions gave rise to a long, expansive historical phase, a multilateral epistemic community, a shared narrative and an intersubjective framework that all influenced the concrete decisions of states above and beyond the need to contain the Soviet threat through international cooperation. Multilateralism is thus the true heart of institutionalism. However, the new theoretical question is whether this rich inheritance is capable of influencing the international system not only after hegemony, but also after the end of the bipolar world. And, if so, how? We concur with Ruggie's argument only up to a certain point. He views as a validation of his approach the peaceful systemic change symbolized by the fall of the Berlin wall, the fallout from which multilateral organizations have helped to manage through their inclusive choices. While we agree with his scepticism as regards the possibility of the emergence of a multipolar logic, we do not share his distrust of any political development of the European Community and Union. He is very optimistic regarding the development of the WTO, but the unrealistic hopes he places in the UN system (with reference to Cambodia, Western Sahara, Namibia and the first Gulf War) and in the NPT reflect a vision of a possible future which, with the end of the 1990s, is clearly receding. The major question that has not been addressed is that of how international organizations and regimes will change following the shift in the preferences of the former hegemonic power. In fact, Ruggie himself is conscious of the threat to the system represented by the resurgent laissez-faire ethos which, since the 1980s and 1990s, has been in conflict with regulatory 'social purpose'. This is one of the elements of early multilateralism whose collapse partly explains current transatlantic tensions over models of society and the government of globalization.[121] However, the twenty-first century started with much harder challenges.

There is a lack of coherence in Ruggie's argument when he emphasizes the differences between consecutive hegemonies. It is true that studies on American identity under Franklin D. Roosevelt and the experience of public intervention ushered in by the New Deal are indispensable to understanding post-war multilateralism (in terms of the international projection of the Roosevelt model).[122] So too are anticolonial values, the open-door ideology and the desire to pull down trade and non-trade barriers without wishing, however, to return to a mere laissez-faire system or the old British Gold Standard one. But it is precisely because hegemonic powers shape the international system in the image of their own domestic model that the profound changes the partnership between the US and EU is currently undergoing cannot but have a considerable impact on the multilateral system.

This historical change is clearly perceptible in the area of political multilateralism. Roosevelt's administration broke with both classic US isolationism and traditional European imperialism – which negated the sovereignty of its partners – as incompatible with international cooperation. This new collective security project could thus take on one of two distinct forms: either a universalistic and inclusive form, as it did in 1945 (i.e. through the UN, even though it incorporated a power of veto for the Big Five, also included the right to sanction and the international community's right to collective self-defence. See art. 51 of the San Francisco Charter), or it could assume a different form (with Truman), consistent with a bipolar vision of the balance of power and directed towards a policy of containment by exclusion of the USSR (through NATO from 1949). To sum up: in contrast to the spider's web of leonine bilateral agreements which the Nazi German government (advised by the famous banker H. Schacht) entered into with numerous European countries and others, the US based post-war construction on two permanent and complementary elements, economic and political multilateral institutions, that have now been thrown into doubt. On the one hand, there was the 'most favoured nation' clause, preventing any trade discrimination. On the other, there was the political principle of indivisible peace, according to which the community of states responds collectively to aggression with common sanctions. It is in this context that the US stimulated the birth of European integration. Political multilateralism is not identical to an alliance. Initially at least, no victim nor enemy is identified, the threat is indivisible and the response is collective. Once the cold war had begun, following the dashing of universalistic hopes, the principle of collective security was adapted to NATO, particularly with the renowned article 5 that deems an attack on one member to constitute an attack on the whole alliance.

In the post-cold war era, it is implausible to imagine the revival of the US–UN relationship of 1945–47. The question, therefore, is: how can we reconcile the gradual decline in American hegemonic functions with the durability of international regimes and multilateral organizations? Certainly, their longevity can partly be attributed to the services they deliver, to the inertia of bureaucratic organizations, to various utilitarian considerations, and to their capacity to adapt to the changing international framework. However, it is generally recognized that the US has progressively distanced itself from the multilateralist spirit that characterized the 1940s and has instead preferred to try to impose its own point of view, with increasing determination and varying degrees of success, on both economic and political matters. In the hardening of the 'IMF orthodoxy' and the so-called 'Washington consensus', we can clearly see these tendencies in the field of economic multilateralism (thanks to the US's power on the IMF Board, where, with 17.11 per cent of the vote, it effectively exercises a veto[123]). Take, for example, the austerity measures and reduction of public and social spending conditions imposed on poorer states which seek loans. Or the baffling success of the US in convincing its partners that its huge balance-of-payments deficit represents the best way of ensuring global liquidity and financial stability.

As far as NATO's political multilateralism is concerned, the lack of enthusiasm shown by the US in 2001 to European proposals to invoke article 5 of the NATO treaty (for the first time ever), as a common response to the September 11th attacks, tells us a lot about the changes under way at the beginning of the new century.[124] Generally speaking, when the hegemonic state distances itself from those international regimes and multilateral organizations which it had originally sponsored, or when it openly tries to simply exploit them for marginal purposes and *post festum* (see NATO role in Iraq after 2004), what follows is either the decline of those same international institutions, or a relative increase in their independence from their original sponsors; at the beginning of this new century, one of the main variables is the emerging role of the EU at their core.

In our view, what is currently emerging is a European vision and practice of multilateralism. New institutionalism and constructivism are particularly germane approaches to the study of European multilateralism. Even the regimes theorist Stephen Krasner acknowledges that the EU constitutes an exception to the 'external anarchy' of international relations.[125] European internal multilateralism developed from the ideas of Jean Monnet and the founding fathers according to federal–functional integration model. The importance of internal ideational factors is highlighted by a vast body of literature, which, although at times apologetic and teleological, has drawn attention to the true importance of the founding 'epistemic community' and the proactive role of the networks of pro-integration movements.[126] Recognizing the importance of the founding values supporting the construction of supranational and intergovernmental rules and procedures is crucial to an understanding of the choices of member states welcoming the constitutional forms that regional integration has implicitly assumed.[127] It also helps to contextualize the relationship between continuity and change in the post-hegemonic phase when internal multilateralism is expected to contribute to a better regional and global multilateral framework.

It was following the collapse of the Bretton Woods system that the then 'small EC' launched its first single currency project (which took 30 years to bring to fruition). Decades later, in the aftermath of the systemic changes of 1989–91, the EU strengthened its multilateralism with regard to both regional (continental stabilization in eastern Europe and the Mediterranean) and global governance. In this regard, it has promoted the institutionalization of development aid, shown a front-line commitment to causes dear to the UN (the end of apartheid, eradication of anti-personnel landmines, the campaign against poverty, etc.) and supported sustainable development and protection of the ecosphere, reinforcement of the WTO, humanitarian aid, the promotion of democracy, the protection of human rights and the bringing to justice of perpetrators of crimes against humanity.

In the current post-hegemonic era, various multilateral organizations balance continuity and change differently. The EU has not only adapted to change, but has blazed its own trail, defining its own priorities independently of the US. Variables such as domestic public opinion, institutional structures, strategic options (both general and specific) and clear-headed leadership all play an important role. In the case of the EU, the great novelty is that it has learnt the lesson of multilateralism so well (indeed, multilateralism is an integral part of its identity), that it now applies it to new challenges and issues, often independently of the US positions. Within existing organizations, the EU is pushing to strengthen the binding nature of multilateral rules and procedures and improve coordination both between international organizations (e.g. the WTO and the IMF) and between the UN and these organizations (e.g. the WTO and ILO). A new dynamic is thus emerging in multilateralism which is more independent of American consensus. The EU also contributes to the spread of regional multilateralism throughout the world (in Africa, Asia and Latin America) by deepening interregional arrangements that go beyond the simple aim of promoting free trade. To conclude, at the beginning of the twenty-first century, not only has multilateral cooperation survived the declining American post-war open hegemony, but, within the framework of Western multilateralism, a regional and global European institutional vision of 'effective multilateralism' is emerging[128] that is distinct from the ad hoc, à la carte or 'utilitarian' multilateralism of the US.[129]

Will the current trend, sometimes like a zero-sum game between the EU civilian power and the US soft power, give birth to a new EU hegemonic state? The prospect of an eventual EU hegemony replacing that of the US is certainly unimaginable, even if the 'bottom-up' emergence of new regional and global actors, of which the EU is the prime example, appears unstoppable. As far as security is concerned, the US looks to many observers as still 'bound to lead the world', whether it accepts its role of 'reluctant sheriff' or not.[130] Furthermore, the EU lacks (and will continue to lack) not only this hard power which, combined with soft power, is essential to hegemonic states but also the state kind of institutional framework.

So does the new multilateralism imply nothing more than a revived universalist and cosmopolitan utopia? Not necessarily. Although it is more binding in nature (if compared with past regimes), new multilateralism is not essentially post-Westphalian or postmodern. It requires states to want to cooperate with each other. Only some of these have profoundly reformed their national sovereignty, by pooling and sharing it, and that is happening at regional rather than global level. Regional actors, combined with regional and global networking of the majority of big states, should contribute to the new complex multilateral trend.

Of the various possible scenarios, the first hypothesis envisages a long uncertain transition during which the world will see the coexistence of very diverse understandings of multilateralism and sovereignty along with different regional, global, civil and military international interests and agendas, which may be more or less cooperative or competitive depending on variables such as time, space and the challenges of the day. What is astonishing is that we are already witnessing a new open-ended time of transatlantic conflicts and realignments, cooperation and competition which is inevitably changing the traditional post-war alliance. This transitional scenario in part remembering the 1990s would allow room for the consolidation of various complementary conceptions of international relations and practices of power, including the EU's one. The second possibility is that, by stressing a 'globalist' strategy (that recalls the bipolar era and 'securizes' the global agenda), the US will seek to diminish what James Rosenau optimistically called the 'bifurcation' of two increasingly divergent international agendas, two levels of global governance: the military and high politics agenda dominated by the US, on the one hand, and the civilian and multilateral agenda, on the other, where EU and multi-level governance are playing a major role. In this conflictual scenario, the US would seek to transfer to the second agenda the power relations it has attained in pursuing the first, thereby establishing a classic hierarchical model of actors and issues, built upon the primacy of military security and the actors who can and will guarantee it. Joseph Nye, among others, contends that the grafting of one agenda onto another is particularly difficult and could possibly engender the opposite effect to that intended.

If this is the case, then the way is free for a new research agenda focusing not only on the above scenario of a long transition but also on the conditions favourable to a 'bottom-up' transformation of multilateralism to which civilian powers – national and neo-regional entities like the EU, first and foremost – can contribute in a proactive way. What is being envisaged as a result of a long process is a multilateral world order which goes beyond the unipolar one. This would not pursue a multipolar vision, however, but would put a firm brake on the phenomenon of fragmentation. We find institutionalist and constructivist approaches to international relations encouraging, for the EU needs to be examined in terms of its present reality on the one hand, and in terms of its dynamics on the other. That is why this new research agenda should include the more innovative institutional and ideational components that are allowing the EU to express its increasing political autonomy such as the European constitutional Treaty, the development of its particular socio-economic model within the context of globalization, and the consolidation of a common international identity in flexible institutional forms, demonstrative of 'intelligent power'.[131]

1.8   The reality of the EU as an incipient, collective civilian power

So far, we have discussed at length what the international system does *not* represent (particularly with regard to the simplified visions of the role of the US) and have sought to demonstrate that the theoretical baggage of international relations theories is of use, even if it is sometimes more useful in terms of what it *disproves* than what it actually *proves*. In the previous sections, we came to the provisional conclusion that, within the context of an international system that tends to be hierarchical and unipolar, but still shows flexibility and heterogeneity, we are witnessing a detachment of multilateralism from the hegemonic power that originally sponsored it. Multilateralism has proved resistant enough to reinvent itself, thus confirming that it is increasingly an evolving system of values, rules, procedures and social planning. Which substantial force is underpinning its renewal (and how)? What impact does it have on the world order? The academic community requires new conceptual tools to interpret the changing international system and the more distinct external profile of the EU. Herein lies the utility of a rethinking of the concept of 'civilian power'[132] in tandem with that of 'new multilateralism'.

Let us provide a deeper and broader accounting of what has been briefly anticipated as our 'realistic' understanding of the EU as a civilian power. By realistic understanding we mean the following: leaving aside for the moment the essentially normative notions of civilian power, in this section we will explore an idea of civilian power which is firmly rooted in the dynamics of the current system of power relations and, therefore, also includes elements that can stand up to neorealist criticism. Rather than opposing real and ideal concepts of power, our aim is to consider the real ways in which the European construction has already tamed and 'civilized' the state sovereignties of its members, transforming what was once an obstacle into a supporting part of its political existence. Notwithstanding its various ambiguities,[133] the EU is already in fact a civilian power. This is the starting point for any analysis, despite the sometimes radical criticisms that are directed at particular EU policies and structures from the viewpoints of a normative theory of democracy[134] or international justice.[135] A political entity can be termed a civilian power not only if it does not intend, but also if it is not able, for various historical or structural reasons, to become a classic politico-military power and pursues its international peaceful objectives using other methods. Admittedly in profoundly different ways, Canada, post-war Germany, Sweden, the India of Gandhi and Nehru, Japan after 1945, the Italian Republic and many other countries besides have all been (and some remain) civilian powers. And, precisely because it includes and transforms also former 'great powers' such as France and Britain (i.e. nuclear powers with imperial traditions and military ambitions), this is one more reason to consider the EU a civilian power. International relations theory and the comparative study of political ideas and institutions can be used to support the thesis that the EU can realistically be defined as an at least incipient, collective civilian power for the following reasons, which link internal and external multilateralism:

1. The EU's common institutions and the routine of cooperation between member states have stabilized peace in western Europe for more than 60 years through social and economic integration. The *acquis communautaire* has clear democratizing and stabilizing effects on member states and candidate countries, even when these have only recently emerged from the tragic experiences of Fascist or Communist dictatorships. This 'internal foreign policy' is also the result of the application since 1952 of the 'Jean Monnet method', the success of which is symbolized by the Single Market, the euro, the consolidation of peace among former enemies and the stabilization of democracy.

European democracy has been enriched with supranational democratic institutions and procedures, transnational networks of parties, unions and associations, and a 'Charter of Fundamental Rights'. Due to the link it makes between individual and social rights, and because it strengthens the roots of the Strasbourg Convention on Human Rights into member states' national systems, while stressing the common European dimension, the Charter has become a salient part of the EU's international democratic identity. The Justice and Home Affairs Cooperation (JHA) also has important external implications, including common actions in international organizations, international agreements on immigration, asylum rights, criminal law and policies on the free movement of people.

2.   The process of European integration has produced increasing convergence around the common ground of what is called the 'European social model'. This highlights the fact that, despite the homogenizing tendencies of globalization, western Europe has developed a dynamic equilibrium between international competitiveness, social cohesion and democratic society that involves an active role for organized social actors and relatively generous Welfare State systems and public services, even if these differ from state to state. This has important external implications for the EU's policies and identity.

3.   The prospect of accession to the EU is a force for peace and democratization across the continent. Within a decade or so, approximately 35 states (including the entire Balkan peninsula) will, in one way or another, be involved in the same legal community, based on political democracy and respect for human rights, in line with the obligations laid down by the treaties.[136] We will deal in Chapter 4 with the problems raised by an endless enlargement process. However, the almost magnetic attraction of the EU to its neighbours makes it an important geopolitical reality and a regional workshop of regulation and multilateral global governance.

4.   The EU develops its economic and political influence through 'common strategies' and partnership agreements with surrounding countries (to the east: Russia, Ukraine and the other states of the former USSR; to the south: the countries of the Mediterranean basin). The new concept of 'neighbourhood policy' may provide a framework for cooperation policies, special partnerships and conditionality. These arrangements translate, albeit with varying degrees of success, into political dialogue, concrete policies, economic cooperation (e.g. the Stability Pact, the Barcelona Process, agreements on immigration policy) and rules of law. If it can better reconcile its eastward enlargement with such

agreements (while keeping them distinct), the EU will demonstrate the unprecedented stabilizing and 'civilizing' capacity of its power on a broad regional level. This will have obvious global implications.

5. In addition to this influence on the near abroad, the EU's role on the world stage has developed, particularly over the past 15 years, to the point where the Union is now recognized as the second global actor. The external relations based on the first pillar of the TEU, the previous EC, are of very high relevance. As the largest trading power in the world and donor of three times as much humanitarian and development aid – 55 per cent of the total amount – and twice as much post-war construction funding compared to the US, the EU has also become the world's second monetary power. It now equals the US in terms of economic power and has begun to explicitly develop its international political identity via its external relations and, in particular, by reform-ing its institutions and the CFSP. As de Tocqueville said, trade represents more than just the 'gentle' method of international communication that Montesquieu suggested. It also facilitates the conduct of effective foreign policy, as the EU experience has shown, by means of agree-ments, non-agreements and conditionality (access to the enormous internal European market is highly desirable and EU exports exceed those of the US by 25 per cent). The EU has promoted significant politi-cal initiatives such as the transition from GATT to WTO, China's mem-bership of the multilateral network, and the US has then followed. Despite the progress made in Geneva (2004), the difficult dialogue between North and South, which had begun at the Doha Conference and then ran into serious trouble in Cancún, still represents a *political* gamble of the first order for the EU. However, acting as a single entity, it has committed itself to promoting a new WTO round of negotiations which is expected to be more favourable to developing countries, although it is being hampered in its efforts by the agricultural lobbies.[137] Furthermore, while it was not an explicit goal of the EU, the euro has become a reserve currency, very competitive with the dollar. Without the euro, not only would the international financial crises of the 1990s have shook and divided the EU, but it is likely that France would have been brought to its knees within a week during its political dispute with the US in 2002–3.[138] International relations theories support this analytical hypothesis, i.e. that there is no longer any great divide between the pre-political and political dimensions of interna-tional action. This has been clearly shown, first and foremost, by the theory of complex interdependence, particularly with reference to the early EC. International political economy theory, on the other hand,

also highlights the interrelation between economic and political power, economic and political conflicts and economic and political security. Susan Strange and others have pointed to the emergence of new international hierarchies based on 'structural power' that is increasingly supported by 'knowledge' resources and technological development. Apart from demonstrating European competitiveness, examples such as the 'Ariane' project, growing space exploration cooperation,[139] the success of Airbus, and the major European satellite project 'Galileo'[140] all testify to the political and identity-marker impact that applied research can have, not least on transatlantic relations. Moreover, Paul Kennedy's historical reconstruction emphasized the importance of economic modernization in comparison to military force as a primary indicator of the growth of powers.[141] Finally, Robert Gilpin, who has traced the emergence of benevolent and malevolent neo-mercantile tendencies in the globalized economy, has drawn attention to the formation of international political entities based on economic and trade policies.[142]

6.   The EU identifies with multilateralism on the global as well as the regional level, often regarding multilateralism as an intrinsic value per se: does it provide opportunities for a positive-sum game which is separate from the pure hierarchical logic of power relations? Comparing the concept of civilian power with Joseph Nye's 'soft power' is useful, although he applies it to the US. Nye's concept risks verging on the classic power theory according to which soft power is only a function of a traditional kind of power that includes the whole range of instruments, whose balance is precarious and influenced by domestic factors as well (elections), and changing stances of ruling US administrations.[143] By contrast, the EU is not seriously expected to become a military power, and it is also for this reason that it so identifies with multilateral institutions. It has defended and championed the institutional strengthening of those international organizations built during the US's hegemonic period, in particular the UN and the GATT/WTO,[144] and promotes the construction of new global regimes as well as the extension of the international civilian agenda. Successful examples in this regard include the continuation in Marrakesh in 2002 and the entry into force in 2004 of the process begun in Kyoto to tackle emissions and the normative innovation of the International Criminal Court[145] (notwithstanding the US's boycott of both). The EU's support for international UN conferences on poverty and underdevelopment (Monterrey, 2002), racism (Durban, 2001) and sustainable development (Johannesburg, 2002) runs in tandem with its overall support for

the UN. However, the internal conflict on the issue of the reform of the UN Security Council clearly shows the non-state nature of the EU as a fully unified political actor.

7.   The EU contributes to global governance by collectively encouraging states in other continents to deepen regional cooperation. In the second chapter, this book aims to highlight that the spread of the regional cooperation among neighbouring countries on all continents as a means of securing peace, prosperity and democracy is a bottom-up process. However, the political and technical support provided by the EU to regional groupings in Africa (SADC in southern Africa and ECOWAS in western Africa), Asia (ASEAN and SAARC) and especially in Latin America (MERCOSUR, the Andean Community and CARICOM in the Caribbean) are all examples of this special kind of multilateralism (see the maps at the front of this book). Each experience of regional cooperation and integration is of course specific to its own historical and economic context and none can fully emulate the unique model of the EU. Chapter 2 recounts the findings of a vast body of international academic work in economics and political science that supports the idea of the structural and multidimensional character of new regionalism in the globalized world and the validity of comparing different regional associations across the globe – especially in terms of the similarities and differences between the varying balances between endogenous and exogenous causes and, most significantly for us here, new regionalism's resistance to unipolarism.[146]

Secondly, the EU has developed a new dimension in international relations, or, to be more precise, in intercontinental relations: that of interregionalism. This has seen the emergence of new structures of partnership and cooperation that encompass trade, economic, cultural and political dimensions. For example, we could mention the cooperation and political dialogue between the EU and Latin America (Rio Process), or that between the EU and the Far East (ASEM), or the ACP Convention which includes most of the world's poorest countries, or the Euro-Mediterranean process launched in Barcelona in 1995. Partnership means the opposite of one-way, colonial-style relations. Furthermore, interregional partnerships are part of transnational relations between civil societies. The content and forms of European interregionalism differ from those of its American counterpart, which limits itself to the promotion of free trade and discourages deeper forms of regional integration. The EU idea of multilateralism, distinct from US interpretation of the term both during and after its post-war hegemonic period, is enriched by several distinctive features: the inclusion of cooperation policies (namely social and development policies), the political dia-logue, the discursive importance attributed to equal partnership and, last but not least, the centrality given to 'new regionalism'. This is not perceived as a temporary derogation within the process of global liber-alization, but as both a mode of governance and an essential pillar of a new multilateralism. It is expected to provide greater legitimacy and effectiveness in the global multilateral system and foster a polycentric world structure that allows space for new actors to emerge on both the economic and political levels.

During the last decade, the Europeans have attempted to tackle vari-ous obstacles and difficulties by transforming their historical informal links into interregional institutionalized partnerships. In Europe's immediate vicinity, these difficulties concerned the lack of sufficient 'bottom-up' regional cooperation among partner countries, the prefer-ence of the EU's eastern partners and Turkey for full membership, and the negative impact of bilateral relations and 'conditionality' with indi-vidual countries. The relatively poor performance of the 'Barcelona Process', begun in 1995, is explained, on the one hand, by its excessive similarity to the Free Trade Area of the Americas (FTAA) and its weak political dimension and, on the other, by the overwhelming weight of the security issues linked to the worsening Israeli–Palestinian conflict.

In general, some of the more disappointing results of the last decade stem from the increasingly negative impact of the new global security agenda and competition with the interregional and, increasingly, bilat-eral relations pursued by the US. However, although EU interregion-alism is not a panacea, it already does represent a new mode of governance which is pushing the EU towards more coherent behaviour in the implementation of its various external relations. If the EU can find a way by which its multidimensional relations with Asia, Africa and Latin America cope better with the various regional security agendas, then interregionalism will become a true political identity-marker of Europe as a global actor.[147]

8. In its multifaceted dealings with partners near and far, the EU can count on the sizeable collective multi-level diplomatic corps. Beyond the EU Commission's external delegations, national diplomats in different countries and regions are increasingly coordinated. The con-crete multiple routine action of around 45,000 diplomats constitutes a formidable tool in driving international mediation and consensus worldwide. For some years, it has been standard practice of the EU Council rotating presidencies to gather the ambassadors of member states together. For sure, the effectiveness of the EU both in its bilateral

relations and within multilateral organizations and conferences could of course be improved. However, a relevant supplementary (and not substituting) tool would be the creation of a parallel diplomatic body that is directly responsible to the new EU foreign minister. Diplomacy provides an excellent illustration of the difference between a *common* and a *unique* foreign policy. The latter is typical of centralized states, and not appropriate for a non-state kind of civilian power as the EU. As far as content is concerned, like other civilian powers, the EU largely identifies with the UN in its foreign policy, including conflict prevention and peacekeeping missions that are to be carried out within the remit of the CFSP.[148]

9.   Though limited in relation to its economic strength, the EU and its member states are playing an increasing military peacekeeping and peace-enforcing role and currently participates in a dozen or so missions around the world – far more than the US (70,000 soldiers in 2004). Not only is the EU always the first to volunteer its assistance in post-conflict reconstruction, but it provides approximately 85 per cent of the international presence in the Balkans, with military missions in Macedonia and, since 2004, in Bosnia. It has contributed to the international force in Afghanistan since 2002 and, since 2003, has taken on responsibility for the mission in Congo. The Rapid Reaction Force, decided upon at the Council meetings in Cologne and Helsinki in 1999 (along with creation of the political and military committee), requires a standing EU corps of some 60,000 troops for peacemaking and peacekeeping missions, independent of any US involvement. The conditions for the use of this force are laid down by the 'Petersberg tasks' as indicated in the 1997 Treaty and that explains why they are not expected to create any 'security dilemmas' for neighbouring countries.[149] Indeed, this military dimension is not in conflict with the nature of civilian power. If anything, the political credibility of the civilian power EU is in fact strengthened by the gradual reduction of the capability–expectations gap.[150]

The existence of EU civilian and multilateral power in the world is thus an incontrovertible fact and well exceeds a mere 'vague influence'. It is thus not only fatuous, but mistaken, to speak of a 'Europe-Venus' in opposition to a 'US-Mars'. This book rejects that type of contrast, so dear to R. Kagan and US neo-conservatives and – albeit for opposite reasons – to European 'beautiful souls' (in the ironic sense of Hegel's term). Contrary to trivial understanding of transatlantic differences the EU in fact acts like a power, looks like a power and is an international power, albeit a very particular one; it combines hard economic power with soft power. We have illustrated how in many ways and to what extent the EU civilian power is emerging, while limiting the US soft power. Furthermore, to a lesser extent it also contains the other's hard power. For example the diplomatic, financial and political strength of the EU and the more shared consciousness of the limits of American power have forced the US to seek in 2004–5 an enhanced cooperation with Europe. On the other hand the EU, certain anti-American fringe elements aside, is well aware of the reality of transatlantic interdependence.

Even to oppose a Kantian EU to a Hobbesian US is misleading. It is important to state clearly that Kant was well aware of the weight of state sovereignties and the threat of 'universal monarchy' as well. It is therefore incorrect to saddle him with an idyllic and naive vision of international relations. As the revision of the Westphalian system is very far from an even partial completion, the EU has to situate its strange power better within the dynamics of the current international system and contribute to its realistic change.

In the following three chapters, we shall undertake a thorough analysis of the various elements that make EU civilian power a collective driving force of a multilateral world order. This brings in both normative and analytical arguments and entails examining the effectiveness and legitimacy of the EU's actions in gradually reforming globalization and the Westphalian system and reducing structural anarchy, both internally and at continental and international levels. In Chapter 4 we define this as a 'structural foreign policy', the nature of which is to foster long-term change of the world structure and the traditional logic of power politics. In Chapter 5, we will discuss the institutional dimensions of the EU's foreign policy.

1.9 Europe: a civilian power at a crossroads?

The primary new challenge which presents itself at the beginning of the twenty-first century is that economic global governance alone cannot guarantee a world order. Terrorism, fragmentation and WMD proliferation, on the one hand, and unipolar security policies, on the other, hinder efforts by civilian powers and multi-level multilateral networks to improve global governance. In the context of a world dominated by the return of security to the top of the agenda and where classical 'Westphalian' trends are back in vogue, being limited to the aspiration of being nothing more than a kind of 'world's Scandinavia'[151] could be seen as equivalent to sticking one's head in the sand, or, at the very least, of playing 'Candide'.

Europe thus finds itself at a crossroads. If the securitization of the international system is going on and the EU responds to the new challenges with mere inertia, it risks becoming a declining civilian power, floundering and divided, the object of a world history written elsewhere. And, in contrast to the post-war period, Europe would no longer be able to take advantage of the spaces created for multilateralism by the benevolent hegemonic power. What negative dynamics, therefore, might lie head for what today represent the strengths of the European civilian power?

1.   Internal peace is irreversible and EU-centred regional cooperation is expanding to include 30–35 members. However, the EU could widen even further to become the setting for a vast free-trade area stretching from the Mediterranean to Vladisvostok and Eilat. The resurgence of ethnonationalism and the increased instability on Europe's precarious south-eastern border (with states of the former USSR, the Caucasus and the Middle East) along with the transformation of the US from external federator to the additional source of political divisions within the EU, could provoke a dangerous combination of the renationalization of foreign policies of individual states and their subjugation to unipolarism.[152] This type of scenario would probably threaten the euro and perhaps even the Single Market. It would certainly endanger the European social model. Fully incorporating an endless number of countries to the east and south into the EU, rather than inventing a new appealing 'partner' status, risks causing the collapse of the traditionally positive interaction between widening and deepening. If, as suggested by past and present leaders such as Thatcher and Berlusconi, the EU were to include not only the countries of central and eastern Europe and Turkey, but also Russia, Ukraine, Israel and Morocco, it would cease to play a political role as a global actor and would become a mere inter-regional association in the mould of APEC or the FTAA, within the context of a world reorganized in concentric circles around its supreme power, the US (see Map 3).

2.   The impact of terrorist violence and the US's new strategic agenda could brutally circumscribe the EU's influence in the world, gradually transforming it into something of a cultural beacon, fit only for ceremonial purposes, much like Greece's role within the Roman empire, but without the linguistic and cultural pride the Greeks never abandoned. Indeed, given the global and 'revolutionary' character of US security policy, it would be fatal for the EU to present itself simply as a market and a diplomatic force that defends the status quo. Diplomacy,

as the management of a situation, is essentially static and impotent in the face of the aggressiveness of proliferation, risks of failing states and the power implications of military actions.

3. Without the EU as its engine, the global multilateral system would become increasingly ineffective, first politically and then economically. The result would be a further crisis of legitimacy. In the absence of a propulsive force or a dynamic and shared leadership, the particularistic fragmentation of interests and unipolarist arrogance would roll back the progress of the past 50 years.

4. The instability of a world whose multilateral dimension is declining would see regional organizations inevitably faced with the unenviable choice of being part of neo-multipolar spheres of influence or becoming dependencies of a unipolar world. European interregionalism would disappear from global governance and pure and simple liberalization would find better ways and more fertile sites in which to prosper through bilateral approaches.

5. The EU's global political activity would be nullified and the would-be 'world's Scandinavia' would be forced to follow the more modest model of Switzerland or the former timid *'Bonner Republik'*. The Franco-German axis would be buried, while eventual moves towards an intergovernmental Directory of the Big Three would unleash disintegrating forces. Among the smaller countries, the illusions of national sovereignty of the new member states would prevail over the pro-integration tendencies of the Benelux and other countries.

In short, the nature of European civilian power would change amidst this scenario of declining multilateralism and a shift in the international system towards unipolarism and anarchy. In an international context characterized by the new wars of the twenty-first century, simple maintenance of the status quo would be patently incapable of dealing with the new global challenges.

The litmus test for the EU as a civilian power therefore lies in its political and constitutional ability to unambiguously step over the threshold of *politics* (understood as the most noble form of human action), albeit in a manner consistent with the nature of the EU, that is a non-state kind of political community. The Union needs to be capable of such a step because it is in its own interest to project the ideational values rooted in the preferences expressed by member states and public opinion, and live up to its growing (and already mature) international responsibilities and the expectations placed on it by Latin America, Africa, East Asia, the Middle East, Russia, the Mediterranean basin and even a section of American public opinion.

The alternative to regression also requires a normative discussion which we will begin here and develop more extensively in the following chapters. Our thesis is that the EU can make up its political deficit without provoking new internal crises, but only if it proves capable of balancing constitutionalization with the intelligent management of enlargement and the Union's political independence.[153] The latter requires a new strategic global vision that develops the foundations upon which the EU's power as a novel type of international actor is based, but without pursuing an ultimately unattainable American model of power. The EU is thus faced with a positive twin option of political autonomy and a model of power which is innovative in terms of its legitimacy and effectiveness. The very existence of the EU has already laid the groundwork for the separation of the concept of politics from that of the wartime use of force. European political culture has relaunched the important notion that (a) declarations of war and the proclamation of a 'state of exception' represent not the zenith, but the negation of politics – especially if tied to a Manichaean vision of evil – and (b) that the criticism of war, combined with the construction of multilateral, supranational institutions, can give voice to a new dimension of politics, no longer identified with its merely state-centred dimension.

In devising an alternative to a notion of civilian power which simply relies on inertial continuity with the achievements of the past, a new and dynamic balance needs to be found, both at research and policy-making levels, between the analytical and normative dimensions of the following issues.

1.   The text of the European Constitutional Treaty is an important milestone as regards the adaptation of the traditional notion of civilian power to the new challenges inherent in constructing a multilateral world order. The EU has set itself the following international objectives: 'to promote peace, its values and the well-being of its peoples', 'offer its citizens an area of freedom, security and justice', 'work for a highly competitive social market economy, aiming at full employment and social progress', 'combat social exclusion and discrimination and . . . promote social justice', 'promote solidarity among member states'.

In its relations with the wider world, the Union shall uphold and promote its values and interests. It shall contribute to peace, security, the sustainable development of the Earth, solidarity and mutual respect among peoples, free and fair trade, eradication of poverty and the protection of human rights, in particular the rights of the child, as well as the strict observance and the development of international law, including respect for the principles of the United Nations Charter.[154]

The Constitutional Treaty makes a deep and direct link between the interests and well-being of citizens and the commitment to the resolution of global emergencies (ecology, poverty, peace, clash of civilizations, etc.) It also asserts its distinctive multilateral identity through the double reference to its values and the UN Charter, which is associated with international law. By stressing the 'development' of international law, and not just its 'strict observance', the new Treaty leaves the door open for its dynamic conceptual evolution and political application to the new threats and challenges (e.g. humanitarian intervention), as discussed within the UN.

These 'institutionalized belief structures' (Keohane) are of key importance, although research needs to verify the extent to which normative beliefs actually influence practical politics. If the EU wishes to play a more effective and coherent global role, it will have to get to grips with international crises at the source, employing its own distinctive means and methods. Furthermore, it will have to use the positive aspects of the successful multilateral regionalism that Europeans have happily applied to our small corner of the world since 1950 to facilitate the step up to the global level. One way of doing this would be to export and deploy the most effective features of EU internal governance (such as the experience of limiting and pooling national sovereignties and of effectively managing national diversities) both to other continents and the global multilateral network level.

2.   The EU cannot successfully reform global governance if it is isolated, inward looking, incapable of communicating the very soul of its governance model. Regional groupings elsewhere in the world are also confronted with a new challenge: that of making the step up to a new stage from inward-looking processes of defending themselves from the negative consequences of globalization and maximizing its benefits. This necessitates the improvement of their political and institutional capacities, by equipping them to interact effectively with the main global actors and influence the regulatory framework. Regional entities can also serve as channels of expression for civil society and as actors in crisis prevention and management. These represent 'regional public goods' which, taken together, can make an innovative contribution to a shared and legitimate notion of a global public good. The EU is

interested in providing coherent support for these potential allies through interregional cooperation, not only at trade level, but also at cultural and political levels.

3. The first part of this chapter offered some evidence for the argument that international relations theories are not at all unanimous in excluding the notion of civilian power, even in the post-2001 strategic situation. On the contrary, recent assertive practices of military power and 'absolute right' (an ironic take on Hegel's understanding of the dominant power which claims to be also the interpreter of the Zeitgeist, the world's conscience[155]) encounter serious limits and lead to the paradoxes of a 'powerless power' or to 'hegemonic instability'. The long transition of the international system may provide space and room for civilian powers to mature. However, the recent new global threats oblige the EU and other emerging civilian international actors to transform themselves from 'influencing' entities into regional and global political powers – elements of an effective and legitimate multilateral order. The time is past for the illusion of postmodern entities, satisfied with displaying their good examples for the world to see and admire. The EU is already the most integrated regional entity in the world, but only by becoming a constitutional political unit can it aspire to greater autonomy. It needs to take on greater global responsibilities (even if this means meeting the financial costs of increased liberty and independence), while endeavouring to avoid open conflicts of power and working to establish a new framework of egalitarian cooperation with the US.

Is the horizontal and vertical coherence among European external policies on the increase after September 11th, despite there still being two distinct decision centres (Commission and Council) and notwithstanding the divisions which have become apparent in addressing the transatlantic relationship? Is the 2003 'Solana paper' a step in the right direction? Does it represent a strategic security vision, consistent with the Constitutional Treaty and capable of moving the necessary preventive policies beyond the largely declaratory and traditionally long-term character of EU foreign policy?[156] Its unanimous approval by the European Council seems to provide further evidence of the continuing ability of the EU to overcome internal crises (in particular the Anglo-French dispute over Iraq) by developing new concepts ('effective multilateralism', 'preventive policies', 'failing states') which meet the urgent need to tackle the informal violence of terrorism and the various international disintegrating forces. The reference to the UN framework for all international actions and the stress on the particular European methods and means are grounded in a distinct analysis of external threats and combines well with the new emphasis on preventive policies rather than preventive strikes. Of course, the compromise achieved through this revival of the EU's common background for external political relations does not necessarily imply quick common political action in the event of international emergencies. To be taken by the EU, such action would require a difficult and complex agreement on the threat, on US policy and on the role of the EU: however, the political performances of 2004 in relation to the crises in Ukraine, Iran and the Balkans went beyond the most optimistic expectations.

4.   As the challenges of global governance are concerned, it would be wrong to focus only on the demand for increased effectiveness and stability. Both the multilateral experience of the EU and its strengthened normative *acquis* have a contribution to make to the crucial question of improving the accountability and legitimacy of regional and global governance. Contrary to conventional wisdom and the well-known traditional scepticism of a large part of liberal democratic theory (e.g. Dahrendorf and Dahl), R.O. Keohane and others recently suggested that the so-called 'governance dilemma' can be challenged in a positive way: not only does the world need more multilateral regulation, but it must also ensure that this responds to appropriate criteria of democracy and accountability consistent with the values of the societies it aims to serve, even if of course, these profoundly differ from national standards and procedures of democracy.

These four points underpin the research agenda to which the following sections and chapters seek to make a contribution.

1.10   Reforming the multilateral system

Strengthening the UN system, and the regulating network in general, is fundamental to international peace in order to prevent single states, groups of states, private interests or malevolent agents from unilaterally influencing the world's political structure. However, the various objectives of a more efficient and legitimate global governance can only be reconciled by reforming multilateralism, its politics and architecture, namely on the basis of its interplay with new regionalism. Let us start by situating our hypothesis within a review of current reform strategies.[157]

1. The astonishing implementation deficit and ineffectiveness of the global institution has given rise to several strategic concepts. The first focuses on policies: according to F.J. Rischard, the expansion of the role of 'Informal networks on global issues' may make faster and more effective the implementation of single norms through informal transnational procedures and action. Chapter 2 will provide some theoretical insights to understanding the new medievalist and technocratic background of this only apparently pragmatic and functional approach. Secondly, the transformation of the GATT into the WTO in the 1990s has indicated another, more institutional, way forward for the political reform of multilateral organizations. This entailed strengthening common rules and implementation obligations, or, to put it another way, sharpening the institution's teeth (through the creation of the 'panels for the settlement of conflicts') in order to enable it to enforce regulations on everyone, including the strongest members. Along this guideline, the hypothesis of a 'WTO constitutionalization' shows the legal advantages, but also the political problems, raised by a too direct emulation of the current EU legal experience. Secondly, limits to this WTO-centred reform of multilateralism can be seen in the persistent, and increasing, asymmetries between North and South and in the areas of social and environmental issues. The WTO will not survive its legitimacy crisis if it does not promote its original objective: the improvement of living conditions through development. This does not necessarily coincide with liberalization and requires global, national and regional institutional innovations. It is within this context that we can appreciate the great stakes involved in the round of negotiations opened in Doha in 2001.

A third hypothesis focuses on strengthening the UN primacy in the global network. It is against this backdrop that we should view several parallel policy proposals anticipated by the K. Annan's 'Millennium agenda'. The UN should be committed to a global employment policy (ILO, Geneva 2001), the fight against poverty, the promotion of development – which was relaunched at Monterrey (UN Conference 2002)[158] – sustainable development according to the rich agenda agreed at Johannesburg in 2002, the International Criminal Court, and, finally, to the difficult task of reconciling these objectives within the UN system.

These multiple proposals are not necessarily incompatible and conflicting with each other. Their value lies not only in their role in providing international public law with new elements such as the WTO and the ICC, but also in that they allow a proactive dialogue between the emerging international public opinion and the global framework. Furthermore, they represent the paradigmatic pillars of a modern and comprehensive concept of security policy, which is the only way to achieve a concerted and definitive defeat of terrorism. In other words, they are pushing to strengthen preventive policies, in line with the EU view of the world, rather than preventive war.[159] However, what is still missing is a convincing rationale, a general reforming principle, addressing both the implementation gap and the democratic deficit.

2.   The lack of coordination between multilateral organizations represents a serious weak point of the current global network, in terms of effectiveness and efficiency. Improving coordination among the 'Bretton Woods' institutions, and between these and the UN system, represents a mid-term objective which is certainly more difficult than the reforming single concrete policies, but easier than the ultimate goal of a global institutional reform.[160] The 'Geneva strategy' of the ILO (2001) takes a step in this direction: it defines the objectives and common deadlines for the new 'round tables' on single common objectives (featuring all the relevant multilateral organizations), and establishes a tighter system of multilateral supervision and controls in relation to the implementation of objectives. The similarity (but not the full identification, given the absence of an executive commission) with the 'open method of coordination' adopted by the EU in Lisbon in 2000 for the better management of national diversity is clear. The latter thus appears as a advanced regional workshop of methodologies (*cum grano salis* and *mutatis mutandis*) applicable to the objectives of global governance.

3.   As regards the reform of the institutional architecture of global governance, it is necessary to distinguish between three challenges: (a) the question of the representation of regional associations, (b) the integration between the UN and the Bretton Woods multilateral system, and (c) the reform of the UN itself.

(a)   Given that the need for more symmetrical participation in global governance by all continents is increasingly acknowledged, the voice of regional organizations needs to be made stronger within economic and political multilateral organizations. Regionalism has enormous potential in terms of enhancing the legitimacy of multilateral governance within states and civil societies and the effective implementation of policies as well.[161] This trend towards the regionalization of global governance is consistent with the EU's very essence, since what was considered as a derogation within US-led post-war multilateralism is, for the EU, a matter of political identity. In political terms, the EU can, through interregional dialogue and agreements, help emerging regional organizations not only to deepen cooperation, but also to make a positive contribution at global level by rejecting recourse to defensive and protectionist policies, on the one hand, while refusing outright subordination to globalism, on the other.

While on this point, we should also note the EU's policy for the development of regional peacekeeping and peace-enforcing organizations to conduct missions in Africa, Europe and Asia. This regional approach may include also tackling more complex crises such as terrorist threats and the Israeli–Palestinian problem. The consciousness of the need for complementarity between the regional organization and the UN is increasingly shared. Given the high interdependence of that region, only a regional organization like the CSCE/OSCE seems capable of bringing peace and stability by establishing an institutionalized network of cooperation to help resolve key problems such as the sharing and exploitation of resources like oil and water. It is only within this type of framework that the interrelation between the specific security requirements (in the broadest sense of the term) of each of the participant states can be taken into consideration.[162]

(b) International research stresses the positive impact that increased UN coordination (based around concrete, fixed-term objectives) of international organizations would have. Though apparently idealistic, this issue cannot be simply excluded at least as a long-term and institutional perspective, provided that the *naïvetés* and failures of the 1970s are not about to come back. According to Jacques Delors and many scholars, it is due to the very lack of coordination both within the UN (due to the excessive autonomy from the secretary-general granted to its agencies), and between it and the 'Bretton Woods system' (e.g. between the World Bank and UNICEF, the WTO and the ILO), the entire multilateral system is suffering from a lack of coherence, rendering it inefficient and weak. As a consequence, both the quest for efficiency and a global concept of security ought to suggest the construction of an 'Economic Security Council', in which the members of the G8, the largest states of the South and about a dozen other non-permanent members (it would better if this were done by rotation on a regional basis) would take the lead in tackling the economic and social causes of conflicts by promoting development and combating poverty. This would replace the lethargic UN Economic and Social Council, an inflated body of 54 members, and would reduce the centrality of the G8 which is too westernized and lacks legitimacy.

(c) The most complex task, and perhaps for that reason repeatedly postponed,[163] is that of a structural reform of the UN itself, 'which has reached a moment no less decisive than in 1945' (Kofi Annan, 2004 Annual Report). Such a reform would have to strengthen the UN's democratic nature as well as its credibility, both of which have suffered from, among other factors, the expansion of the organization's membership from 50 at the time of the San Francisco Charter to the 190 states it counts today. Not least because of the fact that the post-war climate of optimism in which it was set up cannot be revived, the UN finds itself at the very centre of tensions between supranationalism and national sovereignty.[164] The monopoly on the legal use of force by the UN Security Council and the founding impetus for the universal defence of human rights, in particular to guarantee that the experience of the Holocaust never be repeated (Universal Declaration of Human Rights, 1948), could help facilitate its transformation into a sort of world civilian government that could adopt quasi-international 'police' actions under the auspices of a reformed Chapter VII (art. 41, 42, 45 and 46) of the Charter. On the other hand, the recognition of the respect for national sovereignty (art. 2.1 and 7, which recall article 15, paragraph 8 of the doomed League of Nations), and the voting procedures in the Security Council (art. 27), drastically limit the prospects for such a kind of 'post-Westphalian' transformation of the international system. This is borne out not only by events during the cold war (and the abuse of the veto by the USSR, US and other great powers[165]), but also by the controversy that erupted in the 1990s regarding the right to intervene in the internal affairs of a member state on humanitarian grounds. Since 2001, however, we have witnessed a further substantial controversy, i.e. the 'preventive war', designed to overthrow despotic regimes and install democracy. This has very little to do with the type of humanitarian intervention called for by Kofi Annan, particularly in his 'Millennium Declaration', and the preventive policies advocated by various political and cultural leaders, including the EU, in recent years. Will the global emergencies and the pressure of the global civil society foster states and global powers to eventually converge on a way of coming closer to the ideal of 'a democratic organization of democratic states'?

UN reform will prove very unlikely for many reasons. These include US lack of interest (UN reform is very difficult *with* the US, but impossible *without* the US), the possible veto by other Security Council members, the problems in securing the necessary two-thirds majority of the Assembly, and the gap between the excessive and heterogeneous demands regarding the UN's presence in the world and the limits inherent in the decision-making process, the competencies delegated by states and budgetary restrictions. On paper, a radical reform, equipping the UN to meet the challenges facing a twenty-first-century collective security system, should provide consensual solutions to three main issues.

1. The extraordinary potential of the UN General Assembly needs to be better utilized. The Assembly is a universal organ in which all states have the right to speak and vote, but which has become sterile and fragmented. Obviously, democratic principles of majority decision-making and the weighting of votes according to population size (which would give overwhelming power to China, India, Indonesia and others) are inapplicable. Secondly, any proposal that does not take seriously into consideration the abstract nature of the legal principle of equality among states is illusory. It is essential to place more emphasis and focus on an assembly where the great global challenges can be debated by the large and small powers of North and South, where potential enemies can publicly discuss their differences and where a dialogue between the different civilizations is maintained. After all, are these not the universal principles of Western liberal thought? The very serious current corruption scandals and the clear difficulties of the UN can only be tackled if the UN is able to define a general concept as a principle for selecting its priorities and implementing them in a transparent, more democratic and efficient way.

As a step towards transparency and legitimacy, many suggest integrating an annual assembly of a second, complementary and informal chamber comprising NGOs and civil society representatives. That should not, of course, give rise to any illusions over cosmopolitan representativeness. However, reform of the Assembly may usher in a new climate in terms of a commitment to openness, transparency, communication, and the construction of a relevant component of an evolving global democratic public space within the world's political system.

2.   Reform of the Security Council is necessary in order to improve the legitimacy of its resolutions, but it must also strengthen the efficiency of the decision-making process. The current weighting in favour of the north-west of the world is not representative of the majority of the planet nor are its 15 members considered representative of the 190 members of the General Assembly. The only reform to date – that of 1963 – increased membership from 11 to 15. Today, there is a certain consensus on the need to include Japan (which is the second-largest donor) and to increase African, Asian and Latin American representation. However, the list of candidates (including European countries) clamouring for inclusion is long and the hasty enlargement to six new permanent members is controversial. The main problem lies in the competition both between Latin American, African, Arab and Asian candidate states and between EU members. This could perhaps be overcome by their forming regional groupings – a second option proposed by the Wise Men Report of 2004. According to the notion of a 'civilizing' power, the EU should set a good example by merging or rotating its presence in the UN Security Council and not simply coordinating EU member states through the strengthened 'loyalty' Treaty provisions.

Increasing representation, however, is not the sole issue. Indeed, the second important question is that of limiting the right of veto within the Council (an issue which has been dramatically brought to the fore by the crisis in Iraq).[166]

3.   The most important debate concerns the extremely delicate relationship between the legitimacy and strengthening of peacekeeping capacity, i.e. overcoming current military weakness with a better system of UN intervention. The great debate here regards the reform of Chapter VII of the Charter on the use of force and the right to intervene in domestic affairs. Key questions include the UN's ability to order, legitimize or prohibit the use of force in crisis situations and the creation of instruments which are equipped to handle the new challenges. Kofi Annan has been quite successful in countering the image of a faint-hearted UN by strengthening the intervention mandate of the blue helmets and berets with the approval of the 'Brahimi Report',

but has also encountered understandable political obstacles in his attempt to define which rules should sanction and impose the use of force. Examples of this include the obstruction of the 2002 report on the 'threshold for intervention' and the contrasting positions which were revealed during the September 2003 Assembly.

The controversy relates to the adaptation of the instruments used to pursue the UN's original objectives (of guaranteeing peace and defending human rights[167]) to fit the changed conditions. Proposals for a 'disarmament corps' or 'human rights corps' (D. de Villepin) or 'tighter regimes to combat proliferation' (T. Blair) explore new ways of trying to navigate between two significant risks. The first is that of a supine acceptance of a form of unilateralism, by which a 'group of democracies' could intervene in place of the UN (even in the absence of a UN mandate). The second is the risk of non-intervention and inertia, i.e. of being identified as the defenders of an ineffectual system that counts among its failures the Rwandan and Bosnian tragedies of the 1990s or the many examples of problematic post-conflict management.

Those who oppose the failed US doctrine of 'preventive wars' against terrorism and tyrants also have the responsibility of actively contributing to a collective and positive definition of a form of democratic right of intervention, for example in the case of 'unacceptable dictators' who, by general consensus, represent a threat to regional and global peace and the human rights of their own populations. The pleas by Kofi Annan and the international academic community, from Jürgen Habermas's concept of 'internal foreign policy' to Noberto Bobbio's notion of a 'just war' – provided that a consensus within the international community exists – underpin a new approach that, taking its cue from the Gulf War (1991) and the Kosovo intervention,[168] supports a dynamic vision of international law and the global community's responsibilities.

1.11   The EU: the engine for a subsidiary multilateral system combining force and consensus

There are few doubts about the EU being the most interested actor in supporting a regionalization of the global regulation framework. However, the EU member states are often still divided on this issue. To what extent will the mentioned deficits of the multilateral network, the international crisis of 2002–5 and the demands coming from regional groupings leave their mark on fostering progress towards an EU speaking with a single voice and enhancing the legitimacy and efficiency of the global network? In theoretical terms, we are once again faced with the classic problem of the relationship between national sovereignty, on the one hand, and universal rights and principles requiring supra-national protection, on the other. We can see a clear common thread of investigation running through the history of political thought from Kant to Bobbio, Habermas and others that looks in depth at the extremely delicate balance between sovereignty and supranational-ism.[169] In this field of research, the EU's constitutional features offer a sophisticated set of tools including legal procedures, political method-ologies and concrete experiences. After the war, its member states were obliged to internalize multilateralism, but have since increasingly (voluntarily) chosen to limit and share their national sovereignty through treaties of a constitutional nature. Having given birth to the modern state some centuries ago and then effectively tamed it, Europe is currently 'teaching' the world that the rigid defence of the principle of sovereignty undermines the common task of constructing a legiti-mate and efficient supranational authority and its plea for a rule-based global governance is not limited to the simple normative proclamation of international law.

The first important consequence is that the best way forward in terms of crisis prevention and management, the protection of human rights, and the democratization of member states and neighbouring countries, seems to be the linking of the UN to regional organizations. This would help both in exploring a new way between juridical global-ism (Kelsen's style) on the one hand, and national relativism on the other, and in reconciling 'common global public goods' (such as peace and international democratization) with respect for the diversity of security needs of distinct regions. We have chosen to term this decen-tralized vision of multilateralism a 'subsidiary government of world order'.[170] Within this framework, not every crisis and defence of human rights would necessarily be directly referred to the universal system. Instead, many could be better dealt with at regional level. This would leave the international system with the subsidiary tasks that neither states nor regional organizations are in a position to undertake or guarantee.

The second challenge for European political theory is to conduct research (without limiting itself to a simple condemnation or apolo-gia) into what 'ruse of reason' (in the ironic sense of Hegel's term) is hidden in the genuine historical development recently witnessed, i.e. the unprecedented distancing of the transatlantic allies and the revolutionary consequences that the new US strategy is triggering in international relations. A bit like Hegel in relation to Napoleon's politics in Europe – which, although driven by political arrogance, personal ambition and often mistaken strategies of power, nonetheless struck a blow at the *anciens régimes* and theocratic absolutism and contributed to the spread of a rational and legal concept of the state – we can ask ourselves what positive aspects, if any, have come out of the Iraqi crisis of 2002–5. If it serves only to confirm US military and technological superiority and unipolar tendencies, then the concerns about worsening regional and global disorder facilitating the growth of fundamentalism and fragmentation are justified. If, however, notwithstanding the brutality, the unilateral nature of the occupation and its failures, the war has increased the possibility of future wider acceptance of the principle of democratic international intervention in the internal affairs of repressive and dictatorial states, provided there is a consensual decision of the UN community, then this represents a significant appeal to the world's civilian powers to become global political actors and urges them to provide their own multilateral answers to the common global challenges. US political globalism can only be restrained or counterbalanced by a *new* concept of civilian power, supporting multilateralism and the political government of globalization along with an active battle against arms proliferation, terrorism and its roots. This represents the only way to create a credible dialectic pole in opposition to unlawful force.

The political isolation and removal of Saddam Hussein's regime would probably have been widely supported by world public opinion, the overwhelming majority of states and multilateral organizations, had the preparation and execution of the task occurred not in arrogant isolation towards Europe and other countries, but: (a) with the consensus of the international community and Iraq's regional neighbours; (b) within the framework of strict respect (and not a nonchalant version of 'respect') for international law and *jus in bello*; (c) by giving priority to the sovereign wishes of all the components of the Iraqi people during the extremely difficult democratic transition and the process of 'nation building'. This would have required time in terms of careful political preparation of the military intervention and a serious multilateral commitment to the reconstruction phase. In the Messianic view of the US administration, however, Western democracy is a commodity that can simply be exported. By contrast, the experience of Europeans indicates that democratization requires the patient and realistic formation of civil society networks, and a public space that is structured around solid associations and proper political parties, anchored in a system of values that are both local and universal. Only these internal processes can make external 'conditionality', regional pressures and UN intervention effective and legitimate.

The European post-war experience serves as an example of how external pressures and 'conditionality' can be astutely balanced with internal democratizing factors, and the very existence of the EU demonstrates the realism of the required new paradigm in international relations. In the 2004/5, even the US seems to be becoming more aware that, on its own, military force serves simply to win wars and cannot produce enduring successes. When faced with the problems of reconstruction, the US finds itself disarmed and consequently demands international cooperation. If Europeans want to credibly share global leadership, they need to say clearly how force and consensus (albeit in different doses from those experimented with in post-war Europe) should be combined to usher in a democratic process and establish peace. By rejecting what they see as US oversimplifications, Europeans are obliged to propose their own concept of the multilateral use of force within the context of a UN mandate, and to allow the efficiency of civilian power to be measured and assessed. Whether one agrees with it or not, this type of governance, paradoxically now both further away in some ways and nearer in others, could provide the form of a possible new international order, comprising force and consensus, legitimacy and power. This possible distinction (of Hegelian origin) between the motivations driving the historical agents and the significance of their actions would be confirmed and strengthened by the political and constitutional developments of the EU.

1.12   A new transatlantic partnership between equals?

It is clear to anyone familiar with the charters and statutes of the various multilateral organizations that no reform of their institutions can be achieved against the will of the US or without its consensus.[171] Even the gradualist approach which we have discussed in this book – in terms of the reform of multilateral policies and their coordination, the 'bottom-up' enhancement of regionalism and the step-by-step reform of the global institutional architecture – would sooner or later come up against the reality of power relations. Acknowledging the link between the rise of Europe and the crisis within NATO is a starting point, but it is not sufficient.[172] The transatlantic relationship is problematic because the previous type of alliance has changed irrevocably. However, the transatlantic link is irreplaceable and building a new relationship based on the concept of a partnership of two equal pillars, or even of 'friendly rebalancing power' – which has nothing whatsoever to do with the notion of 'balance of power' – represents a difficult but inevitable stake for the EU in the coming decade. The rich network of relationships between the societies on both sides of the Atlantic, along with the shared past heritage and common interests, should facilitate a new dialogue that could lead to a major renovation of the alliance. If both sides are truly to move towards John F. Kennedy's 1961 vision of a two-pillared alliance, then priority needs to be given to strengthening the EU political identity and constructing a specific transatlantic framework which is distinct from that of the EU (and not merged with European institutions, as proposed in 2003 by an authoritative transatlantic networking including M. Albright) and guided by rules and principles for the better management of divergences. Will the US accept that only a stronger and more united Europe can be of help to the US in relaunching and renewing the best elements of their internationalist tradition and in facing new common threats?[173]

One problem is that the US, in spite of C. Rice's art of speaking softly, is primarily interested in increased European military spending within the context of the US security strategy, i.e. in order to share the burden of defence costs. By contrast, the Europeans' interest is to conceive of military force (the Rapid Reaction Force included) in terms of making the EU more credible as a civilian power and not as a poor cousin of US power. This is not only because the US would never accept an increase in European power in proportion to their increased military spending, but it also reflects the profoundly different sensitivities rooted in European public opinion on both the left and right.[174] The European contribution to the alliance will in any case be the product of a different perception of threats. Terrorism is viewed from another perspective in Europe, where the commitment to tackling major problems (economic inequalities, social imbalances, poverty, mass migration, international crime, the drugs trade, etc.) is seen as contextual to tackling terrorism. This is also in the knowledge that the EU possesses more effective means to tackle such problems as a civilian power rather than as a military one.

The EU is facing up to this extremely delicate stage in its evolution by, on the one hand, developing new strategic concepts[175] and, on the other, by equipping itself with new instruments and institutions that will be the subject of discussion in Chapters 4 and 5 of this book. The transatlantic dialogue will be pursued according to a variety of approaches – some of which are complementary, some of which are not.

is the CFSP, the consensual political dimension of the external
..ion of the 25 member states. This has been strengthened and will be
increasingly consistent with the first pillar, although it is still framed by
the unanimous vote, budgetary constraints[176] and the constitutional
limits in the 'Petersberg tasks'. However, it seems inevitable that an
enlarged Europe will have to adopt instruments of internal differentiation, either within the framework of the existing treaties ('enhanced
cooperations' and 'structured cooperations'[177]), or perhaps also outside
of them (following the path of a special settlement as the 'Schengen
Treaty', as discussed by J. Fischer during the four-way Luxembourg
summit on European defence in spring 2003[178]). In whichever case, the
conviction remains that, given the considerable differences in terms of
tradition, status, ambitions and responsibilities among member states,
only a restricted, even if open, 'hard core' of countries (grouped around
France and Germany), whose objectives are consistent with those of the
EU, can give full expression to Europe's international political potential
(whether the Constitutional Treaty is ratified or not).

Herein also lies the key to the inevitable even if controversial reform
of NATO (proposed by Germany in 2004 but rejected by the US), with
the strengthening of the European pillar of the alliance. The EU is
moving from a situation in which the integration of European defence
was supported by Washington to one where this policy, defined in 2003
as a 'wrong kind of integration', often seems to be taking place despite
the US and through a variable geometry model of intergovernmental
coordination. Full supranational integration of foreign and security policy is some way off, however, and the test of European institutional
inventiveness will be whether it can take advantage of the many actions
it can undertake unanimously, while leaving a vanguard group free to
go further, in line with new methods of policy coordination and cooperation. It is in this area that both the constitutional and practical
creativity of the Union is challenged: that 'art of government' of a civilian power which is increasingly aware of its strength and conscious of
its distinctive vision of international relations. In Chapter 5, we shall
argue in favour of deepening the current 'mixed government', whereby
the Commission, Council and Parliament work together to provide
a structure for Europe, including a 'two-speed integration'.

Under which conditions, therefore, is it possible to reconcile the distinctive nature of EU power with a reform of the transatlantic alliance?
The question is hard to resolve, since an alliance is, according to
H. Kissinger, 'a special set of obligations', and it may pretend to have
precedence over multilateral, regional and global rules (e.g. the UN

Security Council monopoly on the legal use of force). Contrary to both the opposing models of 'the junior partner of the US' and 'military independence', the EU cannot cope with this challenge without a reform of NATO, making of it a component of a broader and more effective multilateral network, which encompasses both low and high politics issues, governance and world order (and is not anti-UN oriented). Although it will be difficult to create, this represents the most effective and least disruptive way of managing the European alliance with the US, while keeping the dialogue and cooperation open with other global partners: fulfilling the urgent task of coping with the new threats and shifts of global power. The EU is interested in enhancing the role of the new regional entities and in increasing multidimensional cooperation with the emerging Asian powers (of course Japan, but also India and China, being the 'trilateral model' completely out of order) within a multi-level and multilateral global framework.

For the EU, therefore, strengthening its international political identity means rejecting, in a positive way, the model of Europe as a military power. Europe needs to rationalize its military capacities in line with its vision of international relations. In this, the EU's actions often surpass its declarations and official documents as though it were only partially aware of the meaning of what it is already actively doing. If the practical rejection of war as a means of resolving international disputes were integrated with a complementary and coherent commitment to strengthening supranational peacekeeping institutions, this would represent a supreme act of political sovereignty and an expression of authentic and conscious new civilian power, which is capable of exerting a far-reaching influence on war and peace in the world and changing the structure of international relations. It should also prove more efficient at managing international crises and in the fight against terrorism. Indeed, when the objective is building peace and democracy, whether before or after a crisis, not only does the US not want to do what the EU is committed to doing in the world, it is incapable of doing so. The US can avail itself of a level of economic and military force that the EU lacks, but nothing today suggests that it is possible to manage the world by military force alone. If anything, the contrary is true. If it is possible, therefore, real complementarity requires the construction of a new, more inclusive and more legitimate multilateral institutionalized framework for a common and comprehensive global security. The next years will show whether the US may accept such an evolution of the alliance towards a transatlantic partnership between equals, situated in an open, less asymmetric, multilateral framework.

1.13   Democratic legitimacy and accountability at regional and global levels

As the international community's role in defending human rights and crisis management expands and becomes more intrusive in national societies, it will be increasingly necessary to strengthen its legitimacy and accountability. Accountability requires credibility and control mechanisms, both of which must be developed on various levels: national, regional and global. The national level remains of crucial importance, as comparative research has convincingly shown. Various 'responsible' states have been able to resolve the problems of monitoring humanitarian missions and managing crises by means of different national mechanisms.[179] However, if we take into account the increasing complementarity between the state level and EU and UN mechanisms, then we can envisage a mixed system with regard to both the protection of rights and the management of humanitarian and peace missions, where regional associations may play an increasing role. This would also feature a complementary role for NGOs in promoting accountability both of public agencies and multinational companies.

The democratic legitimization of international politics is a perennial question in the history of political thought. A foreign policy can be perfectly legal and not enjoy international legitimacy. One important school of political thought excludes the possibility of democratizing global and regional governance. This idea can be traced back to de Toqueville and has also been relaunched in recent years by Ralf Dahrendorf.[180] Nonetheless, as Norberto Bobbio argues, no international stable peace is possible without democracy. At the beginning of the twenty-first century, the reinforcement of internal and international democratic legitimization is no longer a utopian luxury, therefore, but a necessity. To a certain extent, it is the essential condition for effectiveness, the prerequisite for international action.

As far as Europe's substantive legitimacy is concerned, the results of Eurobarometer surveys are clear: given that the international performance of the EU (especially in times of acute humanitarian or political crisis) is ranked top of the list of expectations among citizens in the Union, then the EU's actions on the international stage represent formidable factors in terms of legitimizing the Union itself. Vice versa, humiliations, missed opportunities and clear international failures serve to diminish the internal legitimacy of the integration process, as we have seen in the cases of the former Yugoslavia and the first Gulf War. Like Montesquieu's 'Federal Republic', the EU looks to combine, through its multi-level governance, internal legitimacy and external might. The EU may, therefore, provide an interesting case study of the relaunching of a strongly legitimized notion of international politics that links interests and ideals via a public debate on the ends and means of better world governance for peace and social justice. Only by strengthening the democratic legitimacy of its foreign policies will the EU be able to overcome its current paradox: that internal public opinion at times identifies it with the WTO and the G8, while at others it calls on it to channel and politically represent public fears and reactions to unchecked globalization and arrogant unilateralism.

In the case of the EU, the first response to its crisis of legitimacy lies in improving the effectiveness of the external and global multilateral architecture and in identifying a subsidiary system of accountability with regard to the efficiency of the decision-making process. The text of the Convention gives grounds for hope. It provides for a single legal international personality and the improvement of external relations coordination (horizontally, between the Commission and the Council; vertically, between member states and the Union) under the authority of the new minister for foreign affairs. Even if, in the event of a serious international crisis, divergences within the Union might lead to vetoes and deadlock, the coherence of the 'structural foreign policy' will be strengthened (see Chapters 4 and 5).

The second criterion entails legitimization through participation. Transparency, publicity and public dialogue are required to deal with the deficit of legitimacy, as is an element of creativity in channelling the desire for democratic participation, both before and after decisions, onto local, national, regional and international levels. We cannot fool ourselves regarding the levels of daily and permanent interest of citizens in international questions, but nor can we ignore the growth of the levels of information available and public mobilization in response to international emergencies (poverty, ecology, diseases, peace) and during major world crises. In opposition to a vision of politics which is reduced to the mere management and defence of sectional or private interests, the younger generations and national and transnational public opinion continue to show that issues concerning the protection of fundamental rights, humanitarian aid, the commitment to cooperation on development, the reform of global regulation, humanitarian disasters (like the December 2004 tsunami) and the struggle for peace can stimulate considerable and enduring mobilization and collective action by civil society in order to give voice to the interests involved and the widespread consciousness of humanity's common destiny.

Nor should we underestimate the governance dimension of the question of legitimacy, both in terms of its institutional implications (principles, powers and procedures) and its practical side, resolvable without any treaty revision. More difficult than at state level, the legitimization of European foreign policy requires as many national political and parliamentary mechanisms as supranational. For example, an annual session of the European Parliament dedicated to foreign policy and external relations could focus the active mobilization of public opinion in different states on common priorities, encourage the structured participation of civil society, interest groups and NGOs and constitute the high point of an open public debate that would increase internal cohesion and, consequently, the external efficiency of the European civilian power. In conclusion, exporting the democratic practices of the EU and its 'discourse' on legitimacy to the global multi-level governance level is a huge task, particularly in light of the current gap and discrepancies between the EU and the global network.

The EU has spent 50 years evolving a political system and a democratic polity. Respect for democracy and human rights forms the basis of the EU. Although underestimated at the very beginning (Treaty of Rome), from the 1970s (European Political Cooperation) to the late 1980s (Single European Act), the first steps were made towards a foreign policy which strongly supported democracy and human rights. While to an extent reflecting a spillover of the external practices of the Commission, the Maastricht Treaty was an important milestone. With it came the institutionalization of democratic legitimacy, the protection of human rights and the rule of law as a kind of 'soul' of a common nascent European international identity.[181] Despite the difficulties of national democracies, the Union's 'democratic deficit', administrative fragmentation and limits in terms of policy implementation, articles 6 and 7 of the Treaty of Amsterdam (1997), the Charter of Fundamental Rights (2000) and the Constitutional Treaty (2004) show that democratic legitimacy is becoming a key aspect of both the internal institutional development of the EU and its external relations. Of course, that does not mean that the EU is a democratic political system according to national democratic criteria. In Chapter 5 we will argue in favour of defining the EU as a 'mixed government', that is combining diplomatic intergovernmentalism, technocratic governance and democratic principles, which are thus only a part, even if maybe an increasing part, of the EU polity.

Nonetheless, the international system is still dominated by power relations and anarchy. Moreover, international law is based on the principle of the *equality* of states, which has nothing to do with *democracy*. How can this considerable and important discrepancy be tackled? The answers provided by the scientific community can be divided into three broad approaches:

(a) Advocates of 'multilateral constitutionalism'[182] and 'cosmopolitan multilateralism' focus on the global role of the EU as a 'democratic model', a 'rule generator', a 'market facilitating global liberalization', a 'stabilizer and exporter of values to third countries' (TEU, art. 2) and as a 'magnet' using 'conditionality' to promote EU values abroad.[183] For example, the WTO, if 'constitutionalized', could be transformed into a 'cosmopolitan constitution of liberty', a framework for a shared 'social market global economy' with respect for human rights. For its part, the UN could find itself at the top of a pyramidal system of democratic global governance, according to a reinterpretation of Kelsen's classical school of thought. In Chapters 4 and 5, we will critically discuss the philosophical and theoretical roots of this normative neo-cosmopolitan vision of Europe as a 'civilizing power' or 'civil power', and review the interpretations of Duchene, Kojeve, Habermas and others.

(b) By contrast, realists and relativists either deny any democratic deficit at global level or emphasize the structural opposition between the EU's democratic 'exceptionalism' and the international system. Not only is the global network characterized by intergovernmental power relations, conflicts and power shifts which run contrary to the EU's values and practices, but the West itself is divided along ideological lines as regards international legitimacy, which is increasingly opposed to efficiency, particularly after September 11th.[184]

(c) The third approach combines liberal institutionalism with constructivism, while taking into account the 'realist challenge'. This integrates the 'bottom-up' approach, based on the idea of the EU as a normative and influencing example, with the bolstering of the EU's political instruments to enable them to mould global governance in line with EU values. These instruments encompass the common foreign and security policy and the most effective civilian tools available to the EU in its conduct of external relations, i.e. trade, cooperation agreements with developing countries, interregional partnerships, conditionality. In other words, the ingredients of what we call the EU's 'structural foreign policy' (see Chapter 4).

Of course, there are two preconditions for success: first of all, the internal democratic governance of the EU needs to be better translated into consistent policies (fundamental rights policy, etc.[185]) and made more coherent, transparent and accountable to national and European parliaments. According to the experience, all this must be complemented by renewed 'substantive social legitimacy' of the European construction (see Chapter 3). Secondly, the EU is seen as a leading branch of a general move towards global bottom-up democratization by means of an informal and institutionalized process including (a) the formation of a global public sphere, promoting accountability and legitimacy through informal networking, people participation and the creation of sites of public deliberation, and (b) new regionalism, i.e. new political and democratic associations between neighbouring countries showing some progress elsewhere in the world (see Chapter 2). By combining transnational networking at civil society level with coherent interregional partnerships, Europe should be able to spread its understanding of democratic regional cooperation and develop new shared ways of bringing greater legitimacy to regional and global governance.

Finally, a new political idea of Europe as a civilian power has implications not only as regards increasing the democratic legitimacy of multi-level global governance, but also with respect to the creation of a more legitimate world order. To what extent do ideational factors matter? As constructivists show, ideas, rhetorics and narrative discourses are important in explaining actions. As in every international power[186] – and even more, given its very pluralistic polity – there is still a significant open-ended power conflict for many years within the EU regarding which international discourse the common institutions should represent, how this should be consistently spread throughout the world and how it should be transformed into political action. The European institutions represent a real battlefield for debates, conflicts and compromises between states, transnational coalitions, lobbies, cultural groupings and interests which seek to condition the official discourse. What is at stake is both the emerging international political identity of the EU and its contribution to a more legitimate global governance and world order.

Notes

1. See, for example, W.I. Hitschcock, *The Struggle for Europe. The Turbulent History of a Divided Continent (1945–2002)*, Doubleday, New York, 2003, p. 570. W. Wallace, *Regional Integration: the West European Experience*, The Brookings Institution, Washington DC, 1994.

2. See J.S. Nye, *The Paradox of American Power. Why the World's Only Superpower Can't Go It Alone*, 2002, K. Nicolaydis and and R. Howse, 'This is my Utopia', in J.H.H. Weiler, I. Begg and J. Peterson (eds), *Integration in an Expanding European Union. Reassessing the Fundamentals*, Blackwell, Oxford, 2002, pp. 341–65, T. Padoa Schioppa, *Europe as a Civil Power*, Federal Trust, London, 2004 and R.G. Whitman, *From Civilian Power to Superpower? The International Identity of the European Union*, Macmillan, London, 1998. See also the excellent paper by Robert Keohane, 'Realist and Institutionalist Theory after 9.11th', written in December 2004 for the Advisory Group in Social Science and Humanities for the European Research Area, EU Commission DG Research. For more on the political identity of the EU as distinct from the European cultural identity, see F. Cerutti and E. Rudolph (eds), *A Soul for Europe.On the Political and Cultural Identity of the Europeans*, 2 vols, Peeters, Leuven, 2001, with a preface by V. Havel. The three points mentioned in the text constitute the subject matter of Chapters 3, 4 and 5 of this book.
3. The White House, *National Security Strategy of the United States of America*, Washington, 20 September 2002 (http://www.whitehouse.gov/nsc/nss.pdf); G.W. Bush, 'State of the Union. Address to Congress and the Nation', *The New York Times*, 30 January 2002, p. A22; Department of Defense, *Quadrennial Defense Review Report*, Washington, 30 September 2001.
4. On the unexpected force and unity of European and world public opinion against the 'preventive war' and its role in the emerging European political identity, see the article by J. Habermas and J. Derrida, '15 Februar: was die Europäer einigt', *Frankfurter Allgemeine Zeitung*, 31 May 2003, pp. 33–4. U. Eco, A. Muschg, R. Rorty, F. Savater and G. Vattimo simultaneously published convergent articles in several European journals. See also J. Derrida, *Voyous. Deux essais sur la raison*, Paris, 2002. Even the *New York Times* in October of that year defined international public opinion as 'the second superpower'.
5. The mandate for the European Convention, approved by the European Council at Nice in December 2000 (Declaration 23), has since been substantially improved with the Laeken Declaration of the European Council (December 2001), which focuses on the enhanced role of the EU in world affairs. See Chapter 5.
6. R. Lambert, 'Misunderstanding Each Other', *Foreign Affairs*, 82(2), March–April 2003, pp. 62–74.
7. See the conclusions of the European Council of Brussels, 14 September 2001 and the progress made as regards internal security. See also J. Stevenson, 'How Europe and America Defend Themselves', op. cit., pp. 75–82.
8. The term 'revolutionary' is employed here in the sense of accelerated change, as used by S. Hoffman in 'International System and International Law', in K. Knorr and S. Verba (eds), *The International System. Theoretical Essays*, Princeton, University Press, Princeton, 1961.
9. For this definition, see P. Hassner and J. Vaisse, *Washington et le monde. Dilemmes d'une superpuissance*, CERI/Autrement, Paris, 2003. The term 'Wilsonism' refers to the US President Woodrow Wilson who promoted the creation of the League of Nations (1919).
10. Compare the conclusions of the European Councils from 14 September 2001 with those of Salonika in June 2003 and, on a more explicitly critical note,

the positions of the President of the European Commission R. Prodi, the Commissioner for External Relations C. Patten, the International Trade Commissioner P. Lamy, the CFSP representative J. Solana, as well as relevant resolutions of the European Parliament. These were accompanied by a chorus of strong condemnation from J. Chirac, D. De Villepin, G. Schröder and J. Fischer (on the occasion of the 40th anniversary of the Franco-German Treaty celebrated at the Elysée in January 2003). While the sentiments were shared by other countries like Belgium and Luxembourg, the peremptory nature of the comments caused the heads of government of five other EU states (F. Rasmussen, S. Berlusconi, M. Barroso, C. Aznar, T. Blair) as well as those of three accession countries (Hungary, Poland and the Czech Republic, though the latter's government later distanced itself from its President's comments) and several other eastern European governments to take issue with the Franco-German stance and to align themselves with the pro-US minority, including the UK and Aznar's Spain, in the UN Security Council. See note 4 on public opinion's relatively more convergent reactions.

11. See the European Council conclusions of 14 September 2001: the fight against terrorism is conceived of within the context of complex international action which aims to tackle the reasons for the non-marginalization of terrorist groups while simultaneously promoting international justice through North–South cooperation and increased dialogue with the Arab and Islamic worlds.

12. C. Rice, in her presentation to the US Senate of 2005, while not mentioning the 'axis of evil', focused on the following tyrannies: Iran, North Korea, Zimbabwe, Belarus, Myanmar and Cuba. However, President G.W. Bush, in his West Point speech on 10 June 2002, suggested that more than 60 states could represent possible targets for American preventive attacks. See M. Allen and K. De Yung, 'Bush Charts First Strike Policy on Terror Cells', *The International Herald Tribune*, 1 June 2002, pp. 1 and 6.

13. These and other cases of external intervention are analysed in J. Holzgrefe and R.O. Keohane, *Humanitarian Intervention. Ethical, Legal and Political Dilemmas*, Cambridge University Press, Cambridge, 2003, and C. Ku and H.K. Jacobson (eds), *Democratic Accountability and the Use of Force in International Law*, Cambridge University Press, Cambridge, 2003.

14. See R. Kagan, *Of Paradise and Power: America and Europe in the New World Order*, A. Knopf, New York, 2003.

15. See the aforementioned conclusions of the 14 September 2001 European Council and 'A Secure Europe in a Better World', EU strategic document presented by Javier Solana to the European Council at Salonika, 20 June 2003, in Europe Documents, 26 June 2003 (final revision December 2003) (http://ue.eu.int/pressdata/FR/reports/76256.pdf).

16. R.O. Keohane, 'The Globalization of Informal Violence. Theories of World Politics and the Liberalism of Fear' in C. Calhoun, P. Price and A. Timmer, *Understanding September 11*, New Press and SSRC, Washington DC, 2002 and 'The Public Delegitimation of Terrorism and Coalition Politics' in K. Booth and T. Dunne (eds), *Worlds in Collision*, Palgrave, 2002, pp. 141–51 For an analysis of Islamic terrorism compared to other forms of terrorism, see P. Wilkinson, *Terrorism versus Democracy: the Liberal State Response*, Frank Cass, London, 2001, N. Chomsky, 'Who Are the Global Terrorists?' in

K. Booth and T. Dunne (eds), *Worlds in Collision: Terror and the Future of Global Order*, Palgrave, New York, 2002, pp. 128–40, H.W. Kushner, *Encyclopaedia of Terrorism*, Sage, California, 2003 and V.G. Kepel, *FITNA, Guerre au coeur de l'Islam*, Gallimard, Paris, 2004.

17. The revelations of manipulation of information in both the US and the UK regarding the threat posed by Iraq do not add much to the argument of H. Lasswell in *World Politics and Personal Insecurity*, McGraw-Hill, New York, 1935 nor to the research undertaken by R. Aron, other than adding serious questions regarding the guarantees offered by the democratic systems of these countries.

18. Bush, 'State of the Union Address', op. cit., p. 22.

19. The Republican majority in Congress also influenced the Clinton administration by hindering its multilateral approach through support for projects such as the 'missile defence shield' and opposition to the International Court of Justice, the Kyoto Protocol and the ABM Treaty. However the 'continuity thesis', dear to Kenneth Waltz and, in ideological terms, to Robert Kagan, and recognized by Democrats such as Charles Kupchan, risks underestimating the conflicts of the 1990s between the Congress and the President, particularly regarding the balance between 'soft' and 'hard' power.

20. S. Hoffmann, 'The Crisis in Transatlantic Relations', in G. Lindstrom (ed.), *Shift or Rift. Assessing the Transatlantic Relations after Iraq*, Institute for Security Studies, Paris, 2003, pp. 13–20; E.O. Czempiel, *Westpolitik im Umbruch. Die Pax Americana, der Terrorismus und die Zukunft der internationalen Beziehungen*, Beck, Munich, 2002, pp. 176–80. B. Woodward, *Bush at War*, Simon and Schuster, New York, 2002.

21. From an average of US$45bn between 1983 and 1988 to one of US$20–25bn between 1991 and 1999 (statistics from SIPRI). Inter-state conflicts decreased from 39 (1979) to 29 (2003) and nuclear warheads from 65,000 to 20,000. Military budgets decreased from $1300bn in 1987 to 750bn in 1997 (but have since gone back up to $950bn, mainly due to the US defence budget). See J. Hébert, 'Militarisation ou démilitarisation du monde? L'évolution des dépenses militaires mondiales en longue période', *Mondes en développement*, 112, 2000.

22. F. Bergsten, 'Globalizing Free Trade', *Foreign Affairs*, 3, 1996, pp. 105–20. See also the observations on the socio-political contradictions of globalization in the 1990s in P. Hirst and G. Thompson, *Globalization in Question*, Polity Press, Cambridge, 1996; S. Sassen, *Globalization and Its Discontents: Essays on the New Mobility of People and Money*, New York, 1998; Z. Bauman, *Globalization: the Human Consequences*, Columbia University Press, New York, 1998 and U. Beck, *Was ist Globalisierung? Irrtümer des Globalismus, Antworten auf Globalisierung*, Suhrkamp, Frankfurt-am-Main, 1997. Particularly pertinent to the theory of international relations are the questions posed by I. Clark in *Globalization and Fragmentation: International Relations in the Twentieth Century*, Oxford University Press, Oxford, 1997 and R. Gilpin in *The Challenge of Global Capitalism: the World Economy in the Twenty-first Century*, Princeton University Press, Princeton, 2000.

23. Francis Fukuyama (who had contributed to this American ideology in the 1990s with his 1993 article in *Foreign Affairs* and the book *The End of History*

and the Last Man, Free Press, New York, 1992) admitted after September 11 in *Le Monde* and elsewhere that such a historic event necessitated a new periodization. See also 'History and September 11' in Booth and Dunne (eds), *Worlds in Collision*, op. cit., pp. 27–37.

24. Global governance is the object of a wide range of different criticisms by public opinion. These emanate both from the left (the antiglobal movement considers international organizations to be mere pawns of multinational companies and the US) and the right (whose criticisms are voiced at times in the name of total free trade and, at others, in defence of protectionism). Critical reflection has reached the very summit of the WTO itself, as we can see from its former Secretary-General M. Moore's book *A World without Walls: Freedom Development, Free Trade and Global Governance*, Cambridge University Press, Cambridge, 2003, which aims to better reconcile the free market and governance.

25. James Rosenau, the clearest interpreter of this concept, increasingly insists on the concept of a 'bifurcated system' comprising the two worlds of global governance and world politics. See E.O. Czempiel and J. Rosenau (eds), *Governance without Government: Order and Change in World Politics*, Cambridge University Press, Cambridge, New York, 1992, and 'Governance in a New Global Order', in D. Held and A.G. McGrew (eds), *Governing Globalization. Power, Authority and Global Governance*, Polity Press, Cambridge, 2002, pp. 70–86. See also the introduction to Held and McGrew, op. cit., pp. 1–21.

26. Kenichi Ohmae takes a similar line to Fukuyama. See K. Ohmae, *The End of the Nation State: the Rise of Regional Economies*, HarperCollins, London, 1995.

27. See also W. Reinicke, *Global Public Policy. Governing without Government?*, The Brookings Institute, Washington, 1989.

28. The theoretical reference is to H. Bull, *The Anarchical Society*, Macmillan, London, 1977. See also A. Tanaka, *A New Medievalism*, Nihon Keirai, Tokyo, 1996. See also Chapter 2.

29. For example, international conferences and the exponential increase in the number of NGOs – estimated to be approximately 30,000 at the turn of the century – and their influence on governments. To cite some of the more famous examples, we could mention Médecins sans frontières, Greenpeace, The Worldwide Fund for Nature, ATTAC, and numerous other ecological, cultural, religious and trade union organizations, as well as international lobbyists.

30. R. Gilpin, 'A Realist Perspective on International Governance', in Held and McGrew (eds), *Governing Globalization*, op. cit., pp. 237–49. See the second chapter of this book, dedicated to a comparative analysis of regionalism in the world.

31. J.A. Hobson, *Imperialism: a Study*, Pott, New York, 1902. See also the analyses of T. Kemp, *Theories of Imperialism*, Dobson, London, 1967.

32. J.A. Schumpeter, 'Zur Soziologie der Imperialismen', *Archiv für Sozialwissenschaft und Sozialpolitik*, XLVI, 1918–19, pp. 1–39, 275–310.

33. These Latin American and African scholars relaunched the economic theory of imperialism in the 1970s, highlighting the organic and unreformable nature of Third World dependence with respect to the capitalist North. The decline of this theory, which had won considerable support both in the UN

and in CEPAL, was in part due to the failure of economic policies of national 'disconnection' from world markets recommended to various governments.

34. A. Gramsci, *Americanismo e fordismo. Quaderno 22*, edited by F. De Felice, Einaudi, Turin, 1975.

35. R. Aron, *République impériale*, Calmann-Lévy, Paris, 1972, and A.M. Schlesinger Jr, *The Imperial Presidency*, Houghton Mifflin, Boston, 1973 underline the change in comparison to traditional isolationism.

36. For more on the different degrees of decision-making centralization according to the importance and urgency of international questions, see T.J. Lowi, 'Making Democracy Safe for the World: Foreign Policy and National Politics', in J.N. Rosenau (ed.), *Domestic Sources of Foreign Policy*, Free Press, New York, 1967, pp. 295–331. See also C. Wright Mills, *The Power Elite*, Oxford University Press, New York, 1956.

37. Scholars such as R. Rorty, 'Ein Empire der Ungewissheit', in U. Speck and N. Sznaider (eds), *Empire Amerika*, DVA, Munich, 2003, pp. 240–53 point out how the US war on terror has been accompanied by the strengthening of state authority at the expense of civil liberties.

38. J.G. Wilson (*The Imperial Republic: a Structural History of American Constitutionalism from the Colonial Era to the Beginning of the Twentieth Century*, Ashgate, Aldershot, 2002) clearly illustrates the specificity of imperial ideologies in the history of the US and demonstrates that since Alexander Hamilton the idea of an 'imperial republic' is no longer considered an oxymoron, as it was by Montesquieu. Rather, it has been interpreted in messianic, aggressive or colonial terms.

39. N. Ferguson, *The Rise and Demise of the British World Order and the Lessons for Global Power*, Basic Books, London, 2003. For a more critical assessment of the British empire, see E. Hobsbawm, *The Age of Empire, 1875–1914*, London, 1987. For a comparison of the US and the Roman empire, see P. Bender, *Weltmacht Amerika. Das Neue Rom*, Klett-Cotta, Stuttgart, 2003 and U. Speck and N. Sznaider (eds), *Empire Amerika. Perspektiven einer neuen Weltordnung*, DVA, Munich, 2003, with articles by J. Nye, C. Meyer, N. Ferguson, and neo-conservatives such as Max Boot (Irving, William Kristol and P. Wolfowitz and the journal *National Interest* are active advocates of the US as an empire of freedom). For a critical perspective, see P. Hassner, *La terreur et l'empire*, 2 vols, Seuil, Paris, 2003. Huntington's book *Who are We?* (2004) with the thesis of the US as a citadel of godly righteousness and the subsequent debate in *Foreign Affairs* in 2004 on immigration policy (with A. Wolfe) indicate a changing ideological climate, making point (c) even more problematic.

40. M. Hardt and A. Negri, *Empire*, Harvard University Press, Cambridge, Mass., 2000).

41. See D.L. Boren and E.J. Perkins (eds), *Preparing America's Foreign Policy for the Twenty-first Century*, University of Oklahoma Press, Norman, 1999 and, more recently, the spring 2003 issue of the neo-conservative journal *National Interest* whose empire theme was in positive reference to the National Security Strategy. The term 'neo-conservatives' refers to various individuals, journals and groups which exert influence over the George W. Bush administration. These include: Richard Perle, Paul Wolfowitz, Robert Kagan, Max Boot, William Kristol (founder of *National Interest* in 1985), Jeanne Kirkpatrick, the magazine *The Weekly Standard*, and Bruce Jackson and

Thomas Donnelly's 'Project for the New American Century' centre. This group defends the concepts of an 'American empire' (M. Boot, 'Plädoyer für ein Empire', in Speck and Sznaider (eds), *Empire Amerika*, op. cit., pp. 60–70), and the 'preventive war' ('The New American Way of War', *Foreign Affairs*, July 2003) and is hostile to neo-regionalism, i.e. the aspirations of regional organizations such as the EU: regarding liberal democratic imperial theories of the EU as an empire of human rights, see M. Ignatieff, 'Empire Amerika?' in Speck and Sznaider (eds), *Empire Amerika*, op. cit., pp. 15–37.

42. E. Todd, *Après Empire. Essai sur la décomposition du système américain*, Gallimard, Paris, 2002.

43. The association of 'universal' multilateral organizations with the interests of the empire has been shattered by the conflicts the US has had in recent years with the United Nations, the WTO, the Kyoto Protocol and the International Criminal Court. The reference to Kelsen is interesting, albeit excessive (pp. 45–89), given that today we are witnessing the exact opposite – a qualitative and quantitative increase in the political contradictions between American globalism and an international system of justice.

44. The theory of the redundancy of the historic and spatial-temporal dimension is analogous here to Fukuyama's liberal ideology (see *The End of History*, op. cit.). See also Hardt and Negri, *Empire*, op. cit., pp. 21–37. Its criticism of Arrighi, and especially of Wallerstein and the idea of cycles of power, highlights this regression (pp. 225–7). In support of the theory of hegemonic cycles, see R. Gilpin, *War and Change in World Politics*, Cambridge University Press, London, 1981, and P.J. Taylor, 'The American Century as Hegemonic Cycle', in P.K. O'Brien and A. Clesse (eds), *Two Hegemonies. Britain 1846–1914 and the United States 1941–2001*, Ashgate, Aldershot, 2002, pp. 284–302.

45. R. Gilpin, *The Political Economy of International Relations*, Princeton University Press, Princeton, 1987 and Gilpin, *Global Political Economy: Understanding the International Economic Order*, Princeton University Press, Princeton, 2001.

46. See Czempiel's analysis of the costly global reorganization of the US military presence (*Weltpolitik im Umbruch*, op. cit., pp. 144–62). Indeed, on the geopolitical front, the US with its 36,000 troops stationed in Europe is seeking to gain greater influence over eastern Europe through NATO. It has politicized the FTAA project in Latin America and implanted itself in the Middle East with 139,000 troops in Iraq and a further 20,000 in other countries in the area. It maintains a military presence in central Asia and Afghanistan (10,000 troops) and flanks China, from the 31,000 troops in South Korea to its base at Okinawa. We should also not forget that the 7th fleet and the APEC project guarantee its presence in the Asia-Pacific region – the 'American lake'. A new initiative regarding Africa would complete the geopolitical picture. On the strategic level, the US is interested in (a) securing new bases outside Europe and Japan, to allow greater flexibility in organizing attack forces; (b) gaining access to new lines of command for military training; (c) reorganizing its attack forces and hardware, corresponding to its varying objectives of regional dissuasion; (d) improving mobility, in order to be capable of launching long-range military attacks on targets armed with WMD (Department of Defense, *Quadrennial Defense*, op. cit., p. 26).

47. Regarding the evolution of the frontier concept – the cornerstone of the formation of sovereign states – and perceptions of it, see M. Anderson, *Frontiers: Territory and State Formation in the Modern World*, Polity Press, London, 1996.

48. See Chapter 2 and the maps at the front of this book.

49. R.O. Keohane, 'Ironies of Sovereignty: the EU and the US', in J.H.H. Weiler, I. Begg and J. Peterson (eds), *Integration in an Expanding European Union. Reassessing the Fundamentals*, Blackwell, Malden, Mass., 2003, pp. 307–30.

50. Regarding the distinction between economic and political globalism, see M. Telò (ed.), *European Union and New Regionalism: Regional Actors and Global Governance in a Post-Hegemonic Era*, Ashgate, Aldershot, 2001 and the chapter by A. Gamble, 'Theoretical Perspectives: Regional Blocs, World Order and the New Medievalism' in the same volume.

51. A. Stein (*Nation at War*, Johns Hopkins University Press, Baltimore, 1980) compares four wars involving the US and the level of public support for them. In decreasing order of popularity, these are: the Second World War, the First World War, the Korean War and the Vietnam War.

52. A. Gramsci, *Selection from the Prison Notebooks* (ed. by Q. Hoare and G. Nowell Smith), International Publishers, New York, 1971 and the original edition: *Quaderni del carcere*, Einaudi, Turin, 1975, Q. 13, par. 15.

53. Criticisms by the global public opinion interplays with the US society and the American press. It concerns the non-respect of what is since called the roman law *jus in bello* (uncertainties regarding the status of prisoners, the juridical status of the Guantanamo Bay prison, the Geneva Convention and, during the military occupation of Iraq, the widespread abuse and mistreatment of Iraqi prisoners). Second, the shifting domestic equilibrium struck between liberty and security, freedom of information and the need for effective anti-terrorist measures, both within the US and allied states. We do not have the space here to devote adequate attention to these important questions which have been the subject of hard debate, not only by jurists and public opinion in Europe, but also by the media, citizens, associations and Congress members in the US. The main critical argument is that the global struggle for freedom and democracy is undermined by the deterioration of respect of rule of law and by the declining credibility of the international image of Western democracies and rule of law.

54. See C.P. Kindleberger, *The World in Depression, 1929–1939*. Allen Lane, London and Kindleberger, *World Economic Primacy: 1500 to 1990*, Oxford University Press, Oxford, 1996. See also O'Brien and Clesse (eds), *Two Hegemonies*, op. cit., with articles by R. Gilpin, I. Wallerstein et al.

55. The concept of 'public good' is associated in American academic works with that of hegemonic power. The more widely accepted notion of the public good means (a) it is an indivisible product in so far as it is available to all and its extension does not involve a corresponding reduction in the quantity available to each beneficiary; (b) indivisibility, however, does not mean that it is necessary to make it available to others and (c) the impossibility of excluding anyone from enjoying the benefits of the good. See, *inter alia*, J.G. Ruggie, *Constructing the World Polity: Essays on International Institutionalization*, Routledge, London–New York, 1998, p. 51.

56. Gilpin, *The Political Economy of International Relations*, op. cit.

57. R.O. Keohane, *After Hegemony: Cooperation and Discord in the World Political Economy*, Princeton University Press, Princeton, 1984. In his 2004 preface to a new edition of *After Hegemony*, R.O. Keohane argues that

> certainly in 1984 I expected an increasing demand for cooperation. On security issues the collapse of the adversary (Soviet communism) made discord between Europe and the US more likely, and it is natural that such discord had effects on non-security issues as well. Nothing in *After Hegemony* would have enabled one to anticipate the degree of conflict that now exists, in the Fall of 2004, between the United States and its European allies. The book's argument would lead one, however, to expect that the United States could not successfully attain its political objectives through military power, while scorning the United Nations. The failure of unilateralism to achieve American objectives in Iraq supports this position. The argument of *After Hegemony* that cooperation can take place without hegemony also implies that international cooperation does not necessarily require American participation.

58. R.W. Cox, 'Social Forces, States and World Order: Beyond International Relations Theory', in R.O. Keohane (ed.), *Neorealism and Its Critics*, Columbia University Press, New York, 1986 (Cox's article dates from 1981); see also Cox's 1983 article 'Gramsci, Hegemony and International Relations: an Essay in Method', *Millennium*, 12, 1983, pp. 162–75; and Stephen Gill (ed.), *Gramsci, Historical Materialism, International Relations*, Cambridge University Press, Cambridge, 1993. Here we are dealing with an anti-Leninist reproblematization of the 'dependence theory' of Marxists such as Dos Santos, Amin and Gunder Frank, as well as a development of the centre–periphery contrast typical of Immanuel Wallerstein's 'world system' theory which, despite its historiographic value, shares with the former a certain underestimation of the political and institutional conflicts at the heart of the centre in the West (*The Modern World-System*, 3 vols, Academic Press, New York, 1974–89). Neither Cox nor Gill has grasped the political dimension of the European project nor of world neo-regionalism. For a critical review of this 'Italian school', see M. Telò, 'Note sul futuro dell'Occidente e la teoria delle relazioni internazionali', in G. Vacca (ed.), *Gramsci e il Novecento*, Carocci, Rome, 1999, vol. I, pp. 51–74.

59. Gramsci, *Selection from the Prison Notebooks*, op. cit.; see also the original edition *Quaderno 13. Noterelle sulla politica del Machiavelli*, Einaudi, Turin, 1981.

60. Gramsci, *Quaderno 13*, op. cit., par. 19.

61. Ibid., pp. 141–2.

62. Telò, 'Note sul futuro dell'Occidente', op. cit., pp. 51–74.

63. K. Waltz, *Theory of International Politics*, Addison-Wesley, Reading, Mass., 1979.

64. R. Gilpin, *War and Change in World Politics*, Cambridge University Press, Cambridge, 1981.

65. A. Gramsci, 'Americanism and Fordism', in *Selection from the Prison Notebooks*, op. cit. A recent example of confusion between hegemony and dominance is provided by N. Chomsky, *Hegemony or Survival. America's Quest for Global Dominance*, Metropolitan Books, New York, 2004.

66. The symbolic date of this (1931) is pointed out by K. Polanyi in *The Great Transformation*, Rinehart, New York, 1944.
67. Kindleberger, *The World in Depression*, op. cit. The Bretton Woods system reduced uncertainty in international finance and commerce and helped to limit speculation by regimenting short-term capital flow. Regarding this phase, see also Gilpin, 'The Rise of American Hegemony', in O'Brien and Clesse (eds), *Two Hegemonies*, op. cit., pp. 165–82.
68. R.O. Keohane, 'The Economic and Political World System and the Crisis of Embedded Liberalism', in J.H. Goldthorpe (ed.), *Order and Conflict in Contemporary Capitalism*, Oxford University Press, Oxford, 1984.
69. See also L. Brilmayer, *American Hegemony. Political Morality in a One-Superpower World*, Yale University Press, New Haven, 1994.
70. Niall Ferguson contrasts American hegemony with the British empire, which governed its subjects directly. See 'Hegemony or Empire?', *Foreign Affairs*, September 2003, pp. 154–61.
71. E.J. Hobsbawm, *Age of Extremes: the Short Twentieth Century, 1914–1991*, Michael Joseph, London, 1994.
72. For two perspectives on this new phenomenon, see J. Revel, *L'obsession anti-américaine. Son fonctionnement, ses causes, ses inconséquences*, Plon, Paris, 2002 and P. Hassner and J. Vaïsse, *Washington et le monde. Dilemmes d'une super-puissance*, CERI, Paris, 2003.
73. Think, for example, of the debate in *The New York Times* and the American press in general in relation to the growing mistrust, and even hatred, of the US. Think too of the firing of the Bush administration's communications chief in 2003 and of the decision to snub and marginalize the UN only to return there later to secure resolution 1483 in May 2003, and then seek the approval and help of its allies in August of the same year until the consensual UN Resolution 1546. See S. Hoffmann, 'Why Don't They Like Us?', *The American Prospect*, 12, 20, 19 November 2001, pp. 1 onwards (http://www.prospect.org/print/V12/20/hoffmann-s.html).
74. This view does not represent that of the majority in the US. Nevertheless, see D.P. Calleo, *Rethinking Europe's Future*, Princeton University Press, Princeton, 2001, and C.A. Kupchan, *The End of the American Era: US Foreign Policy and the Geopolitics of the Twenty-first Century*, A. Knopf, New York, 2002. The question has also been expertly examined in J. Mearsheimer, *The Tragedy of Great Power Politics*, Norton, New York, 2001.
75. See K. Waltz, 'The Continuity of International Politics', in Booth and Dunne (eds), *Worlds in Collision*, op. cit., pp. 347–53. In 1997 US military spending was greater than that of the next five countries together, in 2000 of that of the next 8. It now exceeds that of the next 10 countries combined.
76. J. Habermas, 'La statue et les révolutionnaires', *Le Monde*, 3 May 2003, pp. 1 and 14.
77. By late autumn 2004, there had been 100,000 civilian casualties in Iraq, according to the respected international medical journal *The Lancet* (19 October 2004). The American economist Paul R. Krugman noted that various inefficiencies and the 'mess that logistical services are in due to their privatisation' (*La Repubblica*, 18 August 2003) could prove a danger 'against serious adversaries such as North Korea'. K. Waltz observed in *Foreign Affairs* (September 2003, p. 193) that 'for a giant, defeat of a pigmy can hardly be

considered proof of the valour of a country and of its methods of engagement'. Disagreeing with the conservative M. Boot, Waltz highlights the imbalance between the two defence budgets ($1.5bn as opposed to $322bn). The majority of observers agree that Iraq's military strength had been decimated by a decade of sanctions and UN controls.

78. As Stanley Hoffman observed during a seminar in Paris in May 2003, resolution 1483 (like resolution 1441 in autumn 2002), is open to different and contrasting interpretations. Resolution 1511 of 17 October 2003 was clearer. However, the strength of the guerrilla campaign, the serious nature of the attacks and the continued lack of engagement of the UN, France, Germany and other countries confirm the difficulty in mobilizing international cooperation, notwithstanding the Sharm el Sheik Conference at the end of 2004.

79. The difficulties encountered in Afghanistan can be partly explained by the historical factor of the long-standing civil war between rival groups (dating back to the fall of the monarchy in 1973) and the seriously limited resources mobilized in comparison with Bosnia and Kosovo: 0.18 men for every 1000 inhabitants compared to 1.39 and 184 (statistics from RAND Corporation, Washington, 2003).

80. M.A. Kaplan, 'Some Problems of International Systems Research', in *International Politics of Community*, Doubleday, Garden City, 1966, pp. 469–501.

81. The White House, *The National Security Strategy*, op. cit.

82. See B. Buzan, *Regions and Powers*, Cambridge University Press, 2003. Buzan discusses the unification of the security complex of north-west Asia with that of South-East Asia and questions realist approaches to the security challenges in Asia. By contrast, the article by James F. Hoge, 'A Global Power Shift in the Making. Is the US Ready?', *Foreign Affairs*, July–August 2004, pp. 2–7, provides 'both a realistic vision of the security challenges in Asia and normative arguments in favour of the US substituting the current ambiguity between rivalry and cooperation with a containment strategy'. See also M. Telò, 'EU Global Role: the East Asian Challenge', in M. Dumulain et al. (eds), *EU and Asia*, P. Lang, Brussels, 2004.

83. People's Republic of China, *China's EU Policy Paper*, October 2003; EU Commission, Policy paper for transmission to the Council and the EU Parliament. *A Maturing Partnership: Shared Interests and Challenges in EU–China Relations*, Brussels, 10 September 2003. The strategic partnership agreement was signed in Beijing by China and the EU on 31 October 2003. For its background in the EU, see EU, *Strategy Towards China*, Brussels 15 May 2001. For an evaluation of the current and potential cultural dimension of the EU–China dialogue, see M. Telò, *Mission Report: China*, for the Advisory Group Social Sciences and Humanities for ERA, European Commission, DG Research, August 2004. Website.

84. Regarding this definition of G8 reform, in the sense of a more systematic rather than occasional opening of its meetings to other states and to civil society, see G. Amato, 'Perché ha ancora senso il G8? Potere e democrazia nel mondo globale', *Aspenia*, 17, June 2002, pp. 9–27 (http://www.aspeninstitute.it/icons/imgAspen/pdf/Aspenia/Asp17_Amato_it.pdf).

85. We refer to the threats by Richard Perle and others regarding the eventual expulsion of France from the Security Council.

86. See A. Gamble, *Between Europe and America*, London, Palgrave, 2003. In the words of Blair's close advisor, Peter Mandelson, the UK found itself alone in 2002–3 in the middle of the Atlantic: far from Europe, on the one hand, and the target of American Defense Secretary Donald Rumsfeld's impatient criticisms on the other.

87. According to Kenneth Waltz (Hobbes scholar and neo-realism expert), the following rules are valid: 'a) every state can use force if it considers its objectives more important than the benefits of peace; b) as it is the ultimate judge of its own state interests, every state can use force in order to implement its own policies; c) given that every state may make recourse to force, every state should constantly be ready to react to aggression or be prepared pay the price for its own weakness'. See K.N. Waltz, *Man, the State and War. A Theoretical Analysis*, Columbia University Press, New York, 1954, especially Chapter 4, 'International Conflict and International Anarchy', p. 160 onwards.

88. S.P. Huntington, *The Clash of Civilizations and the Remarking of the World Order*, Simon & Schuster, New York, 1996.

89. J.J. Mearsheimer, 'Back to the Future: Instability in Europe after the Cold War', *International Security*, 15, 4, 1990, pp. 5–56.

90. R. Seidelmann, 'European Union and Eastern Europe', in Telò (ed.), *European Union and New Regionalism*, op. cit., pp. 187–207 and K.E. Smith, paper for ECPR-SGIR Conference, The Hague, September 2004, op. cit.

91. J.J. Mearsheimer, *The Tragedy of Great Power Politics*, op. cit. We should note that Mearsheimer, along with other neo-realists, is opposed to the war in Iraq in the name of containment.

92. Reworking of data originally in Mearsheimer, op. cit., pp. 347–8.

93. Eric J. Hobsbawm argued in favour of this controversial interpretation in 1995 during a conference held at the Free University of Brussels (Dialogues européens). The edited proceedings of this conference were published in M. Telò and P. Magnette, *Repenser l'Europe*, Editions de l'Université de Bruxelles, Brussels, 1996. Following the Iraq War, Hobsbawn repeated this view in June 2003 in *Le Monde diplomatique*, 'Où va l'empire américain?'

94. Mearsheimer, 'Back to the Future', op. cit.; T. Garton Ash, *In Europe's Name: Germany and the Divided Continent*, Jonathan Cape, London, 1993.

95. E.J. Hobsbawm, *Nations and Nationalism since 1780: Programme, Myth, Reality*, Cambridge University Press, Cambridge, 1990; E. Gellner, *Nations and Nationalism*, Cornell University Press, Ithaca (NY), 1983; B. Anderson, *Imagined Communities: Reflections on the Origin and Spread of Nationalism*, Verso, London, 1983.

96. Here we refer to the political aspects of 'glocalization', a thesis which was trivialized in the 1990s. See B. Barber, *Jihad vs. McWorld*, Times Books, New York, 1995 and Baúman, *Globalization: the Human Consequences*, op. cit.

97. Robert Cooper, *The Breaking of Nations: Order and Chaos in the Twenty-first Century*, Atlantic, London, 2003.

98. Huntington's theory has been used by neo-conservatives. See C. Krauthammer, 'The Real New World Order: the American and the Islamic Challenge', *The Weekly Standard*, 7, 9, 12 November 2001 (http://www.weeklystandard.com/Content/Public/Articles/000/000/000/456zfygd.asp). For a critique of this theory, see T. Meyer, 'The Cultural Factor in the Process of Globalization/

Regionalization', in Telò (ed.), *European Union and New Regionalism*, op. cit., pp. 69–70 and Gilles Kepel, *Fitna, Guerre au coeur de l'Islam*, Gallimard, Paris, 2004.

99. G.H. Joffé, 'European Union and the Mediterranean', op. cit., pp. 207–27.
100. G. Kepel, *Jihad expansion et déclin de l'islamisme*, Gallimard, Paris, 2000.
101. Waltz, 'The Continuity of International Politics', op. cit., pp. 350 onwards.
102. R. Kaplan, *The Coming Anarchy*, Random House, New York, 2000.
103. Waltz, 'The Continuity of International Politics', op. cit.
104. For an attempt to balance declarations of the new threats with a reminder of the values of multilateralism, see the aforementioned 'Solana strategic paper', supported by the E. Council in December 2003, and *EU Strategy against the Proliferation of WMD*, June 2003. Also see M. Smith and others, *Le défi de la prolifération*, ISS, Paris, 2003.
105. Czempiel (*Weltpolitik im Umbruch*, op. cit., pp. 158–70) observes that the US represents a bad example, with its abandonment of the ABM treaty, its lukewarm defence of the Non-Proliferation Treaty, its massive rearmament and, especially, its 'selective' punishment of tyrannies according to their nuclear deterrent. Nuclear proliferation will increase if the US proves that it is the only way for a state to become unattackable.
106. M. Kaplan, 'Some Problems of International Systems Research', op. cit. Kupchan (*The End of the American Era*, op. cit.) gives serious consideration to the scenario of an isolationist US in the future.
107. The US looks as if it considers itself a state above others, *legibus solutus*, to whom common international norms do not apply, e.g. the Kyoto Protocol, the Geneva Convention, the International Criminal Court. In 1966, Morton Kaplan envisaged a similar hypothesis regarding the possible types of international systems which might succeed the bipolar one. Apart from the hypothesis already mentioned (multiple nuclear proliferation contributing to stability) and its opposite based on the clear primacy of universalist organizations, he also discussed the possibility of a highly integrated 'hierarchical system' that could be either authoritarian or democratic, depending on whether it was combined with multilateral organizations, or was imposed 'from above' by the dominant power on reluctant states and actors. In this context, the costs of opposition or exit are high. See Kaplan, *Some Problems of International Systems Research*, op. cit.
108. The 'constitutional rules' provide the institutional basis of societies: if regimes are supported by force alone, they are destined to collapse. The collapse of the USSR, colonialism and slavery are all examples of this. Ruggie does not claim that constructivism is an international relations theory with the axiomatic rigour of realism (on p. 34 of *Constructing the World Polity*, op. cit., he says that constructivism is a 'theoretically informed approach to the study of IR'). In this valuable theoretical work, Ruggie does not acknowledge all his debts to the Hegelian concept of intersubjectivity and the distinction between it and objectivity. The concepts of 'social facts' (opposed to 'brutal facts') and 'collective intentionality' (the social construction of actors) recall Hegel and ideas of the collective spirit and the intersubjective. This is particularly evident in their application to the questions of state sovereignty and human rights. Ruggie also cites Habermas's

theory of communicative action, referring in particular to acts of deliberation and persuasion and the sharing of strategic concepts – the irreconcil-
able utilitarian paradigm. The English constructivist school includes
Herbert Butterfield, Martin Wight, Headley Bull, Barry Buzan and Anthony
Giddens. Serle developed its philosophical basis as a critique not only of
Kenneth Waltz's international anarchy and neo-realism, but also of the
insufficient distance from realism and utilitarianism that, according to him,
limits Keohane's new institutionalism. Ruggie refers to three currents of
constructivism: (a) neoclassical constructivism, rooted in the works of Emile
Durkheim and Max Weber (John G. Ruggie, Ernst B. Haas, Peter
J. Katzenstein, Martha Finnemore, Friedrich V. Kratochwil); (b) postmodern
constructivism, rooted in those of Friedrich Nietzsche, Michel Foucault and
Jacques Derrida (Richard Ashley, David Campbell and R.B.J. Walker, who
promote the study of the linguistic construction of subjects against the
'hegemonic discourse' that a regime of well-established truths would
impose); (c) the third current is the one most closely linked to scientific realism – the naturalism applied to the social sciences by Alexander Wendt
(*Social Theory of International Politics*, Cambridge University Press,
Cambridge, 1999).

109. Ruggie, *Constructing the World Polity*, op. cit., This work refers to the
American and British cases, but makes a number of points which are helpful
when considering the emerging European multilateralism.

110. R.O. Keohane and L.L. Martin, 'The Promise of Institutionalist Theory',
International Security, 20, 1, 1995, pp. 39–51. According to Keohane, international institutions, rather than regimes, ensure 'persistent and connected
sets of rules, formal and informal, that prescribe behavioural roles, constrain
activity and shape expectations'.

111. Keohane, *After Hegemony*, op. cit.

112. An international regime is defined by Keohane and Stephen D. Krasner
(*International Regimes*, Cornell University Press, Ithaca, NY, 1983) as a 'set
of governing arrangements' encompassing a combination of reciprocal
expectations, rules, regulatory systems, organizational plans and financial
commitments which are accepted by a group of states. Krasner insists on
the definition of regimes as 'sets of implicit or explicit principles, norms,
rules and decision-making procedures around which actors' expectations
converge in a given area of international relations', *International Regimes*,
op. cit., p. 2. According to Headley Bull, international institutions help to
secure adherence to rules by formulating, communicating, administering,
enforcing, interpreting, legitimating and adapting them. Ruggie stipulates
that a regime must include principles, norms, rules and decision-making
procedures, around which is found common ground among participants
(*Constructing the World Polity*, op. cit., p. 107).

113. R.O. Keohane (ed.), *Neo-realism and its Critics*, Columbia University Press,
New York, 1986.

114. In the 1950s, functionalism emerged as a theory of the almost automatic
growth of international organizations, related to technological developments
and technical and ecological imperatives (Ernst Haas). According to Etzioni,
the trend is one of transfer of competencies to ever larger authorities, above
and beyond the state. Haas in *Beyond the Nation State: Functionalism and*

International Organization, Stanford University Press, Stanford, 1964, refers to the emergence of 'state like forms beyond the state'. According to Ruggie (*Constructing the World Polity*, op. cit., pp. 45–7), who follows on from Karl Deutsch (in K. Deutsch, S. Burrell and R.A. Kann, *Political Community and the North Atlantic Area; International Organization in the Light of Historical Experience*, Princeton University Press, Princeton, 1957), functionalists remain fundamentally anchored to the notion of hierarchy between subordinate and superior entities in line with the (rational-legal) scheme of authority put forward by Max Weber in relation to national authority. This is mistaken as it underestimates the resilient weight of national sovereignty.

115. Ruggie, *Constructing the World Polity*, op. cit., p. 43: the multilateral institution is not founded just on a vague need for rules, but on specific normative features of multilateral organizing principles.

116. Ibid., p. 109. From p. 107 to p. 120, the author cites various historical examples of multilateral institutions, regimes and practices. These range from the principle of 'extra-territoriality' that underpins the creation of embassies, to the question of coordination between states (an area in which the International Telegraph Union was a pioneer in 1865), to the forms of international political cooperation like the European Concert that proclaimed the principles of the indivisibility of peace and collective responses to aggression (thereby modifying classic power politics). On the economic front, the British system of free trade based on the Gold Standard spread the cause of commercial non-discrimination, first unilaterally, then bilaterally (with France in 1860), and finally multilaterally (an extension of the most favoured nation concept). On the political front, in the inter-war period the habit of multilateral conferencing was developed in the context of a general trend towards institutionalization, encouraged by the League of Nations. See also C. Archer, *International Organizations*, Routledge, London, 1992.

117. R.O. Keohane, 'Multilateralism: an Agenda for Research', *International Journal*, 45, 4, 1990, p. 731.

118. Strangely enough, in Italy, the trade unions and the left were stronger supporters of the Marshall Plan than the governing centre–right coalition. See M. Telò, 'L'Italia nel processo di costruzione europea', in *Storia dell'Italia repubblicana*, vol. III, *L'Italia nella crisi mondiale. L'ultimo ventennio*, F. de Felice (ed.), vol. 1, *Economia e società*, Einaudi, Turin, 1996, pp. 131–243.

119. By this we do not mean to deny the validity of some of the points raised by the aforementioned 'dependency theorists' or by the large body of scholarly work critical of the American superpower, its McCarthyist domestic rigidity (and the related witch-hunts), and its more controversial actions in the bipolar era, from Santo Domingo to the coup in Chile, from Vietnam (recognized as an error by Defence Secretary McNamara) to Cuba (Bay of Pigs) and to Nicaragua. What is astonishing, however, is the confusion between domination and hegemony that is typical of those who seriously underestimate the major historical significance and importance of Americanism in the decades of the post-war hegemony (which it is ridiculous to reduce to simple domination) and who ignore the importance of historical changes and conceptual distinctions, both in comparison with what went before, and came after, this period.

120. J-J. Rey, *Institutions économiques internationales*, Bruylant, Brussels, 1988, and C. Deblock (ed.), *L'Organization mondiale du commerce: où s'en va la mondialisation?*, Fides, Quebec, 2002.

121. Chapter 3 of this book discusses this.

122. On this point, see M. Telò, *Le New Deal européen*, Editions de l'Université de Bruxelles, Brussels, 1989. Also see M.J. Hogan, *The Marshall Plan: America, Britain and the Reconstruction of Europe*, Cambridge University Press, New York, 1987.

123. M. Bøås and D. McNeill, *Multilateral Institutions: a Critical Introduction*, Pluto Press, London, 2003, p. xiii.

124. US refusal in 2001 of the European offer, which had been encouraged by the apparently multilateral line supported by Powell, came as a bit of a cold shower. The NATO Secretary-General, Lord Robertson, spoke of the risk of an unbridgeable gap opening up between the two sides of the Atlantic (NATO Munich conference, 4 February 2002). Only the hard problems besetting post-war Iraq, convinced the US to come back to NATO and look at involving allies, which however succeeded to a minor extent. Germany in 2004 proposed a controversial NATO reform.

125. Krasner, *International Regimes*, op. cit.

126. Among the vast amount of teleological literature on the development of the European construction, we should mention D. Sidjanski, *The Federal Future of Europe. From the European Community to the European Union*, University of Michigan Press, Ann Arbor, 2003.

127. Ruggie, *Constructing the World Polity*, op. cit., p. 22.

128. This concept is explicitly mentioned in the famous Solana paper of 20 June 2003, *A Secure Europe in a Better World* (presented to the European Council).

129. The period immediately following George W. Bush's famous 'axis of evil' speech on 29 January 2002 saw a certain convergence of views within the US administration. Secretary of State Colin Powell declared: 'We believe in multilateralism. However, when it is a matter of principle and the multilateral community disagrees with us, we do not abstain from doing what we consider right and in our interest, even if some of our friends disagree with us' (*Le Monde*, 7 February 2002, p. 5). Moreover, the US *National Security Strategy* of September 2002 states that 'we will not hesitate to act alone, if necessary, to exercise our right of self-defense by acting pre-emptively against terrorists' (p. 6). The shared idea is that the mission determines the coalition and this should not limit the US's freedom to act. This was made clear in Wolfowitz's speech in Werkhunde on 2 February 2002, quoted in Hassner and Vaïsse, *Washington et le monde*, op. cit., p. 80. Also see the comments of Richard Haas, an important State Department advisor, in *Le Monde*, 5 October 2002, p. 5. This kind of varying approach to multilateralism explains, among other things, the US commitment to the WTO (Geneva 2004), to NATO (by rebuilding Iraq), to helping victims of the December 2004 tsunami, etc.

130. J.S. Nye, *Bound to Lead: the Changing Nature of American Power*, Basic Books, New York, 1990.

131. E.O. Czempiel, *Die kluge Macht. Außenpolitik fur das 21. Jahrhundert*, Beck, Munich, 1999.

132. For the history of this concept, see Chapters 4 and 5 of this book.

133. Regarding these limits, see B. De Giovanni's important work *L'ambigua potenza dell'Europa*, Guida, Naples, 2002, and C. Gasteyger, *An Ambiguous Power, the EU and the Changing World*, Bertelsmann Foundation, Gütersloh, 1996.

134. See R.A. Dahl, *On Democracy*, Yale University Press, New Haven, 1998; P.C. Schmitter, *How to Democratize the European Union – and Why Bother?*, Rowman & Littlefield, Lanham, MD, 2000; M. Telò (ed.), *Démocratie et construction européenne*, Editions de l'Université de Bruxelles, Brussels, 1995.

135. See, for example J. Rawls, *The Law of Peoples; with 'The Idea of Pub-lic Reason' Revisited*, Harvard University Press, Cambridge, 1999 and J. Habermas who developed the new Kantian concept of 'domestic international politics'.

136. Articles 6 and 7 of the Amsterdam Treaty already envisage the suspension of the rights of states who continually violate these criteria. The new Constitutional Treaty reinforces this juridical framework through articles I-9 and I-59 and its inclusion of the Charter of Fundamental Freedoms in Part II. On the increasing influence of EU Justice and Home Affairs policy after the Amsterdam Treaty, see J. Monar, 'The EU as an International Actor in the Domain of JHA', *European Foreign Affairs Review*, 9, autumn 2004, pp. 395–415 and A. Weyenberg and G. de Kerkhove (eds), *Sécurité et justice, enjeu des relations extérieures de l'UE*, Editions de l'Université de Bruxelles, 2003.

137. The opening in Doha of a new round of negotiations between the 146 WTO members following the Seattle crisis of 2000 stemmed from an initial convergence between the EU and Third World countries. However, the agenda is complex and difficult: liberalization of trade in services (these represent about two-thirds of EU GDP. Privatization, which remains the competence of the state, is not at issue and the EU insists on respect for the basic principles of universal services), the inclusion of agricultural products on the global market, and access for poor countries to generic medicines. For the EU position, see EU Trade Commissioner Pascal Lamy's speech (on the control of globalization and against the 'law of the jungle') on 8 November 2001 at the Doha Conference *Making Globalization Work for People: Development and Workers' Rights at the 4th WTO Conference*. The WTO impasse at Cancún in September 2003 confirmed first of all the great importance that Third World countries place on the question of the reduc-tion of EU and US agricultural subsidies in order to gain access to the rich northern markets. Secondly, the US–EU agreement proved incapable of restarting global negotiations. This was not only because other countries such as the EFTA member states, Japan and Israel are still protectionist, but also due to the new assertiveness of Brazil and the G20.

138. The share of the euro in official resources was around 20 per cent in 2003 compared with the dollar's 63.8 per cent. However, the euro continued to grow as a reserve currency in 2004 due to the slide of the US dollar.

139. France has long promoted great European space projects, alternating between cooperation and competition with the US. Europe is second to the US in terms of levels of public expenditure devoted to the civilian space sector. See *The European Space Sector in a Global Context*, ESA, Paris, 4/3, 2004.

140. Strongly promoted by the Prodi Commission, the Galileo project for the construction of a European satellite system has significant civilian, economic and military implications and is one of the most important expressions of European independence vis-à-vis the US, which has long opposed EU autonomy in this key field. See Chapter 3 of this book.

141. Paul Kennedy's theory (*The Rise and Fall of the Great Powers: Economic Change and Military Conflict from 1500 to 2000*, Random House, New York, 1987) runs along these lines, even if the author exaggerates US decline.

142. Gilpin, *The Political Economy of International Relations*, op. cit.

143. J.S. Nye, *The Paradox of American Power: Why the World's Only Superpower Can't Go It Alone*, Oxford University Press, New York, 2002.

144. After the Cancún failure, at the end of 2003, Lamy and Prodi promoted a rethinking process aimed at relaunching the multilateral and interregional strategy on a new basis. As far as the UN is concerned, the European Commission presented *The EU and the United Nations* (10 September 2003) in which it proposes the strategic strengthening of cooperation.

145. The Treaty signed on 18 July 1998 paved the way for the new International Criminal Court which came into existence in 2002. In contrast to ad hoc tribunals (such as those of Nuremberg and Tokyo following the Second World War or The Hague tribunal for ex-Yugoslavia), which are criticized as representing the justice of the winners, the ICC's prosecutor is independent. According to Kofi Annan, despite its limits, the Treaty represents a giant step towards the universal respect of human rights and the rule of law ('Le droit n'est plus muet', *Le Monde*, 4 August 1998, p. 10).

146. See Czempiel, *Weltpolitik im Umbruch*, op. cit., pp. 175–81.

147. On point no. 7, see Chapter 2 and Maps 2 and 3 at the front of this book. Also see M. Farrell, B. Hettne and L. Van Langenhove (eds), *Global Politics of Regionalism*, Pluto, London, 2005; J. Grugel, 'New Regionalism and Modes of Governance. Comparing US and EU Strategies in Latin America', *European Journal of International Relations*, 10, 2004, pp. 603–26; also see the papers presented by B. Hettne, L. Van Langenhove, F. Söderbaum, K. Smith, B. Bull, R. Higgott, M. Telò et al. in Section 33 of the ECPR–SGIR Conference 'Constructing World Orders' (The Hague, September 2004). The preference of the Bush administration for a 'hub and spokes' model (rather than the 'open regionalism' and 'building blocks' strategy of the Clinton era) strengthens the EU identity-marker character of multidimensional interregionalism.

148. See the TEU (1992) on the aims of the CFSP:

> to safeguard the common values, fundamental interests, independence and integrity of the Union in conformity with the principles of the United Nations Charter; to strengthen the security of the Union in all ways; to preserve peace and strengthen international security in accordance with the principles of the United Nations Charter as well as the principles of the Helsinki Final Act and the objectives of the Paris Charter, including those on external borders; to promote international cooperation; to develop and consolidate democracy and the rule of law and respect for human rights and fundamental freedoms. (article 11, title V)

The EU Constitutional Treaty stresses these objectives in articles I-3.4 and II-292 and 309. See Chapter 5 of this book.

149. K. Smith, 'The End of Civilian Power Europe: a Welcome Demise or a Cause for Concern?' *International Spectator*, 35, 2, 2000, pp. 11–28. The 'Petersberg tasks' encompass peacekeeping, peace-enforcing and humanitarian missions as well.

150. S. Stavridis, 'Why the "Militarising" of the EU is Strengthening the Concept of "Civilian Power Europe"', *Robert Schuman CentreWorking Papers*, 17, 2001.

151. For a discussion of this brilliant idea, which is also a research agenda and was initially put forward by Goran Therborn with reference to the 1950s–1990s, see below, Chapter 4.

152. See in Chapter 4 the scenario of a 'continental trading state'.

153. The central question is: in whose interests is a politically weakened Europe? This is the point that, since 1989, has pitted the likes of Margaret Thatcher and others who (supported by the US) advocate the rapid and generalized enlargement of the EU against those such as Jacques Delors, who would rather first of all strengthen the EU's political role. We will return to the challenge of enlargement in Chapter 4.

154. Council of the EU, *Treaty Establishing a Constitution for Europe*, 18 June 2004, Luxembourg, articles 3.1 and 3.4. See also R.O. Keohane, 'Governance in a Partially Globalized World', op. cit. and N. Gnesotto, 'EU, US: Visions of the World, Visions of the Other', in G. Lindstrom, *Shift or Rift*, op. cit, pp. 21–42.

155. The paradoxical and exclusive concept of 'absolute right' is the prerogative of an epoch-dominating superpower which justifies its primacy over international law both through historical legitimacy and the claim to be defending universal values. My use of a classic thinker such as Hegel in interpreting current phenomena arises from a very productive and useful series of conversations I had with another of the most important political philosophers of his time, Norberto Bobbio, between the end of 1997 and April 1999. I have discussed this at length in my introductory essay to the French edition of Bobbio's works: N. Bobbio, *L'Etat et la démocratie internationale*, Complexe, Brussels, 1998. See G.W.F. Hegel, *Vorlesungen über die Philosophie der Geschichte*, Werke, 12 (1822), Suhrkamp, Frankfurt am Main, 1986, pp. 133–40. For the postmodern approach, see B. Badie, *L'impuissance de la puissance*, Fayard, Paris, 2004.

156. J. Solana, *A Secure Europe in a Better World*, document presented to the Thessaloniki European Council, 20 June 2003. Mr CFSP's document states that what it calls 'new terrorism' is a strategic threat and that the 'proliferation of Weapons of Mass Destruction is the single most important threat to peace and security among nations. . . . The most frightening scenario is one in which terrorist groups acquire WMD.' Other innovations regarding policies are what seem to be the preconditions for a new transatlantic dialogue, particularly advocated by R. Cooper on behalf of the British government: (a) 'with new threats the first line of defence is often abroad'; (b) 'effective multilateralism' as readiness 'to act when their (international organizations) rules are broken'; (c) the plea to increase the Union's military capabilities. However, the distinctive EU approach is developed: (a) the

use of force as a last resort and only if employed with the approval of the UN; (b) the analysis of threats also encompasses: humanitarian catastrophes such as those in the African Great Lakes or the recent tsunami in Asia, regional instability and persistent conflict (such as the Israeli–Palestinian situation), organized crime, failing states (Afghanistan, Somalia, Colombia, etc.), bad governance, and growing gaps between rich and poor countries, all of which are also considered to be possible roots of terrorism. Civilian means are more effective than military ones against these threats and the EU thus appears able to compete in this area with the US.

157. F.J. Rischard, *High Noon*, New York, 2002, see part 3); Group of Belgian Experts Policy (including J. Wouters, G. Geerhaerts and M. Telò), *Recommendations for Reforming the Institutional Framework – Mastering Globalisation*, final draft, 2003; I. Carlsson, Ingvar and R. Shridat, The Report of the Commission on Global Governance, *Our Global Neighbourhood*, November 1994; Dervis Kemal, *A 'Better' Globalization, Perspectives on Legitimacy, Reform and Global Governance*, with Ceren Ozer, Center for Global Development, Brookings Press, 2004; General Assembly, *Strengthening of the United Nations System*, A/58/817, 11.06.2004; World Commission on the Special Dimension of Globalization, Report of the Director-General; Adam Jones and Farid Kahhat, Global Democratic Governance and Reform of the International Institutions, working document for UBUNTU Network, International Centre for Democratic Culture; David Malone, *Ingredients of Success or Failure in UN Reform Efforts*; Poul Nyrup Rasmussen (ed.), *Europe and a New Global Order – Bridging the Divide between Global Challenges and Global Governance*, a Report for the Party of European Socialists, May 2003; *Report of the Panel on United Nations Peace Operations*, chairman: Lakhdar Brahimi, UN, 2000; Socialist International, *Governance in a Global Society – the Social Democratic Approach*, November 2003; The Foreign and Security Policy Group of Samak, *Common Proposal for Reform of the United Nations*, September 2004; *The Responsibility to Protect*, Report of the International Commission on Intervention and State Sovereignty, co-Chairmen: Gareth Evans and Mohamed Sahnoun, 2001. The World Commission on the Social Dimension of Globalization, *A Fair Globalization, Creating Opportunities for All*, co-chaired by Tarja Halonen and Benjamin William Mkapa, ILO, 2004; UBUNTU Forum Ad Hoc Secretariat and John Foster, *Proposals to Reform the System of International Institutions: Future Scenarios*, Barcelona, 2004.; *Multilatéralisme: une réforme possible*, Henri Nallet and Hubert Védrine – with the collaboration of Patrick Lefas, Denis Tersen and Sébastien Turcat, Ed. Les Notes de la Fondation Jean-Jaurès 1, no. 43, September 2004; *A More Secure World*, Report of the Secretary-General's High Level Panel on Threats, Challenges and Change, UN, 2004; Gemma Adaba, Aldo Caliari, John Foster, Eva Hanfstaengl and Frank Schroeder, *A Political Agenda for the Reform of Global Governance, a Background Policy Paper*, Friedrich Ebert Foundation, New York, 2003.

158. With its objective of halving world poverty by 2015, the UN's 'Financing for Development' conference in Monterrey finally paid attention to the malnutrition of 815 million people, the doubling of the wealth gap between rich and poor over the past 30 years and the political connection

(albeit not automatic) between poverty and support for terrorism. The objective is weakened, however, by its fragile financial basis, the relative limits of the US commitment (increased from $10bn to $15bn) and that of the EU, which although seven times that of the US, still only represents 0.33 per cent of GDP, rather than the previously planned 0.7 per cent. While the 2002 Canada G8 summit offered only $6bn for NEPAD (New Partnership for Africa's Development), the EU programme for ACP countries (detailed in the 2000 Cotonou Convention) pointed to a new political scenario predicated on governance and regional cooperation – a test bench to be studied carefully.

159. Regarding this concept, see the aforementioned 2003 'Solana paper' and P.N. Rasmussen (ed.), *Europe and a New Global Order. Bridging the Global Divides*, PES, Brussels, 2003 (http://www.eurosocialists.org/upload/Publications/74ENPES%20Rasmussen_28_05_2003.pdf).

160. This approach, which distinguishes between 'short-term', 'mid-term' and 'long-term' objectives, provides the basis for the *Maîtriser la globalization*, report presented in February 2003 by an expert advisory group set up by the Belgian Parliament (op. cit.).

161. During the Belgian Presidency of the EU in 2001, Prime Minister Guy Verhofstadt proposed substituting the G8 with a Council made up of regional organizations representing the different continents (EU, Mercosur, Andean Community, ASEAN, African Union, etc). This would work as a forum which could assume the political tasks of coordinating and directing the multilateral network. Also see Czempiel's conclusions in *Weltpolitik im Umbruch*, op. cit.

162. D. Moisi et al., 'L'UE et la crise au Moyen-Orient', *Cahiers de Chaillot*, 62, 2003, pp. 29–36; Czempiel, *Weltpolitik im Umbruch*, op. cit., pp. 30–3.

163. This debate has continued, inconclusively, up to 2004. Nonetheless, it has known a number of important moments: in 1995, marking the fiftieth anniversary of the UN's foundation; 1997, on a proposal from the UN Secretary-General; 2000 and 2001, with the publication of the Brahimi report on peacekeeping, and in the General Assembly in September 2003. The UN Wise Men Report, *A More Secure World: Our Shared Responsibility* (Dec. 2004, op. cit.), contains new hopes and some controversial scenarios.

164. See G.M. Lyons and M. Mastanduno (eds), *Beyond Westphalia? State Sovereignty and International Intervention*, Johns Hopkins University Press, Baltimore, 2000; P. Taylor and S. Daws (eds), *The United Nations*, 2 vols, Ashgate, Aldershot, 2000. Regarding the UN commitment to protection of the 'human security' of individuals and their communities (instead of just the security of states), see UN, *Human Security: Report by the Commission on Human Security*, New York, 2003.

165. See C.A. Colliard, *Institutions des relations internationales*, Dalloz, Paris, 1990 and P. Luif, 'EU Cohesion in the UN General Assembly', *Occasional Papers*, 49, EUISS, Paris, 2003, on the aggregating role of the EU.

166. More than the situation in Iraq, it was the Kosovo crisis that caused problems. In order to avert the risk of a Russian veto, a resolution supported by all other members was avoided. Samuel Huntington has significantly suggested only allowing the US the right of veto, while Britain prefers the

adoption of qualified majority voting (which curiously enough it rejected in relation to the CFSP). There is also dispute surrounding the issue of whether or not to give the power of veto to any new permanent Security Council members. The proposal to set exclusive conditions to membership of the Security Council, such as Blair's 'democratic conditionality' suggestion, remains under discussion.

167. The UN Human Rights Commission, in which countries such as Libya judged others' records, is set to be replaced.

168. The Gulf War gave rise to a transatlantic intellectual discussion about the modern criteria of the 'just war' between Norberto Bobbio, Michael Waltzer, Jürgen Habermas and others. Agreement was easier to reach in 1991 (regarding restoring respect for international law and the importance of consensus among the international community – which does not mean unanimity, but the absence of opposing votes – in the UN Security Council) than in the case of the Kosovo War, due to the problems of international law already mentioned. The French magazine *Esprit* published the main comments of Bobbio on the Balkan wars in its July–August 1999 issue (no. 253). See also M. Waltzer, *Arguing about War*, Yale, New Haven, 2004.

169. M. Telò, Introduction to Bobbio, *Etat et démocratie internationale*, Complexe, Brussels, 1999.

170. The concept of 'Subsidiäre Weltrepublik', whose reference to Kant we share, goes too far. See O. Höffe, *Demokratie in der Zeitalter der Globalisierung*, Beck, Munich, 1999.

171. Nor are certain EU 'internal' changes (with global implications) possible within such a scenario. Examples include the unification of the EU representation within the Bretton Woods institutions (IMF and World Bank), not to mention the linking of the UN and the Bretton Woods system which failed with the UNCTAD initiative in the 1960s.

172. C.A. Kupchan, *The End of the American Era. US Foreign Policy and the Geopolitics of the Twenty-first Century*, A. Knopf, New York, 2002.

173. J. Delors, Associazione Notre Europe, 'Comme nous voyons le nouvel ordre international', *Le Monde*, 29 May 2003, p. 1 (in reply to Madeleine Albright and a bipartisan US document on the transatlantic dialogue proposing US participation within EU institutions).

174. Hassner and Vaïsse, *Washington et le monde*, op. cit., pp. 153–4.

175. See the document presented by Javier Solana to the European Council, *A Secure Europe in a Better World*, op. cit. The idea of a new EU–US relationship of 'complementarity' is advocated by A. Moravcsik, 'Striking a New Transatlantic Bargain', *Foreign Affairs*, July–August 2003, pp. 74–89.

176. The 2002 CFSP budget of €10m is highly revealing of its extremely limited personnel and ambitions. More could be done through coordination with the Commission and by restructuring the Community budget, inevitably to the detriment of the CAP. Moreover, the application of the 'open method of coordination' would be crucial for national foreign and defence budgets to converge.

177. Much has been written about the 'enhanced cooperations', instituted by the Amsterdam Treaty (1997) and made more flexible by the Nice Treaty (2001), but nothing had actually been done by 2003. See T. Jaeger,

'Enhanced Cooperation in the Treaty of Nice and Flexibility in the Common Foreign and Security Policy', *Journal of European Integration*, 7, 2002, pp. 297–316.

178. The Schengen Treaty liberalized the free movement of people between a defined list of countries outside the context of EC and EU treaties (until the Nice Treaty in 2001). During the Luxembourg meeting in April 2003, France, Germany, Belgium and Luxembourg expressed their desire to deepen defence cooperation between them, while not precluding other EU members from joining them.

179. Ku and Jacobson (eds), *Democratic Accountability and the Use of Force in International Law*, op. cit.

180. R. Dahrendorf, *Dopo la democrazia*, edited by A. Polito, Laterza, Rome-Bari, 2001. For Keohane's alternative approach, see *Governance in a Partially Globalized World*, op. cit., pp. 325–45.

181. For the legal basis in the current Treaty of the European Union (TEU), see articles 2 (the Union's objectives), 6 (Internal democratic conditionality and reference to the European convention of 1950), 7 (sanctions), 11 (objectives of the CFSP), 19 (the EU and the UN), 29 (area of freedom, security and justice), 49 (enlargement and conditionality). Also see the *Declaration on Human Rights of the European Council* (1991); the *Declaration of the EU on the Occasion of the Fiftieth Anniversary of the Universal Declaration of Human Rights* (10.12.1998). Also see the EU Commission Communications to the Council on *The EU and the External Dimension of Human Rights Policy: from Rome to Maastricht and Beyond* (1995), *The Inclusion of Respect for Democratic Principles and Human Rights in Agreements between the Community and Third Countries* (1995), and *The EU's Role in Promoting Human Rights and Democratization in Third Countries* (2001). Also see *The EU Annual Reports on Human Rights*, published yearly since 1999 by the Council. And finally, *The Annual Reports on Human Rights in the World*, delivered each year by the European Parliament. In order to improve internal coordination in Community policies, the Commission set up an Interdepartmental Coordination group in 1994 which publishes reports on a regular basis. The EU organized an international conference on this topic in Vienna in 1998.

182. Ernst U. Petersmann, 'Theories of Justice, Human Rights and the Constitutions of International Markets', in *Symposium on the Emerging Transnational Constitution. Loyola Law Review of Los Angeles*, 203, pp. 407–60, E. Cannizzaro (ed.), *The EU as an Actor in International Relations*, Kluwer, The Hague, 2002 and R.B. Porter et al., *Efficiency, Equity, Legitimacy: the Multilateral Trading System at the Millennium*, Brookings Institution Press, Washington, 2001.

183. For this legal normative approach, see Marise Cremona, 'The Union as a Global Actor: Roles, Models and Identity', *Common Market Review*, 2004, pp. 553–73 . For an open political science debate, see the excellent special issue of *Power and Opposition*, no. 2, 2004, edited by D. Held and M. Koenig-Archibugi, with articles by M. Ziirn (on the need to strengthen international legitimacy), A. Moravcsik (denying any EU democratic deficit) and D. Held (on the need for new global institutions).

184. For a critical review, see B. De Witte, *Ten Reflections on the Constitutional Treaty for Europe*, IUE, Florence, 2003, and, in particular, E. Griller, 'External

Relations', pp. 133–62. The US is not as interested in international legitimacy as previously, according to R. Tucker and D. Hendrickson, 'Iraq and US Legitimacy', *Foreign Affairs*, Nov-Dec. 2004, pp. 18–31.

185. See R.O. Keohane, 'Governance in a Partially Globalized World', op. cit., and J.H.H. Weiler and A. Cassese (eds), *European Union. The Human Rights Challenge*, Nomos, Baden Baden, 1991. P. Alston and J.H.H. Weiler, *An Even Closer Union in Need of a Human Rights Policy*, Oxford University Press, 1999 and J.H.H. Weiler and S. Fries, 'A Human Rights Policy for the EC and EU: the Question of Competences', *Harvard Jean Monnet Working Papers*, 4, Cambridge, 1999. Regarding the application of human rights policy to interregional relations, see the examples of the Barcelona Mediterranean Process (1995), the Cotonou ACP Convention (2000) and the Rio Process (1999) discussed in Chapter 2.

186. See the very interesting research by K. Postel-Vinay, *L'Occident et sa bonne parole. Nos représentations du monde de l'Europe coloniale à l'Amérique hégémonique*, Flammarion, Paris, 2005.

2
States, New Regionalism and Interregional Cooperation in the Globalized World

2.1 State and regional integration

This chapter aims to provide an overview of comparative studies of regionalism, i.e. the economic, trade, social and political aggregation between neighbouring states (see Map 1). In studying the dialectic coexistence of integration and fragmentation within the global governance – or what James Rosenau terms *fragmegration*[1] – we need to focus attention not only on fragmentation within the state, but also on the parallel processes of regional aggregation and integration which have characterized the partially globalized world in recent decades. Economic regionalism is a form of fragmentation relating to the global market, but it is also a form of aggregation as regards national markets. The same is true of political regionalism, which would not exist without globalization, but which gains its force from the political will of member states, namely the regional leaders.

Studying the regional political phenomenon, therefore, does not in any way entail ignoring the importance of the state as both international actor and part of multi-level global governance. Even if the 'state-centric' theories of the nation state (understood as a halting of the processes of internal fragmentation and international decline) or the various hypotheses of renationalization of the international system increasingly display their ideological naivety, nevertheless the state is far from being in unambiguous and linear general decline. And this is shown clearly by comparing the heterogeneity of its various national paths, i.e. the differences between large and small states and between diverse and incommensurate continental and regional situations.

The state, in Europe in particular, has been able to adjust to three historical changes during the last 50 years which, according to the large amount of functionalist works on the topic, should have marked its unstoppable and generalized decline: European integration, internal socio-political change and globalization:

1. Without supporting the thesis of those who maintain that European integration may be considered a mere rescue of the nation-state, it must be said that, by the 1960s, we could already witness the extraordinary capacity for state adaptation, not only in France,[2] but everywhere in western Europe and despite the novelty of a functional dynamic of EC integration that went beyond initial forecasts.[3]

2. The enormous changes in terms of internal social composition and national political institutions, due to social and technological modernization, radically altered traditional hierarchical territorial sovereignty and provoked processes of decentralization and pluralistic fragmentation of domestic governance. This made decision-making much more complex, namely with regard to external relations. These changes, however, have not eliminated the ultimate political power of the state to decide on the fundamental steps towards intergovernmental cooperation and supranational integration. This is not only true in terms of treaty negotiations, but also applies to the decision-making process, and policy implementation.[4]

3. The majority of states have also been able to adjust to the recent acceleration of financial, technological and trade globalization. While the state has certainly lost areas of sovereignty, it has also developed at least two strategies in response. These can be seen in the logic of adapting to global competition, as a 'competitor state' and/or reviving regional integration, i.e. taking further steps towards supranational regional integration. The two responses are contradictory, since this latter choice should be seen as a critical reaction to uncontrolled globalization, through territorial cohesion policies and the channelling of internal social and economic expectations and fears by means of a sort of protective shield from the dark sides of global economic competition. However, the three mentioned changes (globalization, regionalism and social change) are also occurring outside Europe and comparative research may

reveal evidence for both strategic options of states, within regional groupings in Asia, Latin America and Africa, with very varying results.

The post-cold war period has massively broadened interaction between the different levels of global governance[5] and the partial redistribution of elements of traditional state authority towards other centres of public, private, supranational, subnational and international authority. Nevertheless states do not dissolve at all or simply retreat. Rather, they often react by strengthening multilateral regimes and regional organizations. They are primarily motivated by the promise of greater policy efficiency and national trade interest. However, international literature has highlighted the political, social and cultural motivations behind regionalist choices, and stressed their channelling of a 'bottom-up' demand for participation. That is why we prefer the concept of neoregionalism.

In this context, the salient question we addressed in Chapter 1 is the possibility of a model for democracy and accountability which is transnational, local–national and regional. Democracy, challenged and reorganized by the changes mentioned above, is being pushed towards extension and renewal all over the world. This renewal is comparable to that which led to the passage from classical forms of democracy, i.e. from the local democracy of the Greeks or Rousseau's Geneva, to the three main modern models, i.e. the federal democracy of the 13 American ex-colonies, the great European national democracies, and the consensual democratic models of the Scandinavian Welfare States. Comparative research is needed. There is evidence that the EU was, and is, able to stabilize democracy in member states and applicant countries which have emerged from long periods of dictatorial rule. How, therefore, is new regionalism elsewhere interacting with democracy?

This chapter critically discusses the thesis of EU exceptionalism as a civilian power through comparative research on neoregionalism in the world. In particular it looks at:

(a) How do states relate to regional integration within the context of the process of globalization? What links and what defines the various processes of regional cooperation in the world?
(b) How can we properly conceptualize this reorganization of regional and global forms of governance, in line with the theory of democracy?
(c) Which role does the EU play, both by its 'model of regional integration' and its interregional policies, in the process towards a multiregional and multilateral world order?

2.2 From regionness to new regionalism: elements for historical periodization at a global scale and in Europe

Regionalism is not a new historical phenomenon. First of all, a natural regional dimension evolved with the development of civilizations and trade and increased economic and cultural exchanges between nearby countries. Examples of this 'regionness'[6] include the Mediterranean area, Scandinavia, the medieval Europe of Charlemagne, the Middle East, South-East Asia, the Indian subcontinent, the Andean zone, the Caribbean, several African subregions, etc. Secondly, there was encouragement from on high, facilitated by the successive waves of internationalization of the economy in the sixteenth, nineteenth and twentieth centuries. These made regionalization a component for the opening-up of national economies, inherent in the logic of capitalism, since the great geographical discoveries. These range from the hegemony first of the Portuguese and Spanish, then of the Dutch and British empires based on free trade – all of which were important historical premises to the current era of globalization. This 'top-down' historical process interacted with the pre-existing 'bottom-up' regional dimension which expressed cultural, economic and social modernization trends. Geographical proximity aided communication within comparatively homogeneous spaces, in which civilizations and political entities developed, including multinational states. This type of regional economic and political spatial dimension has long been underestimated by functionalist and systemic theories and almost completely ignored by liberalism, marxism and all the general theories centred on either the global or national dimension.

Regionalism has, however, characterized, in very diverse forms, two important periods of the twentieth century: firstly, the inter-war years, from the competition for the leadership in modernization between the US on the one hand, and Japanese and Nazi authoritarian imperialism on the other; secondly, the period of American hegemony following 1944–45. Firstly, both Hitler's project for a 'New European Order' and Japanese expansion from Korea and Manchuria to the Indian border and the edges of Australasia (from the early 1930s to 1945) had an authoritarian regionalist economic and political dimension, the failures of which still have relevant consequences, namely the difficult relations between Japan and its East Asian neighbours. Secondly, regional cooperation developed within the framework of the dynamic decades of the American hegemony following the Second World War, and was largely supported by American funding. Contrary to the first one, it was tied to free trade and multilateralism. It was mainly configured in western Europe, Asia and Latin America, however, as a 'top-down' initiative, which explains its economic and political limits. That is why we attach the prefix 'new' to regionalism with regard to the contemporary phenomenon of regional cooperation and integration. International academic scholarship agrees about the distinction with respect to the economic and political phenomena mentioned above and regarding the need to clarify the characteristics of the emergence of new regional actors 'from below' in a post-hegemonic era. These are more autonomous than in the past, more bound to the variegated waves of democratization, more able to provide new modes of multi-level governance.

New regionalism is certainly a heterogeneous phenomenon in today's world. It is already, however, a structural economic and political reality of the global system. Evident variations recall Machiavelli's classic question about what balance should be struck between 'virtue' and 'fortune', between historical–geographical and geopolitical premises, on the one hand, and the political initiative of the elites or the 'epistemic communities', or the states at its origin on the other, between subjective and objective conditions and between domestic demands and the international environment.

Let us begin with the example of the EU, a case which is certainly *sui generis*, but also the key example in any comparative study of regionalism. Obviously, the success of European integration in the last 60 years cannot be interpreted solely as a simple consequence of internal factors. These include the exceptional political and creative abilities of its founding fathers, the excellence of the technocracy that managed the integration process during its initial phase, and the decisive will of the states and part of the internal socio-economic forces that supported it. A vast body of historical literature has shed light on the crucial contribution provided by the favourable international context that allowed integration to succeed after 1945. This had failed after the end of the First World War, despite the commitment of various idealistic movements (federalist and pan-European) and the Franco-German political dialogue from 1926 to 1930 (between the foreign ministers Aristide Briand and Gustav Stresemann). In contrast, after 1945 there were a number of external, 'systemic' variables favouring European unity: firstly, the weight of 'American hegemony' and the transatlantic economic interdependence in the decades following the end of the Second World War.[7] Secondly, the context of the cold war and the 'federalizing effect' of the Soviet threat.[8]

What was the point of equilibrium eventually reached in the histori-cal interaction between external and internal factors favouring regional integration? Among the important internal factors relating to the period from 1950 and the ECSC and EEC treaties, we should note the political will of the six founding states, the spur of the federalist move-ments and the brilliance of Jean Monnet's method (economic integra-tion as a means of pacifying former enemies in the framework of intergovernmental and supranational institutions and procedures). However, the external factor of American hegemony played a decisive role both by supporting and setting clear limits to European integration. This hegemony had a number of deep and 'legitimizing' roots in British multilateralism which are worth recalling because they apparently con-trast with the external role played by the UK until 1973. Two successive phases punctuated its development, after what might retrospectively be considered its historical emergence with the defeat of Napoleon at Waterloo and the beginning of clear British supremacy. The high point of British hegemony, dominated by free trade, symbolically culminated in August 1931, with the end of the Gold Standard based on sterling.[9] Between the 1930s and 1940s, authoritarian and continental regional-ism manifested itself simultaneously against democracy and free trade in its most hostile and malevolent guise, both economically and politi-cally.[10] The Nazi plans against British hegemony, allied to Japanese imperialism, implied a method of international cooperation based on leonine bilateral agreements between the dominant superpower and the other states and excluded both the multilateralism and the 'most favoured nation' clause typical of British hegemony.

The second phase is distinguished by the renewal of this British approach thanks to the creation, as a consequence of victory in the Second World War, of the pillars of American global hegemony and in particular by the transatlantic market promoted by the US. Supported by the men of the New Deal, this era saw the 'Bretton Woods Accords' in 1944, the birth of the IMF and the World Bank and the 'Marshall Plan' which was explicitly aimed at encouraging Europeans to collabo-rate among themselves (in the OEEC from 1948). Keohane and Nye have highlighted the link between complex interdependence (techno-logical, economic and cultural) and hegemony in the schema of transatlantic collaboration. It is certainly true that the European states decided the individual stages and also the 'variable geometry' of the process, but a dynamic was created which de facto forced European states to transform themselves into 'open states'. These are states which are open to trade and international cooperation, with the aim of improving their national performances and offering their citizens those advantages which can best legitimize governments in office. Nonetheless, the fact that the large group of 16 countries of the OEEC was split into two blocks: those which did not wish to go beyond the European Free Trade Association (EFTA), which left national sovereignties untouched, and those which founded the small European Community of the Six, is revealing of the ambiguity of Anglo-Saxon multilateral hegemony. The choice then was already between a deepening and potentially political regionalism (like that conceived by Jean Monnet and pursued by the six) and the alternative option of merely setting up regional free-trade zones (like EFTA). The US followed, or at least tolerated, Monnet's vision for a long time. De Gaulle underestimated the historical opportunity provided by the EC to the French leadership, considering it intrinsically pro-American. In fact, while art. XXIV of the GATT in 1947 expressed US readiness to accept derogations from the free-trade approach of economic and commercial internationalization, for the EC regionalism was much more than a simple derogation. British opposition to the Franco-German design conceived by Monnet continued for decades, consistently with an alternative understanding of multilateralism.

The US, however, consented to the construction of Keynesian states in Europe, provided that this process was framed within transatlantic interdependence. What is noteworthy is that the US accepted the European customs union and the common agricultural policy – confirmation of an approach which was both 'hegemonic' and flexible in the fullest sense of the term, at least until the recent open US criticism of the 'wrong type of European integration'.

The first decade of the EEC was shaped by French influence, although this was often uncertain and contradictory. It is significant that even the two most anti-European moments in French national politics (the 'no' of the Assemblée Nationale to the EDC in 1954 and the 'empty chair' policy in 1965–66) did not halt the overall process of European regional construction. In fact, they led to tangible corrective measures, which neither called the *acquis communautaire* into question nor impeded advances, once the intergovernmental parameters had been established. Hence, in the years following these two anti-European 'French waves', was signed the historical 1957 Treaty of Rome and the 1966 'Luxembourg compromise', which opened the door by providing the right of veto within the Council of Ministers, to the new dynamics of the EC integration of the 1970s. Moreover, above and beyond the rhetoric on the French nuclear 'force de frappe', Gaullist France never deviated from the framework of the transatlantic alliance. For 25 years therefore, we witnessed a complementarity between the deepening EC regional option and US hegemony, and between Europeanism and Atlanticism, as expressed by such great figures as Alcide De Gasperi, Paul Henri Spaak, Jean Monnet and Konrad Adenauer.

Following 1971 and the oil crises of the 1970s, international constraints were reinforced, but so too were the phenomena of regional differentiation with respect to hegemonic power. This happened because the two main complementary elements of the preceding trade-off came into conflict: regionalism and American-controlled globalism. On one side, we had the European Keynesian state, welfare capitalism, about which many theorists and sociologists have written,[11] some of them underlining the similarities between western European and Japanese types of institutionalized capitalism. On the other, was international liberalization, whose stability had been guaranteed by the dollar–Gold Standard parity, suspended *sine die* by President Nixon in 1971. Like Great Britain in 1931, the US declared that it was no longer in a position to support the cost of financing such a fundamental 'international public good', essential for the stability of exchanges and international economics. Thus a new phase of uncertainty and instability opened which, within the context of economic crisis, technological development and the neo-liberal and conservative radicalization of the 1980s, would call into question the previous equilibrium between the European socio-economic model and economic internationalization, between EC regionalism and US globalism.

It is for this reason that the small EEC of the Six set itself its own priorities for the first time. First of all, it accelerated projects on monetary union, namely the 'Werner Plan', a historically important symbol of political autonomy, even if this failed because of its overly ambitious aim of obtaining economic convergence as a premise for monetary union. After the experiment of the 'monetary snake', however, in 1978 the European Monetary System was born. This reflected a Franco-German choice to create a regional zone of monetary stability and therefore to protect western Europe from the turbulence and damaging effects of fluctuations in the dollar and the inability of the US to continue performing the role it had taken on in 1944.

It is significant that European Political Cooperation was also launched shortly afterwards, in 1973, and that, in 1975, European determination convinced the US to sign the Helsinki Pan-European Convention. The Europeans thus began to defend their policy of peace, their socio-economic model and their interests within a context of increased international competitiveness. This also pushed them to reject the heavy pressure of Henry Kissinger for a common front against the Arab world during the two petrol crises of the 1970s. The decade closed with the 'Venice Declaration' on the Israeli–Palestinian conflict, which highlighted western Europe's desire for autonomy notwithstanding the frustrating weakness of its foreign policy.

A decade later, the choice of the Single European Act to launch the '1992 Programme' for the Single Market confirmed and reinforced the regionalist trend backed by independent policies, to the point where it was even viewed in the US as a move towards the creation of a 'fortress Europe'. This climate of suspicion was at the root of the surprising regionalist counter-decision in 1994 by the US to seek an accord with Canada and Mexico resulting in NAFTA, the North American Free Trade Association, one of whose effects was expected to be the reduction of the European presence in Mexico.

Despite the symbiotic links of transatlantic economic interdependence, the US has explicitly reacted to the deepening of European regionalism (which it had helped to generate) by making a defensive and unexpected regionalist choice. Distinct from previous forms of regionalism, all under the American hegemony, we now entered a more ambivalent third phase, in which regionalism both in Europe and in other parts of the world accelerated and deepened, but this time according to a 'bottom-up' process. Now it was no longer entirely subordinate to the US-sponsored globalization, but was more autonomous of it, even functioning as a shield against it. This new regionalism, resulting from the uncertainties and instability of the global context of a 'post-hegemonic era', is oriented to multidimensional cooperation.[12] As a result, regional groups such as MERCOSUR, the Andean Community, ASEAN, the SAARC and the SADC either came into being or were roused from their lethargy.[13]

The growth of new regionalism was not interrupted by the turning point in the system of international relations from 1989 to 1991. On the contrary, it was spurred on to express all of its political potential. On the one hand, the end of the USSR, the communist bloc and the bipolar world certainly constituted the beginning of unipolarism and global leadership for the only remaining military, political and economic superpower. The great breakthrough of the Western economic and political system in the East and the end of the search for radically alternative economic models to the market economy, deregulation and privatization, had an enormous unifying effect on the global economic system, not only with regard to eastern Europe, but also those key developing states such as China and India, in addition to Brazil and, in general, the countries of Latin America. On the other hand, 1989 provoked an upsurge in the tendencies towards fragmentation. Firstly, the end of the Soviet empire gave rise to the often misleading rediscovery of state identities in the republics of the ex-USSR and within the countries of the former Warsaw Pact. This had the effect of reigniting various long-standing border disputes in addition to provoking the radical ethno-centric fragmentation which took place for example in the Caucasus and the former Yugoslavia. The ideology of 'economic globalization benefiting everyone', a global harmony guaranteed by the almost universal acceptance of the market economy and democratic principles, was soon replaced by a variegated scenario made up of both cooperation and armed conflict, of new hierarchies between winners and losers, of the marginalization of Africa and of the protests of the excluded. Regional organizations, however, did not yield to disintegrating internal and external tendencies. Rather, they demonstrated their capacity to resist and, often, to respond to the instability of the multilateral frame-work with choices of both enlargement and deeper and more political cooperation between member states.

In this context, devoid of the past international hegemony, global-ization was not only accompanied by the global village of television and advertising campaigns, but also by its apparent opposite: fragmentation and the fundamentalist rejection of cultural westernization which was seen in several continents through religious, ethnic, nationalist and regional secessionist movements. It is within this context that the new transnational terrorist networks try to establish roots. How does this ambiguity of 'fragmented globalization' without international hege-mony weigh upon the phenomena of regionalization and regionalism? In the absence of a new expansive and credible multilateral order, the challenge to contribute more actively to regional governance also looms large over regional organizations. How can they, and their member states, face this political challenge?

2.3 Globalization, states and regional organizations: three theoretical approaches

Globalization and regionalization are not only economic and trade phe-nomena: they also concern the restructuring of international power hierarchies. For decades, the debate on international relations theories has focused on the future of the state. According to a first school of thought, the pre-eminence of the state-centric paradigm would be re-established as it offers the most realistic equilibrium between global-ization and fragmentation tendencies. Despite the wear and tear upon it, the state would always guarantee, on the one hand, greater policy efficiency, compared to subnational levels (such as regions and cities). On the other, it would constitute a more credible and democratic level of representation for social and political interests compared to the regional and global level or that offered by supranational organizations. Even if they are more representative, the city would be more disarmed in the globalized world (with the exception of global cities, such as Hong Kong, New York, Geneva and a few others). Though more effec-tive, even a supranational regional polity like the EU would be too far removed from its citizens and decentralized interests. The grip of the state would be confirmed in the cases of EU member states, especially in decisive sectors of collective life such as defence, the Welfare State, the relationship between educational and productive structures and the democratic legitimization of political decisions.[14] Territorial logic would find new ways to resist the destructive impact of functional global logic. Those who, following this line of argument, gamble normatively on the resurgence of the state and national republicanism, see regional co-operation as the simple result of the choices of states, of negotiated interests between them and their respective preferences and strategies, which correspond solely to the national public. The declining trend of the state is sometimes integrated by this school, but the realist analysis prompts us to note that not all states decline in the same way and at the same speed. Hierarchies between states are strengthened therefore. This implies a strong capacity for resistance in dominant states, including on a regional level, i.e. the pre-eminence of one or two states compared to the other members of each regional organization. Examples of such dominant states include Germany in the EU (through its axis with France), Brazil in the MERCOSUR, Indonesia in ASEAN, South Africa in the SADC and Nigeria in ECOWAS.

The 'neo-medievalist' school of thought, by contrast, highlights the trends towards what was called the decline or 'the retreat of the state'.[15] There are three corollaries to this thesis:

1. The predominance of global tendencies favouring economic and social convergence rather than national divergences, seen as a legacy from the past. The centrality of TNCs (transnational corporations), other transnational networks and the communication technologies which 'kill' distance and not only permit a boom in trade and the unification of financial markets, but also facilitate the transnational

organization of production. This creates extraordinary pressure on actors to adapt and ostracizes those which are not competitive on the international market, thus surpassing previous forms of territorial solidarity and hierarchy organized by and within states.

2. The de-territorialization of authority. Decision-making power abandons its old state centres and shifts towards new decentralized bases. These are both private (TNCs, NGOs, lobbies, networks, etc.) and public (subnational, transnational, international and supranational) organizations. Nation-states are 'sovereign' in appearance only. They occupy territorial spaces, but are by now unable to control what happens in these spaces.[16] It is within this context that cities and subnational regions would constitute more flexible and adaptable political units for global competition. This can lead to support for subnational decentralization and even, sometimes, secessionist demands (Flanders, Lombardy, Catalonia, Slovenia, etc.). However, functional logic would clearly prevail over territorial logic. This reorganization of the global system according to multi-level governance, which provokes overlapping of authorities and loyalties and does not recognize centripetal hierarchies, has been given the metaphorical term 'neo-medievalism' by some scholars. This is intended to highlight the transience of the 'Westphalian state system', established in 1648 and central to modern and contemporary history.

3. With regard to regional integration processes, the post-state effects are underlined in terms of, on the one hand, the creation of supranational technocratic powers (the ECB for example) and, on the other, the growth of transnational aggregations made up of coalitions of interests or by interregional cross-border communities. These include regions straddling the borders of different countries and other subnational and transnational actors and interest coalitions. Regional organizations would essentially serve as trainers of 'neo-medieval' globalization, agents for the dismantlement of national regulation or the 'regulation of deregulation'.[17] The result is a global system lacking a centre, with various levels of authority which are intertwined and not hierarchically organized. States obviously do not disappear, but they are no longer the main actors.

The third relevant approach is institutionalism. This locates itself somehow between the two above-mentioned interpretative tendencies, i.e. between the state-centred paradigm and neo-medievalism. This interpretative current has its distant roots in the philosophy of Hegel and the sociology of Max Weber and much in common with realism, namely the reference to incentives, power and state interests. However, maintaining physical security is not on the top of world politics and the continuing role of state power does not bring institutionalists to neglect 'the immense impact of multilateral institutions'. Institutions are a crucial variable, both with regard to domestic politics and cooperation between states. Institutions are seen as the result of a combination of functional processes (transnational, subnational and supranational), political will and state preferences. The argument runs that once regimes, multilateral organizations and international institutions are constituted, they may become independent from the previous hegemonic power and, to a certain extent, more autonomous from member states: 'The EU is the most important example of such an institution'. They may have the ability to condition and shape the behaviour of states and frame functional processes, with an implicit reduction of the weight of pure market and/or power logic. We have already discussed the extent to which this approach shares and distances itself from the utilitarian 'rational choice' theory and a costs–benefits calculation in Chapter 1; moreover, there is evidence that some international institutions have the ability to represent contrasting interests, express values, structure preferences, take decisions and form identities, even beyond the simple instrumentalism of member states. Widely applied to the state,[18] this approach is largely being used in relation to regional and global multilateral institutions.[19]

The theory of international regimes made a contribution to this approach, but new institutionalism clearly goes much beyond it. Multilateral and regional organizations may in fact be interpreted as specific cases of the general tendency to build coherent systems of rules, procedures and behaviour with regard to single international issues, which are called 'international regimes'. Their complex polity goes beyond even a set of regimes.[20] An international regime does not suppress member state sovereignty, but limits its activities by routines, procedures and rules which are integrated by the member states themselves, significantly transforming them in their exercise of sovereignty. Regime theory is a necessary part of an account of institutionalism; however it does not provide the whole explanation. As James Rosenau has observed, regimes only deal with certain issues and support cooperation which is limited to certain areas. This fails to cover a number of elements of varying degrees of importance in regional and global cooperation.[21]

When limiting our analysis to regional governance, regional organizations inevitably strive to go further and create forms of cooperation

and integration which involve more sectoral matters of common interest and shared long-term objectives as well. In the case of the EU,
although beginning with just coal and steel (ECSC), the member states
later created common institutions. Other regional groupings such as
ASEAN and MERCOSUR also show a spillover dynamics. Such institutions and legal systems sometimes entail a process of legal integration
and 'constitutionalization' through the treaties, albeit distinct from
'state building'. Regional organizations also frame the mobilization of
internal networks of socio-political actors, transform national public
spaces, involve common memories and, sometimes, feelings of
common belonging and identities. In this sense, the clear existence of
multi-level governance is not necessarily incompatible with democratic
participation, even if these cannot be understood analogously with the
functioning of the national state.

Notwithstanding its distinctive approach, not even institutionalism
takes sufficient account of the fact that globalization (a phenomenon
which is not purely economic and technological, but increasingly political) centres on globalist politics and policy as expressed by the only
superpower, the US. Robert Gilpin, among others, has correctly shown
that global competition is not based on the principle of the free market.
On the contrary, the neo-mercantilist negotiations and conflicts
between national and regional capitalisms entail global and regional
strategies and the first among these is the strategy of the US. Therefore,
geopolitical hierarchies between states and geo-economic conflict of
interests between regional blocks grow worse. Susan Strange has indicated the asymmetries within the neo-medievalist tendency and they
have been interpreted by Robert Cox as a reinforcement of American
supremacy and central to the marginalization of whole countries and
continents on the planet.[22] In their fine analysis, the institutionalists
themselves sometimes underestimate the challenge of international
hierarchies, namely the de facto existence of a sort of 'absolute right'[23]
of the sole powerful superpower, a law that does not need to be recognized within (and by) international organizations for it to be exercised.
This, for example, can be seen in the new policy of selective security and
pre-emptive wars, and in the rejection of both the Kyoto Protocol and
the International Penal Court of Justice. We have already shown in
Chapter 1 that this has led some in the academic community to wonder whether we are not just witnessing the opening up of a new phase
of global governance, but of the world system as well. However, we have
also largely listed the international shortcomings and external limits of
unilateralism. Unipolarist theories of the post-cold war international

system need to be subjected to various precautions not only because of the inert weight of their often archaeological legacies (theories of imperialism, dependence theory, etc.). Furthermore, they ignore the results of domestic sociological analysis of the decision-making process as well, the weight of multiple internal obstacles and limits affecting the efficiency even of the superpower.[24] These domestic factors substantially did already brake the global liberalization policy (fostering the 'emerging markets'), of the Bush senior and Clinton administrations, and have affected the G.W. Bush foreign policy as well. This relates in particular to the oscillations in implementing the APEC and the Free Trade Area of the Americas, but also the incoherences in the management of the Iraqi crisis and the global 'anti-tyranny agenda'.

However, despite such caveats, namely the mentioned international and domestic limits to unipolarism, even the institutional approach is challenged. Current political US globalism should be definitely seen as defining a new international agenda that does not coincide at all with the globalization of the 1990s and imposes a theoretical updating, which is first and foremost to the detriment of the relevance of 'neo-medievalism'. Not least, such updating should be able to cope with the revival of the realist interpretation of the global security agenda.

2.4   Comparative analysis of the major regional organizations: economic, political and cultural factors

The three interpretations of the role of the state in the process of globalization mentioned above all include, albeit in different ways, the phenomenon of regional integration between neighbouring states. In the case of realist approaches, what is occurring is the resurgence of the territorial dimension of governance as a reaction to the predominance of the functional tendencies of globalization. In contrast, according to neo-medievalist theory, regionalism is but one aspect of the general decline of the centrality of the state and of the tendency of authority to move towards entities beyond the state, thus combining anarchy and global deregulation. New institutionalism focuses on regionalism as an important specification of the general phenomenon of the growth of intergovernmental organizations for cooperation between states. Regional organizations coordinate national policies and strategies, and frame private networks.

The question of the causes of the recent strengthening of the phenomenon of regional integration in the world merits further analysis. What internal, international, endogenous and systemic factors contribute to the strengthening of regionalism and neoregionalism in the post-cold war globalized world?

In the first place, with regard to globalization, regional cooperation can be considered as essentially rational from an economic point of view. For example, proximity offers many advantages to economies of scale, trade, the allocation of foreign investments and the reduction of transport costs. Moreover, national economic adjustments to global imperatives become more manageable for public powers if regional mediation is strengthened and guarantees both a supplementary external thrust and increased legitimization for the diffusion of best practices. This is true of the EU, but also applies to other forms of regionalism, including organizations in developing regions. Those states whose GDP per capita is less than the regional organization's average receive a stimulus to make up ground more quickly. The 'convergence rate' is a salient indicator of the success of regional integration. Furthermore, national businesses in each state can make use of a regional market in order to expand and gradually adapt to world competition. Regional organizations can thus facilitate a type of intermediate stage between a choked and narrow national market and a global market that is still perceived as being too full of snares and uncertainties. Albeit not the only one, the transnational business community within member states is often the most diffuse and determined internal bearer of regional cooperation and integration and represents the most tenacious of lobbies. However, building a regional market is something else and involves more than establishing a mere preferential trade agreement (PFA) and/or liberalizing trade: territorial proximity and other factors play an important role indeed, which is *ignored* by pure free-trade theories.

Furthermore, economic rationality is neither the main nor the most convincing explanation for the success of regionalism. In fact, new regionalism can be seen as a political attempt by state authorities to partly regain at regional level the losses of sovereignty related to the financial, economic and social implications of the process of globalization. Domestic social and political pressures reinforce this need for public policies designed to protect states from (and control) the uncertainties stemming from globalization.

Reference to the case of the EU is relevant to both the following interpretations of the recent acceleration of regional cooperation. It can be seen both as a carrier of the process of global opening up and liberalization and as a guard against its destabilizing implications.. Both the attractiveness to states of the prospect of creating a PTA or an internal regional market and the need to strengthen its bargaining power in global multilateral negotiations stimulated this resurgence. In some cases (such as ASEAN and the Andean Community), we are witnessing a revival of old regional organizations that were created in the post-war period and in the 1960s and were in hibernation until the beginning of the 1990s. However, the jolt of globalization that came with the end of the bipolar world and the toughness of the WTO liberalization negotiations contributed significantly to the reawakening of these regional organizations and their development in economic and trade areas, especially given the possibility of tempering the culture of global economic liberalism through regional grouping. The issue of regionalism versus globalization and liberalization is dividing the economic academic and policy community.[25] At the same time, salient national and subnational actors understood that only by constructing united regional blocks could they secure better conditions with respect to IMF and WTO negotiations and interregional arrangements with the US and the EU. Similarly, there was greater awareness that a new window of opportunity had opened up for a multiplicity of actors in global governance.

Another internal factor, partly linked to the previous ones, was, according to various authors, the wish to better protect regional socioeconomic and cultural models.[26] Within the huge global economic convergence of recent decades the US has been able to generalize its model across the world, often at the expense even of those vital local and regional features which have been rooted in local histories for a long time. Existing national differences and regional variations have no longer essentially to do with historical diversities: for example, with regionalisms of the inter-war period (Japan-centred, Germany-centred, etc.). However, world capitalism continues to recreate differences, albeit of a new type and nature. Regionally diversified balances of economic and technological modernization are emerging within the sociocultural environment and the legal and institutional context of each region. The modalities for pursuing the construction of a 'knowledge society' may also significantly vary with respect to the US model of the 'new economy'.

This dimension of new regionalism is also extremely significant with regard to culture and images of the self and others. Following a constructivist approach, it is right to highlight 'ideational factors' such as the weight of identity needs linked to regional integration, the emphasis on similarities between neighbours, on emerging transnational public spheres, and on the various images promoted by regional entities in the world. This argument has nothing to do with static and closed concepts of 'civilization'. It is undeniable that shared memories, values and feelings of common belonging may favour (and be favoured by) appropriate common regional policies.

Of course, internal and external factors interact on the economic, political and identity levels of regional organizations. However, correctly appreciating the external and systemic factors (which are common because they are bound to the international system and its economic and political global evolution) is important in order to better understand the distinctive internal factors. We have already noted the importance of two systemic factors: the acceleration of globalization and the end of the bipolar world.

Thirdly, part of the literature[27] has focused attention on the so-called 'domino effect', i.e. when decisions regarding the strengthening of a regional organization are made in response to the development of another regional organization. We can see this in the case of NAFTA (1992–94), in response to the Single European Act which relaunched the EC in 1987, and in those of MERCOSUR and ASEAN (Singapore Declaration, 1992), which were responses to both. At times, this reaction is born out of a desire for emulation, at others it reflects a fear of increased international competition. In the latter case, a 'fortress' type of protectionist trade policy is envisaged and/or a sort of 'war machine' for global negotiations is created.

As we have already mentioned, the contradictory evolution of multilateral negotiations is another external factor explaining the current development of regional organizations. For example, the final phase of the GATT negotiations, preceding the 1994 Marrakesh accord (and the creation of the WTO), was characterized by major uncertainty and suspicion. On the one hand, it encouraged 'legal' regional trade cooperation (art. XXIV) but, on the other, the tough negotiations prompted many actors to foster a strategic change in the equilibrium between multilateralism and regionalism. It was not by chance that 1994 also saw the birth of NAFTA and this represented a clear signal from the Americans. From 1994 on, the US was resolved to participate as the leader and main engine for a whole series of interregional organizations (APEC, FTAA, etc., see Map 3). This in turn accentuated the asymmetries of the globalized world. It became clear to many states that globalization strengthens national and regional competition and that only regionalist policies allow them to compete more effectively with other trade powers.

The significance and endurance of these multiple endogenous and exogenous factors lead us to conclude that new regionalism has become a structural and multidimensional element of the partially globalized world in the post-cold war era. It is an important factor both for its internal and external implications. Internally, it is important because it frames, shapes and conditions the strategies of businesses, states, organized social forces, etc. Externally, it contributes, in a molecular fashion, in a long-term and structural way, to change not only as regards multi-level global governance, but also in relation to the post-cold war order. It is a tough and resilient phenomenon, even in times of crisis. For example, the 1998–99 financial crisis (the worst since 1945) which first hit South-East Asia, then Russia and finally Latin America, does not seem to have shaken regional organizations. On the contrary, in some cases it has been interpreted as a stimulus for deeper regional cooperation. This already therefore is an important difference compared to the inter-war period and the effects of the 1929 crisis, which triggered the spread of economic international chaos, fostering nationalism and/or authoritarian regionalism. What is occurring in the post-hegemonic era is that the fact that various countries have to deal with the same internal and external challenges, and also (sometimes) the same mandatory recommendations from international organizations (IMF, etc.) in terms of policy implementation, and this forces them to strengthen cooperation among themselves. This is for the simple reason that it is easier to achieve national reform objectives if the government is working in cooperation with other states at the level of regional groupings.[28]

This solidity of the regional phenomenon does not in any way mean identifying the evolving regional blocks with cultural entities which are internally compact and hostile towards one another, of the type Samuel Huntington refers to in his much-discussed work on the 'clash of civilizations'.[29] Comparative sociology tells us that the degree of internal cultural differentiation within regional organizations and even within nations is often greater than the differences between one block and another. It is true of course that, in times of crisis, we see political exploitation of regionalism by populist leaders. We might recall, for example, the 'Asian values' invoked by the Malaysian premier Mahatir or the 'Christian Europe', to which European Christian Democrats turned in order to justify the exclusion of Turkey in the 1990s. But such expressions, related to cultural fundamentalism, are not the result of cultures and regional blocks per se, which never correspond to compact civilizations, but of political manipulation by unscrupulous and populist politicians with a view to asserting internally intolerant and externally aggressive policies.[30] In reality, each regional organization often includes varied cultures and religions like the multicultural

ASEAN (containing five religions) or even NAFTA or Europe itself, most secularized region in the world, whose demographic make-up is being transformed by immigration flows.[31] Finally, new regionalism clearly has antinationalist effects and limits closure and retreat both at national, ethnic and local levels. It also facilitates cooperation and dialogue between countries with heterogeneous culture and standards of life.

In sum, if new regionalism is not merely and essentially a matter of free trade, which relationships exist between the evolving multiple dimensions of regional cooperation? Second, the question for democratic theory is whether common regional institutional structures can facilitate progress towards democratization beyond the sometimes façade declarations of the last 15 years.

2.5 Contributing to regional cooperation and integration theory

When conducting comparative analysis on regional organizations, we encounter a methodological problem. Since Montesquieu (the first comparative social scientist according to Raymond Aron), scholars have been aware of how difficult it is to distinguish clearly between the analytical and normative dimensions through the comparison of regimes. Even if we consider the European model of regional integration not to be exportable and view it as exceptional because of its historical background and *sui generis* institutions, and even if we cannot assess current experiences in the world in terms of evolving approximations of the EU model, nonetheless the variety of these experiences still leads us to classify regional organizations according to a framework that inevitably suffers from comparison with the case of the European Community and Union and its history.

We will not dwell on the purely historical–geographical level of the region, though it is an important substratum of regionalism. As we mentioned earlier, Swedish political scientist Björn Hettne has rightly called it 'regionness' in order to highlight its enduring, *longue durée* characteristics. Here, however, we will try to classify the developments of regional cooperation in terms of its shifts towards deeper integration.

1. By the concept of 'regional society', we mean the various public and private forms of transnational economic, cultural and social relationships within a region of the world. The private sector and civil society are the principal motors of this regionally focused transnationalism. States are not necessarily involved.[32]

2. Secondly, we refer to 'regional intergovernmental fora'. By this, we mean the first step of regional cooperation. This is not yet formalized or furnished with permanent structures. It is oriented towards dialogue more than decisions, but is capable of agreeing on initial procedures, common standards, and on international regimes limited to single issues.

3. Thirdly, we refer to regional cooperation promoted by treaties and various policies resulting from political decisions by governments.[33] Common policies are promoted by international regional regimes, but they mainly concern 'negative integration', involving the removal of obstacles to economic integration trade and investments, consistently with Jan Tinbergen's concept, later taken up by Fritz W. Scharpf.

4. In fourth place, we find the first policies of 'positive integration'. These are common policies such as 'customs unions' which involve a common commercial policy and common tariffs towards third countries. They also entail unity of the emerging regional blocs within international multilateral negotiations and conferences. We can see examples of this in the cases of MERCOSUR and the early EC.

5. The creation of a 'regional common market' implies the passage towards a type of integration which is no longer sectoral, but reflects all economic and commercial activities with huge social and external implications. This stage may be defined as a 'set of international regimes'. However, both treaties and practical common governance do not leave many areas exempt from the cooperation/integration process. Rather, it tends to expand itself gradually, according to Jean Monnet's model – or a functional equivalent – to the point where an economic and monetary union is also conceivable, as in the distinct processes occurring within MERCOSUR and ASEAN.

6. A regional union of states and a regional economic integration include the five preceding layers of 'regionality'. Important steps towards political union are not excluded, however, with the problems raised by the even partial sharing of 'regal' components of national sovereignties (internal and external security). This occurs through various combinations of 'the community method' with the coordination of national policies. It also involves 'exclusive' and 'shared' competences (between states and the regional organization). Common intergovernmental institutions and procedures are envisaged side by side with supranational ones and there is a shared

commitment to the reduction of internal asymmetries. Instead of the controversial and unrealistic concept of a regional 'federal state', we suggest the expression of 'regional polity' (regional institutional architecture).

What is the place of security cooperation within regional cooperation? It is not easy to locate the various forms of regional security partnerships (which are not a purely European phenomenon) within this latently evolving framework. The problem is that they are decidedly differentiated. Some regional confidence-building measures exist independently of economic integration, such as the Shanghai Cooperation Organization (SCO), and also the early bilateral agreement between Brazil and Argentina. Some came into being within the context of successful economic and commercial cooperation (EU). Some are internal to regional organizations and others spill over their borders so as to include neighbouring zones (OSCE and the Euro-Mediterranean Partnership) or countries which, although distant, are relevant to regional security (ASEAN Regional Forum). Some are complementary to military alliances (NATO, in the case of Europe). Some integrate the prevention of internal and international causes of regional security instability (CSCE and OSCE). Some are blocked by external factors, like the wars in the Middle East in the case of the Euro-Mediterranean Partnership.[34] This in no way means that they all evolve in the same way, but one can observe the transformation of the old concept of 'collective security' (see Chapter 1, on multilateralism) into one of 'common security' (i.e. 'my security is inseparable from that of my neighbour') or, even more relevant to Europe, to Karl Deutsch's concept of a 'security community'.[35] Beyond the renouncing of force, this includes internal security conditions, i.e. the problems of society are tackled by institutionalized procedures. The key point is that the emergence of security partnerships at regional level which are independent from economic integration and do not question national sovereignty, weakens attempts to attribute general value to functionalist theories and requires a mobilization of more comprehensive and political interpretations of regionalism, while not forgetting the contribution of constructivism. Hence, our preference for the expression 'new regionalism'.

The importance of this challenging interpretative knot confirms that we still lack a general theory of regionalism that answers the following question: since it is hard to imagine an evolutionary process which leads from the first to the last stage of regional cooperation/integration, how can we explain the dynamics between evolutionary 'bottom-up' tendencies and decisions determined by the political level and inspired by the values of regional actors? The question is open, but we favour explanations referring to various theoretical post-functionalist approaches. Synchronic comparative analyses undertaken at the beginning of the new century must consider emulative effects, imitative interaction between the various regional organizations and reactions and counter-reactions within the context of globalization. But nothing that can be identified as a new evolutionary model of regional integration.

Nonetheless, it would be a serious error to stop at the empirical description of the obvious deep historical diversities, at the unrepeatable nature of each regional phenomenon in the process of aggregation, at the uniqueness of each experience of cooperation between neighbouring states. To consider the single processes of regional integration in isolation would entail, for example, not taking the impulses from the common international environment into account,[36] or the weight of the international economic and political system on present changes, even if the periodization highlighted at the beginning of this chapter has had different effects in various parts of the world. For example, the Soviet nuclear threat and its end, the American hegemony and its decline weighed in very different ways upon eastern Asia, Europe, Africa and Latin America. Multilateralism was thus intensely experimented with in western Europe and unknown in other parts of the world.

Highlighting differences has always been an aim of comparative studies since Charles de Montesquieu and Max Weber. These differences are deeply rooted in history and geography and still affect state preferences, the distribution of resources between them and the degree of convergence/divergence within the partially globalized world. At the dawn of regional systems, various levels of cooperation, integration and decision-making emerge (in part formalized and in part not). The lack of other high-level experiences of institutionalization like the EU has been explained, for example, by referring to the absence elsewhere of a similar example of relatively well-balanced resource distribution and negotiating power between member states. Notwithstanding this, it true that, beyond the domino effect, some forms of regional cooperation explicitly seek to emulate the EU while others consciously ignore the 'European model' and are looking for their distinctive regional way. However, they are all confronted with the influence of EU and US interregional policies.

2.6   US-centred regionalism and interregionalism: from NAFTA to FTAA

Firstly, we should distinguish between regionalism, transregionalism and interregionalism. We have already defined the various forms of regionalism (and new regionalism). By 'interregionalism' and 'transregionalism' we mean relationships established between regions from different continents. But, while by 'transregionalism' we mean relationships established at the level of civil society (before institutional formalization), by 'interregionalism' we mean proper formal accords and the negotiation processes which prepare biregional or triregional intergovernmental agreements. As a first example, we can distinguish between the regional cooperation as represented by NAFTA and the hemispheric interregionalism of the FTAA (including all the Americas), both of which are centred on the US. NAFTA is one of the lightest existing regional organizations. The US decision to create NAFTA (which came into being as a consequence of the Free Trade Treaty signed with Canada in 1989 and extended to Mexico in 1994) is a historically significant sign in the post-hegemonic world: the country at the origin of the 'Bretton Woods' multilateral system resigned itself to regionalism as a second choice, following the difficulties of the GATT–WTO multilateral negotiations and the decisions of the EU to deepen integration and to set its own priorities autonomously from the US and the transatlantic market.

In the first decade after the cold war, in its relations with Europe, Clinton's US appeared to stop coupling security with trade and to prefer agreements without prevailing initial political motivations. In the 1990s, both George Bush senior and Clinton not only launched NAFTA, but also the FTAA project, i.e. the plan to extend NAFTA on a continental scale as a pan-American free trade area by 2005, which would halt what Washington perceived as European intrusiveness in an area which it had considered for a long time (from the 'Monroe doctrine' on) as its back garden. However, this anti-European stance became explicit and political only with the position adopted by the George W. Bush presidency at the FTAA summit in Quebec in April 2001. The EC/EU (since the 'Rio Group' in 1986) has in turn conducted a Latin American policy articulated between the Caribbean (within the framework of the ACP Conventions), the Andean Pact, Mexico, Chile and, above all, MERCOSUR. These relations were resumed within the context of the 'Rio Process', launched in 1999 and continued in 2002 in Madrid and in 2004 in Guadalajara. Similarities and differences between the two types of interregionalism (e.g. the 2000 'Santiago Declaration' and the 'Rio Declaration' of 1999), practised by the US and the EU respectively, are clear. Whichever regional association the US participates in is strongly asymmetric and its institutions are too weak to be able to counterbalance substantial internal imbalances. The EU not only pursues free trade, but also seeks common policies of development, cultural exchange and, in particular, political dialogue. Last, but not least, the EU supports deepening regional cooperation elsewhere, whereas the US opts for diluting regional associations within large interregional agreements.

The FTAA can be seen as a continental size NAFTA, which interprets regionalism through the minimalist vision of the US. Certainly, NAFTA has given birth to commissions for cooperation on the environment and employment issues. There has also been a certain degree of institutionalization regarding trade dispute regulation mechanisms, which is particularly binding with respect to national actors. However, these elements do not give rise to functional dynamics or political decisions in favour of deepening regional cooperation, namely as citizens' rights are concerned. Indeed, the proposals made by the Mexican president Vicente Fox on this issue were rejected by George W. Bush between 2001 and 2004. On the political level, it is significant that on the occasion of the second war in Iraq (2002–4), both Canada and Mexico refused to follow the proposal for 'pre-emptive strike' action unsuccessfully put to the UN Security Council by their superpower regional partner.

George W. Bush has made his distinctive mark on the FTAA project launched in 1994. On the basis of the revival of the intense civil and economic transregional relations that have existed for two centuries, the US wants to accomplish a grand free trade interregional design which includes all of the Americas and is attractive to Latin American export sectors. However, this is encumbered by several factors: domestic opposition of unions and lobbying of weak economic branches; trade asymmetries and the strategic limits of the US vision of interregional cooperation. In fact, notwithstanding the inclusion of the 'democratization agenda' in the 2001 'Quebec Declaration', the FTAA remains confined to light integration in the context of a strange free trade zone, which itself contains many exceptions and derogations. Last but not least it conflicts with the deeper integration envisaged by the new MERCOSUR leadership (Lula, Kirchner, Vasquez), marked not only by unprecedented political convergence, but also by closer objectives and shared mistrust of US domination. Furthermore, the uncertain and unstable 'transatlantic triangle' of the early twenty-first century is complicated by the EU–US discord on the one hand and, on the other, by the internationally proactive Brazilian role in the G20, the WTO and within the so-called 'IBSA' (India–Brazil–South Africa), particularly relevant as it sees the strengthening of a new South–South cooperation. This is also economically appealing for China, Brazil's second export market.

2.7   Latin America and MERCOSUR. American and European interregional projects

Before returning to the interregional game and its impact on global governance, we should focus on MERCOSUR, the regional organization that most closely resembles the EU. MERCOSUR is an example of thriving regional cooperation and has given rise to a broad debate which stretches from comparative studies to regional integration theory.[37] It differs considerably from traditional examples of regional cooperation in Latin America of the 1960s and 1970s which were the product of a 'top-down' process supported and financed by the US and also from the Organization of the American States: the ALEDI, the 'Rio Group' and other groupings which were and still are characterized by vague objectives, political weakness and unreliability. Even if to a lesser extent, the 'Andean Community' shares with MERCOSUR this new regional dynamics since it awoke from its long slumber in 1997, among other things with the decision to transform itself into a free trade area.

MERCOSUR, launched by the Asuncion Treaty (1991), quickly succeeded during the 1990s both as an internal market and regional bloc. Notwithstanding the difficulties which erupted in 1999 (such as the devaluation of the Brazilian real which had serious commercial implications) and were aggravated by the devastating Argentinean crisis in 2001 and 2002, it can be considered significant for its solidity. It boasts a customs union, an impressively developed internal common market and a growing sense of regional belonging, expressed by the variegated 'bottom-up' mobilization not only of states, but also of civil society organizations. Finally, it has a recognized identity in international and interregional relationships. What is particularly interesting is the political dimension, i.e. the political aim of stabilizing young and fragile democracies in the southern cone of the Latin American continent, undermined by the open challenge of poverty eradication which provokes serious social and political crises. In 1996 and 1999, for example, during the two serious political crises in Paraguay, the clause for the exclusion of countries which do not respect democracy was seen to exert a positive influence and push the 'golpist' populist general Oviedo to renounce. A similar stabilizing effect worked during the upheavals of the Argentinean economic and political crisis of 2002. Market integration has interacted with political conditionality and MERCOSUR constitutes a stabilizing factor for the domestic democracy of its member states. This is of course highly significant in Latin America and we will come back to this crucial issue in section 2.11.

It is particularly relevant as regards the political nature of MERCOSUR that the initial step towards regional integration was to be found in the confidence-building measures established between Brazil and Argentina, the two principal protagonists, particularly as regards the nuclear security dimension (the abandonment of nuclear programmes and reciprocal threats). The salience of this political factor recalls the Franco-German relationship after the 1963 Elysée Treaty and also helps explain the stagnation of the SAARC (the community of countries in the Indian subcontinent whose development has been blocked for many decades by the political–strategic conflict between India and Pakistan).

Certainly, compared to the EU, MERCOSUR has only achieved initial institutional development so far: the secretariat of Montevideo has a minimal role, albeit superior to those of the secretariats of the SAARC in Kathmandu and ASEAN in Jakarta. However, a kind of committee of permanent government representatives was created in 2003 to lead the increasing routine form of cooperation. The construction of a judicial system for regulating trade disputes between MERCOSUR countries has successfully passed its initial stages of development with the creation of the Asuncion Court in 2004.

One cause of weakness is the internal structural imbalance between member states. The opposition of the largest state, Brazil, to institutional supranationality is due to the regional primacy of its national economy, which represents 80 per cent of MERCOSUR GDP. In addition, we should recall difficult hurdles such as social deficits and the increase in social inequality. Nevertheless, an early 'Mercosurization' of national civil societies is developing (complementary to an increasing role for NGOs, youth, women's and cultural associations, a Trade Union Forum, business network initiatives, etc.) which could help establish legitimacy for the regional integration process.

As we have already anticipated, the future of MERCOSUR is also significantly conditioned by external factors, especially the evolution of the transatlantic triangle. By this we mean the complex interregional relationships between Latin America and both the US and the EU. These are economic and political relationships, as indicated on the one hand at the biregional summits of 1999 and 2002 between the EU and Latin America and, on the other, by the FTAA summits in Santiago, Quebec and so on. However, the crucial point is that the EU–Latin America relationship is advancing slowly beyond the important 1995 Interregional Framework Cooperation Agreement, firstly because of limited interest and the strong protectionist fears of various European countries (due to the importance of agricultural lobbies, especially French ones), and secondly, because of the recent already mentioned 'polygamic' approach of Brazil and MERCOSUR. As far as the FTAA interregional arrangement is concerned, it is by no means clear whether this interregional project will succeed as envisaged. In addition to the domestic US blocks threatened by the American Congress (less during the first term of the Bush administration), we should also mention the open debate in Brazil and in MERCOSUR concerning the FTAA.

As far as the EU is concerned, its role as a global civilian power is at stake in Latin America. The 'Rio Process', started in 1999, places the dialogue with MERCOSUR within the interregional cooperation between the EU and Latin America. The Guadalajara summit of 2004 was much more successful than the Madrid one of 2002 as far as economic, cultural and political cooperation were concerned. However, there is no evidence of a coherent implementation of biregional and global commitments, namely at level of the WTO and UN. MERCOSUR is not only a trading partner, but also a potential ally in the reorganization of both global governance and the world order. This will not be in the multipolar sense called for by Chirac during his 1998 visit, but rather maybe in a more binding multilateral and less asymmetrical sense, taking into account the opposite stances at the Cancún WTO Conference of 2003.[38] The justifications for greater openness between the EU and MERCOSUR are thus not essentially based on trade, but strategic and political considerations: even if EU–MERCOSUR trade grew by 5 per cent on average per year between 1980 and 2002, in 2002 it still only accounted for 2.44 per cent of total EU exports and 1.83 per cent of total EU imports. That explains why the EU's interests in strengthening its interregional relationship with Latin America are firstly strategic and then economic.

Will MERCOSUR be able to cope with internal challenges, overcome the serious South American financial crisis and its social and political consequences and implement new dynamics facilitating increased regional integration? The elections of the pro-regionalist Luiz Inácio Lula da Silva and Néstor Kirchner (against the pro-FTAA Menem) to the presidencies of the two largest countries in MERCOSUR, along with Vasquez's victory in the 2004 presidential election in Uruguay, encourage hopes that the political initiatives announced in 2003 and particularly in Ouro Prieto in 2004 will be launched and tried out:

- a structural fund, financed according to national GDP, coping with certain internal asymmetries and aiming at increased social cohesion;
- enhanced macroeconomic regional convergence, with the hope of a single currency;
- a regional elected parliament, whose representation criteria and powers are still unclear.

Of course, the political convergence of leadership needs to prove effective in producing outcomes and complemented by two variables: a driving force, that is functionally equivalent to the EU common market, allowing a reduction of huge market discrepancies and asymmetries; secondly, the improvement of the present institutional framework.[39] To sum up, South American regionalism is entering a new phase in its development. Brazil and its regional partners seem to agree about combining the option of deepening MERCOSUR with the creation of a larger Bolivar-inspired South American Community of States (including MERCOSUR, the Andean Community and Chile) which was decided in Cusco in December 2004. The conditions of deepening MERCOSUR and, at the same time, of creating a political South American Community of States are dependent largely upon the Brazilian leadership and the current political convergence of national governments. However, transnational social, economic and cultural networking has never been so influential in supporting and counterbalancing mere intergovernmental cooperation.

In the *longue durée* process of constructing a Latin American democratic regionalism, the next decade will be crucial in two respects. On the one hand, the consolidation of domestic multi-level democracies firstly through the ability of new governments to face the challenges raised by the UNDP Report 2004 on democracy, fragility and social inequalities (*A Democracia na America Latina*) by improving the efficiency of public policies and combining decentralization with state credibility. On the other hand, the maturing of regional and interregional relations beyond the level of mere trade liberalization. These are already structural features of South American governance. However, the concerns provoked by the FTAA, the disappointing delay in EU–MERCOSUR free trade negotiations (2004)[40] and the expanding

South–South relations after Cancún, are challenging MERCOSUR and Latin American countries (like the EU, in its own context) to mature as a new kind of regional and global civilian power.

2.8   ASEAN between Japan, China and the United States. Interregional dialogue with the EU

ASEAN, the most dynamic of the Asian regional organizations, is looking for an Asian path towards regional integration. The multiple plans agreed in 2003–4, to cover various levels of cooperation (such as a common market, cultural and social projects, 'security community') are confirming its dynamics and ambitions,[41] even if, however, they need to take account of the great disparities between member states (technology, labour costs, poverty, exporting power, etc.).

The political dimension of ASEAN is also quite relevant, first of all as its origins and membership. Founded by five countries, it came into being in 1967 to form a united front against the communist threat in South-East Asia (what is, *mutatis mutandis*, similar to the EU) but has also been able to include Vietnam, Cambodia and Laos, that is communist countries and previous enemies. These enlargements, in addition to the membership of military dictatorships like Myanmar, have increased ASEAN's political, ethnic and religious heterogeneity – an important aspect which also emerges with respect to 'global' challenges such as the dialogue between civilizations and religions.

The business community is the main force pushing for deeper regional cooperation and its institutionalization, especially after the 1992 'Singapore Declaration' which went beyond both the fragile early 'Bangkok Declaration' (1967) and the 1976 'Bali Declaration' and launched an 'ASEAN free trade area'. Since 1992, ASEAN has increasingly encompassed new expectations and dimensions of regional cooperation and the present configuration of ASEAN may be only superficially likened to EFTA (the European Free Trade Association created in 1960 by the UK, the Scandinavian countries and other states which rejected the EEC vision of integration, as set out in the Treaty of Rome). In the case of ASEAN, since 1992, spillover effects, shared feelings of common belonging, and political cooperation are making it a unique workshop of regional cooperation.

The 1997–98 financial crisis devastated economic growth in ASEAN countries and provoked social unrest, calls for inward-looking policies and a stop to within-ASEAN immigration, as well as continuous and serious national political crises. Nonetheless, new forms of cooperation were gradually developed to offset external pressure. The action plan for 1999–2004, approved at the 1998 ASEAN Hanoi summit, showed the desire within ASEAN to fortify its objectives and consolidate cooperation. It also called for foreign investment, a common infrastructure programme and coordination of monetary policy. To this end, dialogue and economic cooperation within 'ASEAN Plus Three' (ASEAN plus China, Japan and South Korea) have been strengthened in recent years, in terms of monetary and commercial questions. Last but not least, we should mention the very significant decision to build a China–ASEAN free trade zone before 2010 (2015 for Vietnam and Laos). ASEAN Plus Three involves the fight against poverty and the desire to strengthen common monetary and financial instruments.

At the political level too, the ASEAN experience contains a number of particularly interesting elements. The first is the achievement of a stable peace between former enemies and the use of economic cooperation as a means to overcome political conflicts in a very unstable area. The second is the creation of a sort of concentric circle system around ASEAN. With the success of 'ASEAN Plus Three' and particularly with the 'ASEAN Regional Forum' (ARF), which also includes China, Japan, the United States, the EU, India and the countries with interests in the Asian Pacific region, ASEAN is defending its proactive political role and its desire to contribute to the stabilization of peace in the area, in a delicate period in which the two regional giants (Japan and China) are both expanding their external roles. ASEAN's dynamism, however, is confronted with the interregional strategy of the US in the Pacific (as synthesized in the APEC interregional project, involving America, East Asia and Oceania) to create the world's largest free trade zone before 2020. Observers wonder to what extent it is likely to affect regional entities with much deeper forms of cooperation like ASEAN.

It is true that ASEAN suffers from internal weaknesses: firstly, in terms of its institutional framework which is limited to one summit every year, the meetings of foreign ministers, plus the Jakarta Secretariat) and several intergovernmental bodies; secondly, the aforementioned heterogeneity between, and within, member states; thirdly, the fragility of democracy in this area (in those cases where democracy has taken root). We should also mention the heavy burden of the region's colonial and post-colonial past, as well as its linguistic, ethnic and religious diversity. These weaknesses have hindered more institutionalized forms of collaboration so far. However, regionalism is developing to an extent where it is challenging the traditional principle of non-interference in internal affairs, even if there is still not full consensus on more supranational rules. Several episodes of ASEAN interference in the internal affairs of member states are justified by their external implications: the consequences of the fall of Suharto in Indonesia, the dispute within the leadership in Malaysia, the crisis in Timor, the recent emergence of Islamic terrorism in the region, the impact of the unstable military dictatorship in Myanmar. The Bali summit in October 2003 and the subsequent one in 2004 approved a new programme for a common market and increased cultural and defence cooperation. This marked a genuine move towards establishing an 'ASEAN community' by 2020 (Vientiane summit 2004).

Several endogenous and exogenous factors are generating a new epoch of Asian regional cooperation. Unresolved internal issues, territorial boundaries and demands for self-determination by minorities (Aceh, Mindanao, Papua, along the Vietnam–Laos border, and between Myanmar and Thailand), the effects of the 2004 tsunami disaster and so on, are fostering an enhanced form of multilateral regional cooperation which impinges on national sovereignty and may facilitate a mutual learning process and common action. Interregional regimes established with the EU (ASEM) and the US (APEC) are increasingly multidimensional and political. The question whether they may lead either to a deepening of ASEAN or its dilution deserves a differentiated answer. The interregional interaction since 1996 between the EU and ASEAN within the framework of the ASEM (Asia Europe Meeting) highlights the synchronic dimension and the common reference to analogous external challenges of current globalization and political instability. There is a shared need in both the EU and ASEAN to strengthen the weak side of the US, EU, East Asia triangle (the three main poles of world economic development). ASEM is not institutionalized, above all because of Asian resistance, but it does involve dynamic economic and cultural cooperation in addition to a political dialogue, as demonstrated by ASEM 1 (Bangkok 1996), ASEM 2 (London 1998), ASEM 3 (Seoul 2000) and ASEM 4 (Copenhagen 2002). Recently, ASEM 5 provided an opportunity for convergence on very sensitive issues like the Korean crisis and the war on terrorism within the UN framework, as was in evidence at the Hanoi summit of 2004. However, the EU is developing strategic bilateral relationships with China and Japan, while ASEAN has not yet been considered a strategic partner and the multilateral and multidimensional framework provided by ASEM is still in its initial phase (see EU Commission, *A New Partnership with South East-Asia*, 2003).

Granted, ASEM does not yet compete with the APEC liberalization process. However, the idea of the Clinton administration to set up an open interregional framework of economic cooperation does not seem to tally with the primacy of security issues in the Bush government, as clearly shown by the controversial politicization of the APEC agenda (Santiago, 2004) and his preference for bilateral trade agreements (Singapore, Thailand, Australia). In this evolving environment, Japan is torn between traditional bilateral relations with individual ASEAN countries and an emerging regional multilateral approach ('Tokyo Declaration', December 2003). All in all, ASEAN states find themselves faced with the challenge of launching a new and dynamic period of regional cooperation (open to Japan and China) within the framework of a double interregional dialogue with the US and the EU. They seem to be trying to equip themselves to cope with this opportunity, rather than clinging to illusory notions of national sovereignty.

2.9 The SADC, ECOWAS and African regionalism: politics and economics

Far more than the newborn, institutionally complex, but still vague and ineffectual pan-African organization, the 'African Union', the SADC (Southern African Development Community), ECOWAS (in western Africa) and the minor organizations in eastern Africa are generally viewed as beginning to correct the tradition of inefficiency and the paralysis of regionalism on the African continent. The consequences of colonialism and neo-colonialism and the division between Francophone and Anglophone countries exacerbate an important structural weakness: the composition of demand and production, of imports and exports, is too similar between neighbouring countries to enable them to generate complementarity and develop intraregional trade, which is a decisive indicator for successful regional cooperation. Nonetheless, regionalism is being strengthened both in western Africa with ECOWAS and, even more, in the southern part of the continent (SADC), as a reaction of these states to the risks of marginalization in an increasingly globalized and regionalized world economy.[42]

Begun in 1980, the process which led to the SADC was accelerated with the 1992 Treaty and especially with the active role taken by its new member, South Africa (1994). The origin of the association is political: it stems from an alliance of countries which were opposed to the apartheid system in South Africa. Today there is a series of partially overlapping organizations in the region, of which only Namibia is a member of every single one. These are: the Community of Eastern and Southern Africa (nine members): the Southern African Customs Union

(SACU, five members); the Common Monetary Area (four members); the Cross Border Initiative (seven members). The SADC displays clear internal asymmetries. South Africa represents 70 per cent of the total GDP (and 20 per cent of the population) and its prestigious leadership, from Mandela to Mbeki, contributes to its political importance within the region and beyond. However, the GDP per capita of the richest country (Mauritius) is some 18 times that of the poorest country (Mozambique). Commercial policies are very different, ranging from protectionists to free trade advocates, and therefore there is also great diversity of macroeconomic policies. In some countries regionalism is seen as an alternative to globalization whereas, in others, it is viewed as a step towards the global market. A variegated informal economic network is emerging, which often transcends national and regional borders. With regard to the institutional set-up, the SADC is an intergovernmental organization composed of 14 states. It is directed by summits and councils of ministers. It has a secretariat in Botswana and its work is mainly carried out through sectoral commissions. The original decision that each of these commissions be coordinated by one of the 14 member states has proved sometimes efficient: for example, finance by South Africa, culture and transport by Mozambique, agronomy by Botswana, mining and employment by Zambia.

If we look at globalization from an African perspective, we can clearly see the asymmetries of the world economy: sub-Saharan African net investment flows dropped drastically from 17 per cent in 1990 to 6 per cent in 1996, while those to South-East Asia and Latin America increased during the same period. As a result, the countries of the SADC represent 3 per cent of the world's population, but only 1 per cent of world exports and global GDP. However, the picture is not entirely negative: South Africa, even if in alliance with other countries, is behind the initiative of the NEPAD (New Partnership for African Development, http://www.nepad.org), the best symbol of the African will to recover. Founded in 2001, it links G7 countries' financial aid with good governance and its secretariat is in Johannesburg. From 1997 to 2003 the continent's GDP has grown by 3.4 per cent per year, fostered by exporting countries.

The 1996 Protocol launched a 'SADC – Free Trade Area' in order to increase trade, attract foreign investment and strengthen growth, thus adapting to the requests of the WTO. Various authors,[43] however, have highlighted the decisive effect that the success of complementary policies to liberalization, especially within the education and health sectors, would have. The SADC also needs measures designed to encourage political stabilization and the strengthening of infrastructures and institutions in order to diminish the inevitably destabilizing effects for more closed economies. If we bear in mind the comparative model introduced in this chapter, we can say that while 30 years of collabora-tion have not seen any progress in terms of internal convergence (for example, as regards per capita income), the hard core made up of the five SADC countries which are also linked by a customs union with South Africa (the SACU, South African Customs Union) has halved disparities in per capita incomes. This has been achieved with a speed of convergence superior even to that of the EU over the same period of time and encourages the application of the accomplishments of this hard core to the whole of SADC.

In the best future scenario, the free trade zone will be accompanied by complementary measures, macroeconomic convergence and more binding sectoral policies. The real stumbling blocks are mostly political: internal asymmetry still provokes distrust of South Africa as the regional power in economic, political–military and 'international influence' terms. In particular, the crises in the Congo and the Great Lakes area and the problems related to Mugabe's regime in Zimbabwe (listed by C. Rice as a tyrannical regime) have provoked a widening of the politi-cal divisions between member states and a reinforcement of the medi-ating role of South Africa, on the one hand, along with the creation of subcoalitions – a factor which could weaken regional cooperation – on the other. Despite all this, we can still say that new regionalism in Africa is gradually being consolidated through both the SADC and ECOWAS.

ECOWAS (CEDEAO in French) comprises 16 countries, including the most populous state, Nigeria, and is much more developed than the SADC in its institutional structure (very similar to the EU), but less effec-tive as far as the coherency and consistency of decision implementation are concerned. It aims to construct a common market and, like the SADC, has an inner hard core, including a monetary union (UEMOA). Both organizations (SADC and ECOWAS) are committed to political cooperation.[44]

As regards foreign support, the European states and the EU have been by far the leading aid providers for several decades (compared with other G7 members). However, by setting Africa as a priority they should firstly admit that they share the responsibility for failures and support to corrupt African elites. Therefore, it seems relevant that, as a comple-ment to renewed public aid and trade openness, the EU more recently has been fostering improved governance and regional cooperation. This latter became a distinctive feature of EU African policy. It was enhanced by the 2000 ACP Treaty in Cotonou, which may be classified as an inter-regional partnership and makes the success of regional cooperation a condition for privileged access to the internal European market. Though several regional groupings foster convergence among member states, African regionalism is still weak and challenging both for international relations theory and for EU policies linking regional cooperation with conflict prevention and development aid.[45]

The South African Mbeki leadership of SADC and of the African Union claimed a significant role of regional organizations in the maintenance of peace between member states and across the African continent. Since the results of AU and UN missions in Congo, Sudan and the powder keg of West Africa have been poor for a long time, the EU is enhancing its presence and the Commission plans to increase its financial and political support for the transformation of African regional groupings into permanent peacekeeping and 'stabilizing forces' (according to the prevision for the EU budget 2007–13).

2.10   A structural and multidimensional phenomenon of uncertain destiny

Summarizing this critical overview, we can say that, in the present con-text, the principal differences between the major regional organizations can be classified on the basis of two criteria: on the one hand, the degree of internal integration, i.e. the capacity to create convergence between member states (and therefore to lessen the tendency to fragment through the deepening of unification). On the other, the level reached in terms of its interplay with the global system. With regard to the first criterion, in various regional organizations the fragile nature of their origins has not yet faded and it thus slows down the translation of regional associations onto the level of political institutions. In several cases, the differences between national interests with regard to global-ization, the heterogeneity of national regimes, the fragility of states, the multiple internal asymmetries and the persistent divergence of institu-tional models to be adopted inhibit the pace and success of regional cooperation and integration. This empirical overview confirms what we assert in the theoretical part of this chapter, i.e. weak states produce weak regional associations and in many cases, the reconstruction of states may only take place in tandem with regional cooperation and regional institution building.

We have noted the variety of paths to regional cooperation and inte-gration. The positive dynamic to emerge from private interests and networks towards regional convergence can also be obtained via the intergovernmental path, i.e. without a supranational model akin to that of the EU. Furthermore, the weakness of functional equivalents to EU common market dynamics can, to a certain extent, be balanced through political will. Certainly, the new regionalism is not a panacea with regard to the stemming of phenomena that lead to the disintegration of political authority in several continents. Nevertheless, the positive curbing role established by regionalism as opposed to nationalism and subnational fragmentation is clear, even in situations of serious social and economic crisis. Last, but not least, whether directly or indirectly, regional associations create a political shift towards both democratization and the prevention of conflicts.

Even with regard to the second criterion of successful regional co-operation, i.e. the international impact, it is clear that the EU is the most political in nature of the new regional organizations, which are often born or reconstituted purely for economic and commercial ends. Nonetheless, all regional organizations are increasingly obliged to tackle, often with difficulty, the instabilities of an international economic and political system in which unipolar tendencies and unilateralism count for more than expected. As a result, regional organizations are increasing the political potential of their distinctive civilian role and are certainly not collapsing as both nationalist thought and the various schools of economic and political globalism had imagined.

The future of regional cooperation is faced with three scenarios:

(a) that of regionalisms brought back to the bedrock of globalization and unipolar globalism, through two parallel processes of hyper-fragmentation of light governance on the one hand, and on the other, the hyperconcentration in the US of power in the fields of politics and major economic choices;
(b) that of the creation of closed trading blocs, which are increasingly concerned with their own political security and not just economic protectionism;
(c) the multiple variants of deeper and democratic new regionalism, understood as a dynamic factor in curbing internal political disintegration and as an active contribution to the reform of the Westphalian international system.

It is in this last area that the global and interregional role and active presence of the EU may be decisive. The comparative assessment of the EU-centred interregional relations shows huge differences as the efficiency and effectiveness of economic cooperation, trade, aid to development, political dialogue, security, 'region-building' are concerned: from the globally positive developments of the 'Rio process', to the promising even if still too timid ASEM, from the oscillations of the ACP to the partial failure of the 'Barcelona process'.[46] Only after taking seriously into account the causes of shortcomings and failures would the Union be capable of becoming more than simply an influential workshop for other new regional experiments or an example of successful regional governance, a more active and coherent global political actor, capable of flexible alliances and far-sighted support for new regionalism and multilateralism abroad. This has been proved to be difficult if the relationship between regional organizations is strictly subordinated to global arrangements. After the setback of the WTO Cancún meeting (September 2003), the EU launched a strategic reflection on the balance between its commitment to a global multilateral negotiation process and its support for interregional relations with states and regional organizations which, like a mirror, reflect an image of itself in a multiregional world perspective. We do not yet know whether the result will cope with the rising expectations of near and far partners.[47]

2.11   The EU, new regionalism and democratization

We have established that, despite variations, regional associations are a structural and multidimensional phenomenon affecting local, national, regional and global governance. Furthermore, some evidence exists that the civilian power of the EU supports regional cooperation elsewhere through its interregional and bilateral arrangements and within the framework of its external policies. A question which was posed in the first section of this chapter should, however, be explicitly answered at this point: what is the impact of regional cooperation and integration on democratization?

To respond, we need to divide this key question into three subtopics: the regional contribution to global democratization; the construction of regional democratic polities; the building and stabilization of national democracies.

1.   New regionalism, as a 'bottom-up' process, provides a contribution to the democratization of global governance: successful new regionalism both strengthens and multiplies the number of collective actors which can potentially matter within global institutions. On the

one hand, in realistic terms, if the trade-off between enlargement of the 'club size' and the deepening of common policies is correct, regionalism helps international democracy by stopping nationalism, halting internal fragmentation, and by legitimizing the regional impact of global governance. However, the pressing challenge over the next decade, both for the former 'Bretton Woods' global network and the UN system, will regard how the weight of regional organizations can be institutionalized within their respective decision-making processes.

2.   Democratic regional polities are still far from being a general phenomenon. As a set of regional regimes, the EU is the most democratic polity, while, as a political system in the making, it is criticized for its 'democratic deficit'.[48] As regards regional associations elsewhere, there is some evidence however that, when regional arrangements gradually deepen common policies, sooner or later, the political dimension of regional cooperation, internal spillover, emulation and external pressures provoke a series of dynamics favouring regional democracy: in Latin America, Africa and Asia there is increasing demand, not only for regional parliaments, but also for regional citizenship and regional civil society and identity. This is relevant because the EU example shows both the importance and the limits of regional parliaments and the need for a more comprehensive understanding of regional democracy, beyond the mere formal representative institutions. This gradual evolution is supported by the EU, not only through interparliamentarian dialogue,[49] but also by means of transregional dialogue, civil society networking, and various interregional policies (whose follow-up should be monitored on a regular basis).

3.   Regarding the interplay between domestic democratization and regional integration, we have firstly to distinguish between two processes: on the one hand, new regionalism is distinct from regional groupings of the 1950s and 1960s precisely because, with few exceptions, 'prior change in domestic regime made it possible for these countries to enter into credible arrangements for international trade liberalization and regional policy cooperation'. On the other hand, as regards the 'top-down' impact of new regional cooperation and regional treaties in terms of stabilizing domestic democracies, the current situation is very variegated and controversial. One should take into account the successes of the EU in stabilizing democratic regimes, not only among its own member states, but also in applicant and border countries (both in post-Fascist southern Europe and in post-Communist

eastern Europe), along with the democratic stabilization of MERCOSUR member states (including stopping of the *coup d'état* in Paraguay). Conversely, we should also mention the troubled performance of other regional associations as far as democracy is concerned: namely the SADC (regarding the Zimbabwe crisis), the SAARC (the *coup d'état* in Pakistan), ECOWAS (Ivory Coast and Sierra Leone) and ASEAN (the military regime in Myanmar).

How can we account for failures and shortcomings? To what extent does regional cooperation and regional belonging matter as far as domestic democratization is concerned? It is not enough to say that fragile states back fragile regional associations which are unable to support domestic democratization. Ph.C. Schmitter suggests some criteria to help explain the different domestic impacts: membership should be considered as permanent in nature and promising economic opportunities; it should be backed by complex interdependence at the level of transnational business interests, civil society, etc.; public regional multilateralism should work well and consensually. He correctly emphasizes that there is evidence that *civilian* regional multilateralism is not only more efficient than unilateralism as a stabilizer of democracy, but it also works better than military alliances (as NATO), or global institutions (as WTO); finally, he makes the point that regional associations of neighbouring countries matter more than large continental associations (such as the CSCE, the AU or the OAS).[50]

However, while soft regional associations and the global multilateral network share a clear deficit in terms of accountability and transparency, which explains the increase in transnational critical public opinion, deepening regional groupings may also provoke a negative impact by 'upsetting domestic interest *equilibria*, both between subnational regions (close or peripheral to the new territorial cores) and among domestic political actors', and by creating differential empowerment among institutions. Comparative analysis should, for instance, verify whether regional organizations, thanks to asymmetrical information, exaggerated emphasis on regional commitments and authoritative allocations, strengthen national governments or even 'postdemocratic' tendencies,[51] with respect to parliaments and local administrations and provoke domestic imbalances and instabilities. According to Schmitter, there is no evidence of this type of impact. In part, this is thanks to the role played by the permanent administrative structures of the state, the presence of legal obligations, and, in particular, the weight of transnational interest coalitions.[52]

Nonetheless, successful regional cooperation is reviving territorial authority. Beyond the traditional debate between realism, functionalism and new medievalism, territorial states are not all and generally declining and nor are they being simply confirmed in their classical sovereignty: new regional frameworks are transforming member states into 'open states', committed to international cooperation. This often involves peer review and an increasing multilateral check on domestic democratic standards.[53] Regionalism is not a panacea and depends on trends which emerge within member states; however, comparative analysis shows that variables such as regional institutional settlement, the relevance of legal constraints, citizen participation, the institutionalization of shared values within an evolving regional public sphere and the interregional political dialogue with the EU matter as far as the impact of regionalism as a 'democracy stabilizer' is concerned. However, the main lesson of comparative analysis is that, since there are no cases of regional cooperation evolving into a regional state, democratic legitimacy will not be essentially supranational, but will remain primarily (even if not exclusively) national. That implies a consequence for the EU as an advanced workshop of regional cooperation and integration and its 'mirror effect' in the world: the more the EU, as a polity, demonstrates that it can coordinate diverse national democracies in a manner which is complementary to a transnational and supranational public sphere, the more its civilian global influence will grow in the world. By contrast, the more the EU tries to appear like a superstate in the making, the less appealing it is for regional partners abroad.

Notes

1. J.N. Rosenau, *Along the Domestic–Foreign Frontier. Exploring Governance in a Turbulent World*, Cambridge University Press, 1997 and 'A Transformed Observer in a Transforming World', *Studia diplomatica*, nos 1–2, 1999 (ed. by C. Roosens, M. Telò and P. Vercauteren), pp. 5–14. See also S. Strange, *The Retreat of the State*, Cambridge University Press, 1996. For a critical view, see G. Sorensen, *The Transformation of the State: Beyond the Myth of a Retreat*, Palgrave Macmillan, Basingstoke, 2004 (see pp. 4 and 131, Chapters 9 and 10 in particular); L. Weiss (ed.), *States in the Global Economy*, Cambridge University Press, 2003, pp. 293–316.
2. A.S. Milward, *The European Rescue of the Nation-State*, Routledge, London, 1992.
3. E.B. Haas, *Beyond the Nation State: Functionalism and International Organization*, Stanford University Press, Stanford, 1964.
4. A. Moravcsik, *The Choice for Europe: Social Purpose and State Power from Messina to Maastricht*, Cornell University Press, Ithaca, NY, 1998.

5. J.N. Rosenau and E. Czempiel (eds), *Governance without Government: Order and Change in World Politics*, Cambridge University Press, Cambridge–New York, 1993; A. Prakash and J. A. Hart, *Globalization and Governance*, Routledge, London–New York, 1999, pp. 51–3; O. Young, 'International Regimes Towards a New Theory of Institutions', in *World Politics*, 39, 1986, pp. 104–22.
6. B. Hettne, 'The New Regionalism: a Prologue', in B. Hettne, A. Inotai and O. Sunkel (eds), *Globalism and the New Regionalism*, Macmillan, Basingstoke, 1999, pp. xv–xxix (this book is part of a relevant five-volume project edited by Hettne, Inotai and Sunkel between 1999 and 2001) and M. Farrell, B. Hettne and L. Van Langenhove, *The Global Politics of Regionalism*, Pluto Books, London, 2005; S. Breslin, C. Hughes, N. Philips and B. Rosamond (eds), *New Regionalism in the Global Political Economy: Theories and Cases*, Routledge, London, 2002; W. Mattli, *The Logic of Regional Integration*, Cambridge University Press, 1999; O. Knutsen (ed.), *Regionalism and Regional Cooperation*, Norwegian Institute of International Affairs, Oslo, 1997; L.Van Langenhove, 'Regional Integration and Global Governance', UNU-CRIS, *Occasional Paper*, no. 2004/4, and M. Telò, 'Introduction' to M. Telò (ed.), *EU and New Regionalism*, op. cit., pp. 1–17.
7. We are using the concept of hegemony in the sense already detailed in Chapter 1 and with reference to Robert O. Keohane and Charles Kindleberger (section 1.4).
8. See W. Wallace, *Regional Integration: the West European Experience*, Brookings Institution, Washington, 1994 and Hitschcock, *The Struggle for Europe*, op. cit.
9. I. Clark, *Globalization and Fragmentation: International Relations in the Twentieth Century*, Oxford University Press, Oxford, 1997; K. Polanyi, *The Great Transformation*, Rinehart, New York, 1944.
10. R. Gilpin, *The Political Economy of International Relations*, Princeton University Press, Princeton, 1987.
11. A. Shonfield, *Modern Capitalism: the Changing Balance of Public and Private Power*, Oxford University Press, Oxford, 1965.
12. R.O. Keohane, *After Hegemony: Co-operation and Discord in the World Political Economy*, Princeton University Press, 1984; see the literature mentioned in n. 6.
13. MERCOSUR was set up in 1985 and, since 1991, includes Brazil, Argentina, Paraguay and Uruguay. ASEAN, founded in 1967 by Indonesia, Malaysia, Thailand, the Philippines, Brunei and Singapore, has gradually expanded to accommodate Vietnam, Laos, Cambodia and Myanmar. The SAARC was set up in 1985 by India and Pakistan and also includes Bangladesh, the Maldives, Sri Lanka, Nepal and Bhutan. The SADC now encompasses 13 southern African States, including South Africa, Mozambique and Congo. ECOWAS contains 16 states including Nigeria. Its founding treaty was signed in Abuja in 1975. See Telò (ed.), *EU and New Regionalism*, op. cit. and H. Van Ginkel, T. Court and L. Van Langenhove, *Integrating Africa*, UN University, Tokyo, 2003.
14. This thesis of Gilpin's (*The Political Economy of International Relations*) is shared by Waltz and others. A. Moravcsik (see *The Choices for Europe*, op. cit.) integrates it with the theory of international regimes and an extensive knowledge of the history and structures of the European construction.
15. S. Strange, *The Retreat of the State: the Diffusion of Power in the World Economy*, Cambridge University Press, New York, 1996; for a critical review, see Sorensen, *The Transformation of the State*, op. cit.

16. Strange, *Retreat of the State*, op. cit., pp. 101–13.

17. G. Majone, *Regulating Europe*, Routledge, London, 1996.

18. For an introduction to institutionalism, see J. March and J. Olsen, *Rediscovering Institutions: the Organisational Basis of Politics*, Free Press, New York, 1989.

19. See R.O. Keohane, *International Institutions and State Power. Essays in International Relations Theory*, Westview, Boulder, 1989, and *Realist and Institutionalist Theory after 9.11th*, written in December 2004 for the Advisory Group in Social Science and Humanities for the European Research Area, EU Commission DG Research. In Europe, see the works by Simon Bulmer, Beate Kohler-Koch, Wolfgang Wessels and others.

20. S.D. Krasner (ed.), *International Regimes*, Cornell University Press, Ithaca, NY, 1983, and Moravscik, *The Choice for Europe*, op. cit.

21. J.N. Rosenau, 'Governance in the Twenty First Century', *Global Governance*, 1, 1, 1995, pp. 13–43.

22. R.W. Cox, *The New Realism: Perspectives on Multilateralism and World Order*, United Nations University Press, Tokyo–New York, 1997.

23. G.W.F. Hegel, *Philosophy of Right* (1821), translated by T.M. Knox, Oxford, 1942, paragraph 347.

24. For the theoretical approach to the domestic factors affecting foreign policy and decision-making processes in external relations, see G. Allison, *Essence of Decision*, Little Brown, Boston, 1971, focusing on the US, and, focusing on Europe and Africa, the recent book by C. Roosens, V. Rosoux and T. de Wilde d'Estmael (eds), *La politique étrangère*, Peter Lang, Brussels, 2004, which provides some empirical evidence for the theoretical relevance of this pre-systemic approach.

25. See the anti-regionalist view of J. Bhagwati, in *The World Trading System at Risk*, Princeton University Press, Princeton, 1991, and in J. Bhagwati and P. Arvind, *Preferential Trading Areas and Multilateralism. Stranger Friends or Foes?*, in J. Bhagwati and A. Panagariya (eds), *Free Trade Areas or Free Trade?*, AEI Press, Washington, DC, 1996.; more optimistic on regional cooperation: L. Summers, 'Regionalism and the World Trading System', in *Policy Implications of Trade and Currency Zones*, Federal Reserve Bank of Kansas City, 1991, pp. 46–8 and P. Krugman, 'The Move toward Free Trade Zones', ibidem, pp. 7–42. Optimists insist on the natural character of PTAs, determined by geography, common language and common borders; see also J. Fraenkel, *Regional Trading Blocks in the World Economic System*, Washington, DC, 1997. On the costs of regionalism for club outsiders, see P. Padoan, 'Political Economy of New Regionalism', in Telò (ed.), *EU and New Regionalism*, op. cit., pp. 39–59.

26. C. Crouch and W. Streeck (eds), *Political Economy of Modern Capitalism. Mapping Convergence and Diversity*, Sage, London, 1997, and S. Berger and R. Dore (eds), *National Diversity and Global Capitalism*, Cornell, Ithaca, 1996.

27. R.E. Baldwin, 'The Causes of Regionalism', *The World Economy*, 20, 7, pp. 865–88.

28. On this point see S. Haggard, 'Regionalism in Asia and the Americas', in E.D. Mansfield and H.V. Milner (eds), *The Political Economy of Regionalism*, Columbia University Press, New York, 1997, p. 13. See also R. Higgott, 'The Asian Economic Crisis: a Study in the Politics of Resentment', *New Political Economy*, 3, 3, 1998, pp. 333–57.

29. S.P. Huntington, *The Clash of Civilizations and the Remaking of the World Order*, Simon & Schuster, New York, 1996.
30. See T. Meyer's *Cultural Factor in the Process of Globalization/Regionalization*, on the cultural dimension of the globalization–regionalization dialectic, in M. Telò (ed.), *European Union and New Regionalism: Regional Actors and Global Governance*, Ashgate, Aldershot, 2001, pp. 59–68.
31. The argument of G. Therborn, *European Modernity and Beyond. The Trajectory of European Societies, 1945–2000*, Sage, London, 1995, confirmed by the significant debate in the preamble of the text of the Convention which did not refer to Christianity.
32. P. Taylor, *International Organization in the Modern World: the Regional and the Global Process*, Pinter, London, 1993.
33. See Hettne, *The New Regionalism*, op. cit. and the literature quoted in n. 6, and B. Balassa, *The Theory of Economic Integration*, Allen & Unwin, London, 1961.
34. See also F. Attinà, *La sicurezza degli stati nell'era dell'egemonia Americana*, Giuffrè, Milan, 2003, with regard to the list of various foreseen measures of regional defence partnerships: monitoring and prevention of armed conflicts; crisis management and the re-establishment of peace. And to objectives: protection of minorities, human rights, support for political democratization, assistance to civil society. On the theoretical dimension, see J. Hentz and M. Boas (eds), *New and Critical Security and Regionalism*, Ashgate, Aldershot, 2003.
35. K.W. Deutsch et al., *Political Community and the North Atlantic Area; International Organization in the Light of Historical Experience*, Princeton University Press, Princeton, 1957. Regarding the Deutsch approach in the framework of a review of theories of regional integration, see the 'Introduction' by Finn Laursen in F. Laursen (ed.), *Comparative Regional Integration: Theoretical Perspectives*, Ashgate, Aldershot, 2004, pp. 5–7.
36. See the introduction by Milner and Mansfield in *The Political Economy of Regionalism*, op. cit., p. 18 and the article by J.M. Grieco (*Systematic Sources of Variation in Regional Institutionalization*, op. cit., pp. 164–86) on the systemic causes of national variations.
37. See the chapters by S. Borras and M. Klth and by A. Malamud and R. Perales in Laursen (ed.), *Comparative Regional Integration*, op. cit.; S. Santander (ed.), *Globalisation, governance et logiques régionales dans les Ameriques*, l'Harmattan, Paris, 2004, Cahiers CELA-IS no. 3. See also P. Schmitter, *Nine Reflections on MERCOSUR and its New Democracies Based on the EU and its Old Democracy*, Forum Euro Latino-Americano, Lisbon, 12–13 Oct. 2004.
38. On achievements and perspectives, see the contributions of the Euro-Latin-American Forum and, in particular: *Forging a New Multilateralism. A View from the EU and the MERCOSUL*, IEEI, Lisbon, 2001 and *O Novo Multilateralismo. Perspectiva da Uniao Europeia e do MERCOSUL*, Principia, Lisbon, 2001.
39. See C. Hugueney Filho and C.H. Cardim (eds), *Grupo de Reflexâo. Prospectiva sobre o MERCOSUL*, Ministerio das Relaçôes Exteriores-BID-IPRI-FUNAG, Brasilia, 2002, as well as D. Chudnovsky and J.M. Fanelli (eds), *El Desafío de integrarse para crecer: balance y perpectivas del MERCOSUR en su primera década*, Siglo Veintiuno de Argentina Editores, Buenos Aires, 2001; F. Pena, 'Defensa de la competencia económica en el MERCOSUR', in *Revista La Ley*, 14 May 2001 and 'Reflexiones sobre el MERCOSUR y su futuro', in Hugueney Filho

150 *Europe: a Civilian Power?*

and Cardim (eds), *Grupo de Reflexão. Prospectiva sobre o MERCOSUL*, op. cit., pp. 277ff.

40. Oscillations of both sides explain the failure of the long EU–MERCOSUR negotiations for a free trade agreement before the deadline of the Prodi–Lamy Commission.

41. On this point see R. Higgott, 'The Asian Economic Crisis: a Study in the Politics of Resentment', *New Political Economy*, 3, 3, 1998, pp. 333–57 and 'The Political Economy of Globalization in East Asia: the Salience of "Region Building"', in K. Olds, P. Diecken, P.F. Kelly and others (eds), *Globalization in the Asia Pacific: Contested Territories*, Routledge, London, 1999, and A. Acharya, *Regionalism and Multilateralism: Essays on Comparative Security in the Asia-Pacific*, Eastern University Press, Singapore, 2003. See also M. Beeson (ed.), *Contemporary Southeast Asia. Regional Dynamics, National Differences*, Palgrave, Basingstoke, 2004, the three volumes edited by D. Dewitt on *Development and Security in Southeast Asia (The Environment, The People* and *The Globalization)*, Ashgate, Aldershot, 2003 and D. Webber, 'Two Funerals and a Wedding? The Ups and Down of Regionalism in East-Asia and the Pacific after the Asian Crisis', in Laursen (ed.), *Comparative Regional Integration*, op. cit., pp. 125–59. In a comparative perspective see also: K. Eliassen and C. Borve Monsen, *Comparison of European and Southeast Asian Integration*, in Telò (ed.), *EU and New Regionalism*, op. cit., pp. 11–133; S. Haggard, 'Regionalism in Asia and the Americas', in Mansfield and Milner (eds), *The Political Economy of Regionalism*, op. cit.; R. Foot, 'Pacific Asia: the Development of Regional Dialogue', in L. Fawcett and A. Hurrell (eds), *Regionalism in World Politics*, Oxford University Press, 1995, pp. 2228–49, and the collective book edited by R. Garnhout and P. Drysdale, *Asia Pacific Regionalism*, Harper Educational, Sydney, 1994.

42. See F. Söderbaum, *The Political Economy of Regionalism in Southern Africa*, Göteborg University, Göteborg, 2002, Van Ginkel and Van Langenhore (eds), *Integrating Africa*, op. cit. and S. Page, *Regionalism among Developing Countries*, St Martin's Press, New York, 1999.

43. C. Jenkins and L. Thomas, *African Regionalism and the SADC*, in Telò (ed.), *European Union and New Regionalism*, op. cit., pp. 153–75.

44. After its founding treaty (for economic integration) at Abuja, ECOWAS saw a gradual politicization in the 1980s which resulted in the Abuja Treaty in 1991 and the revised Treaty of 23 July 1993, which attributed priority to peace and security. See also the Lomé Declaration of 1999 on preventive diplomacy.

45. A. Payne (ed.), *The New Regional Politics of Development*, Palgrave Macmillan, Basingstoke, 2004. Regarding cooperation policy F. Söderbaum and P. Stalgren draw attention to the risk of a 'zero sum game' between declining national aid policies and those of the EU ('Unco-ordinated co-ordination', paper, ECPR SGIR conference, The Hague, Sept 2004, section 33) and suggest applying the 'open method of coordination' between national policies (see Chapter 3).

46. Even if an attempt at reviving it is about to occur in 2005 in the context of the tenth anniversary, the diminished tension in Palestine and the dialogue with Libya (see www.barcelona10.org).

47. My personal experience in East and South Asia and in Latin America brings me to the conclusion that an enhanced multidimensional role and a political presence of the EU, despite internal diversities and colonial legacies of member states, is generally and broadly welcome at the beginning of the twenty-first century. The problem may be a kind of capability–expectations gap. See also M. Ortega (ed.), *Global Views on the European Union*, Chaillot Paper, no. 72, ISS, Paris, 2004.

48. On this theoretical debate, see A. Moravscik, 'Reassessing Legitimacy in the EU', in J.H.H. Weiler, I. Begg and J. Peterson, *Integration in an Expanding EU*, Blackwell, Oxford, 2003, pp. 77–98; J.L. Quermonne, *Le système politique de l'UE*, Montchrétien, Paris, 2002; M. Telò (ed.), *Démocratie et construction européenne*, Editions de l'Université de Bruxelles, 1995.

49. A. Malamud and L. de Sousa, *Regional Parliaments in Europe and Latin America: Between Empowerment and Irrelevance*, ECPR, The Hague, September 2004.

50. P.C. Schmitter, 'Change in Regime Type and Progress in International Relations', in E. Adler and B. Crawford (eds), *Progress in Postwar International Relations*, Columbia University Press, New York, 1991, pp. 89–127.

51. By 'postdemocracy', C. Crouch means not only lobbying, but also 'media-democracy', 'gallup-democracy' and populist leadership. See C. Crouch, *Postdemocrazia*, Laterza, Rome, 2003.

52. Schmitter, *Nine Reflections*, op. cit., pp. 4–5.

53. By 'open state' we mean a state which needs to increasingly commit itself to international regimes and regional cooperation (even though this diminishes its national sovereignty) in order to strengthen accountability and internal legitimacy.

3

The Heart of European Integration: the Socio-economic Model between Convergence and National Diversities

3.1 The socio-economic dimension of civilian power

There are two main reasons why we are devoting a chapter to the 'European socio-economic model'. Firstly, Europe cannot develop its civilian power into a classic military one because it consists of Welfare States that spend about twice what the US does on social security (29.9 per cent of GDP in 2001 compared to 14.2 per cent). This structural level of welfare spending prohibits the type of military expenditure feasible in the US (4 per cent of GDP compared with 2 per cent of European states[1]). Secondly, this topic is not only extremely relevant to the internal cohesion and quality of democracy within the EU, but is also central to the distinctive identity of the EU within the context of globalization. The EU presents an interesting case study of the tension between, on the one hand, the drive to speed up neoliberal deregulation and, on the other, the attempt to relaunch old and new forms of way of life and common belonging. These are linked to specific interests and social demands, all intent on introducing some kind of regional 're-regulation'. Drawing on our 1999 article, Jürgen Habermas synthesized three dimensions of this key question: the deep historical roots of welfare Europe, its 'constitutional' dimension and its potential impact on EU identity within the context of globalization.

With a view to the future of a highly stratified world society, we Europeans have a legitimate interest in getting our voice heard in an international concert that is at present dominated by a vision quite different from ours. This would be a way of giving a normative appeal to the European project for those who take a critical view of the impact of economic globalization on nation-states.[2]

If we accept that the route of mere liberal deregulation, resulting from the shift in the international economy towards the 'Washington consensus' in the 1990s, has little to offer the European integration project, it is then interesting to examine the actual and possible socio-economic background for the EU as a civilian power, through the following three theses:

1. The unique relationship between western Europe and globalization can only be understood in the context of the historical process of the last two centuries. The values of social justice, solidarity and democracy, inherent in the great traditions of European thought (social liberalism, social democracy and social Christianity), have become firmly rooted in the various institutional systems of national Welfare States. While these take different forms across Europe, they are linked by a number of important similarities which are distinct from socio-economic models elsewhere.
2. In recent years, the long process of fostering convergence among national social and economic models, as part of a process of reciprocal emulation and the construction of the EU, has seen the addition of a new common framework: the challenges posed by globalization.[3] These have prompted the EU to intensify its efforts to coordinate economic, social, research and innovation policies in order to create a new European compromise between international competitiveness and social cohesion within the framework of the construction of a 'knowledge society' based on common constituent values. The dynamic balance between European convergence and national diversity, between unity and differentiation and between 'positive' and 'negative' integration is only possible by means of innovative institutional provisions which go beyond the age-old debate on the respective merits of federalism and confederalism. This, in turn, requires methods which can reconcile respect for national differences with the advancement of European convergence. Here again, we can concretize the 'constitutionalization' of a social Europe.

3. The renewal of the 'European socio-economic model' constitutes an original response, which is both powerful and simple, to the question of the EU's common identity within the global governance. There cannot be a European civilian power in the sense of a normative European message combined with regulating might, if Europe cannot find new ways of marrying economic strength with social cohesion. Nor can either of these flourish if Europe's socio-historical identity becomes fragmented and 'normalized', according to rules drafted by external forces, rather than renewed and transformed into a driving force capable of shaping the partially globalized world.

3.2   The concept of solidarity in the great traditions of European thought: Christianity, liberalism and socialism

Before being institutionalized within modern national Welfare States, the European notion of solidarity developed within the frameworks of Christian social doctrine, social liberalism and socialism. However, it is rooted precisely in the continent where the notion of the individual was born. The origins of the modern idea of the individual are to be found at the heart of Greco-Roman culture. From the arduous quest of Ulysses to the thought of Socrates, from the stoicism of Cicero and Seneca to the civic engagement of Pericles and Caesar, before coming finally to the Christian concept of the individual and William of Ockham, we can see the complex evolution of the expression of individualism in a vast range of cultural forms such as literature, poetry and philosophy. It is this fact, recognized by historians of civilization[4] as a constituent element of Western civilization, that makes the emergence of the notion of solidarity so significant. Indeed, from its origins in the rights of the citizens of the Greek *polis* to its place as both a republican and a Christian value and an element of the widespread and enduring influence of Aristotelian philosophy, the idea of solidarity has formed the basis of many traditions of contemporary political thought. These include liberalism, from Locke to Stuart Mill, modern Christianity, from Manzoni to Rosmini in Italy, to Lamennais in France and Kolping in Germany, the social democratic ideas of Tawney in Britain, Karleby and Mydral in Sweden, and Bernstein in Germany, all of whom were directly or indirectly influenced by the philosophical theme of the relationship between the individual and society in republican thought from Machiavelli to Rousseau, Kant and Hegel among others. It is particularly significant that the doctrine of natural law itself – although based on Hobbes's more radically pessimistic version of the modern idea of individualism – is at the root of the political community by way of a social contract between individuals.

The idea that the state could facilitate the emergence from within the civil society of greater social justice and solidarity between different social groups emerged forcefully with the French Revolution and the Industrial Revolution, that is between the eighteenth and nineteenth centuries – think, for example, of A. Ferguson's concept of 'civil society' (*Essay on the History of Civil Society*, 1767), G.W.F. Hegel's concept of association/'corporation' (*Philosophy of Right*, 1821) and of the notion of 'organic solidarity' conceived by the French sociologist E. Durkheim (*De la division du travail social*, 1893). This set of ideas spread as a consequence of the severe political and social conflicts of the time. Two intertwined processes were involved: on the one hand, from the top down (and in addition to mere philanthropy), the state was charged with, and committed itself to, containing the devastating impact of the Industrial Revolution on the traditional world in which Christian ideas were rooted and on the modern urban proletariat. On the other hand, from the bottom up, the working classes themselves in various countries endeavoured to promote their own forms of organized solidarity as a kind of counterculture. This involved the provision of popular education and the formation of mutual aid societies – initiatives which were sometimes complementary to those run by the Churches. Over time, workers began to organize themselves autonomously. Spurred on by a variety of sources and conflicting theories from Marx to Proudhon, from Mazzini to Christian social movements, they set up associations and trade unions to defend their interests and rights. New practices of social solidarity and a culture of social justice emerged from these innovations and gave rise to one of modern Europe's most important social and political forces: the labour movement.[5] This was predominantly a socialist movement, but encompassed a wealth of pluralist cultural and political traditions such as the liberal and Christian thought.

Despite the weight of the backlash against them and the extremely rigid and closed conservatism of the 1920s and 1930s, these ideas remained important and were integrated, as 'passive revolution' even by Fascist and Nazi organizations, albeit within the distorted forms of the various types of Fascist and state corporatism. In Scandinavia, Belgium, France, the Netherlands and Great Britain, these ideas developed along democratic and social democratic lines before subsequently asserting themselves in the rest of western Europe after 1945. The strength of the social democratic movement in Europe (in contrast with US 'exceptionalism' which allowed no mass-based social democratic movement to develop) has interested sociologists and thinkers such as W. Sombart and A. Hirschmann. The concept of solidarity as a means of social action, which underpins the creation of workers' organizations, is profoundly different from traditional Christian charity and humanistic liberal philanthropy:

> Those who participate in organizations for mutual help do not wish to do their moral duty; they simply take care of themselves. Help is not given by the rich to the poor, but by the community to the community. All those who need help receive it, whether they are responsible for their misery or not, according to a universal conception of solidarity. It is based on the idea of human dignity, which is considered superior to all other values.[6]

A secularized version of solidarity was stressed as one of the values of the EU in the Treaty establishing a Constitution for Europe (art. I, 2) which should be considered, in this respect, as the transfer to supranational level of a *longue durée* process of secularization of values:

> The Union is founded on the values of respect for human dignity, liberty, democracy, equality, the rule of law and respect for human rights, including the rights of persons belonging to minorities. These values are common to the Member States in a society in which pluralism, nondiscrimination, tolerance, justice, solidarity and equality between women and men prevail.

What has long been at issue is a reworking of the relationship between individualism and the community. This explains how European social democracy and the labour movement, in order to avoid being marginalized as elsewhere in the world, have always tried to respond to the frequent requests of 'revisionists', outsiders and challengers by dynamically refining this relationship. We can see this over time, from E. Bernstein to A. Gramsci, from H. De Man to O. Bauer, and from the 'Bad Godesberg SPD Programme' of 1959 to the 'revisionists' of today such as A. Giddens.

In utilitarian terms, workers viewed collective organization as a collective power resource that could help them strengthen their position vis-à-vis the employers by reducing their dependency on them and helping them obtain a more equitable social compromise. These notions of solidarity, emanating from European civil society and its ideological traditions, have interacted with the top-down movement of successive transformations of the interventionist state: from Bismarck to Lloyd George and from Gaullism to the Christian Democratic governments of the later twentieth century. They resulted in progressively institutionalized inter-class national compromises, often prompted by wars and economic crises. In the 'golden decades' of the post-war period, they were compatible with the internationalization of Western economies. As a result of this twofold process, we can say that solidarity has become a basic principle of social life, together with liberty and equality. In its connections to other values, such as justice, solidarity also implies the possibility of redistributing wealth on a consensual basis, as has happened in the case of the national Welfare States. The specifically European tradition that couples solidarity with justice must be viewed in the light of this understanding of solidarity. This explains how social justice has come to be understood and implemented in European modern and contemporary history. The linkage of solidarity and justice has therefore represented one of the principal forces shaping modern European institutions.[7]

3.3 A Europe of national Welfare States

How did the idea of solidarity develop across different national scenarios in twentieth-century Europe? It permeated traditions and trends, along with social and political movements, to the point where it profoundly changed the nation state, which in turn became the Welfare State.[8] We can identify four main social, cultural and economic factors which have promoted the theory and practice of social justice based on organized solidarity, associationism and public policy. This conception is specifically European rather than Western, since only in western Europe, over a long historical period, was the traditional economic liberal idea that social success or misfortune might be compensated by an 'invisible hand' re-evaluated and corrected, thanks to the three political traditions mentioned above.

1. Trade unions and mass-based organizations represent the first element of this widespread culture of solidarity.[9] National mobilization in the First World War created the conviction (for the first time) that the sacrifices made by workers had earned them the right to a certain level of protection by the state. The transformation of working conditions between the wars, resulting from the importation of Fordism and Taylorism (i.e. the scientific division and mechanization of manual labour), bolstered organized labour movements and

enhanced their negotiating power enabling them to secure better working conditions and social benefits. These two historical factors – the war and changes in the organization of work – accelerated the development of a vast, secularized labour movement in Europe. Economic crises also played a role both in undermining movements (in 1929 in Germany and elsewhere) or strengthening them (as in Scandinavia). After the Second World War, nowhere else in the world did trade unions become as powerful as in Europe, although rates of unionization have varied from country to country and continue to do so.[10] In the 1990s, more than 70 per cent of workers in Scandinavia were unionized as were 30–35 per cent in Germany, the UK and Italy. In Spain and France, only around 10 per cent of workers are members of a union.

While it is true that the type of trade unionism found in northern Europe and Britain remains different from its ideologically divided version in Mediterranean countries, unions throughout Europe do have common characteristics which are distinct from American trade unionism. In Europe, they cannot be reduced to mere lobbies defending the interests of their members because their role is not limited to the economic sphere, but extends beyond it. European trade unions channel a wide range of demands and operate as territorially organized social and often political actors. Trade unionism is thus a vast social and cultural movement which, for many decades, has achieved more success in Europe than anywhere else. Trade unions have contributed to the reduction of wage inequalities, made working lives more independent of the conjunctural performance of different economic sectors than in other parts of the world, and, to some extent, promoted solidarity between workers and the unemployed. Trade unions also serve important cultural functions by fostering mutual help associations and socio-cultural activities and promoting the concept of free time as a social good. Finally, trade unionism has renewed traditional openness to universalistic moral values, such as democracy, human rights and internationalism. Furthermore, it has supported the Welfare State, consumer interests and, albeit for a long time within the priority of mere 'quantitative growth', environmental protection.

Europe is therefore the only region in the world where the unionized labour movement is historically linked to a variegated, but strong, Christian, secular and predominantly social democratic centre-left, which represents the great majority of the labour movement in all European countries. The special link between trade unionism and social democracy, which is characteristic of western Europe, spread to the east after the Communist regimes began to fall in 1989. Its hallmark is that type of solidarity that was, and continues to be, the practice of millions of people all over Europe. Solidarity has been practised in two main ways. Firstly, solidarity is an association between social classes in order to institutionalize charity and aid. It is a modern version of the traditional idea of solidarity between different social groups. Secondly, solidarity is a practice of negotiation between conflicting social interests, in which trade unions use their collective organized power to negotiate with the power of private ownership wielded by employers. For many decades, this so-called democratic and social 'neo-corporatist' culture of solidarity has influenced not only the social democratic movements of central and northern Europe, but also the Christian unions and parties in many European countries. It has thus helped to stabilize the Welfare State.[11] Naturally, this notion of 'neo-corporatism' should not be confused either with authoritarian ideologies of 'corporatism' or with the defence of particularist interests.

2. The second element from which institutions of solidarity emerged in Europe is Christian social thought. Christian ideas began to directly influence European capitalism with the papal encyclicals *Rerum novarum* (1891) and *Quadragesimo anno* (1931) and with Protestant activism in support of labour organizations in northern Europe. The Catholic social doctrine of corporatism, as an alternative to both market capitalism and socialism, was particularly influential in Belgium, Austria, France, Germany, Italy, Spain and Portugal from the inter-war period up until the 1960s. Catholic inter-class corporatism established alliances with the authoritarian corporatist ideology and Fascist regimes. However, Catholic corporatism was a distinctive version of the traditional conception of solidarity as harmony between different social groups, even if it often had the effect of restricting the actions and identities of social movements.[12]

After the Second World War, liberal Catholicism came to the fore.[13] The new German concept of the 'social market economy', developed primarily by Ludwig Erhardt, the CDU 'Haagen Programme', and the European Christian democratic movements encouraged unions and not just economic elites to promote economic reconstruction and growth by combining market institutions with guarantees of social security. This compromise gained widespread support all over Europe through the influence of Christian democratic parties during the golden years of European welfare capitalism. Moreover, in the 1980s, the method of social dialogue between workers and employers at supranational level, launched by the Catholic President of the European Commission, Jacques Delors, can be seen as an attempt to combine this Christian tradition with the northern European social democratic one of free negotiation between social partners. Delors thus sought to transform both traditions into driving forces of the European integration process.

3. The third element permeating European institutions of social justice is the tradition of social-liberal thought. Already during the nineteenth century, liberal thinkers such as John Stuart Mill, Giuseppe Mazzini and Alexis de Tocqueville had realized that working-class poverty posed a dilemma for liberalism. In the 1920s and 1930s, the idea became prominent that laissez-faire capitalism required checking by some form of public regulation. A section of the economic élites in Europe was sensible and open enough to understand that concessions needed to be made in order to avoid the kind of revolt that might threaten social peace and order. National mobilizations in time of war and the sacrifices requested by the élites made political exclusion and social inequalities intolerable. Concessions could create a more socially peaceful climate, facilitating productivity and competitiveness. In other words, social welfare and economic efficiency could be seen as complementary rather than mutually exclusive, in line with the theories of John Maynard Keynes,[14] Lord Beveridge and others. This ideas proved decisive in persuading many governments that economic and social policies cannot be set in opposition to one another.[15]

4. The convergence of the three strands of thought and action described above resulted in the national economic and social compromises which have characterized European Welfare States for decades. Of course, welfare systems vary according to national traditions and historical factors such as the distinctive mix between the aforementioned ideological traditions, the social compromises established in times of crisis or war, the power resources of different social groups and the international economic and political status of the country. However, these systems also share the following relevant elements, rooted in the common relationship between public democratic authorities, liberal capitalism and the participation of citizens.[16]

Firstly, European welfare models are more independent from the market than their American counterpart. Economic regulation by public authorities was designed to prevent negative consequences of market mechanisms rather than simply curb them after the fact. Secondly, through social partnership, trade unions are able to participate in the decision-making process of jointly managed organizations (which are generally tripartite, including employers and public authorities). Furthermore, organized labour is involved not only in the management of companies (industrial democracy), but also in regional and national systems of economic democracy.[17] This combination of territorial and functional representation therefore makes organized labour a major contributor to the formulation of economic policy, beyond even what has been restrictively termed the 'Rhine model'.[18] European welfare capitalism thus claims to be not only more just, but also more efficient than American market capitalism due to the social peace it guarantees, based on the orchestration of social consensus through the institutions of the Welfare State and social pacts. As early as 1938, American political scientists identified the existence of a 'Scandinavian third way' between market capitalism and state regulation. Indeed, this prefigured the global evolution of post-war western Europe.[19] The comparative literature on the subject comes to the same conclusion, even where it is critical of the bureaucratic and incrementalist drifts resulting from these successes.

Finally, social dialogue is viewed not only as a method, but as a value per se. Politics is conceived as a process of both conflict and deliberation between citizens who can reach consensus regarding their common interest. Concertation is a form of political deliberation applied to the social sphere, which runs complementary to political democracy. It is the foundation of a type of social citizenship that completes political citizenship. Social compromises in northern Europe and Germany are conceived of as an alternative to state regulation: when social partners are able to reach a compromise, there is no need for the state to intervene. The instruments for achieving compromise work best in small European states with consensual forms of democracy such as the Scandinavian countries, Austria and Belgium. The importance of state intervention in France and other Mediterranean countries has far deeper historical roots: however, its continuity is both a consequence of the weakness of social partners and the cause of further weakening, which is compensated for by the culture and practice of top-down legislative intervention by the state. However, the German social model not only shares several important features with the small consensual democracies, but also exerts its influence over the rest of the continent.

The reforms achieved through the establishment of the Welfare States were, in part, the result of the intellectual and progressive influence of the labour movement. Liberal, social democratic and Christian democratic parties had similar objectives after the Second World War and several post-war constitutions support principles of social justice. For decades, conservative governments accepted the 'Keynesian consensus', based on the triad of success represented by sustained economic growth, full employment and reforms designed to strengthen the Welfare State. Even when reforms were introduced by left-wing governments, subsequent conservative administrations did not jettison them. Social consensus was so strong in this golden age of capitalist growth, from the 1940s to the 1970s, that some scholars proclaimed 'the end of ideologies'. This consensus depended, however, on specific international conditions that had been made possible by transatlantic economic growth and the shared practice of 'embedded', restrained and regulated capitalism.

In the second half of the twentieth century, democratic politics in Europe, more than elsewhere, have been essentially influenced by the values of justice and solidarity, albeit according to different national models, conceptualized in different ways.[20] These themes have constituted the common framework around which the main internal political cleavages in the recent history of European states were formed, up until the neo-conservative revolution of the 1980s. Elections have thus represented moments of choice between different conceptions of social justice, within the compromise framework of the Welfare State. The question of the extent to which public authorities should be authorized to regulate social and economic life has long been central to European politics. However, other issues, such as sexual equality, environmental protection and equitable treatment of immigrants, have been widely neglected by the main social and economic actors, in western Europe as elsewhere. Despite these historical limits, welfare capitalism and social dialogue were and remain distinctive features of Europe's international identity.

3.4   The European socio-economic model and the challenges of the neo-conservative revolution

The 1980s were a crucial test for the European social model. Social, technological and demographic changes were accompanied by the double challenge of neo-conservatism and 'Reaganism' on the one hand and the consequences of the breakdown of communism on the other.

'Stagflation' and the new monetarist credo put an end to the golden age of 'Keynesian' regulation and social compromise and challenged the view that economic and social policies are interdependent and complementary.

The neo-conservative political and intellectual revolution had two dimensions. From an economic viewpoint, the idea prevailed that social norms and state regulations are detrimental to economic growth, except in the case of 'regulation aimed at deregulation'. Partly due to their ability to accelerate technological innovation, the American and British economies have boasted better macroeconomic results (in terms of growth, productivity and employment rates) than the economies of continental Europe. Mainstream economists observe that, as a result of deregulation and more flexible labour markets, these economies have been able to markedly reduce their unemployment rates, although the quality of the new jobs and their precarious nature are a controversial subject.[21] However, the neo-conservative revolution was also a moral ideology and led to the resurgence of old conceptions of social life. In Great Britain, 'Thatcherism'[22] revived the arguments of the nineteenth century, according to which the poor are responsible for their condition and social services do little other than encourage inactivity and stifle economic efficiency and competitiveness. Consequently, mutual help was to be replaced by self-help, and social regulation was to be reduced to a minimum. This was consistent with a new individualistic ideology promoting the sovereignty of the individual consumer and the privatization of industrial relations, all of which contributed to the development of new inequalities.[23]

These two dimensions of the neo-conservative revolution posed a challenge to traditional political forces and their corresponding cultural traditions in Europe: social Christian, social democratic and social liberal. Their strength lay in their consistency with endogenous and exogenous changes which challenged the very roots of the Welfare State and reformism[24] and the very pillars of the 'great transformation' from the 1930s to the 1970s.[25] The first challenge came from within. The growing social complexity was accompanied by technological and demographic changes which stimulated new social demands. Although overplayed by the media, a vast consensus grew up that work is no longer the primary factor defining the social identity of individuals. This is due, firstly, to the deindustrialization process in post-industrial societies and, secondly, to the reduced significance of work as a value. New social movements developed around new demands and values, such as increased individual freedom and consumer and civil rights. The feminist movement, for example, has become a major political actor both at national and transnational levels. Political participation among the new middle classes tends to centre on individual issues, such as the environment, public health and civil rights, whereas new categories of the poor are ignored by most political parties and may be tempted to support populist and extremist movements. At the same time, employers continue to introduce new technologies leading to the decentralization of factories and prefer to negotiate salaries on an individual or small group basis.

Against this background, trade unions encounter huge difficulties in adapting to new and emerging conflicts.[26] The modes of collective action are changing. Trade unions and political parties are losing members, not only because new technologies promote individualism and reduce the number of employees, but also because economic life is becoming increasingly privatized and new social movements are emerging outside traditional political frameworks and cleavages. The importance of national mass parties is declining in so far as they increasingly resemble the 'catch-all party' along the lines of the American model envisaged by Otto Kirchheimer in the 1960s. Opposition from employers and the critical relationship between trade unions and social democratic and Christian democratic parties in recent years have weakened the traditional social pacts supporting welfare policies. New forms of citizen participation have developed. The declining international authority of the state has weakened social covenants and the ability of traditional collective actors such as trade unions to meet the demands of the majority of the population. Demographic changes and ageing populations, combined with declining employment rates and the effects of the various immigration flows from Africa, eastern Europe and the Near East, also pose a challenge for national welfare systems which were born within relatively homogeneous societies.

The second type of challenge came from outside Europe. Although, from a quantitative perspective, the global economy barely exceeds 20 per cent of the GDP of all countries in the world, the qualitative impact of the globalization of commerce and markets on finance and technology became significant and is likely to increase considerably. The range and salience of globalization are often exaggerated for political reasons in order to justify cuts to welfare programmes in national budgets. Nevertheless, initiatives aimed at promoting social justice inevitably have to take into account the pressure of new interdependencies, ICT technologies, the unification of world markets, the influence of multinational companies and the gradual retreat of the state as an agent of social and economic regulation. These trends were and are located in what the economist John Williamson in 1990 termed 'the Washington consensus' (Washington being the seat of the IMF), i.e. financial liberalization, the decline of the labour movement, privatization, the total opening of economies to capital flows and the removal of all obstacles to global competition.[27]

Despite these formidable external pressures, important European states have managed to retain greater control over their national economies than others, and the decline of traditional state sovereignty has not dramatically weakened the role of all public authorities in regulating social and economic affairs. The era of national economic regulation according to the classical Keynesian model has effectively come to an end. In economic matters, a part of legal authority and effective governance capacity is being transferred from national states to other institutions. Private multinational companies and business networks are becoming increasingly important and have led to the deregulation of labour relations. At the same time, supranational and international organizations are seeking to carve out new positions as technocratic powers. This trend has led to the development of a critical strand in public opinion, which includes the perception of a democratic deficit in the EU as a result of the widening gap between citizens and supranational technocracies.

As mentioned earlier, globalization is an ambiguous process. It encourages the convergence of technologies, lifestyles and social and economic standards while also fostering divergences. Changing economic and social systems and the spread of new communications technologies have contributed to the emergence of new identity claims along with new social and political demands. States and international organizations are looking for new compromises that can reconcile these internal demands and fears with their pressing need to adapt themselves to fundamental changes imposed from outside. At times, their authority is weakened and broken up, at other times it finds new dimensions, as can be seen in the various models of supranational integration (as a form of deregulation or 're-regulation'?) and 'competitor state'(through social and fiscal dumping or as state-led modernization policies?).[28] As regards the reaction to globalization, citizens and interest groups are adjusting differently to the new equilibrium between the markets and public authorities. Some actors, such as private lobbies and transnational companies, are more successful than others in this new globalized scenario. Trade unions and political parties find it more difficult to play a role in highly complex multi-level systems. For example, the competition between cities and regions to attract capital flows through social, fiscal and environmental dumping weakens class ties and national solidarity and increases competition, even within the same state.

Given the uncertainty of the current situation, we can identify a number of different possible scenarios for the future of the European socio-economic model. One is that the majority of peoples and states in Europe will call for the EU to be turned almost into a fortress through the implementation of a defensive trade policy (often defined as neo-mercantilism). This would be aimed at protecting domestic markets from global competition, as well as meeting internal social demands for full employment and distributive justice and/or defending non-competitive economic sectors in agriculture and industry. Fearing globalization, sectors of the labour movement tend to seek protection against the anonymous forces of the global market through state policies promising to preserve and extend justice and solidarity. This can involve building barriers against the free market and, sometimes, against immigration. Such a scenario would cause profound social and political divisions both within the EU and its member states.

Another possibility, in contrast to the previous scenario, is that Europe simply becomes a free trade area, subordinated to globalization and globalism dominated by the US. The internal consequences of this would include the watering down of 'positive integration' and cohesion policies, along with new limits to supranational institutions, policies and procedures. Even 'negative' supranational integration would be halted as far as its spillover effects are concerned. These would facilitate a return to the classic diplomatic game between member states, which would be exacerbated by recourse to the conflicting strategies of 'competitor states'. The relinquishing of common social and economic strategies would lead to the erosion of traditional European modes of social dialogue. This type of change could pave the way for the subordination of European economic and social justice models to standards and parameters that are typically American in origin and nature. The resulting collapse of the European achievements of social cohesion would lead to the fragmentation of social groups (which would be reduced to mere particularistic lobbies), the end of social peace and, possibly, significant populist reactions.

A third possibility is that Europe will develop a new type of regional socio-economic identity that reconciles social regulation and international openness by finding an original equilibrium between the defence of its values and democratic institutions on the one hand, and the necessary opening-up to the global free market on the other. Within that pioneering perspective, the member states and the EU face the following interrelated challenges: to strike a new balance between economic deregulation and re-regulation which is an improvement on that achieved to date at national level; to reform national Welfare States and develop a new sophisticated regional experiment where Europeans can still pursue their common values of justice and solidarity within the context of an increasingly global economy; to implement a modern European 'knowledge society', combining convergence among member states with 'competitive solidarity'.

The success of such an innovative policy also depends upon the evolution of Europe as a social union. The term 'social union' encompasses two distinct elements, one supranational and one national. The supranational element is constrained by the limited budget of the EU and the even more restricted treaty provisions it is granted by member states. From the outset, European treaties have made reference to justice and social cohesion.[29] Both the Structural Funds and the Common Agricultural Policy (now source of much dispute due to its cost and protectionist character) have been important elements of EC/EU transregional solidarity in helping to develop the poorer regions of western and southern Europe. The integration process has created a degree of transnational solidarity. The Treaty of Rome (1957), for example, stipulated that migrant workers from another member state had to be given the same social rights as home citizens. This has facilitated the integration of migrant workers from southern Europe (such as Italians) into northern European countries. From the outset, the EU budget, despite being limited to a maximum of only 1.27 per cent of the GDP of member states, has redistributed funds internally to redress the wealth imbalances between richer and poorer areas, to improve the economic condition of sectors such as agriculture (which still accounted for almost 50 per cent of the EU budget in 2004), and to tackle internal socio-economic disparities through the Structural Funds (about 25 per cent of the budget in 2004). There is much evidence to suggest that the EU budget requires radical reform if it is to meet the three above-mentioned challenges.[30]

Employment, welfare and wage policies remain predominantly national competencies, apart from restricted areas where European directives have been implemented, such as safety in the workplace, equality of men and women in employment, and consultation of workers in processes of industrial restructuring. In all other respects, the Union is restricted to what we could term the 'social dimension of the large domestic market'. In 1989, the Social Charter was drawn up. This was taken up in the European Charter of Fundamental Rights proclaimed by the Nice European Council in 2000, incorporated into the 2004 Constitutional Treaty. In 1992, the Social Protocol, signed on the same day as the Maastricht Treaty, institutionalized the 'social dialogue' (informally introduced in Val Duchesse some years before) between employer associations, trade unions and the Commission. The UK only accepted the inclusion of the Social Protocol in the Treaty in 1997, following the Labour Party's victory in the British general election of the same year. The Social Chapter forms the legal basis for a new system of European social regulation, through the participation and prior agreement of social partners.[31] We will take a closer look later at another aspect of the Amsterdam Treaty: the coordination of national employment policies, launched at the Luxembourg European Council in December 1997.

In fact, the main challenge facing an enlarged Europe of 25 or 30 member states will be the coordination of national welfare and economic policies. Not only are these countries new to the culture of democratic federalism, but they are also defensive of their recently gained sovereignty. That is why it is unrealistic to expect an expansion of the 'community method' of supranational integration, particularly as far as social policy is concerned. The eastern expansion of the EU is often seen as a serious threat to traditional European mechanisms of social solidarity. The cost of cohesion policies on such a large scale and the growing disparity within the Union between standards of living, welfare and consumption levels and degrees of labour organization are all factors which appear to favour mere 'negative integration' rather than common social policies. Nonetheless, the European social model looks attractive in eastern Europe, for all the new members but Slovakia, and this test bed should be viewed as a chance to examine, almost on a continental scale, the degree to which the European social model can spread and expand beyond its previous borders, through the coordination of countries at the centre and on the peripheries of Europe.

Successful enlargement would provide a considerable part of the EU's contribution to global governance. In this context, however, the challenge of how to regulate the relationship between reform of the European social model within an enlarged EU on the one hand, and globalization on the other, becomes both more complex and more urgent. Secondly, through its external relations, the Union is trying to marry its internal modes of solidarity with support for multilateral global policies designed to narrow the gap in wealth and social amenities between North and South in the world. Within the third scenario, the EU is seeking more coherent ways to help reform and coordinate the policies of multilateral trade, labour and financial institutions, such as the ILO, WTO, IMF and the World Bank. We refer to this EU, combining internal cohesion and external solidarity, which is committed to cooperating with weaker regions and helping them boost their economic and political stability, as the 'world's Scandinavia', referring to the role played by Scandinavian countries in Europe since the end of the Second World War.

Is this last scenario a mere Utopian dream? It would be premature, for several reasons, to jump to such a conclusion, as we argued during our earlier discussion of the current EU civilian power (see section 1.8). In the current uncertain international climate, however, this civilian influence needs to become more coherent, more competitive and politically tougher. Europe is not an island in the global economy. Indeed, its proportion of the world's population will decrease from 13 per cent in 1993 to 9 per cent in 2025. This demographic change in itself requires that classic ideas of justice and solidarity be reconsidered in a new framework which takes account of international socio-economic trends, migrations and the risks and opportunities arising from globalization. Only by renewing its concept of modernization and the balance between international competitiveness and justice can the EU hope to shape the whole continent and influence others, along with democratically regulating its domestic market and contributing to a reform of global governance.

The historical conditions exist for the development of a new kind of European regionalism which is open to the rest of the world, but proud of its own socio-economic identity as a proactive and innovative factor in global governance.[32] The crucial test, however, will lie in its capacity to reach new compromises between tradition and technological innovation, economic productivity and social cohesion, the state and the market, and deregulation and re-regulation. All this must occur within an innovative framework and be undertaken with the same spirit of courage and originality that saw the construction of the EC and, in parallel, the establishment of the various national Welfare State systems in Europe.

3.5   Reforming the European social model: national and European solutions

As we have highlighted, solidarity mechanisms have rarely transcended the boundaries of nation states and, even then, only in very limited ways. This is due to the fact that social and employment policies remain predominantly national competencies. Nevertheless, all member states are facing the same challenges of international competition, globalization, falling birth rates and the demographic implications of an ageing population, etc. And all looking for similar solutions. This convergence between European government agendas has intensified since the early 1990s when the Maastricht Treaty established the criteria for joining European Monetary Union.

The key question throughout Europe is whether the specificity of the European social model, or rather of European social models, belongs to the past or whether it can be adapted to the partially globalized world of the twenty-first century. The answer partly depends on another question: can European countries import lock, stock and barrel the competitive American social and economic model which, during the boom of the new economy in the 1990s, posted faster rates of growth and employment than Europe? The comparison between EU countries and the US shows that different economic models reflect different social and institutional environments. These, in turn, reflect different values and strategic choices regarding the form globalization should take at domestic level. For example, while wage differentials in Europe remained stable in the 1980s and 1990s, the poor and the lower middle classes in the United States lost about a quarter of their wealth. This is not just a consequence of economic change, it is also the result of political options that derive from different traditions of justice and solidarity. These contradictions explain why such issues, which have been at the heart of political debate in Europe for many years, have not yet been able to find consensus solutions.

Within the context of a globalizing economy, how can public goods continue to be provided in Europe on the basis of a specific equilibrium between public authorities and private economic actors, organized democracy and technological innovation? Under what conditions can social democracy, Christian social doctrine and social liberalism continue to inspire the search for new forms of social equilibrium at subnational, national and supranational levels, notwithstanding the changes of the 1980s and 1990s?[33] The serious dilemmas facing social solidarity, between internal demands and external commitments, require responses which do not reflect defensive and introverted visions or overly Eurocentric internationalism.[34]

Various combinations of social security and economic flexibility have proved effective in the Netherlands, Scandinavia and the UK, while voluntarist, state-led employment policies have been implemented in France, Belgium and Germany. In all these cases, with the exception of

France, national social pacts between trade unions, employers and governments have been revitalized and play a crucial role in stabilizing domestic consensus. The innovative element is that these pacts are often instituted locally or regionally, rather than only at national level. They are renegotiated on a regular basis and are sometimes open to new actors and tackle new issues, such as environmental policy, consumer rights, etc. Important parts of the public sector have been privatized, but the Welfare State is still preferred to an American-style welfare system which provides assistance only to the poorest and most marginalized sections of the community. Despite these common features, national fiscal policies in Europe differ greatly in terms of the balance they strike between reducing taxes, cutting indirect labour costs, introducing new progressive taxes such as eco-taxes and increasing funding for pensions.

Major challenges lie ahead for European social models and the EU, whose international reputation partly relies on its social policy successes. The prospect of a single European Welfare State for all of Europe is completely unrealistic, given the deep-rooted influence of national traditions. The main question therefore is: what kind of solidarity can be conceived and implemented at transnational and supranational levels? In other words, what kind of mixed, multi-level system of governance would be most appropriate and what would be the respective role of nation states, regions, local authorities, and the system of supranational government?

It is clear that states and regions must play their part by reforming their national and subnational solidarity systems in order to adapt to the recent structural changes in the world economy. But what is the role of the EU? Can it counterbalance the negative impact of international market forces by introducing new European public policies or mainly by coordinating national policies? If it fails, not only will the EU see its democratic deficit increase, but it will also see its 'substantive legitimacy' diminish.[35]

3.6   The question of convergence: the 'Lisbon Strategy' and the 'Open Method of Coordination'

The reason for the large international interest in the 'Lisbon Strategy 2000–10' (despite the shortcomings revealed at its mid-term evaluation) is that its very essence is the attempt to provide an innovative and common response to this important set of questions and to the dilemmas which paralysed the EU in the 1990s. The European Council finally acknowledged in March 2000 that, in terms of technological and economic achievements, Europe was lagging dramatically behind the new economy of the US. That is why the European Council launched a ten-year socio-economic modernization programme aimed at promoting a European knowledge economy according to distinctive European values, that is greater European convergence, while also respecting national differences. The Lisbon European Council concluded that a global long-term strategy is required to fundamentally restructure the European socio-economic model. This strategy includes regional, national and European common policies, all converging towards the same shared objectives. New common work methods are also required, given the desire of states for greater convergence but also their unwillingness to delegate more powers to supranational authorities. This gave rise to the innovative proposal to introduce the Open Method of Coordination (OMC), i.e. a new form of European governance which merits further attention.[36]

Why is there a need for greater European convergence? This was a valid question even before the rise of neo-nationalist and populist right-wing movements in Europe indicated increased support for an explicit renationalization of policies. In fact, although it may seem obvious to convinced Europhiles, the prospect solemnly proclaimed in the Preamble to the Treaty of Rome of 'an ever closer union among the peoples of Europe' is far from being an intrinsic value of public opinion in many European states. It is even less important to those not in the Eurozone and who really do not want EMU to lead to any greater economic and social union. Very convincing arguments (as well as common interests and also utilitarian reasons) must be put forward, therefore, if all European governments are to be persuaded to allow the Union to tackle key questions such as economic and technological modernization and the reform of the Welfare State. While these themes are increasingly central to national agendas, they are also areas in which the Union has very limited competencies. Consensus was reached, however, at the Lisbon European Council for the following three reasons, which emerged from extensive dialogue between the EU political agenda and experts from the social sciences.[37]

Firstly, the urgency of the external threat proved significant as it was perceived as a common interest. In the run-up to Lisbon, the Helsinki European Council (December 1999) had forcibly stated that Europe was lagging behind in the construction of an 'information society'. The was reflected in the low European growth rates compared to those of the US and an unemployment rate in Europe which was double that of the US. These poor results can be partly explained by the fact that new ICTs are being rolled out at a much slower pace in Europe and are not being used as productively as in the US. Following a classic model that recalls Servan-Schreiber's 'American challenge' or Albert's 'two capitalisms', and that has nothing to do with anti-Americanism, we can identify the threat of a decline in the relative competitive position of the EU compared to the US and Japan as the key consideration. Not only does this provide the main incentive in overcoming resistance to a great 'leap forward' of European convergence, it might also help generate a kind of civic patriotism towards Europe as it embarks on a new modernization path within the context of global competition.

Secondly, by 2000, the 'costs of a non-Europe' that is of insufficient convergence and the attachment of some European governments to the model of the competitor state were already becoming apparent. Within the EU, states are aware that, now more than ever, information is a source of wealth and power and some states are using new technologies to strengthen their competitiveness at any cost. Hence, rather than being an extraordinary resource for development, ICTs represent another divisive element, both on a global scale and within the EU, by extending the costly and destructive competition between member states (already present in fiscal and social policies) into the field of technology. The decline of internal cohesion threatens to damage the market, the euro and European solidarity, i.e. common values and interests.

The third reason is more controversial and concerns the sustainability of national Welfare States. Even though some scholars continue to defend the importance and credibility of national policies in maintaining and adapting the national Welfare State, there is an emerging awareness that such defensive strategies are too fragile in the context both of global competition and the deregulatory force of European law.[38]

The combination of these three factors discussed above gradually convinced the entire European Council – from the centre-left governments which were the clear majority at the time (including Blair and the Franco-German alliance) to conservatives like Aznar – to work towards greater coordination of medium and long-term national modernization policies. This does not constitute a new 'process' in addition to those of Luxembourg (employment policy), Cologne (macroeconomic policy) and Cardiff (economic policy), but rather coordinates these processes within a coherent ten-year strategy. It represents a significant turning point and an initiative which is more than mere rhetoric. It could relaunch the EU at the highest level of technological competition, with progressive objectives relating to the information society, R&D, economic reforms, social cohesion and innovation. This would also have the effect of reducing the two great asymmetries of the Maastricht Treaty: (a) between a highly federalized Monetary Union and a still decentralized economic union; (b) between EMU as a whole and social union, i.e. deeper integration between European societies.

3.7   Modernization policies for a European model of a knowledge society

The choice of method to be used in applying the Lisbon Strategy is relevant both for the future of European integration and for the communication between the EU and other regional associations abroad. The new Open Method of Coordination was, at least during the period from 2000 to 2005, the sine qua non for the unanimous vote of the European Council, thus confirming the central role of governance issues. This ambitious 'ten-year strategy to make the EU the world's most dynamic and competitive economy according to European values' is aimed at helping states formulate and implement better national policies with a stronger European bent. The famous Delors Commission White Paper in late 1993 had also been intended to 'square the circle', by reconciling competitiveness with social cohesion. Despite its merits, however, it was not implemented. In part, this was because no new methodology was then formulated that could break down opposition within the European Council.[39] The strategic innovation of Lisbon, already formulated by the Presidency as a global strategy in January 2000, was approved in March 2000, and relaunched by the spring European Council of Gothenburg (2001) and Barcelona (2002) and Brussels (2003, 2004 and 2005). It consisted of several complementary policies:

- modernization policies (lifelong learning, social protection, the fight against social exclusion, research and development, active employment policies, education and training policy, democratization of internet access, etc.);
- 'negative integration' and deregulation (energy, gas, electricity, etc.);
- a new economic policy mix aimed at stability, featuring in particular, for the first time after a decade of austerity, policies supporting macroeconomic growth (objective: 3 per cent);

- microeconomic measures: reform of the financial markets, support for business (especially small and medium enterprises), technological innovation, e-commerce;
- reform of national social models and relaunching of social dialogue, in response to common technological and demographic challenges;[40]
- striking a dynamic balance between economic and environment policy.

The extremely delicate combination between common European objectives and indicators and diverse national starting points is sought by means of an innovative method. This is the new Open Method of Coordination (OMC) of national policies, which is proposed as a kind of halfway point between, and complementary to, the community method and simple intergovernmental cooperation. The new method includes various social actors and hinges on the principle of respect for national differences. The origins of the OMC can be traced back to the multilateral 'monitoring of policies' agreed by the Council in 1997 and which had been implemented by the 'Luxembourg Process'. This innovation, called the 'European Employment Strategy' (EES), had already been outlined at Essen in 1994, but was only codified in 1997 by the Employment Chapter (Title VIII, art. 125–130 ECT) of the Amsterdam Treaty and put into practice by the Luxembourg Council of Europe (December 1997). The EES is well known for its frequent warnings to defaulting states. The second legal roots of the new method are to be found in article 99 of the EC Treaty, which regulates the approval and implementation of Broad Economic Policy Guidelines (BEPG). It also provides for multilateral supervision of national economic policies. The European Councils of Lisbon and Feira in 2000 brought in four innovations.[41]

1. Given this limited legal background, the OMC was specified with regard to four stages and sought to stress its 'openness' with respect to national and regional differences, social and economic forces and civil society[42]:

   (a) The Council sets out common European guidelines for the short, medium and long term of the policy in question.
   (b) The Council formulates quantitative and qualitative indicators, deadlines and terms of reference through *benchmarking* (designed to link objectives with deadlines) in order to disseminate national best practices and foster reciprocal emulation.

(c) As a result, each government must draw up a national plan for each policy, aimed at translating common guidelines into specific national and regional targets.

(d) At regular intervals, the Council organizes a monitoring and evaluation process of the progress (relative to particular national contexts) made by each government. In certain cases, it may issue critical recommendations to governments.

The Commission actively participates in the process, particularly with regard to points (a), (b) and (d).

2. A wider application of the strategy is adopted for employment policies, the knowledge society, economic reforms, lifelong education and training, research and development (with the aim of creating a 'European Research Area'). Albeit with greater difficulty, this also extends to enterprise policies, sensitive areas of welfare policies such as social inclusion, pensions and, at some point in the future, public health policies.

3. The Broad Economic Policy Guidelines (BEPG) approved once a year by the ECOFIN Council, are intended to create greater synergy between macroeconomic, structural and employment policies. However, they must themselves be integrated into a global strategy 'designed to promote growth, employment and social cohesion, as well as the transition to a knowledge economy'.

4. For the ten years following the introduction of the strategy, the spring European Council has the task of evaluating progress in its implementation, including the BEPG, and relaunching it for the following year. This evaluation is carried out on the basis of a Commission synthesis report which includes common indicators and deadlines.[43] In Gothenburg in 2001, the Council decided to include an environmental dimension as a third criterion qualifying modernization. In 2002 in Barcelona, the original strategy was reinforced when the controversial energy deregulations were counterbalanced by a commitment to the importance of public services and the famous 'Galileo Project' (fundamental to the political autonomy of the EU in the field of satellite technologies). In Brussels in March 2003 further progress was made in integrating the various areas of application of the OMC, a topic which we will return to later. The Brussels spring European Council in 2004 further harmonized the various policies. The mid-term evaluation of the Brussels European Council in 2005 relaunched the early objectives, adapting them to the enlarged EU and strengthening national implementation and its monitoring.

3.8   The Lisbon agenda implementation: achievements and shortcomings

Five years are not sufficient in order to draw firm conclusions on the Lisbon Strategy, particularly as the optimistic objectives in 2000 for economic growth have had to be revised in the light of an unfavourable international economic climate. Indeed, for the first time, the priority attached to tackling excessive public deficits, set out in the 1992 Treaty and the 1997 Stability and Growth Pact, has been called into question. The quite positive view, prevalent in the already extensive international literature up to 2004,[44] is based on the improvement in employment rates (5 million jobs created in the first three years), the spread of technological innovation, progress in deregulating the energy market, and the launch of various national plans promoting consistent policies in areas such as employment and social inclusion. Other achievements include new strategies for the modernization of competition policy, the improvements of the European financial market, the 'single sky' directive, the advances made in coordinating national lifelong education, the first small steps towards coordinating national pension system and public health reforms, as well as some advances in coordinating and enhancing research programmes towards a European Research Area.[45]

   The flexibility of the strategy itself has been a positive element, as it is enriched by the different priorities of various Presidencies; however, it risks fragmenting its coherence. As regards the OMC, it applies, albeit in very different ways, to a number of areas and it has even spread to other key sectors where governments have no intention of ceding competencies to the EU.[46] Moreover, it proved a relevant issue in Convention debates of 2002–3. The OMC has been welcomed for many reasons. It is a means towards European integration, primarily in the field of socio-economics. Governments are keen to import best practices from other countries in order to improve policy efficiency and increase domestic public support. Moreover, as R. Keohane observed, the strength of soft governance is that it fosters interdependence and offers governments greater incentives to gain influence in important policy areas, which in turn explains government readiness to tolerate the cost of restricted national autonomy. Although it is significantly less stringent than the EMU's regulative framework, there is some evidence that the OMC exerts both a moral and political pressure on governments, from the Council's guidelines discussions, to the elaboration and implementation of coherent national plans, as well as the obvious pressure exerted by the Commission in its role as the monitoring and issuing body of critical recommendations which various actors (such as the media, parliamentary opposition, social groups, etc.) may bring to the attention of the public at national level.[47]

Three main difficulties have emerged however:

1. The fragmentation of the various reform and innovation policies resulting from the intricate European multi-level governance system. This is partly due to the distinct responsibility of various specialized councils and the clear inability of the General Affairs Council in its current format (made up of national foreign ministers) to provide horizontal coordination of these bodies.
2. The tendency of the ECOFIN Council (composed of national finance ministers) to compensate for this fragmentation by imposing through the BEPG a de facto hierarchy under its leadership, that is under the 'Stability and Growth Pact', as a problematic framework for the various policy sectors.
3. An implementation deficit: the consistency between government commitments made in Brussels and their actual national policies is not what it expected.

This has two clear implications: on the one hand, as regards the compromise struck in Lisbon between 'deregulation' and 'positive' integration, we can see a shift towards deregulation policies, with destabilizing consequences for the balance between the economic and social/environmental aspects of the strategy. Moreover, the very aim of the Lisbon conclusions is called into question in terms of the political will to match the global character of the strategy with coherent management, i.e. *political* management, over and above the various specialized councils, including ECOFIN. This was the main reason for the role attributed to the European Council as the key body for policy orientation (including the BEPG) and strategic leadership.

What then emerges from the Commission's annual synthesis report in 2003 and 2004 and the Wim Kok mid-term report *Facing the Challenge* in November 2004 regarding the overall performance of the Lisbon Strategy? First, the Lisbon agenda is strongly reaffirmed at the heart of European socio-economic modernization; second, there is a clear and urgent need to adapt it in the light of an enlarged EU, the national implementation deficit, and the increasing gap in relation to the modernization trends of US and Japan. Greater synchronism is called for between the different strands of the Lisbon Strategy regarding the deadlines for benchmarking and schedules, which should be fostered by social dialogue and redeployed on a three-year rather than an annual cycle. This regards European guidelines, national plans and monitoring. Finally, the priorities are redefined. These are employment policies (which, given the poor economic climate, assume a more central role), industrial policy and the promotion of an 'enterprise culture', economic reform and completion of the Single Market, the balance between competitiveness and public services, the importance of sustainable development, the relaunch of social protection and inclusion (the fight against poverty in the second cycle of the national plans), and, finally, pension system reform and research development, both in line with the OMC.[48] However, in 2005, as a result of its mid-term evaluation, it is absolutely clear that the Lisbon Strategy necessitates a rethinking of the relationship between the Commission and the Council (as far as the leadership is concerned), a clearer assumption of responsibilities by national governments and regions, as regards implementation, as well as a greater openness to social and parliamentary actors, both at European and national levels.

The key to striking a good balance between the various policies lies, therefore, both in the centrality of the question of leadership and in the issue of openness of the coordination method to the public. There is, therefore, a strong link between socio-economic policy and the institutional framework. That explains why conflicting approaches emerged as regards practical governance and Constitutional Treaty reform.

3.9   The controversy surrounding supranational European democracy

The leadership and democratic deficits of the modernization strategy are closely related. In fact, the kind of fragmentation discussed above does little other than exacerbate the democratic deficit which has been criticized (for different reasons) by both the European Parliament ('Bullmann Report', II, 2002) and organized social actors like the ETUC and UNICE. However, the democratic legitimacy of the Lisbon Strategy and the OMC is a controversial issue in the academic community. Its achievement would constitute a substantial relegitimization not only of the strategy, but of the EU itself. As regards the legitimacy by participation, both Scharpf and Moravcsik, among others, deny that this is provoking a democratic deficit as both the strategy and the method are essentially intergovernmental and both the European Council and the Council of Ministers have full legitimacy based on national democratic procedures.[49] Other commentators, however, are of the opinion that the

Lisbon Strategy is also developing in the transnational and supranational dimensions, according to a multi-level governance system that involves not only national governments, but other actors including the Commission, transnational social and economic interest coalitions, etc.[50] As a result, the call to integrate national legitimacy (through national parliaments and national social pacts) with greater and more transparent supranational legitimacy seems justified in the context of a European form of democracy which is itself transnational and supranational.[51]

Reducing the democratic deficit could also help to create greater policy efficiency. A process of internal aggregation of the various demands of social and political participation would counter the current fragmentation and would provide a catalyst for more authoritative leadership, both from a reorganized Commission as well as from the European Council. In concrete terms, besides strengthening the powers of control of national parliaments over their respective ministers, it has been requested to reduce the valid frustrations of the European Parliament regarding the control of social and economic government.[52] Two suggestions for improvement have been made:

1. An annual session of the EP could be dedicated to discussion of the modernization strategy. This would follow meetings of various representative bodies, not only involving the COSAC (delegations from national parliaments), but other concerned standing committees of national parliaments, the Committee of the Regions, the Economic and Social Committee and the Social Forum. There also needs to be a broad process of consultation with national and transnational public opinion on the different options for the European model in the context of globalization. Ideally, this EP session would conclude with a vote, before the spring European Council, as in 2000.[53]
2. As regards social legitimacy, a new tripartite central organization should replace or integrate the many fragmented current modes of dialogue with organized social actors, thereby strengthening the legitimacy and coherence of the strategy. For example, by institutionalizing the 'European Social Forum' (the tripartite meeting which precedes the spring European Council) and making it a reference point for national and regional social tripartite fora on the Lisbon Strategy.

It is not, therefore, solely a question of increasing the input, in quantitative terms, of actors in the decision-making process, but of structuring their participation in order to enhance their impact on key decisions. This would have the effect of strengthening the joint leadership of the strategy. Otherwise, the mere proliferation of appeals for greater democratic participation and checks would end up reducing the efficiency of the strategy and result in its greater fragmentation and weakened political leadership. The open question remains of whether strengthening the leadership and the role of the Commission is just one of the many issues that need to be resolved in the area of informal and practical governance or whether the issue at stake in fact demands revising the treaties.

3.10   The 'mixed government' of socio-economic modernization

The search for compromise between intergovernmental procedures and a more significant role for the Commission has prompted discussion of a 'third way' between the community method and simple intergovernmental cooperation. This would constitute a new form of governance: a kind of 'oriented subsidiarity'. In fact, the July 2001 'Commission White Paper' affirms that the OMC already offers the possibility of 'joint management' of policies between the EU and national governments.[54]

The European Council has taken up the role of strategic leader, posing many practical and institutional questions (with regard to the Council and to the Commission),[55] as well as providing and renewing the necessary political impetus on a regular basis. The legitimacy conferred on the European Council by the willingness of heads of state and government is indisputable. So too, however, are the risks assumed by governments arising from their involvement in a new regime of European interaction which is aimed at greater convergence. This regime gives the Commission greater room for manoeuvre along with exposing the actions of governments to monitoring, criticism and 'recommendations' from Brussels which, while not legally binding, can still have significant political implications. Certainly, some governments make use of 'European directives' as a kind of scapegoat to help public opinion digest unpopular reforms. However, this kind of 'abuse' along with divisive choices which run contrary to social consensus catch up with governments after a while and the broad impact of Europe on national societies tends to be centripetal and consensual. This is also due to the fact that it is becoming ever more evident that the role of the Commission has been growing since 2000. Even in the context of European Council leadership, the role of the Commission is the factor that distinguishes the OMC from the mere benchmarking technique employed by other multilateral, intergovernmental organizations such as the OECD, the ILO and the IMF. In fact, through its annual synthesis report to the spring European Council and other decentralized inputs and offices, and given the lack of continuity implied by a different Presidency every semester, the Commission is fulfilling an ever greater role in providing expertise, initiative and coordination of various policies. It is also playing the part of 'guardian' of the coherence and continuity of the strategy.[56]

The Commission will be able to carry out this task if its way of working can be retuned[57] in line with a few essential priorities and backed up by treaty reform. This *recentrage* should be complemented by provisions strengthening the responsibility of states as regards national policy implementation, in line with the Wim Kok report, *Facing the Challenge* (2004), and the March 2005 Presidency Conclusions. A final point to note regards a political priority accepted by the Commission, i.e. the revision of the relationship between the Lisbon Strategy and the Stability and Growth Pact, with the aim of ensuring a more favourable and dynamic macroeconomic climate. The recurring tensions since 2000 (and which have been exacerbated by the economic climate from 2003 to 2005) regarding French and German budget deficits and the creeping hierarchization of policy-making could perhaps be mitigated by establishing a more balanced link between stability and research investments. Gunnar Myrdal explained back in 1932–33 the rationality of anti-recessionary policies, provided that their quality is assured, which currently means, policies for investments and research. The problem of the mid-term revision of the Lisbon Strategy is, however, that it is simultaneously facing the above-mentioned macroeconomic urgency, the domestic implementation deficit of 11 'Lisbon' related policies, the EU debate on the budget and cohesion and an enhanced international competition. Only a mixed government would have the chance to combine all the conditions of coping with such a multiple challenge.

3.11   The impact of the 'Lisbon Strategy' on the international role and identity of the EU: the case of research policy

According to Georg Gadamer, science has shaped the form of European history, and is defining the modern European identity, as distinct from art, religion and philosophy (*Das Erbe Europas*, 1989). If research policy is at the heart of the strategy to build a European knowledge economy

The Heart of European Integration   183

that is not only because research and innovation are the main driving forces behind both successful socio-economic modernization and improving external competitiveness. According to the Lisbon Strategy, the European knowledge economy will be characterized by the following distinctive features:

(a) consistency with the values of social cohesion and opposition to new digital divides;
(b) reforming, and not dismantling, the special link between research and public higher education institutions, including the development and improvement of partnership agreements with the private sector;
(c) developing democracy: making access to ICT as broad as possible (involving lifelong learning, reforming the public administration);
(d) combining support of excellence with dissemination.

These objectives have huge potential international implications as far as the EU's global role is concerned, beyond mere trade policy. A European knowledge economy, if achieved, would strengthen plurality within the partially globalized economy, and increase the strategic autonomy of Europe, as both a regional and a global research power.[58]

The spring 2002 Barcelona European Council detailed the objectives of reaching the 3 per cent target of EU GDP for research policy by 2010 and creating a European Research Area (ERA). This relates to both applied and basic research. The achievement of these quantitative and qualitative goals depends upon both EU policy and national private and public actors. In 2004, the Prodi Commission proposed to double the budget of the Framework programme, the EU research policy's main instrument. However, the EU budget accounts for less than 10 per cent of the total research budget of member states. The mid-term evaluation of the Lisbon agenda revealed that only Sweden and Finland were in full compliance with the Barcelona objective, while the EU average was still below 2 per cent of GDP in 2004, less than both Japan and the US. Numerous comparative surveys, including the Wim Kok mid-term report *Facing the Challenge*, note that Scandinavia has shown itself to be an excellent example of the European model: it boasts the highest levels of public expenditure not only for R&D and higher education policy, but for *all* policies included in the Lisbon Strategy. As far as the other member states are concerned, the main problems are to be found within the states themselves, i.e. in stagnating levels of government funding, ineffective incentives, flawed fiscal policy mixes and, particularly, in insufficient business funding. The Lisbon Strategy advocates combining the Framework programme (FP, EU budget) with the 'open method of coordination' of national research budgets,[59] which has been included in the Constitutional Treaty. Of course, policy coordination of the Lisbon agenda at national level is also needed, as emphasized by the EU Luxembourg Presidency Conclusions in March 2005.

The second set of problems is related to the heterogeneity of the EU internal market. One of the main challenges facing the EU is to combine diversity with convergence, and to transform internal variety into a resource for external competitiveness at global level:[60] however, the serious delay regarding the 'EU patent system' (aiming at reducing both the costs and complexity of protecting intellectual property rights) highlights the negative consequences of resilient linguistic rivalries and prevents the EU from taking full advantage of ICT for economic growth.

Why is research so relevant for the EU's external role as a civilian power? The successful developments of the European Space Agency and the international technological excellence of the Airbus enterprise provide good examples of European research potential. However, the famous 'Galileo' Global Navigation Satellite System is particularly salient as far as the internal and international potential implications of the Lisbon Strategy for international competitiveness are concerned. In 2004 it represented an investment of more than €2.5bn (combining two-thirds private finance with one-third from the EU budget) and it is planned to be operational with 30 satellites by 2007–8.[61] Its launch, eventually decided by the Transport Council in December 2004, is one of the main strategic international successes of the Prodi Commission, which not only had to deal with scepticism from Britain and others, but also strong US opposition from the Pentagon.[62] The main difference between Galileo and its principal rival, the US Global Positioning System (GPS), is that Galileo is conceived of by the Council as a 'civilian program under civilian control'. That does not exclude military applications, decided on by a unanimous Council vote within the framework of the ECSP. Even within the limits of the 'Petersberg tasks' (see Chapter 4), the European common defence policy will need Galileo if it wants to be more autonomous, even within NATO. However, even as a purely civilian program, the fact that Galileo is moving Europe away 'from US dominance' (and technological policy) towards fair industrial competition in mass markets for users and equipment is of major economic importance (the relevant market is expected to be €8bn in 2005).[63] The inclusion of India, China and other countries as partners and financial co-investors in the project may be a turning point: firstly, it is fostering a spillover effect in accelerating European industrial, technological and research cooperation with the two Asian giants and beyond. Secondly, it is establishing the EU as a distinctive kind of research power, which is perceived by partners as an alternative model to the US: more cooperative, open and, under certain conditions, prepared to share high-level technologies.

Even research in the social sciences and the humanities has a crucial role to play, as regards internal cohesion and international cooperation. More than ever, the sixth and seventh FP will foster social research, transnational mobility, the renewal of public and private partnerships, the spreading of knowledge through networks and centres of excellence, the construction of long-term infrastructures, and increased interdisciplinary research. According to G. Gadamer, precisely the European linguistic heterogeneity and various historical legacies may again make Europe a pole of international attraction and cooperation, in opposition to the US 'brain drain' model. However, not only for the humanities, but for all disciplines and research branches, these objectives require policy coordination by member states and the opening up of the ERA at a global level in terms of visa policies, the recognition of diplomas and careers, adequate funding for universities, communication infrastructures, the improvement of living standards and accessibility and, in the long run, the establishment of a single centralized autonomous European Research Council.[64]

The coming decade will be decisive. Either the EU will prove able to implement the Lisbon and Barcelona objectives regarding research and build up an ERA or, notwithstanding its intellectual and scientific legacy and potential, it will be 'colonized' by the US and the emergent Asian centres, worse than the 'Graeculi' during the Roman empire, because a true US empire will never exist. What is at stake is the development of a European conscious leading class which has not, like now, its Alma Mater in the US, and is aware of its regional and global responsibilities.

However, something new is maturing, and not only a common world view. Rather, what research and technology progress are fostering is a consistent institutional mechanism of implementation and an effective and multi-level system of governance of common decisions, including a harmonization of internal research and political structures. The growing awareness that failure would have huge implications for both the civilian power of the EU and its international identity may provide the necessary input for achieving in the early twenty-first century what Europe failed to do in the latter part of the twentieth.

3.12   From the reform of social governance to the strengthening of the legal basis of economic government and a social Europe?

The European Convention (the consultative body established by the Laeken European Council in the run-up to the 2003–4 IGC) tackled the question of the future of the European socio-economic model from its inception on 28 February 2002 until the final draft on July 2003. Among those involved in the debate were European and national parliamentarians, the Commission, governments and the social partners, as observers. Perhaps due to concerns that the Europeanization of the Constitution might weaken social consensus within member states, a lot of time was devoted to examining the problems of social Europe. Signed by the 25 MS, supported by the ETUC and EP and ratified by the majority of EU states, the new Treaty was rejected in 2005 by French and Dutch referenda, confirming the *longue dureé* centrality of socio-economic issues.

There are three points to emerge from the Constitutional Treaty which are of great symbolic significance as far as the future of the European social identity is concerned. First and foremost, the Nice Charter of Fundamental Rights became the second part of the Constitutional Treaty, including its articles on social rights. Second, for the first time, the values of social justice, solidarity and full employment are emphasized (art. I-2 and I-3). Third, social dialogue has finally been constitutionalized (art. I, 47). The last was one of the main reasons for a Constitutional Treaty[65] and is more relevant than leftist criticism which centred on the risks involved in deregulating public services and on 'negative integration'. We have already underlined that European social history and constitutional theory show that national social integration and cohesion have resulted both from civil society through a kind of citizens' contract and from the legal framework provided by the political community.[66] The constitutional framework could be confused with political orientations depending on varying political majorities. Of course, social rights only have value if they are linked to consistent and effective policies and tasks for actors and institutions. While mentioning the gap with the legal force of national law, we are drawing attention to the question whether the Constitutional Treaty strengthens the Lisbon Strategy and the OMC as a concrete policy means of enhancing the internal and international cohesion and the identity of the European socio-economic model. In this regard, the Convention and the IGC were faced with three possible options:

(a) Institutional status quo: this option has been supported by different camps and for different reasons. These have paradoxically ranged from the conservative Aznar government in Spain to the staunch defenders of traditional federalism. This implied keeping the practice of the Lisbon Strategy marginal, separate from the revision of the treaties. Certainly, the illusion that changes of such relevance to European governance could take place without consolidating and clarifying their institutional and legal framework was an initial illusion of the Lisbon Strategy.[67] Those who, several years later, still defend the juridical status quo, seek to harm the chances of positive integration implied in the OMC, even at the cost of exacerbating the democratic deficit and reducing the efficiency of the Lisbon Strategy.

(b) In contrast, a second ambitious option aimed at modifying the division of competencies between the Union and member states. This would entail either directly linking the OMC with the Community method or extending it to other social areas of EU competency. This could have been achieved, for example, through reform of article 137.2(b) of the TEC, allowing framework directives that ensure a greater binding force, while still respecting different application methods for the various national models (or rather the models of groups of states, according to a tripartite distinction between Scandinavian, Bismarckian and Anglo-Saxon welfare models).[68] Integrationalist consolidation of the legal basis of the OMC, reconciling convergence and diversity, would be a tempting solution.[69] More indirect links to the Community method might also be possible. Nonetheless, it was rather predictable that all the objections made between 2000 and 2002 against the transition from simple intergovernmental cooperation to the OMC, or those made at the Nice IGC against the extension of QMV and the Community method for social policy, would be firmly reiterated from 2002 to 2004, during the Convention and the IGC. The British Labour government, for example, has wished to be seen to take a resolute stand on this in order to placate domestic Eurosceptic public opinion.

(c) The third option was oriented to bring about an institutional reinforcement of governance, transparency and OMC legitimacy, while maintaining a realistic respect for the current system of division of competencies between member states and the EU. It would also promote different contributions from the various European institutions involved in governing the strategy.

The Convention's decision to opt for this last approach was largely confirmed by the IGC and the final draft of the Constitutional Treaty (2004). However, a related dispute divided the supporters of this third approach during the Convention. The Working Group on competencies made a first attempt in June 2002 to finalize the list of competencies and to invoke OMC in the area of 'complementary competencies', i.e. those sectors where the EU could only provide 'supporting measures' for national policies. The only merit of this limiting proposal, which was rejected as being too rigid in the Plenary Assembly by both the PES (Party of European Socialists) and the EPP (European Popular Party), was that it specified that the OMC is not in competition with the Community method. The second proposal, which divided the Presidium and the Assembly, sought to include the OMC in the *first* part of the Treaty. This had the great advantage of establishing a general set of procedures whose adaptation to different policy areas could be left to the appropriate European authorities. The third proposal, which was ratified only at the last moment by the Presidium and the Assembly (thanks to cross-party, transnational and interinstitutional lobbying), is set out in a text included in four articles of the *third* part of the Treaty (regarding Union policies[70]). These articles include the essential elements of intergovernmental coordination, but on the Commission's initiative; it refers to policies and programmes in four areas (social policy, industry, research and public health) and aims to ensure 'the establishment of guidelines and indicators, the organization of exchange of best practice, and the preparation of the necessary elements for periodic monitoring and evaluation'.

All in all, the Lisbon Strategy and the OMC can only benefit the interplay between the new EU governance and the institutional settlement. It is difficult to imagine any serious and lasting dynamic interinstitutional balance without what Montesquieu termed 'mixed government'. What we mean by this is that the contributions of key institutions such as the European Council, the Council of Ministers, the Commission, and, of course, the European Parliament are very welcome elements in the search to produce greater EU efficiency, legitimacy and effectiveness on socio-economic governance. On the basis of the Constitutional Treaty, the path to a normative strengthening of the European socio-economic model might look easier. This is complemented by relevant and realistic progress with regard to the reform of economic governance and the BEPG. Such reform envisages a significant reinforcement of the role of the Commission along with the Council's capacity for binding intervention, parliamentary control of macroeconomic coordination (ex art. 99 of the TEC) and further strengthening of the 'Eurogroup' (member states in the Eurozone).

3.13   The socio-economic model and European identity

Although not a panacea, the new constitutional Treaty and the modernization strategy entail great potential, both for the integration process as well as the deepening of European identity within the context of globalization. The keys not only to the EU's internal legitimacy, but also to its international identity, are to be found in the renewal and the strengthening of common features of the socio-economic model.[71] Romano Prodi stressed the need to keep in mind the price the EU would pay for subjugation to a neo-conservative *pensée unique*.[72] The recent populist shifts in European politics are further confirmation of the devastating implications of applying purely utilitarian and technocratic logic to European construction as part of a mere 'negative integration'. Improvement of the political leadership and institutional framework of the modernization strategy would be ineffective without an enhanced social mobilizing force. What is needed is not only a stronger European modernization policy, but also media visibility and the ability to engage social, individual and collective energies. This has plainly been underestimated so far, as shown by the 2005 French referendum. A technocratic and elitist Europe would risk further fuelling populist Euroscepticism, fostered by social insecurity. A large-scale reform project therefore cannot succeed if it is not presented effectively to public opinion. This implies some kind of 'mythical' dimension, albeit expressed in a moderate and rational form. The 1992 'Single Market Project' and the launch of EMU illustrate the capacity of the EU to mobilize social, economic and political resources for a programme which is well presented to the public and whose aims are clear to citizens. This difficult task of European democratic leadership can only be accomplished through an intense synergy of European institutions.

The civilizational legacy of national Welfare States to be adapted to the twenty-first century needs greater European convergence, while respecting national diversity. The project for a European knowledge society fosters research, social cohesion, industrial policy, growth, economic government and, indirectly, it may be a driving force for a renewal of Europe's international identity. Conversely, the current distortion of this strategy into a mere process of 'negative integration', unequivocal deregulation and social rhetoric would constitute a serious failure for the EU and its legitimacy for the simple reason that if there is no difference between Europeanization and liberal globalization, then the very reason for the creation and deepening of the European project and its international identity would be negated.[73]

Notes

1. OECD Annual Report 2004. However, several reasons (lack of coordination and rationalization) make it possible that European defence budgets 50 per cent less than in the USA, currently provide only 20–30 per cent of real military capacity.
2. J. Habermas, 'Why Europe Needs a Constitution', *New Left Review*, 11, September–October 2001, pp. 5–26. Habermas refers to the article by M. Telò and P. Magnette, 'Justice and Solidarity', in F. Cerutti and E. Rudolph (eds), *A Soul for Europe: on the Political and Cultural Identity of Europeans*, vol. 1, Peeters, Leuven, 2001, pp. 73–89. Habermas's article was previously published in *Zeit der Uebergaenge*, Suhrkamp, Frankfurt a.M., 2001.
3. I. Clark, *Globalization and Fragmentation: International Relations in the Twentieth Century*, Oxford University Press, Oxford, 1997; J.N. Rosenau, 'Governance in the Twenty First Century', *Global Governance*, 1, 1995, pp. 13–43; see also C. Crouch and W. Streeck, *Political Economy of Modern Capitalism. Mapping Convergence and Diversity*, Sage, London, 1997; A. Prakash and J.A. Hart (eds), *Globalization and Governance*, Routledge, London–New York, 1999.
4. See A. Laurent, *Histoire de l'individualisme*, PUF, Paris, 1993; P. Kennedy, *The Rise and Fall of the Great Powers: Economic Change and Military Conflict from 1500 to 2000*, Random House, New York, 1987; A. Toynbee, *Civilization on Trial*, Oxford University Press, New York, 1948.
5. D. Sassoon, *One Hundred Years of Socialism: the West European Left in the Twentieth Century*, Tauris, London, 1996.
6. Telò and Magnette, 'Justice and Solidarity', op. cit., p. 76. See also R. Zoll, *Was ist Solidaritaet heute?*, Suhrkamp, Frankfurt a.M., 2000 and S. Sternø, *Solidarity in Europe*, Cambridge University Press (forthcoming). S. Sternø rightly emphasizes the distinctions within each tradition, in particular in the socialist one, between the social democratic notion of 'solidarity' and the 'liberal' concept of 'justice'.
7. Ibid., p. 112.
8. For the significance of this transformation of the modern state, see G. Ritter, *Der Sozialstaat: Entstehung und Entwicklung in internationalen Vergleich*, Oldenbourg, Munich, 1991.
9. Zoll, *Was ist Solidaritaet heute?*, op. cit.
10. P. Rosanvallon, *La question syndicale*, Calmann-Levy, Paris, 1988.
11. P.C. Schmitter, 'Still the Century of Corporatism?', *Review of Politics*, 36, 1974 and 'Interest Intermediation and Regime Governability in W. Europe and N. America', in S. Berger (ed.), *Organizing Interests in Western Europe*, Cambridge University Press, Cambridge, 1981.
12. Schmitter, 'Still the Century', op. cit.
13. The catholic idea of looking for a third way between socialism and liberalism between the nineteenth and twentieth centuries was expressed among others by H. Pesch, L. Bourgeois, Ch. Gide and A. Fanfani and initially

entailed many ambiguities regarding democracy. J.F. Durand, *L'Europe de la Démocratie Chrétienne*, Complexe, Brussels, 1995; J.M. Mayeur, *Des parties catholiques à la Démocratie chrétienne*, Colin, Paris, 1980; M.P. Fogarty, *Christian Democracy in Western Europe, 1820–1953*, Routledge and Kegan Paul, London, 1957; E. Poulat, *Eglise contre bourgeoisie. Introduction au devenir du catholicisme actuel*, Costerman, Tournai, 1994; W. Becker and R. Morsey (eds), *Christliche Demokratie in Europa*, Bohlau, Cologne, 1988.

14. J.M. Keynes, *The End of 'Laissez-faire'*, London, 1926; R. Skidelsky, *Keynes*, Oxford University Press, 1996.
15. R. Titmuss, *Essays on the Welfare State*, Allen & Unwin, London, 1958.
16. See the vast comparative literature on the European Welfare States, for example P. Flora and A. Heindenmeyer (eds), *The Development of Welfare States in Europe and America*, Transaction Books, New Brunswick, NY, 1981; J.H. Goldthorpe (ed.), *Order and Conflict in Contemporary Capitalism*, Oxford University Press, Oxford, 1984; P. Baldwin, *The Politics of Social Solidarity. Class Bases of the European Welfare States, 1875–1975*, Cambridge University Press, 1990. As the critical debate: H.L. Wilenski, 'The Problems and Prospects of the Welfare State', in *Industrial Society and the Welfare State*, Macmillan, New York, pp. 5–52; N. Luhmann, *Politische Theorie im Wohlfahrtstaat*, Olzog Verlag, Munich, 1981.
17. G. Lehmbruch and P.C. Schmitter (eds), *Patterns of Corporatist Policy-Making*, Sage, London, 1982.
18. M. Albert, *Capitalisme contre capitalisme*, Seuil, Paris, 1991.
19. On this point, see M. Telò, *Le New Deal européen*, Editions de l'Université de Bruxelles, 1989.
20. G. Esping-Andersen, *The Three Worlds of Welfare Capitalism*, Princeton University Press, Princeton, 1990; id. (ed.), *Welfare States in Transition. National Adaptations in Global Economics*, Sage, London, 1998.
21. W. Beck, L. van den Maesen and A. Walkers (eds), *The Social Quality of Europe*, Kluwer, Amsterdam, 1997.
22. R. Skidelsky (ed.), *Thatcherism*, Blackwell, Oxford, 1988.
23. J.P. Fitoussi and P. Rosanvallon, *Le nouvel age des inégalités*, Seuil, Paris, 1996.
24. N. Luhmann, *Politische Theorie im Wohlfahrtstaat*, Olzog, Munich, 1981; J. Waddington and R. Hoffmann, *Trade Unions in Europe*, ETUI, Brussels, 2000.
25. The end of the 'regulatory state' was looming. The regulatory state was reclassified as a break between two periods dominated by economic liberalism, preceding and following the 'great transformation', as the historian K. Polany (*The Great Transformation*, Rinehart, New York, 1944) termed the birth of the Keynesian state and the end of the self-regulated market under British hegemony.
26. M. Regini (ed.), *The Future of Labour Movements*, Sage, London, 1992.
27. European Commission, *Employment in Europe*, Luxembourg, 1997 and M. Olson, 'Varieties of Eurosclerosis. The Rise and Decline of Nations since 1982', *IUE J.Monnet Chain Papers*, Florence, 1995.
28. P. Cerny, 'Paradoxes of the Competition State', *European Journal of Political Research*, 3, 1997, pp. 100–20; H. Wilke, *Supervision Staat*, Suhrkamp, Frankfurt a.M., 1997; S. Unseld (ed.), *Politik ohne Projeckt?*, Suhrkamp, Frankfurt a.M., 1993 (in particular, J. Esser, 'Die Suche nach dem Primat der Politik', pp. 409–30); R Voigt (ed.), *Des Staates neuer Kleider*, Nomos,

Baden-Baden, 1998 and F.W. Scharpf, *The Problem-Solving Capacity of Multi-level Governance*, Schumann Centre, EUI, Florence, 1997.

29. See the Preamble to the Treaty of Rome (TEC) and the articles on common values, as well as the Preamble to the Treaty on European Union (TEU).
30. Regarding EU budget reform, see the report drawn up by an expert group set up by the Commission, presided over by André Sapir (*An Agenda for a Growing Europe*, July 2003).
31. G. Falkner, *EU Social Policy in the '90s*, Routledge, London, 1998; H. Wallace and A. Young, *Participation in the European Union*, Oxford University Press, Oxford, 1997.
32. See the articles by G. Therborn ('Europe, Scandinavia del mondo'), M. Albert ('Il capitalismo europeo nel quadro della mondializzazione: convergence e dif-ferenze'), A.S. Milward ('L'impossibile fuga dalla storia'), R. Bellamy ('Una Repubblica europea?') and others in M. Telò (ed.), *Quale idea d'Europa per il XXI secolo?*, special edition of *Europa/Europe*, 5, Rome, 1999. See also G. Therborn, 'Europe in the 21st Century: the World's Scandinavia?', in P. Gowan and P. Anderson (eds), *The Question of Europe*, Verso, London, 1999, pp. 357–84.
33. Many authors have written on this topic. See E. Matzer, *Der Wohlfahrtstaat von Morgen*, Campus, Vienna, 1982; A. Touraine, *Comment Sortir du libéral-isme?*, Fayard, Paris, 1999; A. Giddens, *The Third Way*, Polity Press, London, 1998; T. Meyer, *Die Transformation der Sozialdemokratie*, Dietz Verlag, Bonn, 1998; R.A. Dahl, *Dilemmas of Pluralist Democracy: Autonomy vs. Control*, Yale University Press, New Haven, 1982.
34. J. Hoffman (ed.), *The Solidarity Dilemma: Globalization, Europeanization, and Trade Unions*, ETUI, Brussels, 2002.
35. This expression is taken from J.H. Weiler, 'Comunità europea', in *Enciclopedia delle scienze sociali*, vol. II, Istituto della Enciclopedia italiana, Rome, 1996.
36. *Presidency Conclusions* (Lisbon European Council), Ref. Council of the EU, SN 100/00; *Presidency Conclusions* (Santa Maria da Feira European Council), Ref. Council of the EU, SN 200/00; Presidency of the EU, *Note on Ongoing Experiment of the Open Method of Coordination*, Ref. Council of the EU, 9088/00, 14 June 2000.
37. The Portuguese Presidency recruited various experts in the fields. Their find-ings are published in M.J. Rodrigues (ed.), *The New Knowledge Economy in Europe. A Strategy for International Competitiveness and Social Cohesion*, Elgar, Northampton, 2002 (articles by R. Boyer, G. Esping-Andersen, M. Telò, A. Lundvall, L. Soete, R. Lindley and M. Castells).
38. See F.W. Scharpf and V. Schmidt (eds), *Welfare and Work in the Open Economy*, vol. I, *From Vulnerability to Competitiveness*, vol. II, *Diverse Responses to Common Challenges*, Oxford University Press, Oxford, 2000; M. Ferrera, A. Hemerijck and M. Rhodes, *The Future of Social Europe*, Oeiras, Celta, 2001; V.A. Schmidt, *The Futures of European Capitalism*, Oxford University Press, 2002, and W. Streeck, *Neo-Voluntarism: a New European Social Policy Regime?*, in G. Marks, F.W. Scharpf, P.C. Schmitter and W. Streeck (eds), *Governance in the EU*, Sage, London, 1996, pp. 64–93.
39. European Commission, *Growth, Competitiveness, Employment White Book*, in *EC Bulletin*, supplement 6, 1993.
40. The 12 January 2000 document (Presidency of the EU, *Document from the Presidency*) was the outcome of a consultation process between the

Presidency and a group of experts. See Rodrigues (ed.), *The New Knowledge Economy in Europe*, op. cit. The *Presidency Conclusions* (cited, above, in n. 36). The Conclusions of the European Councils of Lisbon (23–24 March) and Feira (19–20 June) benefited from the essential input of the Commission, the contribution by the 14 other governments (thanks to two tours of the capitals of Europe by prime minister Antonio Guterrez and Maria Joao Rodrigues), a rich exchange of letters and documents, the contributions of social and economic actors and of the network of the prime ministers' *sherpas*, who met four times in Brussels during the first semester of 2000.

41. See the 'Introduction' to the previously cited volume *A New Knowledge Economy in Europe*, edited by M.J. Rodrigues, in particular the section 'Europe at the Crossroads'.

42. Presidency of the EU, *Note on the Ongoing Experience*, op. cit. According to Delors: 'the economic and social resolution adopted in Lisbon is a step in the right direction'; 'it is interesting to note that in the economic and social sphere, we are looking for new methods of governance: the directive is inappropriate, simple cooperation is insufficient' (testimony of J. Delors before the EU Committee of the French Senate, Paris, 5 April 2000, in *Bulletin Europe*, 28 April 2000, pp. 3–5).

43. On this topic, see A. Lundvall ('International Benchmarking as a Policy Learning Tool', in Rodrigues (ed.), *The New Knowledge Economy in Europe*, op. cit., pp. 203–30). Lundvall gives a good explanation of the necessary distinction between purely technocratic benchmarking and its use in the context of the Lisbon Strategy: it is more open to diverse national starting points and aimed at encouraging progress, keeping countries on the right path and distinguishing between common indicators and specific national objectives within an agreed time frame.

44. P. Pochet and C. De la Porte, *Building Social Europe through the Open Method of Co-ordination*, P. Lang, Brussels, 2000; J. Goetschy, 'The European Employment Strategy', *ECSA Review*, 13, 3, 2001; J. Goetschy and P. Pochet, 'Regards croisés sur la stratégie européenne de l'emploi', in P. Magnette and E. Remacle (eds), *Le nouveau modèle européen*, Editions de l'Université de Bruxelles, 2000, vol. II, pp. 79–97. D. Hodson and I. Maher, 'The Open Method as a Mode of Governance: the Case of Soft Economic Policy Co-ordination', *Journal of Common Market Studies*, 39, 4, pp. 719–46; A. Larsson, 'The Social Agenda from Lisbon to Barcelona. Achievements and Expectations', paper, J. Delors Centre, Lisbon, 31 January 2002; F.W. Scharpf, *The European Social Model: Coping with the Challenge of Diversity*, EUI, Florence, March 2002; M. Telò, 'Strengths and Limits of the OMC', in Weiler, Begg and Peterson (eds), *Integration in an Expanding European Union*, op. cit. L. Magnusson, P. Pochet and J. Zeitln, *The OMC in Action*, P. Lang, Brussels, 2004; and the special issue of the *Journal of European Public Policy*, edited by S. Borras and B. Grere, 'The OMC in the EU', vol. II, 2004.

45. The evolution of the Council as regards education is particularly important for both lifelong learning programmes and new indicators and methods related to student mobility (which will be strengthened by additional funds from European, national and local budgets: see Nice European Council Conclusions, December 2000). The Research Council of Ministers (included in 2002 in the new Competitiveness Council) launched an extensive process

aimed at developing, among other things, a European Research Area (ERA) which combines European and national policies and resources, establishes European indicators and coherent and coordinated national plans with appropriate benchmarking criteria. The Employment and Social Policy Council has made relevant progress both as regards employment and in the more difficult area of social protection policies (including national plans to combat poverty and the pension system reform). A key role was played by the Belgian Presidency, namely by Minister F. Vanderbroucke. See his 'Toward a European Social Policy: Turning Principles of Cooperation into Effective Cooperation', paper, London, 11 November 2000 and *The Future of Social Policy*, Max Planck Institute, Cologne, 2002.

46. For example in the areas of internal security and immigration. This was proposed by Commissioner Vitorino to the Council in 2001 and was looked at again in Salonicco by the 2003 European Council, despite obvious resistance from states and difficulties in its application. Two other relevant areas of national policies coordination are defence cooperation and also youth policy (see White Paper, 2001).

47. The Lisbon Strategy is a long-term process which encourages continuity in government policy, regardless of changes in electoral majorities. It acts, therefore, as a centripetal force within national politics. In this sense, it may depoliticize issues such as the fight against unemployment and Welfare State reform. On the other hand, it affirms the political priorities: growth policy, rather than the mere control of spending; it also expresses a political vision of European socio-economic modernization, which is distinct from the US model. As regards European political cleavages, the strategy reflects a new dynamic and unstable compromise, symbolized by the positive reception it got from Blair and Aznar and the unanimous vote in the European Council. Although it cannot be considered a centre-left strategy, it is nonetheless a definite product of the hegemony of progressive governments in Europe during the period 1997 to 2001. Having said that, the Blair government's interpretation differs from both that of the strategy's main promoter, Guterrez of Portugal, and that of the French government under Jospin. Inevitably, each government exerts an independent influence on the implementation of the strategy. Obviously, therefore, each spring, the European Council is the scene of confrontation between different interpretations of the balance between deregulation and re-regulation and between positive and negative integration. Organized social actors heighten these confrontations by exerting pressure on incumbent Presidencies and on the Commission. The European Trade Union Confederation (ETUC), for example, often takes a different view from UNICE, the Union of Industrial and Employers' Confederations of Europe. Private lobbying matters. The Social Forum, which takes place before each spring European Council, is often an occasion for mass demonstrations and debate between opposing interests and interpretations. Similar to national social pacts, provided it masters the bureaucratic and '*routine*' bias, the negotiation framework instituted by the Lisbon Strategy provides an advanced battleground where heterogeneous, and often opposed, interests and demands may be expressed, as the premise to a compromise which is constantly renewed and to which both the Commission and the Council contribute.

48. European Council 20–21 March 2003, Brussels, 'Presidency Conclusions', in *Europe Bulletin*, 23 March 2003.
49. A. Moravcsik, 'Reassessing Legitimacy in the EU', in Weiler, Begg and Peterson (eds), *Integration in an Expanding European Union*, op. cit., pp. 77–99.
50. On the question of European multi-level governance, see F.W. Scharpf, *The Problem-Solving Capacity of Multilevel Governance*, IUE, Florence, 1997; G. Majone (ed.), *Regulating Europe*, Routledge, London, 1998; Marks, Scharpf, Schmitter and Streeck (eds), *Governance in the EU*, op. cit. and in particular P.C. Schmitter, 'Imaging the Future of European Polity', pp. 121–49. Also, B. Kohler-Koch (ed.), *Regieren in Entgrentzen Raume*, Westdeutscher Verlag, Opladen, 1998.
51. M. Telò, 'Government and Governance in the EU. The Open Method of Coordination', in Rodrigues (ed.), *The New Knowledge Economy in Europe*, op. cit., pp. 242–71 and M. Telò (ed.), *Démocratie et construction européenne*, Editions de l'Université de Bruxelles, Brussels, 1995. See also the similarly themed works of Goetschy, Pochet and De la Porte, cited above in n. 44.
52. The European Parliament passed an important resolution in March 1999 concerning the strengthening of its role within the framework set out in art. 99, para. 5, i.e. macroeconomic and BEPG coordination.
53. European Parliament, *Resolution of the European Parliament on the Lisbon Special European Council*, Ref. B5–0236, 0239 and 040/2000, March 2000.
54. European Commission, *White Paper on European Governance*, July 2001, and preliminary materials: Working group Report 4A, *Expertiser les processus de coordination des politiques nationals*, Brussels, July 2001 and M. Telò (ed.), *L'evoluzione della governance europea*, special edition of *Europa/Europe*, 2/3, 2001 with articles by J.H.H. Weiler, E. Kirchner, P. Magnette, R. Dehousse, M.J. Rodrigues and others.
55. 'Le Conseil européen s'est autoproclamé gouvernement économique', declared Jacques Delors, after Lisbon in March 2000. 'By strengthening its political role balancing that of the European Central Bank, the European Council has given its response to the problem of EU leadership' stressed the Swedish Prime Minister, Göran Persson (*European Bulletin*, 23–25 March 2000). The European Council has proclaimed: 'l'Etat c'est moi' indeed. This exceptional role of the European Council recalls the positive observation made by Jean Monnet at its birth, in 1974, when it was intended as a 'provisional government' (see J. Monnet, *Mémoires*, Fayard, Paris, 1976, pp. 591–2). On the Council of Ministers and the European Council, see J.P. Jaquet and D. Simon, 'The Constitutional and Juridical Role of the European Council', in J.M. Hoscheit and W. Wessels (eds), *The European Council 1974–1986: Evaluation and Prospects*, IEAP, Maastricht, 1988; J. Cloos, G. Reinsech, D. Vignes and J. Wyland, *Le traité de Maastricht, genèse, analyse et commentaires*, Bruylant, Brussels, 1993; F. Hayes-Renshaw and H. Wallace, *The Council of Ministers*, St. Martin's Press, New York, 1997; M. Telò, 'The Council of the EU: the Decision-Making after Nice', in P. Zervakis and P. Cullen (eds), *The Post-Nice Process: Towards a European Constitution?*, Nomos, Baden-Baden, 2002.
56. See the Synthesis Report, *Communication from the Commission to the Spring European Council in Barcelona. The Lisbon Strategy. Making Change Happen*, Brussels, 15 January 2002.
57. This self-critical expression is also contained in the European Commission *White Paper on Competitiveness* of 1993, op. cit. A strong precedent had been

set in the excellent *Rapport pour le Commissariat Général au Plan*, prepared by the group of experts led by J-L.Quermonne, *L'EU en quête d'institutions légitimes et efficacies*, La Documentations française, Paris, 1999, pp. 66–7.

58. M.J. Rodrigues, *European Policies for a Knowledge Economy*, Elgar, Cheltenham, 2003; B. Van Pottelsberghe, 'Les politiques de science et de technologie et l'objectif de Lisbonne', *Reflets et Perspectives de la Vie Économique*, 2004, pp. 69–86; M. Telò, 'Préface' to M.J. Rodrigues (ed.), *Vers une société européenne de la connaissance*, Editions de l'ULB, Brussels, 2004, pp. vii–xvii.

59. Part III of the Treaty is consistent with part I (art. I-14.3), establishing EU research policy as a shared competence between the EU and member states. While art. III-248 mentions the objective of a European Research Area, art. III-250 focuses on the coordination of national policies. Art. 251 and 252 establish the rules and objectives of the multi-annual Framework programme.

60. R. King (ed.), *The University in the Global Age*, Houndmills, Palgrave Macmillan, 2004.

61. J. Lembke, 'The Politics of Galileo', *Pittsburgh University European Policy Paper*, no. 7, 2001.

62. In June 2004, the US agreed to sign a technical 'interoperability agreement' between GPS and Galileo.

63. Arnaud Salomon, 'A Question of Independence and Sovereignty', *CNES Magazine*, no. 6, 1999, pp. 20–1 (Salomon is Director of Space and Aeronautics in the French Ministry of Research).

64. These recommendations are shared by a large number of national and European advisory groups, including the European Commission, DG research, the 'Social Science and Humanities Advisory Group for ERA' (2002–5, chaired by M.J. Rodrigues), the Danish Social Science Research Council (The Working Group on Research Infrastructures in Humanities and Social Sciences 2004, www.forsk.dk); the ESRC, UMIST, *Final Report on Success for Social Science in the EU*, 7th FP (March 2004).

65. Habermas, *Why Europe Needs a Constitution?* op. cit.

66. This discussion has been open since Hegel: see *Philosophy of Right*, op. cit., paragraphs 142, 258 and A. Von Bogdandy, *Hegels Theorie des Gesetzes*, Alber, Freiburg, 1989, pp. 119–25.

67. See my critical remarks in M. Telò, 'Governance and Government in the EU', op. cit. and G. de Búrca, 'The Constitutional Challenge of New Governance in the EU', *European Law Review*, December 2003, pp. 814–36.

68. Scharpf, *The European Social Model*, op. cit.; he refers to Esping-Andersen, *The Three Worlds of Welfare Capitalism*, op. cit.

69. Scharpf, *The European Social Model*, op. cit., pp. 109–34. See also my critique, *Strengths and Deficits of the Open Method of Coordination*, op. cit., pp. 135–42.

70. Council of the European Union, General Secretariat, *Treaty Establishing a Constitution for Europe*, 18.6.2004, Luxembourg, art. III-213 (Social Policy), art. III-250 (Research Policy), art. III-278.2 (Public Health), art. III-279.2 (Industry).

71. Cerutti and Rudolph (eds), *A Soul for Europe*, op. cit. For further discussion of identity and constitutionalization, see J. Habermas, *Die postnationale Konstellation: politische Essays*, Suhrkamp, Frankfurt, 1998; see also J. Habermas, *Der gespaltene Westen*, Suhrkamp, Chapter 5 on European identity.

72. R. Prodi, 'Cinque motivi per credere nell'Europa', *il Mulino*, January–February 2002, pp. 40–7.

73. This has also provided an opportunity for significant interaction between the agenda of the EU and that of the academic community, particularly in the social sciences which receive for the first time special encouragement through the European Research Area project and the Framework VI programme for research. See European Commission, *Third European Report on Science and Technology Indicators. Towards a Knowledge-Based Economy*, Brussels, 2003 and the website of the Advisory Group Social Services and Humanities ERA.

4
The Development of the European Union as an International Actor

In 50 years, western Europe has moved from a vision of itself which was primarily concerned with internal integration issues to one which entails a comprehensive and dynamic approach of the EU's role in the governance of the partially globalized world. While there is still a clear gap between the significance of Europe in international economics and trade as compared to its political role on the world scene, the EU is, nonetheless, more than simply a sophisticated workshop of regional integration. Moreover, it promotes aspects of this historically successful experience through the influence it exerts and its interregional relations with other continents. As we argued earlier, the future of new regionalism and the role of the EU are now decisive and interdependent variables in the creation both of an improved multilateral regulatory system for the partially globalized world and of a more stable international order capable of reducing the uncertainties of the post-cold war era.

How did this mindset gradually develop over time from the European Community – a small introverted entity under the protective arm of the US – through to the EU, the relatively most autonomous regional organization of the post-cold war world which is now establishing itself as a new global actor? What path led the EU to expand its concerns beyond its 'internal foreign policy' – the management and enlargement of the historical result of peace achieved in western Europe between neighbouring states which were formerly enemies – and to start dealing with former colonies, neighbouring areas and attempt to shape the future of multilateralism and peace? It is worth reflecting on this multi-dimensional and long-term development and, in particular, on the interaction between the economic and political aspects of EC/EU external relations, the evolution of which has been marked by turning points, defeats and substantive progress. Research must combine the instruments of foreign policy analysis with systemic international relations theory and the current debate is highly controversial as far as comparative analysis and theoretical approaches are concerned.[1]

4.1 The growth of the EC/EU as a global economic actor

The first half-century of the European integration process has been marked by both change and continuity. On the one hand, member states are still decisive actors of multi-level European external relations. On the other hand, even at its origins and during the most difficult periods of the bipolar world, the European Community was considered a significant example of the inadequacy of the classic state-centric model, the declining role of force in international relations and the growing importance of transnational interdependence.[2] The famous definition of 'security community'[3] reflected the political salience of the dynamics of socio-economic regional integration between previous enemies. The first definition of Europe as a 'civilian power' was based on the Tocquevillian idea that is theoretically legitimate to define trade policy as the first significant element of foreign policy. Since the Treaty of Rome, the Common Commercial Policy and the Customs Union, the cooperation with previous colonies, have represented the heart of the EC's external economic relations indeed.[4] In just a few decades, the European Community has become a competitive economic and trade power. Since 1996, it has controlled about 20 per cent of world exports[5] and member states are the main foreign investor in the so-called emerging economies. Although European states are no longer the dominant economic powers they used to be prior to the Second World War, four members of the G8 are EU members and, like the US, the EU represents a fifth of the world economy.[6]

It would be mistaken to think that such statistics relate simply to the strength of individual western European countries. On the contrary, the extraordinary increase of the overall economic weight of the EU is largely due to the successful regional integration process. Since the Treaty of Rome and, in particular, the Single European Act (SEA) and the Maastricht Treaty, the EC/EU has evolved into an increasingly resourceful international actor within the global multilateral network. This is a consequence of the external implications of its dynamic internal market and common policies such as competition policy,[7] agricultural policy, the international effects of the euro and Monetary Union, the commitment to development cooperation (including the ACP process), humanitarian aid policy, and participation in international conferences and organizations. Last but not least an important dimension is what is known as 'treaty-making power', i.e. the power to sign treaties, as a result of which the EC/EU has developed an extremely dense network of institutionalized international agreements at bilateral and, increasingly, multilateral and interregional levels with single countries and regional groupings. In all these spheres, the EU acts either as a supranational entity (as is the case within the WTO and international and interregional trade agreements) or through simple cooperation and coordination of member state policies. The EC/EU has a wide range of legal instruments relevant to its external relations, which still represent the essence of its foreign policy.[8] The crucial part it has played as far the WTO is concerned, since its very foundation in Marrakesh on 15 April 1994, and its efforts in Doha (November 2001) to open a new controversial negotiation cycle (the 'Development Agenda'), highlight the distinctive role of the EU in the multilateral civilian arena. Although this might appear paradoxical given that the EC was born as a derogation to GATT rules (on the basis of art. XXIV regarding regional PFA), it is important in the light of the central role that the WTO is increasingly assuming in global governance.[9]

International scholars have highlighted many other relevant political implications of current EC/EU civilian external relations. For example, association and interregional agreements often explicitly support regional cooperation among EU overseas partners. Hence, the 'Cotonou Convention' with the ACP (Africa, Caribbean and Pacific) countries supports regional agreements in Africa (SADC, ECOWAS, etc.), the Caribbean (CARICOM) and the Pacific. The 'Rio de Janeiro Process' provides a frame for agreements with the Southern Common Market (MERCOSUR) and also groups such as the Andean Community. The Asia–Europe Meeting (ASEM) supports regional cooperation through ASEAN and 'ASEAN Plus Three' (China, Japan and South Korea). During the 1990s, the association agreements with central and eastern European countries and the Euro–Mediterranean dialogue (the 'Barcelona Process') highlighted (admittedly with varying degrees of success) the strategic preference of the EC/EU for multidimensional cooperation (economic, cultural, commercial and political). As the inclusion of 'political dialogue' in every interregional agreement of the EU illustrates, the political impact of this approach is considerable. Even if in the near abroad region-to-region cooperation may have been negatively affected by bilateral conditionality, the growth of EU economic and political influence in eastern Europe and the Mediterranean can hardly be questioned.

Secondly, the traditional boundary between the economic and political aspects of an international presence no longer represents the type of insurmountable barrier it did in the nineteenth century. This holds true for state policies and, even more so, for the EU. For example, the external representation and implications of the common market and single currency are obviously political issues, despite depending on the first pillar of the EU. The political impact of trade disputes and negotiations, particularly the many difficult challenges relating to the WTO Uruguay and Millennium Rounds, are a salient aspect of this interplay. The political dimension of external economic, environmental and trade relations is becoming ever more evident, and the classic realist criticism of the weakness of the EC, seen as merely a commercial and economic entity and, as such, a subordinate component of the bipolar balance of power, was widely and fundamentally questioned after the end of the cold war. In this chapter, we shall attempt therefore to assess the current relevance of the scepticism authoritatively expressed by Robert Gilpin and others about the external results and processes of EC/EU regional integration, allegedly wholly dependent on the pretended *pax americana* and the residual power of states.[10]

4.2 A non-teleological history: the vicissitudes of the CFSP and CSDP

The history of the Common Foreign and Security Policy (CFSP), unlike a teleological history, does not consist of a series of steps in the 'right' direction, aimed at constructing a new fully fledged international political actor. The history of European cooperation in these sectors is marked by failures and abrupt U-turns back in the direction of the renationalization of foreign and security policies. Nevertheless, taking a *longue durée* view, we can trace a significant evolution from the low profile of the early decades after the Second World War, through the advances and fluctuations of the decade following the end of the bipolar world, up to the present day, notwithstanding the 'crucial test' of 2002–4 provided by the war in Iraq. Even if the growing expectations of third countries and the ambitious aspirations included in the Treaty on European Union (TEU, Maastricht 1992) seemed to envisage a more convincing evolution than the subsequent reality of the CFSP, we may still be justified in saying (paraphrasing Galileo Galilei): 'nevertheless, it does move!' A brief review of the history of political cooperation may help us shed more light on its significance and limits.

Following the dramatic breakdown of the European Defence Community (EDC) in 1954, both the military and political dimensions of integration became taboo subjects for a long time as the history of the 'Fouchet Plan' (1961) and of the 'Spinelli Treaty' (1984) clearly show. However, the 1969 Hague summit, the first of the 'post-de Gaulle' and the new 'Brandt era', was a first step forward. The six heads of state and government launched an appeal for a 'united Europe capable of assuming its responsibilities in the world of tomorrow'. Willy Brandt endeavoured – with several notable successes – to Europeanize German Ostpolitik, one of the results of which was the highly significant 1975 Helsinki Treaty (CSCE). For his part, Georges Pompidou began setting out the strategic meaning of North–South cooperation, moving it beyond the mere inertia of France's post-colonial links. Against the new and dynamic background that led to the approval of the 'Davignon Report', we find the first decla-ration of political cooperation in 1973, when the nine member states established EPC (European Political Cooperation) and agreed on the principle of consultation before taking foreign policy decisions. Although ineffective, the 1978 'Venice Declaration' on the Arab–Israeli conflict is the most famous example of this innovation, and it was no coincidence that the Declaration saw the adoption of a different stance from that of the US.[11] The 1986 Single European Act which institutionalized EPC, partly involving the European system in the process, was another step forward. At that time, the EC identified nine areas for the development of EPC: the Conference on Security and Cooperation in Europe (CSCE), the Council of Europe, East–West relations, Cyprus, the Middle East, Africa (South Africa and the Great Lakes region), Latin America and the US. During the 1980s the international climate was not conducive to major progress: the resurgence of the cold war allowed little room for manoeu-vre between the deployment of missiles and pacifism. Germany in partic-ular was both the symbol and the victim of this, as shown by the split in the SPD regarding Chancellor Helmut Schmidt's 'twin-track decision' and the commitment within the movement for peace, which was read by some as a sign of an early, naive transnational 'European patriotism'. The policy of political dialogue continued, however, and was extended to Latin America.[12] From 1985 on, it would achieve remarkable successes with the end of the 'second cold war' and the beginning of the 'Gorbachev era', which would allow Europe to greatly increase its room for manoeuvre.

The end of the Soviet nuclear threat along with that of the USSR itself in 1991 not only created an important 'peace dividend' for national defence budgets, but also reduced Europe's reliance on the US nuclear umbrella. A fresh array of options opened out before the EC. In the new post-1989 international context, defined by the decline of Russia and the considerable new weight of a united Germany, the joint letter by Kohl and Mitterrand in 1991 was of historical importance, albeit still insufficient to bring about a political Europe. The decision of the new Germany to deepen European cooperation, rather than asserting its reunited national identity and full sovereignty with a *Sonderweg*, was the launching pad for further unitary development of the EU as, at least in western Europe, moves towards the 'renationalization of foreign policy' were contained.[13] In 1992, the double decision at Maastricht to create both monetary and political union (including a CFSP) went some way towards correcting the internal imbalance of the integration process: the gap between the massive international importance of the EC as a global economic and trade actor on the one hand, and its relatively minor political role on the other.

Achieving the objectives laid down in the Maastricht Treaty turned out to be a difficult task. The second pillar (CFSP) was created independently from EC procedures, although it belonged to the same entity, the new European Union.[14] The Lisbon European Council in 1992 represented a step forward towards the definition of tangible common international priorities.[15] From the mid-1990s, a series of EU 'common strategies' were specifically approved in relation to Russia, Ukraine, the Mediterranean and the western Balkans. These were complemented by the launch of 'political dialogue' with applicant states, neighbouring countries and global partners, including Japan, India, Australia, Canada, the former Soviet republics, Russia, the US, Latin America (the 'Rio Group', the 'San José Group', MERCOSUR and the 'Andean Pact'), Israel and China. The amount of 'common actions' (the Amsterdam Treaty stipulates that these require a qualified majority vote if included in the framework provided by a 'unanimously approved strategy') have been limited, thus confirming the still largely declaratory nature of the CFSP ('common stances'). We should mention the following however: the numerous actions in the western Balkans, including the support for electoral processes in Bosnia, political and economic restrictive measures against the former Yugoslavia (Serbia), the administration of the city of Mostar, the defence of the Stability Pact for Central and Eastern Europe, launched in 1993; the deployment of observers at the 1993 Russian elections; the support for the peace process in the Middle East and the appointment of a special envoy, the aid programme for the Palestinian Authority and the support for the electoral process; the embargo on Iraq from 1996; the support for democratic transition in

South Africa and various ad hoc interventions in Rwanda, Afghanistan, Burma and elsewhere. As regards security, we should recall the commitment to energy development in the Korean peninsula, the total ban on chemical and biological weapons, and the efforts made against the proliferation of nuclear weapons and anti-personnel mines. The 1996 protection measures against extraterritorial legislation of third countries have interesting transatlantic implications.

The EU has thus become specialized in conflict prevention, crisis management and post-war reconstruction.[16] All this has been achieved with a very limited budget and staff (350 officials and €350,000 in 2002). Following the ratification of the Amsterdam Treaty in 1998, these officials became answerable to Javier Solana, the Council secretary-general, also known as 'Monsieur PESC' or 'Mr CFSP', appointed by the Council within the framework of the second pillar and without involving the Commission.[17]

The European Councils of Essen (1994), Cologne (1999), Helsinki (1999) and Laeken (2001) gradually paved the way for the so-called 'European defence policy' (CSDP). The main milestone to date was the decision in Helsinki to create a rapid reaction task force.[18] Defence policy was further debated by the European Councils of Seville and Copenhagen in 2002 which looked at issues such as: the first CME (Crisis Management Exercise, May 2002), peacekeeping police missions – specifically the commitment from 2003/4 to the military missions in Macedonia, Congo and Bosnia – as well as the integration of the objective to fight terrorism. It is important not to create confusion as to the significance and limits of these steps: they are framed within the 1992 'Petersberg tasks' (humanitarian, peacekeeping and crisis management missions, including peace-enforcing missions) which were included in the 1997 Amsterdam Treaty. Furthermore, the Seville European Council specified that the CSDP does not mean the creation of a European army, but rather the maintenance of a consensual framework on the part of all member states, which of course also includes neutral members and their traditions. Finally, we should also note the strict limits on supranationality and on strengthening national financial commitments by member states and the deep roots of these: article 28 of the TEU sets very tight controls on the budgetary commitments of the EU, the need for Turkish consent to access the structures and facilities of the Alliance is problematic, cooperation in the field of armaments and institutional cooperation within NATO are still uncertain (despite the agreement of 16 December 2002), and, above all, the transatlantic tensions during the 2002–4 period.

Up to 2003, international commentators considered the overall achievements of the first decade of CFSP to be rather poor. The actions implemented by the CSFP were few and not particularly meaningful. Although the Amsterdam Treaty increased its visibility (the spokesman 'Mr CFSP') and authorized a more flexible decision-making process, the procedure maintained the right of veto, i.e. the expression of divergent interests and visions of the member states as far as the EU role and transatlantic relations are concerned.[19]

However, a series of very contradictory results marked the 1998–2000 period. On the one hand, the promise of the 'Saint-Malo spirit' (meaning the December 1998 meeting between Chirac and Blair on the CSDP[20]) went unfulfilled and Europe has continued to be technologically and operationally dependent on American leadership. This is especially true within the context of the militarization of local crises and revival of 'power politics' by the US. By contrast, European states and peoples have proved reluctant to provide for their own military safety. While this attitude has been encouraged both by the post-1989 'peace dividend' and the budgetary cuts linked to the Maastricht criteria regarding Monetary Union, it cannot fail to have an impact on the credibility of the CFSP and CSDP, if they are assessed according to classical realist criteria.[21] On the other hand, however, it is also true that decades of collaboration, institutional spillover and the new willingness of member states to react collectively to certain external challenges have produced innovative results. This is particularly true of the 2000 Nice Treaty (although it only came into force in 2003), which could, for example, facilitate the launch of 'enhanced cooperation' within the CSFP, with only eight partners, irrespective of the total number of member states. Variable geometry, and/or the creation of vanguard military groups (Eurocorps, several co-operation groups on armament matters, etc.) seem the more practical way forward within – but often outside – the framework of the CFSP and CSDP, particularly in an enlarged Europe. The crucial question is whether this 'two-speed' structure will take place through the Constitutional Treaty, framed in terms of more flexible acts of 'enhanced or structured coopera-tion', or outside, in line with the precedent set by the Schengen Treaty for example.

Objectively, the increased political weight of the EU in global gover-nance is not determined mainly by the CFSP and CSDP, but by its great continuing civil relations at continental and global level. Historically, if we had to identify the core of the EU's main contribution to global governance, we could say it lies in western European peace and, since 1989, in the pan-European architecture stabilizing the continent through a network of association agreements which pave the way for the entry of 10–15 new member states. Furthermore, it is worth pointing out that, over a ten-year period, the EU has significantly strengthened its international presence as the second civilian global actor. In addition to managing interregional and bilateral agreements in Africa, Latin America and Asia, including the 'political dialogue', this involves providing initial answers to international expectations regarding the increased global role of the Union and moving the EU beyond its traditional commercial dimensions and cooperation policies. Political dialogue with Asia, Latin America and Africa can only increase European responsibilities in terms of the restructuring of post-cold war world order. The question is whether the long-standing and wide gap between declarations of intent and economic power on the one hand, and political actions, operational capacity and diplomatic coherent representation on the other has really been bridged.[22]

Paradoxically, the enlargement of the EU and its global interregional action – fields only marginally covered by the CFSP – have turned out to be its two most significant foreign policy successes, especially if compared with its disappointing results with neighbouring Russia, the quasi-fiasco of cooperation policies with the southern rim of the Mediterranean, and the Union's decidedly unsteady debutant performance when faced with military conflicts (in the former Yugoslavia, the Middle East and the Gulf War).

It is worth looking for a moment at the quantitative extension of the presence of the EU and its member states across the world after the end of the cold war[23] and the clearer qualitative profile of the EU's 'international identity'.[24] The EU is now recognized as the second global actor by third countries. After the end of the cold war and the collapse of the USSR, the EU is far less dependent than it used to be on American nuclear protection and risk assessment. This historical discontinuity is crucial to any explanation of the global role of the EU. Prior to the Maastricht Treaty, the EC was little more than a mere economic entity whose international role was strictly framed within the Western alliance, even if there may have been a few original elements in East–West and North–South relations. Regardless of national rhetoric, the reality was that European states, including De Gaulle's France, were under the defensive umbrella of the US. However, in the new international context of the 1990s, the success of enlargement and the desire of member states to take full advantage of the new external opportunities and responsibilities led to the emergence of a new European regionalism, rich in external relations and implications. This relates not only to the intensification of integration policies, but also to the more active contribution of the Union – as a single entity and not just the sum of its member states – to the creation of new international economic and political regimes. The other novelty is that this qualitative and quantitative growth of the EU's contribution to global governance is happening in unprecedented forms and by means of procedures which differ greatly from the classic power model.

4.3   The roots of the ambiguity of European power

The debate on the contribution of the EU to global regulation and its international identity as a civilian power can be divided into three main stages: (1) the long period of the cold war and bipolar world order; (2) the 1990s; (3) the current phase which began with the return of the security question to the heart of the international agenda. In this section, we will examine the conceptual distinction between the development of an inter-national political role for the EU and its unrealistic transformation into a classic military power. Although it becomes fashionable after every inter-national military crisis, the rhetoric surrounding European security and defence policy cannot hide the self-evident truth of the widening quanti-tative and qualitative gap between the US and Europe in terms of military power, technological potential and defence budgets. To this list, we should add the growing gap in terms of the respective strategic tactical abilities of the US and Europe to successfully intervene anywhere in the world within a few days.[25] Thus, if the assertion that Europe is a military power is untrue today, it remains at best a risky dream in the future. Moreover, it distracts the EU from those goals within its reach and creates a constant feeling of inadequacy, rather than encouraging the Union to enhance the various innovative contributions of European practice to international relations and the new vision these reflect. This brings us to the key point: the concept of 'civilian power' can be an original contribution to twenty-first-century international relations and not a sad euphemism, synonymous with semi-sovereign power, weakness and lack of capacity.[26]

For as long as there remains a frustrating ambiguity about that choice, the EU will not only be left on the sidelines, but will be profoundly shaken whenever it is faced with the re-emergence of the politics of power in the post-cold war world (e.g. the first Gulf War, Kosovo, Afghanistan, the Iraqi War). In fact, notwithstanding the end of the cold war and the successes of the EC/EU (the Common Market and Monetary Union), the so-called 'French model',[27] identified 20 years ago by Headley Bull among others, still seems beyond Europe's reach and suitable neither for an international entity like the EU nor for its heterogeneous member states. There is no evidence, however, to support the thesis that a European political power 'comparable with the dignity of nations with the wealth, skills and historical position of those of western Europe'[28] must invariably lead to a new version of the 'French model' or a futile effort to catch up with US military power.

This raises the question of why the military power model cannot be applied to the EU. As shown in Chapter 3, the indisputable fact is that the majority of European states, political parties, associations and citizens, rightly or wrongly, refuse to devote a significant share of their wealth (4 per cent of GDP, instead of today's 2 per cent) to the creation of a military power comparable to the US providing the guarantee of security in the classic sense of the term. The second insurmountable obstacle lies in different national visions of the relationship with the United States and, consequently, the future of the Alliance.[29] Thirdly, the controversy surrounding Europe's institutional configuration is such that many believe greater supranational unity would be a weakness, rather than a strength, in the context of defence policy. Even a stronger EU Council Presidency as the expression of a single European voice in the international arena was a source of opposition and fears during the Convention. This problem of the centralization of external relations exists because the wider and more diverse these relations are, the greater coordination difficulties they create among the various relevant sectors (trade, cooperation policy, foreign policy and humanitarian aid) and among member states, particularly between the larger and the smaller ones.[30]

While the first difficulty looks insurmountable, those depending on institutional reforms and the political will of member states could perhaps be overcome. The question, therefore, of what type of pre-military international entity the EU might become in the twenty-first century is still open and numerous potential scenarios can be imagined. Each of these presupposes a different and sometimes opposite meaning of 'civilian power', beyond the first formulations of the term provided during the cold war. These accounts do, however, still constitute an essential starting point when dealing with the concept of 'civilian power'.

F. Duchêne presented his pioneering concept of 'civilian power Europe' against the background of a European community which had already become something more than a mere economic power by the early 1970s. Duchêne focused on the Community's capacity to play internal and external civilizing roles, to improve relations among member states and to spread civil and democratic standards around the world. As he wrote, 'this means trying to bring to international problems the sense of common responsibility and structures of contractual politics, which have been in the past associated exclusively with "home" and not foreign, that is alien, affairs'.[31] Despite the limits imposed by bipolarism, in the 1970s the EC began to evolve into an international entity, albeit one lacking both security and foreign policy dimension. It proved able to exert a degree of influence not only within its borders, but also on states, international and regional organizations, multinational corporations and other transnational bodies through a wide range of diplomatic, economic and legal instruments. As a result, several American international relations scholars, among them R.O. Keohane and J.S. Nye, started stressing the theoretical implications of this successful cooperation and integration process in criticism of the neo-realist school. Two of the most frequently mentioned of these arguments are that the concepts of power and foreign policy are no longer as clearly defined as in the past and that traditional distinctions between politics and economics, and between high and low politics, have become rather obsolete within international relations theory.[32]

The 1989 Franco-German initiative, which proposed that member states strengthen the political dimension of European integration in order to tackle the new challenges of the post-cold war period, and the Maastricht Treaty (1992) creating EMU and political union (including the CFSP) showed the EC/EU member states' desire to considerably increase their presence and assert their international identity.[33] External acknowledgements and expectations have also helped, since EU institutions encourage international and interregional accords with a view to improving both its visibility and internal legitimacy. Thus, the 1990s were marked by a significant growth of both internal and external expectations as far as the EU global role is concerned. This produced a reservoir of innovative ideas regarding the post-cold war globalized international system and the role of new actors such as the EU.

The current and future *terminus ad quem* of that evolution was, and still is, largely unknown. According to many commentators, the EU is becoming a global political actor. That status, however, raises the question of what criteria should be used to assess the capacity of an *actor* which differs from both the traditional nation-state model and, in particular, from the US and is no longer a mere international *entity*. Compared with the EU, as far as foreign policy is concerned, states have six main features: not only an established community of strategic interests, but also a centralized decision-making system, supported by an organization of communication and representation channels with the external world, not only an efficient regional crisis prevention and management system, but also an autonomous and sufficient military capacity, and a mobilization system in case of emergency.

The apparent deficits of the EU have taken on a dramatic character during the third, and current, stage of the debate on 'civilian power' following the problems posed by global terrorist violence, proliferation threats and 'preventive wars' at the top of the international agenda. To what degree can the EC/EU consider itself a genuine international actor which behaves in a coherent and satisfactory manner in its external relations, without being more politically credible? Whereas in the bipolar world, and to some extent during the 1990s, the EC could operate as a second rank power, there is no evidence that an enlarged Union, operating in the partially globalized and politically unstable world of the twenty-first century, can exist politically or even preserve the achievements of the 'small' European Community.

The theoretical problem is how, and to what degree, can a regional 'civilian power' evolve politically without following the traditional 'French model' of *Europe puissance*, extensively illustrated by Headley Bull. It is still unclear what a Union not based on the state model can be in terms of the redefinition of power. Of course, the crucial *external* variable is the scope provided by the evolving international relations system, as we have seen in Chapter 1. However, the internal political and theoretical challenge is: what kind of political civilian power is required to overcome the current images of a 'Candide' Europe or of an 'ambiguous power' or 'status quo supporter entity', and to allow the EU to operate effectively as a more autonomous regional and global actor within the context of the global system of the twenty-first century?

4.4   The widening and deepening of the EU: the institutional variable

To answer the question just posed, we need to identify the relevant variables. The first of these is internal and regards the *institutional balance* between the enlargement in 2004 to include 10 – and in the future even more – new member states and the constitutional revision of the treaties. The second one is internal/external. The events of 1989 and the end of the bipolar world produced two consequences which are not easily reconcilable: on the one hand, the applications addressed by neutral and post-Communist countries are irresistible because of the right to apply is, at least within certain limits, beyond question; on the other hand, however, the quantitative and qualitative implications produced by such a huge widening challenge the very nature of the EU in terms of both the coherence and the political nature of its approach to international affairs.[34]

Even before the 2004 enlargement, the decision-making and implementation processes within both the CSFP and external relations were hindered by weak central coordination, which caused inconsistencies and incongruities within the 15 member states of the EU. Decentralization keeps the decision-making process on two levels (national and supranational) and creates further complications as enlargement increases internal differentiation (in terms of traditions, external relations, interests, capacities, etc.). In the case of Europe, most commentators agree that we are faced with a complex system of multi-level governance which is very different from the American polity. Europe will always lack that extraordinary central factor, balancing the complexity of the internal decision-making process in the US, which Arthur Schlesinger termed the 'imperial presidency' – meaning the highly centripetal decision-making process developed in the US between the two Roosevelts (Theodore and Franklin Delano), i.e. between the end of the nineteenth and the mid-twentieth centuries. The hypothesis we deepen in Chapter 5 is that EU will never become a state. However, even if it is inevitably very far from the US model of power and not yet ratified, the solution suggested by the Constitutional Treaty is a kind of rationalized 'mixed government' based on a 'triumvirate' capable of enhancing the consistency of the body of external relations: a legitimated, full-time, stable Presidency of the European Council (no longer a rotating one), coordinated with a Presidency of the Commission, better legitimated (by a vote of Parliament). Thirdly, a 'minister for foreign affairs', as a member of both the Council and the Commission (moving beyond their current division as two distinct decision-making centres). It is too soon to know whether this triumvirate would be revealed as a conflicting settlement or facilitate the coordination of decisions and policies, namely on sensitive international issues, rich in political implications, relating not only to the second pillar, but also to the former first and third pillars. This is expected to partially counterbalance the tendencies towards policy renationalization and the 'routine' of internal polyarchy and fragmentation of national, sectoral and local interests, both private and public, which are involved in the decision-making and implementation processes. In the case of more controversial political questions, however, any attempt to use the qualified majority voting procedure in the Council is and will remain unlikely to succeed. The current Treaty of Nice is an even less efficient 'mix'.

The opposite is true in the US. As the famous political scientist Theodore J. Lowi[35] noted, it is precisely in the case of the most delicate issues concerning foreign policy that the above-mentioned fragmented governance and internal polyarchy are effectively supplanted by a unified 'elitist' decision, while, on minor and low politics questions, by contrast, decisions are taken and implemented according to a fragmented and/or polyarchic model. In Europe, the essence of foreign policy decision-making is likely to remain subject to long intergovernmental, interinstitutional negotiations and discussions between institutions and member states as in the US routine low policies,[36] with inevitable consequences in 'situation of emergency' (C. Schmitt's concept), situations such as international military crises. However, institutional reform and informal trends may matter, at least towards a more oriented subsidiarity.

In the long term, even after enlargement, vertical coordination will benefit from the routine of external relations. National ministries across Europe bear the signs of a 'Europeanization' process, namely the habit of working together with the other partners and regularly taking their opinions and interests into account when formulating national preferences. This common framework has changed the way high-ranking national officials work (this is particularly true of those who regularly participate in the various specialized Councils of Ministers or Coreper). Some observers note how, even without justifying any teleological hopes, there does exist a certain 'institutional spillover', i.e. an incremental dynamic towards increased unification. This explains half a century of concrete progress along with the fact that engaged rhetoric and common ambitions regarding the integration process can sometimes be turned into genuine progress, even in the cases of traditionally Eurosceptic member states.[37] This dynamics should not be overstated as a 'fusion process', however, especially when the core of national sovereignty is at stake.[38] Integration requires the political will of member states not only to simply cooperate, but also to delegate competencies and increasingly centralize the foreign decision-making process.

In the 25 member state EU, vertical coordination is also hampered by the fact that several causes of the persistent decentralization of the European political system are structural. Firstly, they are to be found among the heterogeneous national interests and different visions of the Union's future, as shown by the endless debate between those states and actors which stress the need for greater internal cohesion and loyalty and the defenders of the structures and practices of national sovereignty.[39] This problem exists since the failure of the EDC in 1954 and the British entry in 1973, and it does not appear to have been particularly exacerbated by the later entry of those neutral countries which, for example, contributed to the Amsterdam compromise on the 'Petersberg tasks'. Greater difficulties are inevitable, however, with the accession of countries which have only recently regained their status and symbols of national sovereignty after decades of subjugation to the Soviet empire. These states do not always make the distinction between national sovereignty that is limited by an external authority by coercion and sovereignty which is being voluntarily shared. Even if they seemed, at least in 2003–4, to prefer delegating to NATO and the US rather than to the EU as regards security and foreign policy, the above-mentioned functional and institutional factors are likely to enhance their acceptance of increased European coordination.

Theoretically, the current institutional framework of EU external relations requires multiple approaches in order to be correctly interpreted. As far as the first pillar and EMU are concerned, intergovernmental approaches (focusing on the interaction process and cooperation policies between member state governments) differ from functionalist accounts in underestimating the centripetal spillover caused by common interests in the gradual development of common policies and institutions. However, they are right when, in contrast to functionalist approaches and federalist aspirations, they stress that the second global actor is neither a state, nor a republic of republics, nor a state-like unitary and consistent actor, but the most advanced case of regional polity. The institutionalist approach is essential, because it allows us to explain the modes and aims of vertical and horizontal coordination and helps us trace the evolution of a clearly *sui generis* political system which, while undoubtedly comparable with other political systems, has no single President or diplomatic corps, nor a real government including a minister for foreign affairs. As regards horizontal coordination, the Constitutional Treaty improves the relationship between the Commission and the Council. As for vertical coordination, the key issue lies in carefully gauging the scopes and limits of member state loyalty to the Union. Since participation in European common policies strengthens the international weight of member states, a very relevant achievement would be to institutionalize common international interests and to improve the coordination of national policies within international organizations, conferences and negotiations.

To conclude, we can say that, on the one hand, the EU is clearly different from the traditional state model and from the concept of a state power in particular. On the other hand, however, it is not simply equivalent to a collection of international regimes. It lacks the appropriate means either to incorporate the sum of member state foreign policies, or to achieve its goals in all the various power sectors: ideological, political and economic, financial, technological and military. However, thanks to its institutions and policies, it does exercise a wide and variegated influence on the world. In the case of other regional associations like the EU, gradually constructed institutional frameworks have a particularly significant impact on actual evolution. Of course, there are no legal sanctions for the lack of political will. However, comparative research shows that changes in rules and juridical structure have an impact on the policies and behaviour of member states. Indeed, they provide a clearer explanation of both the driving forces and the limits of half a century of results, and of the very particular configuration of the EU as a special global actor and a 'strange power'.

4.5   The EU and globalization, new regionalism and multilateralism: three scenarios

The three scenarios examined below (Europe as a continental trading state, 'fortress Europe' and Europe as a new civilian power) are based on the different impact that the various potential institutional frameworks resulting from the widening and deepening of the EU will have on the place of European new regionalism within the post-cold war world. The aforementioned internal/external variables are combined with a series of purely external variables indeed. Sketching different scenarios can be useful in assessing the uncertainty surrounding the future development of the EU and its international role. It also helps us avoid trivial comparisons and contrasts between what Europe *is* and what it *ought to be* and simplified accounts of the ongoing debate between different normative positions. The evolving international identity of the EC/EU will be analysed therefore not only in terms of internal dynamics, but also within the context of international political trends.

4.5.1   Europe as a continental 'trading state' in the global economy

This first scenario envisages new regionalism being watered down within the context of the creation of an endlessly widening EU, in which the current enlargement to 25 member states – and the likely future increase to 35 member states in the next 15 years[40] – would not only become incompatible with the further development of the integration process which was started 50 years ago, but would also jeopardize those results achieved to date. It seems exaggerated to imagine an EU in danger of turning into a large free trade zone, a mere geopolitical 'space', as Valéry Giscard d'Estaing put it. Rather, the impression is that a continental EU would resemble a large and deregulated market integrated by a softer legal framework, a sort of Council of Europe or CSCE, i.e. light pan-European organizations playing not insignificant roles at legal (protection of human rights), security and economic levels. The first scenario only postulates an apparent continuity with the current unification level; however, as a consequence of enlargement, it foresees a worsening of the trends leading to ineffectiveness not only in terms of external political action, but also as regards internal cohesion policies. This would be mainly due to the maintenance of an institutional status quo which cannot cope with the governance of an excessively enlarged EU.

'Apocalyptic' commentators underestimate the fact that the enlargement of the EC/EU to include eastern Europe and the Mediterranean could, however, lead to a very broad and innovative regional area of cooperation, albeit rigorously framed within a globalization and world order governed by the US. The literature presents two versions of this scenario. The first (and rosier) hypothesis envisages the confirmation of the EU's role as a propagator of the historical benefits of European integration (peace, stability, democracy and prosperity) on a continental scale, with positive repercussions also in neighbouring areas (Middle East, North Africa, CIS). The gloomier hypothesis envisages enlargement towards a 35-member EU not only causing a change in the nature of the EU, but a decline. This would occur for the following three reasons:

(a) given the wide economic gap between different parts of Europe, the EU budget would be unable to rise to the huge financial and social challenges posed by enlargement in relation to cohesion policies. Moreover, the national European welfare models and the 'social market economy' would be threatened by fanciful attempts to import the American model of globalization, with serious consequences for internal cohesion between and within both states and regions, for social peace and even for the single currency;

(b) at institutional level, the rejection by several old and new member states of the very idea of supranationality would produce a purely intergovernmental organization, paralysed by reciprocal vetoes and the weakness of the decision-making process and the narrow common budget;

(c) the rejection by the majority of member states of the prospect of a more autonomous European political union would lead to the end of the CFSP and CSDP. Institutional inertia would provoke substantial economic and political decline along with the end of the EU as a global political actor, and lead to increasingly fragmented and less accountable internal governance. This would not result in a mere free trade zone, but a 'condominium' lacking any political profile, according to Philippe Schmitter's famous definition, i.e. a mixture of forms of membership and governance mirroring territorial and functional criteria.[41]

This second variant could imply the end of monetary union, given the contradictions that would emerge due to insufficient market integration and the lack of a counterbalance to what was aptly described by Tommaso Padoa-Schioppa as the solitude of the European Central Bank in governing the European currency. The Single European Market would be downgraded to the status of a mere component of the transatlantic, continental and Mediterranean free trade area within the context of global liberalization. The *acquis communautaire* would not disappear, but would certainly undergo gradual erosion as regards common policies. Obviously, since the residual intergovernmental regimes would no longer be a precondition for a political community, that structure would be very fragile when faced with international pressures. The regional integration model would be profoundly transformed and reconfigured as a regional grouping of states within economic and political globalism led by the US.

This new kind of EU could be compared to the semi-sovereign West Germany during the 1949–90 period. Europe could maintain its international image as a relatively prosperous and ecologically and socially aware continent. It could also remain unchanged as a powerful economic and commercial entity. However, the context of global international competition/cooperation would be neither as friendly nor as stable as in the golden years following the Second World War, mainly because the US is no longer the hegemonic cooperative leader it used to be, and Asian competitiveness would easily threaten the European share of the global market. Moreover, internal demographic changes such as ageing populations and immigration flows would force radical changes upon the socio-economic model, with destabilizing consequences. Admittedly, such threats are overestimated by protectionists and there is as yet no evidence suggesting real marginalization of Europe, either now or in the near future. Summing up, even if in contrast to the optimism of the 1990s, this enlarged Europe would, according to various scholars, be like Dante's 'ship without a helmsman in a terrible storm', it could continue to exert a certain level of international soft influence, despite political integration having been halted and globalization being governed by third parties.

On the other hand, less optimistic readings highlight the fact that a Europe similar to the 'Bonn-Germany model' would need a competitive edge to ensure its survival in the global economy and to maintain social integration and economic prosperity. The domestic and international conditions which marked the years of the German and Italian economic booms have disappeared. So too have the previous competitive edges.

This scenario would therefore eventually weaken the EC/EU and its member states as an economic and commercial giant, in addition to crushing any aim of developing a global political role. For such a type of 'continental trading state', even any reference to the timid, but prosperous, Federal Republic of Germany, the nice 'Republic of Bonn', recalling the famous image of the economic giant and political dwarf, is illusory and optimistic. In both readings, Richard N. Rosecrance's definition is still valid. As he wrote, a 'trading state' is a political system in which economic growth has no implication on political and military power, because this remains safely in the hands of the leading power in the alliance.[42]

At present, the main supporters of this kind of evolution are not only to be found within the G.W. Bush administration, but also among the strong economic networks, technocratic groups and transnational coalitions of interests that exist in every European country, not only in the UK. The idea of giving priority to a so-called 'fortified transatlantic community', encompassing the EU and the only superpower in an increasingly asymmetric alliance, is shared by several political forces and leaders in both old and new member states. The implications of this have emerged during the Iraqi crisis and the Convention debates. Habermas intends something similar when he envisages a possible neo-liberal alliance between Eurosceptics and Eurocrats.[43] On the surface, he might seem to be wrong as Eurocrats have defended the *acquis communautaire* in the past. If we delve deeper, however, we find that he may be right since part of the European technocracy is characterized by a deep-rooted, anti-political tradition and a functionalist search for 'niches for experts', all conducted with rigorous deference to international power hierarchies.

Enormous obstacles would have to be overcome, however, in order to bring about such a scenario. Solid industrial, economic, commercial and strategic interests are opposed to any radical shift of the classical European project of deepened regional integration. These include very dynamic and successful European technological achievements such as the Airbus carriers, the European Space Agency and research and the 'Galileo' project for an independent satellite network. European interests are underpinning the recurrent commercial disputes within the West, and explain the failure of the Multilateral Agreement on Investment in 1998. Moreover, at least a section of European elites is aware of the dangerous domestic implications (in terms of greater social instability and the rise of neo-populist political opposition) of such a neo-Atlantic, neo-liberal scenario. Last but not least, the cleavage of 'autonomy versus dependency' would again politically divide the European Council.

What would be the implications of this scenario for new regionalism worldwide? In the 1990s, one could have responded that such a 'continental trading state' would belong to a wider global trend linked to the American global strategy of 'emerging markets' and the creation of huge free trade interregional US-centred arrangements such as the Free Trade Area of the Americas (FTAA) with Latin America, the Asia-Pacific Economic Cooperation (APEC) with the Asia-Pacific countries, and, indeed, with Europe too. Of course, any evolution of the EC/EU towards this scenario would have important implications for the other regions of the world. Every country and region would be forced into the limited choice between either adapting their economy to the imperatives of such a political reorganization of global markets or embracing catastrophic isolation. Nationalist and fundamentalist movements would react against the more binding aspects of this kind of globalism, since countries would be deprived of an alternative regional structure in which to initiate a more gradual and less destabilizing process of economic and political cooperation. Even less would be done to combat the current marginalization of the poorest countries, which would also lose the contractual strength provided by solid regional organizations and a potentially important ally in the EU. Global governance would thus be more unstable and asymmetric.

In these early years of the new century, we may add that the international system is ever more characterized not only by (seemingly liberal) American globalization, but also by growing political hierarchies worldwide, which are ignored by neo-liberal theses. In the scenario outlined here, the world order would be characterized by an unprecedented concentration of power, and by national/subnational fragmentation. The defeat of political regionalism as a kind of dynamic third way towards multilateral global governance, between unipolarism and anarchic fragmentation, would thus have vast implications for the very political structure of the world itself.

4.5.2   The second scenario: from 'fortress Europe' to a neo-mercantilist power

In the uncertain context of the partially globalized post-cold war world and as a reaction to external tensions, pressing internal demands and fears, economic failures, the lack of technological innovation and the emergence of informal terrorism, the EU could strengthen its more introverted and defensive tendencies by increasingly limiting its openness and global interdependence. The combination of hard trade disputes and internal social requests for economic security could lead the EU to introduce protectionist and defensive economic policies.[44] It could also provoke chain reactions leading to obsessions about internal and external security in the face of global instability. The politicization of internal security demands could become particularly evident in the event of major crises on the eastern and/or southern borders of the Union,[45] as has been highlighted by the introverted responses during the crises in the western Balkans and populist reactions to illegal immigration, terrorist threats and the question of Turkish accession into the EU. While economic and security needs are not necessarily connected, the former do create favourable premises for the latter and vice versa. In particular, irrational internal security demands could help strengthen the link between the two needs.

It is not necessary to go so far as to imagine some sort of 'institutional Big Bang' and a drive to 'fortress Europe', brought about by new conflicts or threats (whether real or presumed) in the surrounding world, or even by the decline of the international economic and trade system. Rather, as a reaction to difficulties in federal and functional integration, it is more credible to envisage a new intergovernmental structure, based on the revival of the logic of member state territorial sovereignty as an institutional principle and a directorate of major states emerging in conjunction with the partial failure or scaling down of enlargement towards the east and south-east, considered more of a problem than a resource.

Fears of immigration flows and anxieties about external terrorist threats, combined with the weight of lobbies representing protected industries and the arms industry, could act in support of the rhetoric for a protectionist Europe and a notion of *Europe puissance* in the narrow military sense, thus reviving the discourse of trade wars and international power. Even if internal socio-economic requests were to be the starting point, a logical consequence could be increased support for a view of political and military power as the only solution to disputes and conflicts when economic, legal and ideological powers fail.[46] A political and military 'European power' would adopt a multipolar perspective with respect to the US and the rest of the world, well beyond the simple notion of *influence* mentioned above and of *civilian power* as well.

To what degree can such a scenario be considered realistic in the early years of the twenty-first century? Various institutional circles, cultural and political trends, networks of industrial and agricultural interests and economic lobbies, not only in France but within each EU member state, openly support the idea of Europe as a protectionist and military power. Let us focus on three main driving factors. First of all, the difficulties which the EU has had to face during the last decade in dealing, in a very short time, with the demanding task of widening/deepening, as well as the unknown factors in the unprecedented enlargement to the east (and south-east) and a difficult internal reform process, have provoked facile and widespread populist reactions. Secondly, fears are generated by a type of global competition which sees Europe as a potential loser, and in which the failure of the 'Lisbon Strategy' (see Chapter 3) would be beneficial to rivals. Finally, we have seen the spread of myriad and crude anti-American reactions, encouraged by the unilateral arrogance of the US. This would of course be a costly scenario. However, even alternative scenarios entail costs. In this case, funding would be required for the social consequences of broad enlargement to the east and liberalization. In sum, such a scenario deserves more attention than it received in the 1980s and 1990s.

Nevertheless, there are important caveats attached to this scenario of a neo-mercantilist and sovereign 'fortress Europe'. Such an entity could not avoid causing serious divisions both between and within European states. As regards the political and military side of the demand for a stronger and more centralized European power, there are immense differences between the various national traditions. These include those between the two nuclear powers and the rest, between neutral powers and nuclear powers, between the five countries with most experience in terms of foreign policy and the use of military force, between small and large countries, between junior partners of the US and those who favour independent stances, and, finally, between dogged supporters of the symbols of national sovereignty and hardened federalists. There is also a significant political difficulty: while trade protectionism and the manipulation of fears regarding immigration and terrorist attacks may attract, rather than repel, voters, no European politician, whether from the right or the left, would dare base an electoral campaign on support for the growth of the military budget, given the repercussions on living standards, welfare provisions and democratic accountability. Indeed, the simultaneous emergence of such internal problems would end up causing the division and possibly the disintegration of the EU.

Let us imagine, however, that the EU somehow proves capable of managing these internal economic and political difficulties. What would be the external implications of a neo-mercantilist European power for other regions and global governance? One of the outcomes would be a drift towards multiple conflicts between competing blocs – both regional and national. Europe already currently conducts a policy of interregional agreements and preferential trade agreements,[47] including the

Mediterranean southern rim, Russia, Africa, Asia and Latin America. Opposition to American globalism could become explicit and strategic. The FTAA and APEC could more openly develop as part of an effort by the US to isolate the EU. Asian giants could strengthen trade competitiveness, regional power alliances and exclusive identities. 'Most favoured nation' status, the linchpin of multilateralism, could be radically transformed into a trade war weapon. Agreeing and implementing global multilateral agreements would become increasingly difficult due to growing tensions within the global trade, financial and monetary systems. Other regional entities would imitate the mercantilist stance of the EU and the US. Multilateral organizations would be thrown into crisis and paralysed. Predictable responses would include the strengthening of defensive regionalism and economic nationalism in America and Asia. The EU and every other regional organization would emerge profoundly changed in the event of commercial and political conflicts between trade blocs. They would be either internally divided or would become part of the sphere of influence of their respective dominating state on a regional scale.

The costs of greater competition between blocs could be very high, especially in developing countries and marginal areas. These would become victims of the struggle between spheres of influence and would be forced to side with one or other of the opposing parties. The changing global environment will have an impact on big countries such as China, India, Brazil, Indonesia and South Africa, pushing them towards nationalism and inward-looking policies. NATO and the UN would also suffer in the event of transatlantic disputes. The theories on the opposition between regionalism and globalization would be openly confirmed and would match Robert Gilpin's gloomy forecast which envisages malevolent mercantilism shifting towards military rearmament, in a multipolar logic.[48]

Furthermore, although not highly militarized, the EU would represent a decisive factor in the shift towards a multipolar world. Naturally, in theory at least, there are numerous possible forms which a multipolar world could take. It is worth noting that the radical transformation of multilateralism into tough bargaining between trade blocs and the emphasis placed on power politics (whether the main actors are megastates or regional blocs) do not differ greatly from the ideas recently expressed not only by several American and Asian leaders, but also by some European ones. Given the uncertainties of the international system, the transformation of regionalism from a 'benevolent' to a 'malevolent' form cannot be completely ruled out. Nevertheless, paradoxically, what is lacking most in this scenario is realism, because the legacy of half a century of international relations history – marked not only by bipolar confrontation, but also multilateralism in the West – cannot be easily erased. In particular, we should consider the interests of states in cooperation, the role of international and multilateral organizations, and the extraordinary development of transnational relations and new regionalism in support of peace and cooperation among states. In the light of these considerations, not even the emergence of American unipolarism can be seriously interpreted and dealt with in classic 'balance of power' terms.

4.6   A civilian and political power: the third scenario

Various schools of thought have investigated the idea of the EC/EU as a new kind of international civilian actor, capable both of defending its fundamental socio-cconomic and institutional achievements and better managing new international challenges and threats. To what extent are normative approaches relevant? According to constructivist theories of international relations,[49] ideas, ideational factors, 'social purposes' and the self-images of actors both influence political action and are issues of power conflicts. As anticipated in Chapters 1 and 3, scholars and a part of public opinion support the idea of 'Europe as the world's Scandinavia' – emphasizing both the socio-economic content of the external influence of the European model of society which can balance freedom, justice and solidarity, and the commitment to the UN. Second, the foundation of the concept of the EU's special mission, of its 'international political responsibility' or 'historical memory' of past tragedies is underpinning an idea of Europe as a normative power. Both of these lie at the heart of the conception of the EU as a very special kind of soft power, clearly distinct from the concept of soft power applied by Nye to some of the external policies of the US. The first of these can trace its roots back mainly to Sweden, while the second originated from within the founding states and particularly in Germany. The EU institutions, however, have been able to increasingly integrate them in their discourse. To what extent are they useful, however, in explaining why the constant reference in European treaties, the EU's declaratory diplomacy and its participation in global organizations such as the WTO, the UN and the ILO, to the values and principles of international justice and multilateralism, might be more credible and effective than the traditional rhetoric of other institutions and states?

We have already discussed the notion of the EU as 'the world's Scandinavia', and so reference is only made here to its imaginative strength, in the sense of the example set by its external civilizing role, based on the welfare model and traditional influence on the UN system. The second notion recalls the distinctive role of shared memory of the past in Europe, particularly after the three decades of 'European civil war' from 1914 to 1945. In EU understanding, applying the notion of 'responsibility' to international relations means stressing a theoretical innovation as regards realist and neo-realist tradition. The appeal for responsibility in foreign policy challenges the classical notion of state sovereignty. It not only questions the division between domestic democratic policy and international policy – a perennial gamble of democratic theory ever since Rousseau, Kant and Tocqueville – but also commits the EU to maintaining its tragic historical memory and transmitting this understanding to new generations of Europeans and new member states. An analysis of what 'international responsibility' really means must also include accountability towards domestic democratic public opinion.

The distinctive European relationship to its past underpins a concept of civilian power which fundamentally differs from the US notion of 'soft power' and the Japanese kind of civilian power. On the one hand, the EU is constructing its political identity by a selective reading of the legacy of 2500 years of humanistic civilization, from the Greek *polis* to Roman law, from Renaissance 'republican' culture and the Enlightenment as a shared and secularized background for its unification process. On the other, it emphasizes the process of democratic learning from past tragedies and the aggressive policies implemented by Europeans (Fascism, Nazism, Communist dictatorships, colonialism, intolerance, etc.). Indeed, it uses this background as a resource to help foster understanding with others near and far and to improve and democratize global governance. We can recognize similarities and differences between the learning processes resulting from the experience of Fascist dictatorships in Germany, Italy, Spain and Portugal on the one hand, and, on the other, for example, the post-war experience of Japan which turned Hiroshima into a consensus facilitating national pacifism and the rejection of war in its Constitution (art. 9) and in support of its foreign policy as a civilian power. However, Japan was not yet capable of building confidence and trust with previous enemies and victims such as Korea and China.[50] The historical and theoretical relevance of the Franco-German reconciliation for the construction of the new European political identity is still underestimated.[51] This comparison thus provides a better explanation of why Europe not only feels globally more responsible for the world's public welfare and global good government than, for example, the US, China or other states, but is also increasingly developing a multilateralist European identity, that is becoming a shared value influencing EU institutions and policies. This is reflected in greater coherence with cosmopolitan values, the values of the UN, and the commitment to defending mankind's common interests (disarmament, peace, the environment, economic growth, social justice, the fight against crime, terrorism, epidemic diseases, drugs, etc.).

The lessons of history and memory are important in shaping the conscience of nations and in influencing national and supranational preferences in many political spheres – in particular, those linked to the identity and international status of the political subject in question. This was, and still is, relevant in many European states, within both the framework of post-Fascist democratic reconstruction (Germany, Italy, Spain, etc.) and the revival of national traditions of loyalty to democratic values (Britain), republican principles (France) or active commitment to the policies of peace and development cooperation (Sweden and neutral countries in general).

These types of plural European 'virtues' need propitious circumstances (*fortuna* in Machiavelli's understanding), however, in order to express themselves in a unified fashion, and just such an occasion is provided by the new window of opportunity open to Europe after 1945 and particularly following the end of the bipolar world. The first 50 years of European construction provided a collaborative and constructive framework for national memories to be largely shared and re-elaborated with previous enemies, towards an emerging common understanding and assessment of the past tragedies, and against the pluralism of conflicting and vindictive memories.

With the new post-1989 international environment which minimized the significance of nuclear threats and reduced the importance of traditional military security issues, the influence of 'idealist foreign policies' became stronger, especially in the national political cultures of Germany, Italy, Belgium, Scandinavia and others. This factor has played a role in European construction and has impacted significantly on the defence budgets of all European states which – unlike the US – have exploited the so-called 'peace dividend'. Realist criticism against European military weakness became less cogent therefore, as an effective contribution to global governance seems achievable though innovative instruments, schedules and modes of action which differed from those of a classic military power.

To what extent and how in the 1990s did the political dwarf of the Western world therefore begin conceiving and operationalizing its distinctive international political identity? First of all, we should note the difference between the related, yet distinct, concepts of influence and power. Influence is well interpreted by the notion of Europe as 'the world's Scandinavia'. This concept denotes much more than a mere economic entity and presents itself as an alternative to the two scenarios discussed above. We understand 'Scandinavian Europe', in fact, rather than as a normative concept as an analytical one, consistent with both economic and social achievements and a shared scientific awareness that there is not sufficient evidence to support the idea that the American social model can be imported. Chapter 3 shows that Europe has so far maintained its principal common social characteristics despite critical domestic and international factors. The spread of social justice and solidarity as values influencing social partners and the various national political party systems along with the relatively well-developed Welfare State continue to shape the continent in line with an internationally recognizable identity. Moreover, the EU consists of a very precise set of international regimes and supranational institutions, a systemic integration process, a 'social mega-network' and a 'concentric circles' type of legal area which is governed by European Community law at its heart, and by the Court of Strasbourg, the Council of Europe and the OSCE in its broader circles. The Union's coherent set of common values in terms of science and society (including control over genetic engineering, opposition to the death penalty and so on) is surviving the impact of globalization much more so than elsewhere.[52]

Nevertheless, one thing is becoming increasingly clear: since the current type of globalization leaves no room for a pluralism of socio-economic models if they cannot be firmly asserted at world level, traditional 'influence' is increasingly complemented by other dimensions of civilian power, namely by common EU policies. Faced with the strong pressures in favour of global economic convergence, the defence of European national social models (and their supranational dimension) would be untenable if Europe cannot renew and strengthen itself on the world scene. This consideration lay at the heart of the strategy approved by the Lisbon European Council for the 2000–10 period which, as we argued in Chapter 3, rejected both neo-mercantilism and the mere adaptation to globalization. Rather, it expressed the desire of member states for reform and the development of a 'European model of the knowledge economy'.

This kind of strategic approach already goes beyond the notion of European 'influence' and stresses the vital diversity of regional socio-economic models within the global market economy. However, we provided evidence that the EU is expected to more consciously and directly contribute to the rare 'public good' of a better type of world governance. Admittedly, the very existence of the EU has thus far managed internal diversities by curbing radical market policies and domestic protectionist trends among its member states, but its ability to creatively tackle future protectionist or deregulatory demands is open to question.[53] The 'world's Scandinavia' scenario risks failure if it gradually degenerates into some sort of 'world's Switzerland' – the illusion of an island of wealth, extraneous to the destiny of global governance. It is worth noting that the provincial reticence of Sweden and Denmark regarding the euro is not helping Europe become the pillar of a new global multilateralism. To some extent, the international implications of the euro and its political potential are symbolic of the gap between the 'Scandinavian Europe' model of EU international identity and that of a new European civilian power.

This point is both fundamental and new even if ignored by isolationist approaches defined by C. Offe's 'welfare-chauvinists'. Even the best national models are dramatically inadequate when faced with the challenges and threats of the twenty-first century. National approaches, distinct from solidarity within the EU and the development of a stronger common political identity, are thus anachronistic. Of course, a common political identity must be pluralist and its development based on multi-level concentric circles: it needs to complement local and national identities and, at the same time, reconcile 25 (and perhaps 35 within the next 20 years) different national identities. In addition to Scandinavian and northern European identities, common and pluralist ground for a shared European identity has to be found in every national political culture, that is, in pacifist Germany, republican France, Italy (divided between pacifists and Atlanticists), Great Britain (notwithstanding its 'special relationship' with the US), the Iberian peninsula (which controversially combines strong support for Europe, the Atlantic partnership and nationalism), the neo-sovereign current inclinations of several new member states[54] and the distinctive demands of the smaller members of the Union. All these together may contribute to the construction of a European international identity (including its values and practices), if they distinguish republican citizenship from state nationalism. Indeed, both intergovernmental cooperation and the Community institutions are more necessary now than ever in terms of reviving citizens' participation, spreading this heterogeneous legacy out from the EU borders and turning it into effective and coherent external action.

The EU cannot be compared to a spiritual power like the Catholic Church. If it neither strengthens its decision-making process and institutional capacities nor makes further progress towards a stronger new model of civilian power, then 'Scandinavian Europe' risks falling into a 'Candide' Europe scenario in which it would become the weakest link in prospective global power struggles. 'Scandinavian Europe', even if Europeanized by the Lisbon Strategy, cannot therefore survive without both the desire and the ability to confidently and clearly express its vision of the world in international and interregional bodies through a vast array of policies from trade links and development cooperation to foreign policy.

To conclude, in comparative terms, the EU is already a peaceful, democratic and civilian power. It is inspired by common values, conserves the memory of its past and espouses loyalty to the UN. It was able to enshrine these elements within the treaties by means of binding provisions for both present and future member states. The Constitutional Treaty goes beyond articles 6 and 7 of the TEU, which already stipulated firm support for democracy and human rights and threatened sanctions on member states which violate these. However, we will verify later in Chapter 5 to what extent the Constitutional Treaty provides the normative dimension for this new kind of civilian power, starting with common principles and values, even beyond what is already stated in Chapter VII of the TEU, which clearly stresses consistency with the universal objectives of the UN and the OSCE. Secondly, we will verify how it strengthens the political Union and also the decision-making process, rendering them better able to coordinate the EC/EU's external relations, contribute to global security, promote democracy in the world by peaceful means, facilitate conflict-prevention missions aimed at keeping and enforcing peace both in neighbouring and far-off areas, manage crises and post-war reconstruction, govern trade conflicts, reform North–South relations and, when necessary, defend common strategic interests.

4.7 A structural foreign policy

What concepts can explain the very particular forms of action of the EU as an international civilian power in the making? The EU does not have a classical foreign policy and its concept of foreign policy should include the various external relations, both the ends and the means, economics and politics, efficacy and democratic legitimization, direct accountability and multilateral commitment. The issue at stake is not to conceptualize a second-best solution, but to address a salient theoretical dimension: what are the terms of a foreign policy designed to reform the classical Westphalian model of inter-state relations? Our concept of 'structural foreign policy' is meant to provide an answer. It therefore includes not only the CFSP *stricto sensu*, but also the various dimensions of external relations, i.e. the set of external relations belonging to the first EC pillar.[55] More specifically:

(a) the concept of a 'structural foreign policy' demands greater attention to long-term gains rather than purely utilitarian short-term cost–benefits criteria as regards international relations. Even if it welcomes assessment of its effectiveness, it provides an original answer to the question about the optimal timetable for the foreign policy of a modern world power;

(b) a 'structural foreign policy' is expected to modify the basic structural conditions in which all actors will operate in the future, leading to an environment more favourable to peace and the values of civilian powers. According to F. Braudel, power is the capacity of creating a favourable conjunction of circumstances;

(c) it should also have a particular impact on the economic, social, political (democratization) and ideational components of partners: states, regions, economic actors, international organizations, etc., so as to influence their foreign policies (support for regional and interregional cooperation; the promotion of democracy and respect for human rights; the prevention of violent conflict);

(d) it is implemented through peaceful and civilian means and encompasses the set of external relations of the three pillars, moving beyond the narrow CFSP field. This regards not only diplomatic relations, sanctions and political dialogue, but also policy areas such as preferential trade agreements, immigration, development and monetary policy.

The contrast between the EU's 'structural foreign policy' and the classic foreign policy of traditional powers tends to be oversimplified, as in the case of the banal contrast between US strength and EU weakness, when we are discussing two concepts of power.[56] Within international relations theory, the main references are provided by the institutionalist critiques of Kenneth Waltz's 'structural' neo-realism,[57] by constructivism and, to some extent, by international political economy (IPE). Unlike Marx, by 'structure' Kenneth Waltz means the political basis of the international system, in particular the persistent anarchic connotation of inter-state relations. The definition of 'structural foreign policy' should logically focus on an international actor's capacity to consciously pursue gradual changes in this anarchic structure, firstly by making lasting cooperation and stable peace feasible between neighbouring states. The very existence of the EU represents the most successful example to date of 'internal' structural foreign policy. That was, after all, the reason why it was created when the US was implementing its own structural foreign policy in Europe through the Marshall Plan and multilateralism. However, political relations between Brazil and Argentina, between South Africa and its neighbours, between Indonesia, Thailand, Malaysia, the Philippines, and the Communist (and formerly Communist) members of ASEAN, such as Vietnam, Laos and Cambodia, are already beyond the level of international cooperation and demonstrate the possibility of long-term limiting of international anarchy and distrust between previous enemies through new regionalism. These successes are the result of the combination of both internal and external stimuli which promote trade, economic and multidimensional cooperation. The European Commission, by supporting new regionalism elsewhere, both technically and by other means, practises a 'structural foreign policy' at global level.[58] Of course, as a comparative analysis of regional variations shows, this type of EU policy only works when there are multiple 'bottom-up' preconditions and factors within the partner regions intent on tackling security problems, preventing conflict and reducing fragmentation.

The concept of 'structural foreign policy' relies therefore on the theoretical background of the critiques of neo-realism which emerged within American and international political science during the 1970s and 1980s.[59] According to these, a whole series of 'international regimes' emerge, which establish different sets of shared rules and procedures, exchange mutual information and create reciprocal expectations among member states. All these elements exert a positive influence on their preferences and options. Moreover, transnational common interest coalitions and de facto solidarity are encouraged, uncertainties regarding the behaviour of neighbouring states are limited, and a positive-sum game can be hoped for through institutionalized cooperation.

Regional associations are a good example of deepening international regimes. Not only do they serve to combat anarchy between and within member states, but candidate countries are also subject to the influence of the internal rules of the club they have applied for. More generally, the increasingly thick network of decentralized, multiple, informal and formalized associations and regimes that has developed within the globalized economy offsets the neo-realist conception of structural anarchy and the classical practice of state sovereignty in so far as the current world governance deficit, typical of the post-hegemonic age, did not seem to necessarily foment overwhelming tendencies towards anarchy and fragmentation during the 1990s. International regimes, and new regional territorial entities even more so, constitute a real and potential third level of governance, between fragmentation and unipolar concentration of political power. All in all, the EU's structural foreign policy is not a voice crying in the wilderness, but benefits from broader objective trends.

Secondly, the European structural foreign policy can also be interpreted as an extension of the legacy of Jean Monnet's method, which envisaged the creation of peaceful political relations through economic interdependence and integration. This is illustrated by the Union's external relations and, in particular, by the so-called international and interregional 'pactomania' of the EU, which promotes preferential trade agreements and cooperation agreements throughout the world. Critical opinions, based on fears that the EU may develop a new Eurocentric policy of influence, have been expressed against preferential trade agreements, relationships based on 'conditionality' and requiring not only economic adjustments, but also greater respect for the rule of law and good internal and external governance. However, as we mentioned in Chapter 2, comparative research on regional groupings in Africa, Asia and America demonstrates that such external support for regional agreements can only be effective if internal factors, resulting from the economic and political orientations of member states and civil societies, are also independently pushing for regional cooperation. On the contrary, regional cooperation fails or stagnates when there is excessive asymmetry between internal and external factors.

Thirdly, international political economy supplies instruments fit to enrich the concept of structural foreign policy with a significance regarding the nature of international power today. We refer here to the concept of 'structural power' as opposed to the traditional realist notion of 'relational power', based on power relations. According to Susan Strange, 'structural power' increasingly shapes the structures of global governance. By its structural power, the EU indirectly conditions the modus operandi of other actors and prompts them to modify their behaviour without forcing them to do so. In the globalized era, structural power based on security may be combined or counterbalanced by economic and financial power, and particularly by structural power based on knowledge and information, the growing importance of which tends to influence both the international economy and world politics.[60]

This innovative approach, reforming 'Westphalia', suggests that foreign policy students pay greater attention to the current difficulties of the EU in developing its model of a 'knowledge society', rather than to its flaws as a military power. If it could redress this lag in terms of technology, infrastructure and the broad socialization of information, research and innovation, then a regional entity and world trade leader like the EU could partly counterbalance its extremely limited military power. In his own way, Nye validates this notion of structural power by including it in his concept of soft power.[61] However, in the case of the EU, 'soft power' is not appropriate, because, contrary to the US, structural foreign policies are by far the main pillars of the European civilian power. These distinctive features may underpin a European international identity compatible with the dignity of nations sharing the wealth, capacity and historical status of western Europe (to paraphrase the already mentioned quotation by Headley Bull).

In sum, a 'structural foreign policy' limits international anarchy by supporting international regimes and their legitimization processes, and consolidating regional organizations elsewhere. Moreover, it expresses a changed perception of threats and power criteria, strengthening a type of structural power linked to civilian relations and the knowledge society as opposed to classic military power .

In Chapter 5 we will verify whether the Constitutional Treaty makes a significant contribution to the improvement of the institutional framework for a structural foreign policy. Institutional strengthening of the vertical and horizontal coordination of external policies was, along with improved foreign policy structures, a vital issue for the European Convention and the 2003–4 Intergovernmental Conference.[62] We should add that the legitimacy of structural foreign policy is higher than that of the CFSP. Classic foreign policy tends to be spectacular, leading to short-term results, stirring nationalistic anxiety and aggressiveness against whomever the external enemy of the time may be. By contrast, structural foreign policy does not benefit from any of these powerful sources of potential 'substantive popular legitimization'. Of course, the more the CFSP enhances its salience within the structural foreign policy of the EU, the less it can be effectively implemented without better legitimization and clearer accountability. Internal democracy, citizens' participation, accountability are the sine qua non of increased CFSP effectiveness. The strengthening of the monitoring role played by the European Parliament could provide part of the answer.[63] The rest of the solution is to be found in a permanent dialectic interaction between national and European institutions and a growing European public sphere, both transnational and supranational. This emerging public sphere is complementary to national public spheres and encompasses various expressions of European civil society such as the media, associations, political parties and networks. Public opinion in Europe is more informed about global challenges than anywhere else in the world and enriched not only by the pacifist passion of the younger generations, but also by new instruments of lifelong learning and democratic dialogue on the great issues concerning mankind such as peace, hunger and the environment. It is precisely the task of national and EU institutions to channel this potential input and translate it into a driving force of common and coherent structural foreign policies implementing the EU's distinctive international identity.

4.8   The challenges of the next decade: Turkish membership and the EU's south-eastern border

Among the internal and external conditions underpinning the EU as a new kind of civilian power, the situation regarding its south-east border is particularly relevant, because it entails implications which are both internal (at institutional and policy levels), external (the Union's relationships with its new possible future neighbours, i.e. Iraq and Iran!) and global. While the next section will deal with the *external* framework, namely the evolving transatlantic relationship, here we will focus on the evolving *internal/external* precondition of the EU's south-east border. The recent negotiations with Turkey and Ukraine's turn towards western Europe confirm the extraordinary attractiveness of the EU as a continental pole of stability, democracy and prosperity. At the same time, however, both Turkey and Ukraine present serious challenges for the EU as a civilian power. In recent decades, the EU has taken on a central role in promoting democratization: the history of the European construction itself provides a vivid illustration of the EU's ability to foster the democratic transformation and stability of member states and neighbouring countries. This successful structural foreign policy was relaunched in 2004, as highlighted by the role of Mr CFSP, Javier Solana, in calming the Ukraine crisis and the constant political pressure on Turkey to implement its commitments to restrict the role of the army, end its persecution of the Kurds, reform the Constitution, implement human rights and the rule of law, and to seek a settlement to the Cyprus question. Although perhaps monotonous, the EU's strategy in this area has been more effective than the 'transformationalist strategy' of the US and has not involved playing the military card.[64]

Both these external/internal policies are consistent with the distinctive features of the EU as a civilian power. In this sense, the positive recommendation of the EU Commission on 6 October 2004 regarding the beginning of 'open-ended' negotiations with Turkey[65] and the like-minded European Council decision of 17 December 2004 are coherent with the Union's successful history of bringing poor post-Fascist and post-Communist countries into the European mainstream. To say that this broad enlargement is more consistent with the US–UK agenda than that of the EU is wrong. Indeed, this will not be the first time that the consequences of successful EU integration in fact go far beyond the US agenda. However, the size of Turkey, its demographic trend and geo-political and religious features make this enlargement a hard and decisive step in the history of European regional construction,[66] not least because of its link to the new 'inter-civilization' challenges and security questions of the post-2001 era and the ambitious aim of nurturing a Muslim democracy.

Both anti-Islamic populist pleas for a 'fortress Europe' and Eurosceptic advocates of a future EU as a mere combination of a 'continental trading state' and NATO are unavoidable parts of the debate on Turkey both inside and outside Europe. In fact, they do not represent anything new. What is new, however, is that supporters of a secularized and democratic vision of a 'civilian power Europe' are being challenged to find new ways of combining two different sides of the EU's role in global governance: enlargement and global foreign policy:

(a) On the one hand, we are witnessing a 'bottom-up' concept of EU civilian power which provides a practical example of global governance through its *internal* cooperation/integration policies and its democratic institutional settlement. Turkish membership would extend the current common stable democratic and legal space, based on trade and economic integration, beyond the geographic borders of Europe. The global role of the EU would be strengthened by its clear openness to a modern Muslim country, which, in turn, would serve as a model of fair, rule-based, legally structured, democratic, multi-ethnic and multi-religious regional governance, on the borders of the unstable Middle East. Indeed, following this logic, several states support extending EU enlargement even further eastwards and southwards.

(b) Many commentators, however, believe that enlargement on such a grand scale carries a serious risk of diluting the integration process and, in particular, diminishing political unity within the EU. The role of the EU as a 'democracy stabilizer' would also be affected by unlimited enlargement and huge stress would be placed on the sustainability of those social cohesion policies which we defined in Chapter 3 as the very soul of civilian power Europe. Furthermore, what message would Turkish membership send to the broader Muslim world? Even if comparisons with the Byzantine empire are misplaced, it is legitimate to wonder if the EU's reputation within the external Islamic world would be more improved by accepting Turkey into the EU than by offering true integration as European citizens to the many millions of Muslim immigrants in Europe. Finally, if it becomes absorbed by heavy enlargement priorities, the EU as a political union risks seeing its role as a global player weakened. It is this very role which needs to be bolstered and not undermined in terms of its internal cohesion and institutional capacity to act coherently at regional and global level.

The EU is thus again faced with the challenge of finding a dynamic and successful compromise between enlargement and the Union's global role. The 1993 'Copenhagen Criteria' (requiring a market economy, the rule of law and the *acquis communautaire*) should not be isolated from the rest of the Treaty and a fourth implicit criterion is required: the maintenance of the dynamics of EU political integration. According to this approach, the EU's regional role as a peace and 'democracy stabilizer' should not just be identified with enlargement, but should also take the form of long-term distinctive *external* relations and partnerships. If not, not only those states bordering the EU, but others such as Israel, Russia or even Quebec could one day apply for membership! Establishing a clear and open south-eastern border is crucial to the future efficiency and legitimacy of the EU and its international role. Dialogue and cooperation with border countries, both with former Soviet republics (such as Ukraine, Belarus, Moldova, Georgia, Armenia) and with Islamic countries such as Morocco could be deepened within the framework of the new special neighbourhood Commission policy and in the spirit of the 'privileged relationship' provided for by the Constitutional Treaty, art. I-5.[67] Why, therefore, have such reasonable arguments proved so weak and ineffective during the past decade?

Over that period, the EU's European continental agenda has been conditioned by fragmented demands and US priorities and the EU has not done enough to strategically manage this situation. Since 1989, the EU has set up a stable external concentric circle of border countries cooperating within special partnership arrangements, while renouncing full membership. With the sole exception of the troubled, but institutionally relatively stable, 'strategic partnership' with Russia, ambiguities persist regarding the other eastern border countries. In this context, Ukraine will be the main challenge, particularly after its political crisis in late 2004. Undoubtedly, the 'Three-year EU–Ukraine plan' aimed at strengthening bilateral cooperation will be influenced by the Union's need to improve relations with the neighbouring Russian power. However, it will also be conditioned by the evolution of the EU–Turkey negotiations.[68] As regards Turkey, definitively belonging to an external circle of partners is now completely out of the question. The impact on Turkey's difficult democratization process of a firm European 'no' would be massive. Moreover, Europe would send a very negative message to the wider Muslim community. This would be reinforced by those in politics and the media who like to present Europe as a closed fortress and a 'Christian club'.

Summing up, in the 'new civilian power scenario', it seems plausible that the ten-year negotiations cycle will be long and deep enough not only for Turkey to genuinely democratize its institutions and society (the rule of law, rights of women, minority rights, democratic scrutiny of the army and its budget, etc.) but also to foster a kind of 'learning process' for both sides. Both have accepted the prospect of negotiations without guaranteed outcomes. Negotiations may bring both parties towards a gradual mutual adaptation to enlargement which can combine successful Turkish membership with the establishment of new instruments to facilitate improved regional and global EU *external* actorness. In this virtuous trade-off scenario, the EU would find new ways to continue its very successful 'internal foreign policy': the *longue durée* enlargement process as an effective method of spreading democracy, prosperity and peace on a continental scale. This would represent an important contribution to global governance per se. Nonetheless, in this case it seems plausible that a hard core of EU countries (powered by the Franco-German engine of EMU), will emerge and these will be strongly committed to a deeper, coherent, efficient and independent political Union.

However, nobody should dismiss the possibility that the 'open-ended negotiation process', starting in 2005 and planned to continue over the next 10–15 years, will result in a gradual mutual understanding based on a 'second-best' solution. The heavy (but still not transparent) costs in terms of the budget, overstretch and institutional complexity for the EU, on the one hand, and, on the other, of lost sovereignty and profound domestic social reforms for Turkey, may lead both parties to look for an intermediary settlement, which falls between the current multidimensional link (association since 1963, military alliance since 1952, customs union) and full membership.

Whatever the eventual outcome, a long 'learning process' will occur. This will be of fundamental importance for the political identity of the EU as a civilian regional and global power. The Union will thus find itself at a crossroads as far as its full transformation into a political actor is concerned. Its immediate 'comprehensive' security challenges will not be limited to the Balkans, but will encompass the whole continent and its neighbours (including Russia/Ukraine, the Caucasus, the Middle East, and the routes to energy sources). Moreover, these security challenges are among the most difficult to tackle of the new world order. Turkish negotiations may push the EU to seek to devise what has been missing over the past decade: a strategic plan which provides responses to the following questions: How can the EU cope with its regional/global responsibilities without advancing on the achievements of the 'Solana strategic paper' of December 2003? How can it deal with these issues without going beyond the veto right in foreign policy? How can it create a suitable security policy, which is consistent with the Union's civilian ambitions, but can meet the new challenges? The Turkish negotiation process thus requires EU leaders and citizens to think about, and decide, what kind of EU they want. Of course, Turkey will also have to transform constitutional changes from paper into practice. In addition, it will also be cajoled into a process of self-criticism (undergone, in previous decades, by Germany and other member states). The European political identity includes memory of the past and rejects 'denial'. Thus the Turkish nation will have to look at elements of its history such as the Armenian genocide and its long-standing nationalistic understanding of national sovereignty. As argued above, civilian power also implies a union of memories.

Stipulating that Turkey raise its level of democracy will also force the EU to improve its own democratic legitimacy. The shared aim to marry liberal democracy with constitutional patriotism requires greater citizen participation and communication both in Turkey and the EU. Negotiations with Turkey thus provide an opportunity to tackle the growing internal legitimacy deficit of an enlargement process which many perceive as too hurried and too wide. At the very least, it will be very hard to limit the negative impact of enlargement on the Constitutional Treaty ratification process. Public opinion should, however, be given the time and opportunity to positively adapt to a widening

Europe, which is perceived as consistent with its profound aims. Enlargement has huge implications in terms of the Union's common political identity which are possible only within a territorial space defined by geographical proximity and common historical roots. No observer can dismiss the hypothesis that, under certain conditions, Turkey and even Ukraine could in the future participate in a shared European Political Union founded on the common implementation of democratic rules and institutions provided for by the Treaty. However, for this to happen, Europe would need a strategically more credible leadership, capable of handling debate on enlargement and the Treaty reform and able to tackle the existing fears, identity issues and social demands for internal cohesion.

Finally, Turkish accession has numerous implications for international politics. As we mentioned earlier, a part of the research community has questioned whether Turkish membership of the EU (strongly supported by the US) will strengthen the transatlantic junior partnership of the EU, or whether the inclusion of a 'European' Turkey will serve to spur the EU on in further expressing its international autonomy as a pillar of a new multilateralism, as it has begun to do during the Iraqi crisis.

4.9   The challenges of the next decade: transatlantic partnership and new multilateralism

How do transatlantic relations appear in the light of the new threats and in the aftermath of the serious EU–US rift of 2002–4? A politically growing EU is facing the issue of a new type of military and political cooperation with the US at a time when perceptions of uncertainty and threats among Europeans differ from those of Americans. Since 1989, while not dreaming of some kind of postmodern paradise, Europeans have no longer seen traditional international nuclear wars as a security priority; and, since 2001 they do not see the growing list of existing despotic regimes as a new incumbent threat.[69] Many transatlantic networks are looking for innovative solutions able to combine an innovative identity for a European international role with a renewed transatlantic partnership. However, this transition time is proving harder than expected. The challenge goes beyond reforming NATO, which is being transformed from a Western defence organization into an enlarged political forum on pan-European and global security issues. It is a major challenge that will define the coming decade and the outcome of which remains uncertain. Indeed, the historical roots of both this partnership and American primacy are not only to be found in US military and economic power, but also in the victories over Fascism, Nazism, Stalinism and militarism.

In the current era, the US does not look as approvingly as before on the developing political role of the EU. Even if the unfriendly *divide and impera* approach of 2001–4 is tempered by the offensive of C. Rice's diplomacy over the next years, the awareness is largely shared that the kind of transatlantic alliance which was a feature of the post-Second World War decades cannot be repeated. Both the US has changed and the EU is now too strong to be reduced to playing something similar to the post-war junior partner role of the timid post-war West Germany and Italy. While a divorce would be catastrophic, the transatlantic relationship is likely to be characterized over the next decade by instability and fluctuations,[70] depending on external challenges (the Israel–Palestinian conflict, Iran, North Korea, China, etc.), bilateral trade controversies, global issues (financial instability, fight against poverty, the environment), but also depending on domestic politics, on both sides of the Atlantic. Regarding those of the US, this is the main source of the confrontational trade, economic and monetary policies of the Bush administration. Isolationist tendencies will be contained and, given its important economic, political and cultural interests, the US will not leave Europe as it did (to its later regret) in 1919.[71]

However, not only conflicting economic and geopolitical interests, but also various changes occurring within both partners and in their mutual perceptions are of a structural, long-term nature. While debate on the scope and continuity of the new US September 2002 Security Strategy remains open, the statistics regarding the US military budget in conjunction with a practice of new security sovereignty which de facto limits the sovereignty of others are incontrovertible. It has become a statement of the obvious to forecast that the past identification between the European and transatlantic agendas is destined to change, as well as to acknowledge that, despite their shared solidarity against terrorism and proliferation, the differences between the EU and the US in terms of perceptions of the security threat and conceptions of the post-cold war world are not occasional or simply the product of some misunderstanding.

It will be impossible to manage this divergence between the allies by seeking recourse to transatlantic models dating back to the 1950s. Furthermore, it would be ridiculous to seek to tackle it simply by means of a timid increase in the military budget (the only kind of increase that would be accepted by European public opinion), whether or not the European military is conceived as subordinate (Great Britain or Italy) or autonomous (France). The Rapid Reaction Force represents something different as it can be included in the innovative context of a responsible and up-to-date civilian power, acting under a multilateral UN mandate and within the limits of the 'Petersberg tasks' (TEU). In sum, from the EU point of view, we are conceptually dealing not with a classic bilateral alliance, but a partnership within a triangle including the US, the EU and the UN.

A new transatlantic peer-to-peer dialogue will partly also depend on European internal variables. The first of these is Germany, the big civilian power. In fact, it is Germany first and foremost that can transform and blend the French national independence tradition and the legitimate aspirations of other European countries into a common new effective multilateral power. The new Germany has shown that it can conceive of a more realistic balance than others between continuity and discontinuity, i.e. a more political civilian power and a new transatlantic partnership. This is what makes the German 'tamed power' (Katzenstein, cit.) a potential – and, in part, already an effective – leader of European new regionalism, as regards both security and trade policies. Of course, we might question whether the German leadership and the traditional Franco-German engine will be able to encourage the UK and others to take the necessary steps in this direction. The 'Solana paper' of December 2003 represents a first, but only a first, positive achievement. The second variable is comprised of the European institutions and the outcome of the constitutional reform of the Treaty and its ratification. A core of countries that wish to progress further than others must be allowed to do so within the context of the common treaties, as otherwise de facto groupings will emerge beyond the scope of the treaties. The two-speed Europe, already foreseen by the Treaty, is a serious answer to a concrete problem. It seeks to reconcile the unity of the enlarged EU of 25 (and, in the future, around 35) member states with the expression of the political will for greater political autonomy of a hard core of EMU members, which is open to the others, but determined to give voice to the maturation of Europe's global responsibilities.

The third variable will be the effectiveness of the emerging distinctive EU's view of regionalism and multilateralism. The idea of the EU as a civilian power is not at all a legacy of the 1990s which is now fading with the emergence of the new security threats. On the contrary, it belongs to the *longue durée* of the European idea. If anything, only the contradictory aspects of this concept belong to the past, because the decline of nuclear threats and the evolution of both structural power and relations between states have improved the chances of carving out a new status for the EU as an international actor and a new and credible power. Much more so than in the past, the EC/EU seems capable of finding allies and partners elsewhere to help construct a less asymmetric type of global governance. However, the question is whether, as in the past, at the inception of the Greek *polis* and the modern state, Europe can now put forward a new approach to face the challenges of the twenty-first century: that of new regionalism as a pillar of effective and new multilateralism.

The EU and US visions of multilateralism have distinct background and features. The EU urges multilateralism to be effective enough to shape regional and global governance, to entangle national powers and deal with emergencies.[72] Regionalism is not simply an instrument by which old multilateralism can be restored. Rather, it is the driving force for a reformed world governance which goes beyond a mere update of the old article XXIV of GATT. As far as the EU is concerned, the third scenario introduced above (of a new political and civilian power) and the first one (of a continental trading state) both encompass the inevitability of growing economic interdependence and further globalization. However, the third and second (of a 'fortress Europe') scenarios are akin in terms of the analysis of the conflicts and obstacles produced by the globalized economy and the potential significant political dangers. Protectionism can only be defeated by a combination of greater global regulation (as provided by informal governance) and reformed multilateral governance. New regionalism can provide the best support for multilateralism and limit both arrogant unilateralism and nationalist, ethnic or privatizing fragmentation of authorities. As we saw in Chapter 2, it is likely we will witness the continued growth of regional groupings and their evolution as new political actors.

According to the EU a 'strengthened regionalism' and multidimensional interregionalism could provide contributions to global multilateral governance, combining the legacy of previous multilateral values with the prospect of a less asymmetric world order. If this were to come about, new regionalism would unite what many observers consider incompatible, i.e. economic opening-up and the territorial representation of economic, cultural and political differences. A new principle of territoriality is emerging from the space between the defence of obsolete national sovereignty and functionalist and politically hierarchical globalism. And the EU is better equipped to cope with this pluralistic, multiregional and multilateral evolution of the world order than the US.

While in the 1930s, regionalism was an implacable enemy of multi-lateral world agreements and, in the 1960s, it was part of international multilateralism dominated by American liberal hegemony, today a new balance can emerge in which new regionalism and interregionalism interact beneficially with a new system of multilateral global regulation. We can foresee a mixture of continuity and discontinuity compared to previous decades. For many years within the framework of the bipolar world until the 1970s–1980s, democratic capitalism had a multilateral vocation which was accompanied by an American hegemonic multilateral cooperation policy. After the crisis and the dissolution of the USSR, this was replaced by the so-called 'Washington consensus' and the dynamic of the emerging markets in the 1990s. Finally, it has been greatly restructured by the new global security agenda at the beginning of the new century.

Summing up, the most important variables of the evolving transatlantic partnership depend on both internal and external factors. What is new is that the heterogeneity of the international system and new regionalism offer the EU opportunities to develop alliances and partnerships on a global scale with a view to strengthening multilateralism. The EU is already committed to consolidating this type of alliance and cooperation with six strategic partners (the US, Canada, Japan, China, Russia and India) and regional organizations. Other civilian powers, including Canada, Brazil and Japan, are also interested in a neo-multilateral approach. Strategic partnership with China, Russia and India is designed to include them within the multilateral framework. This kind of trend can contribute to bridging the current gap between economic globalization and the global political structure, according to the EU vision.

Last but not least, we are currently witnessing an ambiguous proliferation of 'global responsibilities' within international politics. We have already indicated the term 'responsibility' as one of the components of the new concept of Europe as a civilian and political power. Indeed, sometimes the political power of various states exploits the rhetoric of global values, the defence of human and democratic rights and the urgent need for improved global governance.[73] On that point, the relationship of 'distant proximity' between the EU and the US will evolve during the next decade within NATO and the UN. A responsible EU must prove how new regionalism and multilateralism, rather than supporting a conservative status quo, can efficiently deal with the challenges of terrorism, humanitarian intervention and democratic interference. The EU has a historical responsibility to present a reliable third way, distinct from both globalist authoritarian regulation and the threats of proliferation/fragmentation. As far as the current normative debate on the improvement of world governance and respect for human rights is concerned, it is worth considering this potential third way between juridical globalism and relativism, and between cosmopolitan ideals on the one hand and, on the other, obsolete and anarchic myths of national sovereignty.

The EU cannot succeed as a global actor without changing the international environment and its political structure. Various commentators wonder to what degree Europe, thanks to its memory of the past, its values and its civilian power, can be the cradle of a new universal idea of peace and cooperation through its contribution to democratic, pluralistic, multicultural and multilateral governance at national, regional and global levels. Obviously, this is only feasible if other global, regional and state actors converge towards the same goals. The next decade will answer the question whether the US accepts being included in a new multilateral perspective. The new challenges of the twenty-first century confirm that whereas military and economic unilateralism corrodes universal values and does not stop fragmentation, the EU's structural foreign policy, if more effective and legitimate, may strengthen multilateral governance, provide greater economic justice and better protection of human rights, thanks to increased structural symmetry between actors, greater respect for differences and the input of a transnational and pluralistic worldwide public sphere.[74] On the other hand, beyond pure normative and postmodern understanding of the EU's global role, a political concept of civilian power cannot progress without both simultaneous conditions, the internal strengthening of institutional capacities and the external advance of a new global multilateral and multiregional order, gradually changing the world's anarchic structure and increasingly revising the Westphalian system.

Notes

1. See also K.E. Smith, *European Union Foreign Policy in a Changing World*, Cambridge University Press, 2003 and C. Rhodes (ed.), *The European Union in the World Community*, Lynne Rienner, Boulder, 1998; M. Smith, *Europe's Foreign and Security Policy: the Institutionalisation of Co-operation*, Cambridge University Press, 2004; R. Ginsberg, 'Conceptualizing the European Union as an International Actor: Narrowing the Theoretical Capability–Expectation Gap', *Journal of Common Market Studies*, 37, 3, 1999, pp. 429–54. H. Smith, *European Union Foreign Policy*, Pluto Press, London, 2002; B. White, *Understanding European Foreign Policy*, Palgrave, Basingstoke, 2001. See also www.fornet.info.

2. R.O. Keohane and J.S. Nye (eds), *Transnational Relations and World Politics*, Harvard University Press, Cambridge, Mass., 1972; E.B. Haas, *The Uniting of Europe. Political, Economic and Social Forces*, Stanford University Press, Stanford, 1958.
3. K.W. Deutsch, S. Burrell and R.A. Kann, *Political Community and the North Atlantic Area; International Organization in the Light of Historical Experience*, Princeton University Press, Princeton, 1957.
4. As regards the economic dimension of external relations, the 1957 Treaty of Rome represents the legal basis of the EC's external responsibilities mentioned above. The treaties regulate the cases in which the European Commission can partly act on behalf of the member states and whether communitarian procedures (exclusive initiative by the Commission, qualified majority voting in the Council, competence of the European Court of Justice, and, more recently, opinion or co-decision for the European Parliament) or intergovernmental cooperation methods should be applied.
5. In 2002 the EU accounted for 18.8 per cent of world trade in goods and 23 per cent of world trade in services. See EU Commission 'Making Globalization Work for Everyone. The EU and World Trade', in *Europe in the Move*, Brussels 2002, 10 (htpp://europa.eu.int.comm/publications/booklets/en.pdf).
6. According to data provided by the World Bank and the IMF, no western European economy is third rank in terms of prosperity, and also immediately behind the United States and Japan as regards GDP per capita. Moreover, the gap between these states and those of the developing world is progressively widening.
7. Mario Monti recently highlighted the scope of such implications in 'The External Aspects of EU Competition Policy', *European Foreign Affairs Review*, 7, 2002, pp. 235–40. The impression created by the prevented merger between two American IT giants is well known.
8. Art. 133 (formerly 113) of the Treaty of the EC provides one of the key legal foundations for external common action and allows the Commission to make trade agreements with 'one or more states or international organizations'. Although still subject to the unanimous agreement of the Council of Ministers, the Amsterdam Treaty (1997) refers to the extension of the Commission's mandate to include 'international negotiations and agreements on services and intellectual property', such as the delicate issues of the problematic new WTO Round. Pursuant to art. 300–301 (formerly 228 and 228A), the European Commission can negotiate international agreements with states and international organizations. Articles 302–304 (formerly 229–231) provide the legal basis for the participation of the EU in international organizations: the WTO, the European Bank for Reconstruction and Development (for eastern European countries), the Council of Europe, the Organization for Security and Cooperation in Europe (OSCE), the United Nations and some of its organizations and agencies. In addition, a particularly significant provision of the Treaty in political and economic terms is art. 310 (formerly 228) of the TEC which refers to the power to conclude 'agreements establishing an association involving reciprocal rights and obligations, common action and special procedures', applied to the states and organizations involved. There are different types of associate status such as those applying to states belonging to the ACP convention and the eastern European and

Mediterranean states. The CEEC and Mediterranean states which applied for membership in the 1990s had special and distinct 'European agreements', which were conceived of as a sort of prelude to membership. It is important to emphasize that, since the beginning of the integration process, successive enlargements (art. 49 of the Treaty on European Union – TEU) have been an essential part of European foreign policy, as shown by the British and Iberian accessions and, particularly since 1989, Scandinavian enlargement and the accession of EFTA and central and eastern European countries.

9. Ch. Deblock, *L'Organization mondiale du commerce: où s'en va la mondialisation?*, Fides, Quebec, 2002.
10. R. Gilpin, 'The Politics of Transnational Economic Relations', in Keohane and Nye (eds), *Transnational Relations and World Politics*, op. cit. and id., *The Political Economy of International Relations*, Princeton University Press, Princeton, 1987.
11. With the inception of its role as an international political actor, the EC has contributed since the 1970s to the decline of the international hegemony of the United States. It is difficult to explain EPC solely in terms of an internal development. Rather, the effort to coordinate national foreign policies represented the autonomous reaction of the EC to an unstable international environment.
12. The 'Contadora group', a forum for dialogue between the EC and Central America, was the far-sighted result in 1984 of an initiative by Hans Dietrich Genscher, the German minister for foreign affairs, in collaboration with Costa Rica.
13. S. Hoffmann, R.O. Keohane and J.S. Nye (eds), *After the Cold War, International Institutions and State Strategies in Europe 1989–1991*, Harvard University Press, Cambridge, Mass., 1993; C. Hill (ed.), *The Actors in Europe's Foreign Policy*, Routledge, London–New York, 1996. See, in particular, the introduction by C. Hill and W. Wallace.
14. The preamble to the TEU highlights the goal of 'reinforcing the European identity and its independence in order to promote peace, security and progress in Europe and in the world' (para. 9). Art. 11 (formerly title V, art. J) of the TEU is the legal foundation of the CFSP, which belongs to the political Union and strengthens the former EPC in order 'to assert its identity on the international scene' (art. 2, formerly art. B, para. 2).
15. See European Council, *Conclusions of the Presidency*, Lisbon, 26/27 June 1992, which stressed the importance of enhancing the consistency of EU external economic and political relations. It also highlighted common interests and joint action areas: eastern Europe and Russia, the Mediterranean area, Latin America, the Middle East, developing countries. Interregional relations are also mentioned: 'The easing of international tensions with the end of the cold war provides new possibilities and resources for development but also favours the emergence of new forms of co-operation, namely at the inter-regional level' (p. 24). Between the mid-1990s and 2004. the EU focused on six main multidimensional and bilateral 'Strategic Partnerships', with the US, Canada, Russia, Japan, China and India, respectively.
16. On this topic, see K. Jorgensen (ed.), *European Approaches to Crisis Management*, Kluwer, The Hague–London–Boston, 1997 and the statements of relevant actors: Chris Patten (commissioner for external relations),

'Debate on Conflict Prevention/Crisis Management'; speech given in the European Parliament, Strasbourg, 14 March 2001; P. Nielson (commissioner for cooperation and development and humanitarian aid), 'Building Credibility: the Role of European Development Policy in Preventing Conflicts', speech to the conference of the Foreign Policy Centre, London, 8 February 2001. Conflict prevention is defined as 'the coordinated and timely application of specific political, diplomatic, economic and/or security related measures and activities taken in response to a situation threatening peace. The aim of which is to defuse tension, prevent escalation and contribute towards an environment in which a peaceful settlement of violent conflicts or potential conflict is more likely to occur' (EPLO – European Peace Liaison Office Conference: *Building Conflict Prevention in the Future of Europe*, November 2002). In 2003–4 the EU made significant progress as its 'Petersberg' missions both in former Yugoslavia (from SFOR to EUFOR, the EU takes the lead in the implementation of the Dayton agreement; Althea) and Congo (Arthemis).

17. The Amsterdam Treaty achieved progress in a number of areas: the symbolic creation of a 'Mr CFSP' (he remains only a spokesman, subject to the Council, not involved in the Commission, although he/she has been provided with his/her own analysis team); a decision-making system improved by the use of majority voting on common actions if the strategy has been approved unanimously. Moreover, it paved the way for the 'enhanced cooperation' clause that the Treaty of Nice allows to be applied within the second pillar, albeit not yet for defence. The Amsterdam Treaty also strengthened the power of the Commission to conclude treaties and conduct trade negotiations (although this is limited to the amended art. 300 and 133, i.e. subject to the unanimous vote procedure in the Council as regards services).

18. The Helsinki European Council decided to create a new instrument with the establishment of a European 'Rapid Reaction Task Force' by 2003 (this force would consist of 60,000 troops capable of being deployed rapidly in areas bordering the EU and consistent with the terms of the Petersberg tasks). See M. Rutten (ed.), *De Saint-Malo à Nice*, Institut UEO, Paris, 2000. See also the regulation approved by the Council during the Helsinki meeting on 20 February 2001, which created the RRF (Rapid Reaction Force), *Instruments on Conflict Prevention and Civilian Crisis Management Available to the European Union*, aimed at contributing to the civilian aspects of crisis management within the CSFP and CSDP and providing rapid funding to meet urgent civilian needs.

19. See M. Telò and P. Magnette (ed.), *De Maastricht à Amsterdam. L'Europe et son nouveau traité*, Complexe, Brussels, 1998. See, in particular, the introduction and the article by Remacle. The Amsterdam Treaty procedure is intergovernmental and its very strict provisions for 'enhanced cooperation' not only gave Eurosceptics guarantees, but also the right to block high-level political decisions.

20. See Rutten (ed.), *De Saint-Malo à Nice*, op. cit.

21. See K. Shake, 'Rhetoric and Reality', in J.H.H. Weiler, I. Begg and J. Peterson (eds), *Integration in an Expanding European Union. Reassessing the Fundamentals*, Blackwell, Oxford, 2003, pp. 301–6; R. Kagan, *Of Paradise and Power: America and Europe in the New World Order*, A. Knopf, New York, 2003.

22. C. Piening, *Global Europe. The EU in World Affairs*, Lynne Rienner, Boulder, 1997, pp. 193–7; M. Holland (ed.), *Common Foreign and Security Policy. The Record and Reforms*, Pinter, London, 1997.

23. See Piening, *Global Europe*, op. cit. and D. Allen and M. Smith, 'Western Europe's Presence in the Contemporary International Arena', *Review of International Affairs*, 16, 1990, pp. 19–37.

24. J. Manners and R.G. Whitman, 'Towards Identifying the International Identity of the European Union: a Framework for Analysis of the EU's Network of Relationships', *Journal of European Integration*, 21, 1998, pp. 231–49. According to the authors, the EU implements its 'active identity' by means of a considerable array of instruments.

25. See the articles by A. Deighton ('The European Security and Defence Policy'), N. Gnesotto ('New World, New ESDP') and K. Shake ('Rhetoric and Reality'), in Weiler et al. (eds), *Integration in an Expanding European Union*, op. cit.

26. R. Kagan, 'Power and Weakness', *Washington Policy Review*, 113, 2002, pp. 30–45.

27. By 'French model' the author means 'endogenous nuclear weapons, control of foreign bases, loyalty to NATO but insistence on a different personality within it' (in H. Bull, 'Civilian Power Europe: a Contradiction in Terms', in L. Tsoukalis (ed.), *The European Community: Past, Present and Future*, Blackwell, Oxford, 1983, p. 160). Of course, the international environment of the 1970s and early 1980s influences Bull's appeal for a distinct European nuclear deterrent, based on French and British collaboration.

28. Ibid.

29. Hill (ed.), *The Actors in Europe's Foreign Policy*, op. cit.

30. The 1997 Amsterdam Treaty openly expressed the hope for better coordination of these aspects by strengthening art. 3 of the TEU (formerly art. C). This not only prescribed greater consistency among the various elements of external action, but better coordination between the Council and the Commission. Nevertheless, the current multiple responsibility system including 'Mr CFSP' (the secretary-general of the Council and Western European Union – WEU, a post occupied in 1999 by Javier Solana), the external relations commissioner (Chris Patten, in the Prodi Commission) and the rotating Presidency of the Council is clearly not an efficient way to conduct foreign policy.

31. F. Duchêne, 'The European Community and the Uncertainties of Interdependence', in M. Kohnstamm and W. Hager (eds), *A Nation Writ Large? Foreign Policy Problems before the European Community*, Macmillan, London, 1973, pp. 1–21.

32. Keohane and Nye (eds), *Transnational Relations and World Politics*, op. cit.; R.B.J. Walker, *Inside/Outside: International Relations as Political Theory*, Cambridge University Press, Cambridge, Mass., 1993; W. Carlsnaes and S. Smith (eds), *European Foreign Policy: the EC and Changing Perspectives*, Sage, London, 1994.

33. R.G. Whitman, *From Civilian Power to Superpower? The International Identity of the European Union*, Macmillan, London, 1988.

34. For a pessimistic view of the political implications of enlargement on the EU, see C. Saint-Etienne, *La Puissance ou la mort. L'Europe face à l'Empire Americain*, du Seuil, Paris, 2003.

35. T.J. Lowi, 'Making Democracy Safe for the World: Foreign Policy and National Politics', in J.N. Rosenau (ed.), *Domestic Sources of Foreign Policy*, Free Press, New York, 1967, pp. 295–331.

36. G. Allison, *The Essence of Decision*, Little, Brown, Boston, 1971. Some European countries have three levels of foreign policy decisions because, as is the case in Belgium, at subnational level, regions have external competences and exercise what has been termed 'paradiplomacy'.

37. See, for example, the Declaration to enhance the role and consistency of the Union entitled *Common Strategies*, submitted by the Council for General Affairs to the Vienna European Council (December 1998), Tony Blair's proposals concerning defence cooperation (April 1999) and the aforementioned progress made in 1999 and 2000 as regards defence and security policy.

38. W. Wessels and D. Rometsch, *European Union and Member States: Towards Institutional Fusion?*, Manchester University Press, Manchester, 1996.

39. The analysis of the various national interests and aims provided by Hill (ed.), *The Actors in Europe's Foreign Policy*, op. cit. is particularly useful. Moreover, in his 1998 article ('Closing the Capability–Expectations Gap?', in J. Peterson and H. Sjursen (eds), *A Common Foreign Policy for Europe?*, Routledge, London–New York, 1998, pp. 18–38), Hill noted four external common interests shared by EU member states: providing a second Western voice in international diplomacy; stabilizing eastern Europe; managing the globalized economy and world commerce; developing relations with the South.

40. In addition to the candidates which are already in negotiations (Romania and Bulgaria) or will start in 2005 (Turkey), we should mention the 25 signatory states of the Athens European Council in March 2003: the western Balkans (Croatia, Bosnia, Macedonia, Serbia-Montenegro, Albania) and the remaining EFTA members (Norway, Liechtenstein, Iceland, Switzerland). These latter states may be gradually more tempted to apply as and if regional integration becomes more diluted. The final list includes 37 states, at least according to the Commission's 2003 statement on the frontiers of the EU. This still excludes consideration of possible applications by Ukraine, Belarus, Georgia, Armenia, Azerbaijan and Moldova, members of the OSCE. No EU statement has yet listed Russia, Israel and Morocco as possible members, contrary to the hopes expressed (and met with little support) by some European ministers and heads of government.

41. This gloomy version of 'multi-level governance' sees the end not only of the teleological conception of the EU, but also of the functional spillover which dominated the first three decades of European regional integration. The author does not believe either the 'state' or the 'confederation' scenarios connected to territorial logic to be realistic; see P.C. Schmitter, 'Experiment in the Present Euro Polity with the Help of Past Theories and Imagining the Future of the Euro Polity with the Help of New Concepts', in G. Marks, E.W. Scharpf, P.C. Schmitter and W. Streck (eds), *Governance in the EU*, Sage, London, 1996, pp. 1–15.

42. R.N. Rosecrance, *The Rise of the Trading State: Commerce and Conquest in the Modern World*, Basic Books, New York, 1986. On the socio-economic dimension of this scenario and 'EU as regulation of the deregulation', see Chapter 3.

43. J. Habermas, *Die postnationale Konstellation: politische Essays*, Suhrkamp, Frankfurt a.M., 1998.
44. Gilpin (*The Political Economy of International Relations*, op. cit.) distinguishes between 'benevolent' and 'malevolent' types of neo-mercantilism. See also B. Hettne, 'The Double Movement: Global Market versus Regionalism', in R.W. Cox (ed.), *The New Realism: Perspectives on Multilateralism and World Order*, United Nations University Press, Tokyo–New York, 1997, pp. 223–44, and 'The New Regionalism: a Prologue', in B. Hettne, A. Inotai and O. Sunkel (eds), *Globalism and the New Regionalism*, Macmillan–St. Martin's Press, London–New York, 1999, pp. xv–xxix.
45. G. Bertrand, A. Michalski and L.R. Pench, 'Scenarios Europe 2010: Five Possible Futures for Europe', Working Paper, Forward Studies Unit from the European Commission, Brussels, 1999.
46. N. Bobbio, 'Stato', 'potere', 'governo', in *Enciclopedia Einaudi*, vol. XIII, Einaudi, Turin, 1981, and *L'Etat et la démocratie internationale*, M. Telò (ed.), Complexe, Brussels, 1998.
47. See A. Sapir, 'The Political Economy of EC Regionalism', *European Economic Review*, 42, 1998, pp. 717–32.
48. J.N. Bhagwati and A. Panagariya (eds), *Free Trade Areas or Free Trade? The Economics of Preferential Trading Agreements*, AEI Press, Washington, 1996. On this controversial issue, see Chapter 2.
49. See section 1.7, and Ruggie, *Constructing the World Polity: Essays on International Institutionalisation*, op. cit., in particular the 'Introduction', pp. 1–40 and the first theoretical section, pp. 41–131.
50. On the Japanese evolving notion of 'pacifist power' see M. Telò, 'L'UE, la gouvernance mondiale et l'ordre international. Le cas des relations avec l'Asie de l'Est', in M. Dumulain (ed.), *L'Europe et l'Asie*, P. Lang, Brussels, 2004, pp. 79–93, K. Matake, 'The Evolution of an Actively Pacifist Nation', *Gaiko Forum, Japanese Perspectives on Foreign Affairs*, spring 2004, pp. 12–20 and J. Gilson, *Japan and the EU*, Palgrave, 2000.
51. We agree on this point with J. Habermas, Chapter 5 of *Der gespaltene Westen*, Suhrkamp, Frankfurt a.M., 2004.
52. G. Therborn, 'Europe in the 21st Century: the World's Scandinavia?', in P. Gowan and P. Anderson (eds), *The Question of Europe*, Verso, London, 1999, pp. 357–84 and *European Modernity and Beyond*, SAGE, London, 1995. J. Rifkin (*The European Dream*, 2004) shares the analysis of the distinctiveness of the European way of life while underestimating the new challenges it is facing in the new global environment, namely after September 11th.
53. Two opposing perspectives are provided by D. Piazolo, 'European Regionalism and Multilateral Trade Negotiations', *Journal of European Integration*, 21, 3, 1998, pp. 251–71, and S. Bilal, 'Political Economy Considerations on the Supply of Trade Protection in Regional Integration Agreements', *Journal of Common Market Studies*, 36, 1, 1998, pp. 1–31.
54. P. Drulák (ed.), *National and European Identities in EU Enlargement, Views from Central and Eastern Europe*, Institute of International Relations, Prague, 2001; I.B. Neumann, *Users of the Other: the East in European Identity Formation*, Manchester University Press, Manchester, 1999; K. Henderson, *Back to Europe. Central and Eastern Europe and the EU*, UCL Press, Leuven, 1996.

55. In other understandings, it also includes enlargement policies, and the external implications of common policies: S. Keukeleire (*Het structureel buitenlands beleid van de Europese Unie*, Kluwer, Deeventer, 1998) explored this point, which is a significant aspect of the empirical part of this concept. Here, I think it best to focus on the theoretical aspects. See also White, *Understanding European Foreign Policy*, op. cit., H. Smith, *European Union Foreign Policy*, op. cit. and Ginsberg, 'Conceptualizing the European Union', op. cit. In French see also C. Roosens et al. (eds), *La Politique Étrangère – le modèle classique à l'épreuve*, Peter Lang, Brussels, 2004.

56. Kagan, *Power and Weakness*, op. cit.

57. K. Waltz, *Theory of International Politics*, Addison-Wesley, Reading, Mass., 1979 and R.O. Keohane (ed.), *Neorealism and its Critics*, Columbia University Press, New York, 1986.

58. M. Telò and S. Santander, 'Le néorégionalisme et l'UE dans le cadre de globalization', in P. Magnette and E. Remacle (eds), *Le nouveau modèle européen*, Editions de l'Université de Bruxelles, Brussels, 2000, vol. II, pp. 153–66.

59. R.O. Keohane and J.S. Nye (*Power and Interdependence*, HarperCollins, New York, 1989) examine the importance of transnational relations and the birth of new private and public actors within the international system as well as the decline of traditional hierarchies and power issues. The authors question the traditional division between a state's domestic and foreign policies and explore the world of international cooperation as a possible positive-sum game. Such liberal institutionalist models highlight the impact of commercial interdependence on the construction of global and regional institutions. See also S. Haggard, 'Regionalism in Asia and in the Americas', in E.D. Mansfield and H.V. Milner (eds), *The Political Economy of Regionalism*, Columbia University Press, New York, 1997, pp. 47–8; S.D. Krasner, *International Regimes*, Cornell University Press, Ithaca, NY, 1983.

60. S. Strange, *States and Markets*, Pinter, London, 1988.

61. J.S. Nye, 'Limits of American Power', in *Political Science Quarterly*, 117, 4, 2002–3, pp. 545–59, and also *The Paradox of American Power: Why the World's Only Superpower Can't Go it Alone*, Oxford University Press, New York, 2002.

62. The new Treaty is aimed at improving the internal consistency of external relations: (a) by strengthening the political leadership of the European Council and its President as regards general orientations; (b) by splitting the Council of General Affairs in two in order to remedy its current fragmentation and depoliticization. This would see, on the one hand, a Council responsible for the CFSP, presided over by the new minister for foreign affairs, and on the other, a Council of General Affairs, made up of ministers responsible for coordinating and managing the implementation of EU policies; (c) by improving and legitimizing (through the partial involvement of the European Parliament) the Commission's executive, external representative and negotiating roles. On the Constitutional Treaty, see Chapter 5.

63. The example of controlling arms exports is enlightening: in the US, parliamentary control is more developed than in the EU or its member states (except Sweden), but this does little to prevent the growth of arms exports. A code of conduct and transparency are not enough: they need to be accompanied by a more widespread democratic political culture typical of a 'civilian power' in order to achieve a reduction in arms exports.

64. The challenge of global democratization against tyrannies has been put at the top of the international agenda by the George W. Bush administration (increasingly since 2001).The growing list of desired 'regime changes' has been set by P. Wolfowitz, D. Rumsfeld and, even if by a more appealing balance between hard and soft power, by the successor of C. Powell as secretary of state, C. Rice (who included also Iran, N. Korea, Belarus, Cuba, Zimbabwe and Myanmar). Comparing the US with the EU, until 2004, distinct ideational factors and institutions provided distinct foreign and security policies.

65. The Commission recommendation contains several anomalies: (a) the lack of any credible estimate of the costs for the CAP and other common policies (this has been postponed, despite its implications for the EU's structural policies and internal cohesion); (b) the rejection of any foregone conclusion and the 'permanent *clause de sauvegarde*', i.e. 'consistently with the TEU and the Constitution, the Commission will recommend the suspension of negotiations in case of grave and persistent violation of the principles of freedom and democracy, of respect of human rights, of fundamental liberties and rule of law, on which the EU is founded. Concerning that recommendation the Council states by qualified majority voting procedure.'

66. If it joins the Union, Turkey will not only be the poorest EU member state (35 per cent of the population live on less than four dollars a day), but it will also eventually have the largest population (which currently stands at 71 million). Moreover, its geopolitical situation involves the EU in a highly sensitive border area with Iraq, Syria and central Asia, where around 150 million Turkish speakers live. Its strong growth rate (9 per cent in 2004) should serve to attract foreign investment, but will not reduce the unemployment rate (10 per cent in 2004). See O. Roy, *La Turquie aujourd'hui*, Universalis, Paris, 2004.

67. See F. Attinà and R. Rossi (eds), *European Neighbourhood Policy: Political, Economic and Social Issues*, Jean Monnet Project, Catania University, 2004. According to the new Treaty, this kind of 'special agreement may include rights and mutual obligations and the possibility to conduct common actions as well'. They aim at establishing 'a space of prosperity and good neighbourhood, based on the EU values and characterized by close and peaceful co-operation relations' (*Treaty Establishing a Constitution for Europe*, op. cit., art. I-57 paras 1 and 2).

68. M.A. Molchanov, 'Ukraine and the EU: a Perennial Neighbour?', *Journal of European Integration*, 26, December 2004, pp. 451–73.

69. Even a section of French scholarly (and policy advising, as the EU Institute of Security Studies, Paris) work on the subject considers the need to overcome the old debate between French and British security policies, both focused on the nuclear threat. See N. Gnesotto, *La puissance et l'Europe*, Presses de Science Politiques, Paris, 1998.

70. S. Sarfati, *La tentation impériale*, Odile Jacob, Paris, 2004; P. Hassner, *La terreur et l'empire*, Seuil, Paris, 2003; B. Badie, *L'impuissance de la puissance*, Fayard, Paris, 2004; J. Rosenau, *Distant Proximities*, Princeton University Press, 2003; Keohane, *Ironies of Sovereignty*, op. cit. and *Power and Governance in a Partially Globalized World*, Routledge, London, 2002; D.A. Lake, *Entangling Relations. American Foreign Policy in Its Century*, Princeton University Press, Princeton, 1999.

71. D.L. Boren and E.J. Perkins (eds), *Preparing America's Foreign Policy for the 21st Century*, University of Oklahoma Press, Norman, 1999.

72. See section 1.7. See also the Commission *Communication on Multilateralism* and the 'Solana paper' on security of 2003.

73. B. Badie, *Un monde sans souveraineté. Les Etats entre ruse et responsabilité*, Fayard, Paris, 1999, pp. 223–85.

74. Habermas, *Der gespaltene Westen*, op. cit., Chapters 3 and 5; also 'Die Europäische Nationalstaat unter dem Druck der Globalisierung', in *Blätter für Deutsche und internationale Politik*, 4, 1999, pp. 425–36 and as philosophical background, 'Kant's Idee des ewigen Friedens – aus dem historischen Abstand von 200 Jahren', *Kritische Justiz*, 28, 1995, pp. 293–319.

5
The Process of Treaty Reform: the International Dimension

5.1 The constitutional process

As we have seen, despite the various internal and international obstacles and internal political setbacks, there exists in Europe a multiple legacy of broad interests and rooted aspirations which is strong enough to create a new regional and global political actor, different from the traditional state. Taking an interdisciplinary focus, ranging from the history of political thought to international relations theory, in this chapter we will look at the conceptual basis of the EU as regards the constitutional dimension of its development.

To paraphrase Hegel's famous beginning to the *Constitution of Germany*, our starting point (widely accepted in European studies) is that the EU polity does not constitute a state.[1] Furthermore, in contrast to the young Hegel's Machiavellian-like inspired tones regarding the construction of the German state, we must add that not only is the EU not currently a state, but it never has been one in the past and, realistically, never will be, even by means of a constitutional treaty. The EU lacks, and will continue to lack, access to some of the main prerogatives of classic external sovereignty of the Westphalian state, i.e. the centralization of internal and external security policies and the power to declare war. Moreover, its political existence as a unitary entity is called into question whenever the world enters into a 'state of exception'.[2]

However, because of this very limit, conducting a more thorough analysis of the nature and international implications of such a *sui generis* entity is a particularly interesting task from a theoretical point of view. This is the issue on which we would like to focus our attention here. The main reason why international political thought is interested in the conceptual and philosophical implications of the historical development in western Europe of a non-state political form, its power of expansion and attraction (both as a force democratically unifying the continent and in terms of its global presence[3]), is above all the following: if the agenda had included the birth of a new state, i.e. if the European Communities of the 1950s had actually developed into the United States of Europe, as the founding fathers imagined and wished (in other words a single federal political body), the theoretical interest in the transformation of international relations and the very concept of sovereignty would have been more modest. Undoubtedly, it would have been less than the interest aroused by the totally unprecedented type of political system created through the European treaties. The first international implication of the development of the association of the western states in Europe following the end of the Second World War is the 'internal foreign policy' effect, i.e. embracing socio-economic integration and renouncing war as a way of solving disagreements between neighbouring countries. In other words, through the emergence of a 'security community',[4] armed conflict between the protagonists of western European history became inconceivable. However, this important historical achievement runs the risk of being considered less significant in the event of a negative answer to the following question arising from phenomena such as globalization, the end of the bipolar world, and the new global security agenda after September 11: can the political development of the EU realistically be such as to enable the Union to play a peacemaking and balancing role in twenty-first-century international relations?

Interest in this question has notably increased as a result of the exceptional opportunity offered by the debate on the definitive constitutional set-up of the EU. In general, a constitution is the 'very structure of an organised political community, the necessary order deriving from a sovereign power and the institutions exercising this power'.[5] In the case of the EU, the new Treaty could be expected to be the instrument by which everybody stipulates clear and relatively stable agreements on who governs, how they govern and the limits of power that need to be taken into account.[6] The 'Laeken European Council Declaration' in December 2001 insisted on the inclusion of the Union's global role on the agenda as a key starting point for the redefinition of the EU's institutional architecture. The lively academic debate in the 1990s on the relevance of a constitutional perspective in the absence of a European state and *demos*[7] has been enriched therefore by a constituent praxis that encompasses and exceeds it. The EU is indeed undertaking a refounding process that, from the Convention to the Intergovernmental Conference, the explicitly constitutional new Treaty and its ratification,[8] is clearing up some of the thornier aspects of the international dimensions of the Union.

The EU is thus dealing with a new and decisive chapter in a theoretical debate that traces its roots back to the dawn of the European Community of the Six. The developments of the last 30 years have shown the error of those who had forecast that the EC would become a 'superpower'.[9] However, the empirical fact of the EU not being a classic political and military power is only one aspect of the question. The EU has developed a political system and international role which is distant and distinct from the classic power model. It has taken a path unfamiliar to realist and state-centred thought.[10] This has produced a twofold historical result: on the one hand, it is recognized that the EU reveals its marginal role in hard military crisis situations, whether these be regional (Balkan wars) or global (Middle East, Iraq, etc.). On the other hand, if we take into account all external relations but the military power, the EU is also recognized as the second global actor. Therefore, the question addressed here is whether (and, if so, how) this new kind of political entity, which we have defined as a 'civilian power', can achieve the constitutional features of a political power in terms of producing united and effective international actions consistent with a shared international political identity based on constitutional principles. This question is in turn linked to another question, which we examined in Chapter 1: in the context of twenty-first-century international relations, is there (or can there be) space for a non-state political actor, internally legitimized and effective, to play an incisive role? In other words, will the European Union be capable of dealing with a highly political international agenda, in which security is once again the central issue?

5.2 The concepts of 'civilian power' and 'shared power'

In Europe, the roots of the notion of 'civilian power' are to be found not only in the Enlightenment, liberalism, Christianity and democratic socialism, but also in the tragic legacy of the twentieth century. This had a direct impact on the post-war Constitutions of the defeated powers such as Germany and the new Italian Republic. Thus, article 11 of the 1948 Italian Constitution refers to the 'repudiation of war' as a 'means for settling international disputes', the willingness to accept 'limitations of sovereignty where they are necessary for a legal system of peace and justice', and the promotion of 'international organizations furthering such ends'. The concept of civilian power and the European notion of protection of human rights refer to the memory of the tragedies of the last century, the Holocaust and the self-critical historical memory developed by the peoples of Europe after 1945. There are similarities with the Japanese post-war Consitution (see art. 9). However, in Japan it has not yet played a significant role in improving relationships with previous regional enemies and victims. By contrast, in Europe, this radically innovative political culture pervaded the epistemic community of the founding fathers at the heart of the early EC integration. We have already examined the theoretical dimension of the debate on civilian power within the theoretical and geopolitical context of the second half of the twentieth century, characterized by the bipolar world and the cold war.[11] In fact, most commentators acknowledge that the EC emerged and prospered in part due to the external federating element provided by the tensions of the bipolar world, even if this did mean that all member states relied on the powerful American ally for nuclear security and political leadership, and renounced a proactive political role for Europe.[12] However, the political potential of the EC and its member states was already there, even if limited (and not only as the 'downsized' defeated powers) by the logic of the bipolar international system.

The post-1989 era, the end of the bipolar world, the demise of the Soviet nuclear threat and the collapse of the socialist system have certainly not provided the idyllic conditions for the 'end of history'. They have, however, furnished Europe with a new window of opportunity and created the geopolitical space for a world accommodating new economic and political actors in what has been redefined as 'global governance'.[13] In this new scenario, the important decisions of the Maastricht Treaty to institutionalize the first steps of a common foreign and security policy and construct federal monetary union (in other words, touching on the 'sovereign competence' of member states) have led to the revival of the theoretical issue of 'another power'. This has stimulated a new debate on the variety of international actors, realism and legitimacy of a European path to international actorness and power.[14]

In François Duchêne's pioneering work, it is not methodologically clear to what extent the concept of civilian power is normative or analytical: the 'European Community could have the opportunity to show the influence that can be exercised through wide political cooperation that has emerged mainly to implement new forms of power'.[15] The basis of such potential influence is provided by the values declared and practised at both internal and external levels. These include human rights, democracy, peace and the settlement of conflicts, justice and tolerance, combined with the non-military instruments used by the EU to conduct external relations and international actions and, above all, the possible dissemination of elements of the regional integration experience to other continents, as a way of achieving democracy and lasting peace. Even if Headley Bull's realist criticism of EC civilian power as a 'contradiction in terms' was appropriate during the nuclear confrontation stage between the two superpowers, the issue now is whether it is completely obsolete against a background of the conflicts in the Balkans in the 1990s, Europe's continuing military subordination to the US and the EU's difficulties in facing the challenges of the post-September 11 period. The disappearance of the traits typical of the half-century defined by the nuclear threat and the balance of power between the US and the USSR offers Europe new choices and opportunities. The question is whether conditions have matured in Europe for a notion of civilian power that can answer the good objections of realism. We shall begin by discussing the concept of political power, which is central to the redefinition of the concept of civilian power.

Referring to Robert Dahl, Norberto Bobbio argued that the framework of the classical notion of power is that of a negative-sum game ('A's power implies B's lack of freedom') and that, in the case of conflict between political power and economic or cultural power, the political always prevails.[16] This traditional notion of power, which dates back to Machiavelli and Bodin, was adjusted to fit the modern state by Max Weber, who defined it as the capacity to impose one's will even when faced with opposition. It was on this basis that European political theory influenced the realist and neo-realist school of international relations, particularly in terms of the version that dominated American political science after the Second World War.[17] In Europe, Hinsley, Schmitt and others focused on the basic feature of sovereign power, the *jus ad bellum*, namely the right to declare war in the context of the inter-state system.[18] The internal sovereignty of the supreme power of the state is the prerequisite for the affirmation of its external sovereignty amid an inter-state system which, although to some degree organized by international law, lacks a central authority.

This notion of sovereign power is notoriously subject to criticism both in Europe and the US. Its alternative is provided by the two main versions of constitutionalism as 'shared sovereignty' which has deep roots in the history of political thought and institutions: the federalist tradition (especially its American version), on the one hand,[19] and 'mixed government' on the other. This latter version was expertly presented by Norberto Bobbio as a theoretical (and also historical if we think of examples such as the Republic of Venice) notion of power, far from the classic modern realist tradition, defined by a compromising balance between different procedures, principles, social forces and institutions.[20] The two versions of 'shared sovereignty' should not be confused: for example, Hegel underestimated the American federal form and defined it as a pre-state – 'neither a true state, nor a true government'.[21] However, he defended the mixed constitution of constitutional monarchies as a complementary combination of different principles. According to this school of thought (which has its far roots in the celebration of Licurgus by Polibius), the mix of monarchic, aristocratic and democratic principles constitutes the maximum degree of wisdom, since it is only this Ciceronian *aequatum et temperatum* system – mixed constitution in the modern world – that ensures stable governments and guarantees a balance between different forces and principles.

The theoretical question that has long been posed is whether such institutions inevitably turn out to be fragile because they are intrinsically 'monstrous' (in Chapter 29 of *Leviathan*, Hobbes uses the image of the man 'that had another man growing out of his side') or because, in exceptional historical situations, the real sovereign eventually emerges (as claimed by Carl Schmitt, for example). Or, on the contrary, it could be the increasing internal polyarchic pluralism and the multiple external interdependence that inevitably defuses the unitary concept of sovereign political power, to the benefit of various forms of 'shared sovereignty'. The very existence of a complex political system like the EU stimulates a new line of theoretical research on sovereignty. Of course, its political development during the decades of the bipolar world avoided encroaching significantly on issues not only of peace or war, but also of political union, and this aspect clearly prevented it from being considered a sovereign power. It is no coincidence that its political constitution has been compared to the two forms of shared sovereignty. However, it is its original civilian nature that poses an unavoidable conceptual challenge. To what degree is this specifically intrinsic aspect of the EU compatible with its growth as a global power?

In Chapters 1 and 4 we provided a positive, albeit conditional, answer by referring to the rich and variegated renewal process which has taken place within international relations theory over the last 20 years or so, and to the questioning of the theoretical premises of the classic meaning of political power and international power beyond the neo-realist school: the theory of regimes, the 'theory of complex interdependence', institutionalism and constructivist theory. In this section, we will put forward further arguments by summarizing some results which complement research conducted on the history of political ideas and comparative institutionalist studies.

1.   The *longue durée* tendency as regards the decline of classic state sovereignty due to the complex global interdependencies of the market, trade, socio-cultural processes, the mass media and the technological revolution. In this context, we refer to the decline of the primacy of military and security issues (not only the nuclear deterrent) on the international agenda and the growth in the political importance of trade, cultural, economic and technological links, etc. This has had inevitable consequences on the hierarchy of international relations and carries implications for the growing significance of civilian (aid, trade and diplomacy) as compared to military means in terms of international influence.[22]

2.   The variety and plurality of international public and private actors, national and international actors, multinational companies, transnational networks, as well as the emergence of functional approaches aimed at reorganizing authority within the context of globalization and diminishing the centrality of the state as the organizing factor of political space.[23]

3.   The questioning of the unitary nature of international action by the state, due to the internal complexity of the decision-making process, the participation of civil society groups and the growing importance of MNCs, transnational interest networks and coalitions.[24]

4.   The overcoming of the classic realist distinction between two spheres, i.e. domestic and international, inside/outside, anchoring peace to the internal democratic constitution of each of the units of the system (an idea rooted in Kant's thought).

5.   The clear insufficiency of the state when faced with the major emergencies of global governance, peace, the environment, economic and financial instability, hunger, poverty, infectious and endemic diseases, humanitarian disaster, etc. This inevitably encourages cooperation among states and the functional strengthening of multilateral institutions, both regional (such as the EU) and global. This can lead to an enhanced role for international organizations and regimes and the strengthening of their capacity not only to manipulate and bind, but also to guide the autonomous preferences of member states.

6.   The growing international influence of 'structural' power (based on knowledge, know-how and technology) as compared to military or economic power.[25]

7.   The importance of multilateralism and also the relevance of its broad non-utilitarian interpretations. These not only anchor it to the typical values of historically changing hegemonic power,[26] but also pave the way for its renewal: from a constructivist viewpoint, there is

a need for a rethinking of the notion of international power, given the presence of a non-military political entity (like the EU) which wants to be a global player in the name of its interests and values and is inter-subjectively recognized as a relevant multilateral actor by many external partners.

8. The European Community and European Union understood as case studies and workshops for all these innovative traits. The EU is the most advanced example of a difficult and contradictory historical development that has gradually led the various European states to accept shared and civilized sovereignty: the progressive limitation of the *jus ad bellum* during the twentieth century, from the 'Kellog-Briand' Pact on the UN Charter to the political role of the Security Council, from the emergence of international law and increasingly binding multilateral organizations to the voluntary and progressive limitations of national sovereignty introduced by the 'Schuman Plan' (1950) and strengthened by every European treaty since then, up to and including the Treaty of Nice (December 2000) and the draft of the European Convention (2003).

9. Finally, comparative research on politics and institutions shows that the transformation of sovereign power involves both the Union and each member state as object and also subject within a growing 'Europeanization' process, in the sense of a civilian power. Germany, in particular, which, represents the challenging heart of the European construction, has paradoxically recovered – and at the same time limited – its international sovereignty since 1990 (see the Maastricht Treaty, 1992) and during the two Iraqi crises to the point where it has attracted criticism for 'Teuton timidity' (and even worse). For decades, Italy has made use of the far-sighted article 11 of its Constitution as a lever for the internal integration of European treaties which are increasingly aimed at reinforcing supranationality. There is a clear similarity in the paths taken by Italy and Germany, at least until 2001.[27] France has learned to reconcile its republican national identity with the political strengthening of the EU better than in the past.[28] The Franco-German engine, the symbol of the overcoming of classic power politics, now seems to combine the German feelings for peace and the French attachment to national pride, and clearly goes beyond both respective illusions, i.e. those of 'Great Switzerland' and Gaullist *grandeur*. Finally, thanks to the stimulus provided by the inclusion of the 'Petersberg's' (peacekeeping) civilian and military tasks in the Amsterdam Treaty, states with traditions of neutrality (such as Austria and the Scandinavian countries) have proved they are not an obstacle to political union. Indeed, they are helping to mould its most innovative civilian features. Of course, this 'Europeanization' of

national policies encounters resistance among those states and groups who conceive of Europe as a mere large market overshadowed by NATO. Today a modest conception of civilian power,[29] subordinating the idea of Europe to that of the West, can be found within post-Communist countries, among the Mediterranean right and in Britain, where it is based on a deep-rooted bipartisan sovereign state culture. Despite the more markedly pro-European stances taken by the Blair government from 1997 to 2000 (Amsterdam Treaty, 'Saint-Malo' understanding on European defence with France, support for the Lisbon Strategy), the constant priority given by the United Kingdom to its 'special relationship' with the US is potentially detrimental to the political role of the EU. Nevertheless, even in Britain a section of public opinion realizes that greater commitment to both monetary union and the EU political union might be in the national interest. If the British government could really overcome the old idea of Europe as a subset of 'Western' global policy, it would be able to increase its influence over the EU and shape its role as a world civilian power. It would be helped in this respect by its past as a great multilateral trading power at a time when Britain dominated the seas, but was weak militarily. If this does not occur, however, the most likely development will be the emergence of two concentric circles or a 'variable geometry' Europe: a common market and law area, separate from a group of core nations more committed to international political autonomy.

In brief, the development of a new theory of sovereign power as 'shared sovereignty' is thus interwoven with the (albeit difficult) 'Europeanization' of large European states, which has been taking place for decades. The heart of this lies in the transformation of member states (and not just the EU itself) into civilian powers not only 'by defect', as evidence of the limited sovereignty typical of defeated countries, but also as a choice which has been renewed 50 years after the end of the war by the losers, the winners and neutral states. As regards the future, however, fundamental variables include the willingness of member states to take the step of equipping both themselves and the EU with those elements and provisions that can make the civilian power option credible in the twenty-first century: (a) appropriate resources and means (including military ones) to support and implement the 'international policing' actions required by the peace policy: (b) stronger common institutions and a shared strategic vision. Of course, the different conceptions of the EU's global role and the relationship between Europe and the US constitute formidable factors of uncertainty.

Thus, the EU finds itself at a crucial historical crossroads. The continuity of Europe as a peaceful civilian power is deeply rooted in history, both in terms of ideals and practices. These roots are both modern (from humanism to the Enlightenment. In modern history, the balance achieved by the European Concert can be interpreted as multilateral, as is also obviously the case for British commercial multilateralism) and pre-modern (the ideas of an open Europe and supranationality are rooted in classic Greek, Roman and Christian philosophies). From the federalism of the origins to the New Deal, up to the Marshall Plan and the 'liberal' decades, American culture has also played an important role in the political revival of the values of multilateralism, shared sovereignty and the limits this implies for state sovereignty. Nevertheless, the new challenge which emerged in the 1990s centres on the relationship between this legacy, enriched by decades of European integration, and *political* union, i.e. the transformation of the Union is occurring in a new international context that is linked to historical events and changes. From the fall of the Berlin wall to the resurgence of violence and war, events and changes have shown that the Union's (albeit important) adjustment to the challenges of global governance in the 1990s is still not sufficient. Institutionalist political theory is again being challenged and, in part, this is because the cosmopolitan theories on the world order, even if relevant, are not really appropriate.

5.3 The EU and global governance: beyond cosmopolitanism

In this section, we will take a step back for a moment. After the end of the bipolar world, we saw a revival of cosmopolitan thought in which the interpretation of the destiny of the EU plays a significant theoretical role. This revival was encouraged by real phenomena such as the end of the cold war, the spread of democracy (or at least the 'façade democracies') to 81 new countries, technological and trade globalization (in both its friendly and threatening sides), and the multiplication and deterioration of local and global emergencies (in particular concerning poverty and the environment), whose size is increasingly overwhelming for the limits of every nation state. Although the starting point was provided by different disciplinary approaches and cultural perspectives, research in the social sciences and political philosophy has provided new support for innovative normative visions of the world order and normative conceptions of the role of the Europe as *civilian and civilizing* power.

1. The neo-cosmopolitan approach, taking in the decline of the nation state and the revival of a role for a reformed UN,[30] increasingly identifies the establishment of a European political community as an obligatory passage, a first step towards a legitimate and accountable system of global multi-level governance, structured according to an organic and rational scheme involving 'regional' parliaments and governments. New cosmopolitanism is thus more flexible and judicious than previous versions. Despite widespread criticism of the limits of nation states, the convergence between cosmopolitanism and Europeanism cannot be taken for granted, since the regionalist – and not only neo-mercantilist – political option is hard to combine with the global vision of the new cosmopolitans. They underestimate two issues: first of all, from an analytical perspective, it is necessary to take into account the dogged internal resistance of European nation states, despite increased global interdependence (or perhaps even because of its destabilizing impact). This leads to greater attention being paid both to the civilizing effect stemming from cooperation between states and to the deep crisis of traditional federal visions of the EU. Secondly, new cosmopolitanism is faced with an external challenge: the changed security situation at the beginning of the twenty-first century. This aspiration was widely subscribed to during the 'Clinton decade' and was conceived of not only in terms of a broad global networking system, structured around various levels of authority and international and transnational cooperation, but also as an opportunity to spread democracy, thanks to the birth of promising universalist regimes aimed at the protection of human rights,[31] new stakeholders in civil society and the formation of a transnational public opinion. In Chapter 1 we provided evidence that the new international security challenges and agenda have rendered obsolete not only the mediatic Fukuyama's nice wording but also many serious optimistic prospects for global governance and world order.

2. Although distinct from the classic neo-cosmopolitan trend, a multi-faceted current of thought is emerging which harks back to the theme of the EU as a community of values. This emphasizes the universal implications of the original nature of European law[32] and enriches the most noble economic–commercial interpretation of civilian power. This latter idea, beyond the Lockean notion of trading relations, also involves the enhancement of the potential positive impact of the EU/EC's high degree of integration in the commercial field on the WTO – the multilateral institution at the heart of global governance today. Both academic literature and the European Commission[33] highlight this potentially exemplary

impact on global governance and view it as one of the most markedly political points of the global contribution of European regionalism.

While a number of commentators have already expertly dealt with the scope, limits and constitutional implications of the current forms of European supranationality, some overlook the necessary strengthening of the political and constitutional conditions of civilian power conceived of as political power, as well as its international autonomy. The result is the correction of the state-centred federalist approach, either in the sense of a community of values capable of influencing multilateral institutions,[34] or in the sense of 'transnational federalism' (the prerequisite for transnational governance).[35] In this case, we refer to the classic approach adopted by the European Commission,[36] i.e. of an EU which 'provides a good example' for the rest of the world of successful democratic governance and is hypostatized, appearing almost as a sort of miniature government of globalization.

3.   In this context, Jürgen Habermas's synthesis stands out. Taking stock of Kantian cosmopolitan thought, he places the link between the EU and the global economic and political multilateral system against a more explicitly political theory background which encompasses both the role of European states and the political dimension of their socio-economic regulation. In fact, the use of the term 'federal state' should not hide the fact that the EU is also an *unprecedented institutional structure* according to Habermas; when he expands on the external dimension of the famous European 'constitutional patriotism', supporting a wider global consensus on values (peace, respect for human rights, support for refugees, the fight against inequalities, etc.), he stresses the issue of the primacy of *political integration*. Of particular significance is his assertion that 'a federation will not suffice'.[37] The boundary between inside and outside (the state) must be overcome in the sense of achieving some coherence between democracy and international relations. Furthermore, within the EU, national political parties and public spaces need to be more 'synchronized' and states must recover a social regulating function (different from the neo-liberal vision) by strengthening cooperation both in this area and against the violation of the ecosystem, international organized crime and the new terrorist threat. This is the foundation for a 'global-scale domestic policy which, even in the absence of a world government, can at least make multilateral transnational organizations more consistent'. In line with Kant, Habermas fears the danger of a world state; nevertheless he does not hesitate to warn that the EU runs a *double* risk: on the one hand, that of becoming a 'fortress Europe' which, through mercantilist choices, is more closed

in terms of asylum and immigration policies. On the other hand, the convergence of Eurosceptics and Eurotechnocrats around pure market logic – and ethics – may create a block, an institutional status quo and an economistic regression of the EU, which would stop any universal projection of the European construction experiment.

These new interpretations of the civilian link between European integration and global governance hark back not only to great philosophical traditions, from Locke to Kant, from Myrdal to Keynes, and from the founding fathers to Delors, but also to the deep trends which have emerged in European society. These include contemporary public opinion which pays greater attention to issues such as the importance of international law, the protection of human rights, the political role of the EU as a commercial entity, the persistent socio-economic differences amongst Welfare States in western Europe and the increasing need for European convergence, including the modernization and institutionalization of the social model at supranational level.[38]

Neo-cosmopolitan approaches show clear limits: with the exception of Habermas, the influence of the cultural climate of the 1990s is apparent, as clearly expressed in Rosenau and Czempiel's image of *governance without government*, i.e. the gradual decline of the logic of international power relations and the growing marginalization of security issues in favour of decentralized, civilian and peaceful governance. A second limit is that, in this context, rather than an effective power, the new civilian power risks becoming a 'good intention', based on common values, nice wording and pacifism or an entity which uses the influence of its social civilization, combined with its commercial role and its presumed exemplary democratic practice to realize the hope expressed in 1950 by Alexandre Kojève in a letter to Léo Strauss, when he said 'the world state might be realized through the gradual expansion of the European approach to integration across the entire globe'.[39]

There is no doubt that we are dealing with a valuable historical and theoretical legacy, which goes well beyond Duchêne's hopes. However, neither spreading the European example nor grafting it onto a cosmopolitan approach provides an appropriate response to the new challenges of comprehensive security in the twenty-first century.

With regard to the realist and neo-realist tradition, the legitimacy of the civilian power concept will not be achieved until it provides an answer to questions of war and peace. This means taking account of the new web of modern and postmodern threats, asymmetric hostilities (informal terrorist networks) and international disorder which defines the globalized world in the post-cold war era. Similarly, unlike neo-medievalist and neo-liberal visions, which envisaged the end not only of the state, but also of politics, we must face the fact that security is once again at the heart of the international agenda and that the only superpower – despite occasional fluctuations – is pursuing a classic idea of sovereign and military power and is reluctant to leave any room for civilian alternatives to its approach to power relations which go beyond that of a timid façade.[40]

This book provided some evidence that an innovative theoretical response is possible, which goes beyond both realist national interest theories and cosmopolitanism, while taking stock of their findings and challenges. Currently, we are witnessing the politicization of contradictions within global governance, as well as active resistance on the part of the multilateral and multiregional world and (admittedly weak) multipolar shifts against the move towards the hierarchical redefinition of a world centre. While the US began relinquishing its role as a multilateral hegemonic power, in the sense of a combination of domination and consensus,[41] civilian powers have devoted increasing attention to international cooperation, as can be seen not only from our analysis of the EU, but also with regard to political trends in regional organizations and large countries such as Japan, Brazil, Canada and Indonesia.

Attempts to provide theoretical answers to this question, which ignore the European institutional reality once again, repeat and exacerbate the mistake made by those who separated theories about the 'decline of Europe' from the analysis of the important results achieved during the last 50 years by the EC/EU in overcoming the classic concept of sovereignty and their theoretical implications. Today, at the risk of raising the temperature of internal debate, the EU is discussing how it can synchronize and institutionally qualify its international voice in terms of a politically mature civilian power, based on the new political will of its states. In fact, the study of the preferences of European states is a crucial step because, despite Europeanization, they have never substantially relinquished their competencies in terms of foreign policy.[42] Today, however, they must choose whether to bridge the gap between expectations and actual EU capacity[43] and therefore promote the EU as a participant in world political leadership, worthy of the continent's history.

The novelty of the 2002–3 period is that the political implications of identifying the EU's core activity as relating to both economic and political multilateralism have become apparent. The Security Council of the UN has power thanks to the EU and the EU expresses its policy regarding war and peace issues thanks to the UN. According to Robert

Keohane, the current tough transatlantic confrontation involves two theories and practices of sovereignty. The elements already substantiating the peculiarity of European power were mentioned in the research approaches outlined above. The novelty is that exogenous factors and external challenges and expectations are pushing the Union and states to overcome residual ambiguities. In Chapters 2–4 we have sought to illustrate the unique and special nature of the EU's external relations, i.e. the most salient aspects of its 'structural foreign policy', that is its influence on the anarchic political *structure* of international relations. We shall now deal with its specifically institutional dimension.

5.4   A 'mixed government' for the European Union of the twenty-first century?

In the search for a new political and juridical synthesis aimed at strengthening the EU's international role, the main questions are the following:

(a) What political autonomy can the EU achieve within the context of the evolving transatlantic partnership and given the divergent international interests and visions of member states? In other words, what kind of common foreign, security and defence policy will be possible in the future?

(b) What type of unitary and legitimate institutional framework can be devised in order to bolster the coherent government of external relations and the political role of an enlarged EU in the world?

As the way of Treaty reform, the pressures for a more democratic, open and transparent process of treaty revision succeeded and the European Council Laeken Declaration (December 2001) created a European Convention, half of whose 103 members were either members of the European Parliament or national parliaments. Observers and scholars agree on the unprecedented value of the Convention exercise, chaired by Giscard d'Estaing and open to 25 countries plus 3 candidate states. This provided a unique arena for deliberative and consensual democracy at the supranational level. Moreover, the Convention has been effective. Although granted 'advisory' rather than 'decision-making' power, the convergence achieved between February 2002 and July 2003 in relation to a whole series of issues (where the working groups' reports have been taken on board or the Presidium's mediation accepted by the Assembly) gave rise to a number of important institutional innovations. These were very largely maintained by the Intergovernmental Conference (2003–4):

- The definition of article 7, part I, regarding a single legal personality for both the EC and the EU. Although no legal implications can be expected for the unification of procedures regarding the various aspects of external relations, this convergence clearly impacts on both the unification of the TEC and TEU treaties and the EU's international role.[44]
- The inclusion of the Charter of Fundamental Rights (proclaimed by the Nice European Council in December 2000) as the second part of the new Constitutional Treaty[45] connects rights and politics, takes on significant international meanings and confirms the EU's identity as a democratic power both in terms of old and new member states and in relation to neighbouring countries and the global scene.
- The willingness to improve horizontal coherence between the various external relations also implies a more rational organization and unification of those responsibilities which are currently divided between two 'centres of gravity': the Commission and the Council. This is to be achieved by means of a new minister for foreign affairs, who will have the double role of vice-president of the Commission and representative of the Council (art. I, 28).[46]
- Various articles emphasize solidarity between member states and the Union (art. I, 5 and I, 40.5). Article I, 16 states that the 'Union competence in matters of foreign and security policy shall cover all areas of foreign policy and all questions relating to the Union's security, including the progressive framing of a common defence policy that may lead to a common defence'. Furthermore, it stresses the obligation to 'actively and unreservedly' support the CFSP 'in a spirit of loyalty and mutual solidarity' and compliance with 'the Union's action in this area. States should refrain from actions contrary to the Union's interests or likely to impair its effectiveness.' Although the international events of 2002/3 remind us that there are no juridical solutions capable of preventing political disagreements, experience has confirmed the existence of an institutional chain spillover effect. This increases hopes that, if member state acceptance of this step of the constitutional process and principles can be secured through ratification, a more pro-European attitude will result.
- The multilateral 'solidarity clause' (art. I, 43) in the event of an attack on a member state, mirroring article 5 of the WEU Treaty and article 51 of the UN Charter (art. I, 41.7). Furthermore, article I, 43 extends

the solidarity clause in the event of 'a terrorist attack', including prevention, protection of population and assistance to a member state
in its territory.[47]
- There is a larger application of 'enhanced co-operation' (art. I, 44)
  between a minimum of one-third of the member states (only 8 in Nice).
- Regarding European Security and Defence Policy, the IGC provided
  real progress: the way is open for an in principle non-exclusive 'permanent structured co-operation' (art. I, 41 and III, 318), provided
  that member states have sufficient 'military capabilities'.
- A 'European Armaments, Research and Military Capabilities Agency'
  was created, aimed at strengthening the industrial and technological
  bases of the defence sector and assisting the Council (art. I, 41.3 and
  III, 311).
- The unanimous voting procedure has been retained as far as the
  ECSP and the ESDP are concerned (art. I, 40.6), although several
  'passerelles' to QMV are possible (art. I, 40.7).

Despite these limits to the supranational principle, and notwithstanding
the explicit reference to the 'NATO obligations of certain member states'
(art. I, 41.2, strange in a 'Constitution'!), the Constitutional Treaty
expresses the political desire to set common European priorities, including ones relating to the EU's international more autonomous role.[48]

This generally positive shift towards the politicization and growth of
the coherence of the EU's international role brings us back to a key
issue – that of central government in an enlarged EU. Or, to put it
another way: how can the coordination of decisions and policies be
ensured given the greater internal difference within the wider EU? This
'squaring of the circle' is pursued by means of an innovative version of
the classic 'mixed government' model. Indeed, various considerations
encourage us to focus on this approach, which goes beyond the old
debate between federalists and confederalists:

(a) the Constitutional Treaty can only be the result of a compromise
    between the various constitutional cultures of member states as well
    as the result of a balanced strengthening of all four main European
    institutions: the Commission, the Parliament, the European
    Council and the Council of Ministers;
(b) the decline of the federal state model is also due to the difficulties
    encountered in reconciling diversity and unity, given the weight of
    member states (the Council defends its prerogatives) and the wide-
    spread objections to the idea of turning the Commission into the
    sole governing centre of the EU. The EU federal state scenario

appears unrealistic if we look not only at the Treaty issued by the IGC in June 2004 but also at the July 2003 draft Constitutional Treaty, whose article 1 does not include the oxymoron reference to a 'Federation of States' either;

(c) the major EU enlargement process currently under way will have significant and far-reaching institutional implications for the decision-making process.[49]

In what sense can 'mixed government' be said to represent the most suitable institutional dimension for the EU as a political and civilian power? The interest in the 'mixed government' concept was already mentioned with reference to the prior functioning of the EU[50] and is being revived as a source of inspiration for the current reform process, particularly as the embodiment of the principle of double legitimacy regarding states and citizens.[51] In fact, many aspects of the European institutional system already correspond to a mixed government system: the expression of the will of the people (the European Parliament) is combined with the active contribution of states (the European Council and the Council of Ministers) and with the Commission, the technical expertise body which is the expression of the common interest of the Union. In contrast to a system founded as federalist *ab initio*, it is the gradual emergence of common competencies that determines the federal management of common policies, whereas – with the exception of the currency – essential competencies remain in the hands of states (domestic order, foreign and defence policy, education, the Welfare State, and constitution-making power). These too, however, are increasingly conditioned by the common framework of the Union. Therefore, the evolving *institutional architecture* is marked by some federal traits and displays the empirical characteristics of a political management structure which is articulated on several levels. This includes a permanent negotiating process and a system with functional and territorial bases, largely lacking a hierarchy, which many researchers term 'multilevel governance'.

The Constitutional Treaty rationalizes these traits, which are now characteristics of European integration, and simplifies the current political system without radically replacing it with another one. It can stress its political potential and improve efficiency and democracy, even without turning the Union into a federal state. Indeed, in the light of the implications of eastern enlargement, which were clearly discernible during the Convention and the IGC (in terms of the attachment to external symbols of national sovereignty typical of countries whose sovereignty was limited by the Soviet empire for decades), the consolidation at a quasi-continent-wide level of the degree of supranationality achieved by the EC/EU in the management of common competencies, as well as shared regulations and values, would already be a remarkable historical achievement, particularly if complemented by several clauses safeguarding the integration dynamic. Given, therefore, the nature of the EU and the consequences of enlargement, what institutional approach can constitute a meaningful step towards political union? What new equilibrium can be achieved between five decades of *acquis communautaire* on the one hand, and, on the other, divided national public opinions, conflicting internal and external expectations, in order to enhance and improve the efficiency of the EU's global role?

Beyond (and notwithstanding) the opposing approaches envisaging a federalist big bang or the preservation of the status quo, the simultaneous strengthening of the four main institutions – Parliament, the Council of Ministers, the European Council and the Commission, even if asymmetrical – may foster a dynamic reconciliation of the principles of technocracy, democracy and state cooperation. This combination is the main feature of the new Constitutional Treaty indeed, as far as the government of domestic and international policy functions is concerned.

The European Council is to have its essential political role strengthened by the stabilizing of its Presidency, even if the latter looks more as a chairperson than a true president.[52] The same holds true for the Council of Ministers, although the creation of a new 'law-making Council' was rejected by the IGC: the minister of foreign affairs will centralize very relevant external powers. The qualified majority vote in the Council of Ministers is being extended to many new areas regarding external relations. The EP is a clear winner in terms of its powers of legislative co-decision, which becomes the general rule, but not as the CFSP is concerned. The Commission looks like the loser to many observers; however, its executive power is also being strengthened though the direct election by the Parliament. However, one of the reasons why there is no longer serious justification for federalist hopes that the Commission will turn into a fully fledged government is precisely, according to many observers, the final welcoming by the IGC (contrary to the Convention draft) of the Commission's proposal for one Commission member for each member state: how do you take decisions by majority voting in that new internal context?

Summing up, even if the dispute between large and small states regarding its composition and the new QMV has given cause for concern, the

Constitutional Treaty provides a relatively well-balanced strengthening of the four institutions, according to a compromise essentially based on the Franco-German paper of January 2003. Admittedly, many expected that the majority vote would be applied to the CFSP, but we cannot say that the EU's international role is being globally weakened: rather, the Presidency of the European Council and the minister for foreign affairs are likely to increase the EU's international presence and visibility. The powers of the Commission in terms of other external relations are safe-guarded. Moreover, the provisions envisaged as far as the 'closer cooperation' and 'structured cooperation' Treaty provisions are concerned are likely to permit greater flexibility and initiative of the willing states.[53]

The Constitutional Treaty provides a clear improvement of the way the EU may carry on its external trade policy from the point of view of both efficiency and legitimacy: (a) co-decision of the European Parliament and the Council, which votes by QMV procedure; (b) exclusive EU compe-tences, with the exceptions of culture, services, public health and audio-visual system. This dynamic compromise is assigning greater international negotiating power to the Commission, but a unanimous vote is necessary in the Council on politically sensitive issues such as culture, which is seen by certain states as the means to defend European values and sensibilities from the negative effects of globalization. The minister of foreign affairs provides the coordination between the Commission and the Council, which masters the CFSP and CSDP. This example confirms that the 'mixed government' offers the most pertinent conceptualization of a situation in which the management of national diversities, the equilibrium between the two sources of legitimacy, the need for efficiency and the synthesis between the supranational and intergovernmental methods cannot be achieved by strengthening one institution and one principle at the expense of others.

'Mixed government' should in no way mean 'fragmented govern-ment' in practice, particularly as regards external relations (which was not stopped by art. 3 of the Maastricht Treaty, see the current TEU), as would ensue from the maintenance of two separate parallel adminis-trations, i.e. the Commission and the Council.[54] The current situation diminishes the consistency of the policy-making and the coherence of the EU's international action. The difficulty lies in successfully re-conciling the reinforcement of the Commission Presidency with the new long-term Presidency (rather than the rotating one) of the new European Council. It would be necessary to establish a rational divi-sion of tasks among central authorities, while leaving space for the new EU foreign minister and allowing for regular checks by Parliament, which, by contrast, is only consulted and informed as per art. I, 40.8 and I, 41.8. This complex compromise solution proved to be the only possible one according to the current 'political nature' in the EU. It is certainly the strongest and most legitimate institutional lever under the present circumstances fostering the EU's characterization as a new civilian and political power. This type of mixed EU Presidency, expressing a personalized form of supranationality, could increase the expectations of citizens regarding the EU's international role and encourage further enhancement of its capacities.

Of course, if the redefinition of central institutional powers is not accompanied by the strengthening of the elements which make up the essence, rules and international uniqueness of the EU's internal democracy, then the Constitutional Treaty risks failure. That is why the national ratification process is crucial and uncertain. However, both the Constitutional Treaty and its long and controversial ratification process serve to encourage the further development of a European transnational, democratic, critical, European public sphere. Such a process will only be successful if it occurs in synergy with renewed national democracies and a modernized European social model. The next decade will be crucial for the three main internal pillars of the European civilian power: the institutional reform process will interact not only with the uncertain enlargement process, but also with the Lisbon agenda.[55] If we consider the 'constitutionalization' of the EU within a broader, *longue dureé* process of the growing political dimension of regionalism, both in Europe and elsewhere, we inevitably come to the conclusion that this profound and variegated democratic trend is of extreme historical relevance for the future world order, whatever the local and global challenges it may face.

In the partially globalized post-cold war world, the EU represents the main real innovation in terms of political and institutional originality: it is more than a mere international regime and goes beyond the traditions of cosmopolitanism and republicanism. However, it is called upon to communicate more and more with other regions in the world and to contribute to the reform of the world order. Regardless of the classic meaning of sovereignty, the EU's international autonomy, international decision-making capacity, and the credibility and coherence of its external actions will be the crucial test for the political nature of the institutional construction. The text of the new Constitutional Treaty may make a further contribution to the gradual reform of the Westphalian system. Of course, the expectations for a more effective (generalized QMV) and democratic (Parliamentary scrutiny power) foreign policy are legitimate. The Preamble could also have been more courageous in mentioning the European tragedies of the past. A more clear-cut way of expressing Europe's political identity could actually have been achieved by means of an explicit article in the new Treaty rejecting war as a method of conflict resolution, complemented by the commitment to coherent support for peacemaking initiatives by international institutions. However, the EU is a diverse, multinational and pluralistic entity and historians do confirm that ideal Constitutions have rarely been applied.

We already focused in Chapter 2 on the deep link between regional cooperation and democratization. In this regard, the EU institutional reform process can be seen as the tip of the iceberg. Underneath lies the demand for a rule-based global governance that is firmly rooted in democratic participation, more accountable, more legitimate and channelled by regional organizations.

Since a durable international peace cannot realistically result only from a global legal system and it is possible that the most positive multilateral legacy of the twentieth century may hinder any process of anarchic fragmentation as well as the development of unipolar forms of 'universal monarchy', how will the universal value of the European experience be expressed? Taking a Hegelian perspective, in order to be stable, the political government of the 'global system of needs' and global civil society not only needs good governance and honest administration, but also solid political and 'ethical' roots from both functional and territorial viewpoints. In other words, it needs a widespread network of cooperation, driven by civilian powers, including regional political organizations, which are capable of creating fruitful mediations between nations and a new multilateralism. Moreover, it requires a fresh, positive and expansive new shared leadership. This can no longer be embodied by pure military power, aspiring to be the expression of the Zeitgeist and based on an 'absolute right': on the contrary, it can only be the expression of collective and pluralistic leadership, combining cooperative power and global legitimacy. The 'divided West'[56] on which we focus in Chapter 1, was a necessary step, even if we demonstrated that it cannot provide the end of the story through the revival of the classical multipolar system. Within a new, equal, coherent and rule-based cooperation among the network of multilateral organizations, the EU looks capable of assuming a major role, provided that the controversial institutional debate turns into a true political union. Indeed, together with enlargement and the modernization strategy, this political step is the third decisive factor determining the role of Europe within the structure of the world in the twenty-first century as an established, collective, civilian power. Only by strengthening this innovative long-term trend may the European Union truly be able to change the world's political structure.

Notes

1. See *Hegel's Political Writings*, translated with notes by T.M. Knox, Oxford, 1964.
2. I refer to Carl Schmitt's extreme term to help understand what remains an open problem for political theory. See *The Nomos of the Earth in the International law of the Jus Publicum Europeum*, London, 2003. On the English-speaking debate regarding the Schmitt thought, see the papers presented in section 11 of the ISA-ECPR Conference, The Hague, September 2004.
3. See J. Habermas, 'Why Europe Needs a Constitution', *New Left Review*, 11, September–October 2001, pp. 5–26, and *Die postnationale Konstellation: politische Essays*, Suhrkamp, Frankfurt a.M., 1998. Also see B. De Giovanni, *L'ambigua potenza dell'Europa*, Guida, Naples, 2002.
4. K.W. Deutsch, S. Burrell and R.A. Kann, *Political Community and the North Atlantic Area; International Organization in the Light of Historical Experience*, Princeton University Press, Princeton, 1957.
5. N. Matteucci, 'Costituzionalismo', in N. Bobbio, N. Matteucci and G. Pasquino, *Dizionario di politica*, UTET, Turin, 1983, p. 249. See also C.H. McIlwain, *Constitutionalism, Ancient and Modern*, Cornell University Press, Ithaca, NY, 1940. As regards the role of the constitutionalism of the EU against the background of the history of European constitutionalism, see R.C. van Canegem, *A Historical Introduction to Western Constitutional Law*, Cambridge University Press, Cambridge, 1995; P. Magnette (ed.), *La Constitution de l'Europe*, Université de Bruxelles, 2000.
6. F. Cerutti, 'La Costituzione europea di fronte a pace e guerra', *Quaderni del Forum*, XVI, 1, Florence, 2002.
7. J.H.H. Weiler, *The Constitution of Europe: 'Do the New Clothes have an Emperor?' and Other Essays on European Integration*, Cambridge University Press, Cambridge–New York, 1999, and also the articles by Habermas and D. Grimm included in P. Gowan and P. Anderson, *The Question of Europe*, Verso, London, 1997.
8. Council of the EU, General Secretariat, *Treaty Establishing a Constitution for Europe*, 2 vols, July 2004.
9. J. Galtung, *The EC: a Superpower in the Making*, Allen & Unwin, London, 1973.
10. Keohane, 'Ironies of Sovereignty: the European Union and World Order', op. cit.
11. See Chapter 4 and the references to F. Duchêne, 'The European Community and the Uncertainties of Interdependence', in M. Kohnstamm and W. Hager (eds), *A Nation Writ Large? Foreign Policy Problems before the European Community*, Macmillan, London, 1973, pp. 1–21 and H. Bull, 'Civilian Power Europe: a Contradiction in Terms', in L. Tsoukalis (ed.), *The European Community: Past, Present and Future*, Blackwell, Oxford, 1983, pp. 150–7.

12. Among others, H. Wallace and W. Wallace, *Policy Making in the European Union*, Oxford University Press, Oxford, 1996.
13. J.N. Rosenau and E.O. Czempiel (eds), *Governance without Government: Order and Change in World Politics*, Cambridge University Press, 1992.
14. As shown also by catchphrases referring to the EU such as 'the ironies of sovereignty', a 'gentle power', an 'ambiguous power'. See the texts cited by Keohane, 'Ironies of Sovereignty', op. cit., De Giovanni, *L'ambigua*, op. cit., T. Padoa Schioppa, op. cit.
15. Duchêne, 'The European Community and the Uncertainties of Interdependence', op. cit., p. 19.
16. N. Bobbio, *Stato, governo e società. Per una teoria generale della politica*, Einaudi, Turin, 1986.
17. K. Waltz, *Theory of International Politics*, Addison-Wesley, Reading, Mass., 1979.
18. E.H. Hinsley, *Sovereignty*, Cambridge University Press, Cambridge, 1986.
19. Keohane, 'Ironies of Sovereignty', op. cit.
20. N. Bobbio, 'Governo misto', in Bobbio, Matteucci and Pasquino, *Dizionario di politica*, op. cit.
21. G.W.F. Hegel, *Vorlesungen über die Philosophie der Geschichte* (1832–45), Suhrkamp, Frankfurt a.M., 1986.
22. R.O. Keohane and J.S. Nye, *Power and Interdependence*, HarperCollins, New York, 1989.
23. W. Wallace, The Nation State – 'Rescue or Retreat?', in P. Gowan and P. Anderson (eds), *The Question of Europe*, Verso, London, 1997, pp. 21–50.
24. M. Castells, *La société en réseaux. L'ère de l'information*, Fayard, Paris, 1997.
25. S. Strange, *States and Markets*, Pinter, London 1988; also *The Retreat of the State: the Diffusion of Power in the World Economy*, Cambridge University Press, New York, 1996.
26. J.G. Ruggie (ed.), *Multilateralism Matters. The Theory and Praxis of an Institutional Form*, Columbia University Press, New York, 1993. As regards Ruggie's position, see section 1.7 of this book.
27. This parallelism was rightly emphasized by G.E. Rusconi, *Germania, Italia, Europa. Dallo stato di potenza alla potenza civile*, Einaudi, Turin 2003, particularly in Chapters 10–14. See also P. Katzenstein (ed.), *Tamed Power. Germany in Europe*, Cornell, Ithaca, 1997 and W. Heydrich, J. Krause, U. Nerlich, J. Nötzold and R. Rummel (eds), *Sicherheitspolitik Deutschlands: neue Konstellation, Risiken, Instrumente*, Nomos, Baden-Baden, 1992, in particular the article by H.W. Maull, 'Zivilmacht: die Konzeption und ihre sicherheitspolitische Relevanz', pp. 771–886. Twenty years after Duchêne, this German perspective, although excessively anchored to a normative conception, is important because it is connected to the national development of the main European power.
28. M.G. Cowles, J. Caporaso and T. Risse, *Transforming Europe*, Cornell University Press, Ithaca, NY, 2001.
29. Ibid., Chapters 10–11.
30. R. Falk, 'The United Nations and Cosmopolitan Democracy: Bad Dream, Utopian Fantasy, Political Project', in D. Archibugi, D. Held and M. Köhler, *Re-Imagining Political Community. Studies in Cosmopolitan Democracy*, Polity Press, Cambridge, 1998, pp. 309–30.

31. D. Beetham, 'Human Rights as a Model for Cosmopolitan Democracy', in ibid., pp. 58–70.
32. Weiler, *The Constitution of Europe*, op. cit.
33. P. Lamy and J. Pisani-Ferry, *L'Europe de nos volontés*, Fondation Jaurès, Paris, 2002.
34. Weiler, *The Constitution of Europe*, op. cit.
35. K. Nicolaydis and R. Howse, *The Federal Vision*, Oxford University Press, Oxford, 2001; also 'This Is My EUtopia: Narrative as Power', *Journal of Common Market Studies*, 40, 4, 2002, pp. 767–92.
36. European Commission, *White Paper on European Governance*, Brussels, July 2001.
37. Habermas, *Die Postnationale Konstellation*, op. cit.
38. Habermas, 'Why Europe Needs a Constitution?', op. cit. as part of the international debate on the EU Constitution in Gowan and Anderson (eds), *The Question of Europe*, op. cit., articles by D. Grimm, J. Habermas and J. Weiler, pp. 239–95.
39. L. Strauss, *On Tyranny*, Free Press, New York, 1991, p. 256, mentioned by Nicolaydis and Howse, 'This Is My EUtopia', op. cit. The appropriation by American neo-conservatives of Léo Strauss's liberal thought is an obvious abuse.
40. R. Kagan, 'Power and Weakness', *Policy Review*, 113, 2002, pp. 3–28.
41. See Chapter 1 of this book and R.O. Keohane, *After Hegemony. Cooperation and Discord in the World Political Economy*, Princeton University Press, Princeton, 1984.
42. A. Moravcsik, *The Choice for Europe: Social Purpose and State Power from Messina to Maastricht*, Cornell University Press, Ithaca, 1998.
43. C. Hill, 'Closing the Capacity–Expectations Gap?', in J. Peterson and H. Sjursen (eds), *A Common Foreign Policy for Europe?*, Routledge, London–New York, 1998, pp. 18–38.
44. Convention Européenne, Secretariat, Rapport final du Groupe de Travail III, *Personnalité Juridique*, CONV 305/02, chaired by G. Amato, Brussels, 1 October 2002. The Convention draft has been translated in the Treaty (art. I-7). The legal personality of the EC had already been acknowledged since the Rome Treaty (TEC).
45. This had already been developed through the positive efforts of the working group (*Rapport du Groupe sur la Charte*, chaired by commissioner A. Vitorino, September 2002) and was confirmed by Giscard d'Estaing's draft (Convention Européenne, Secretariat, Presidium, *Avant-Projet de Traité Constitutionnel*, CONV 369/02, Brussels, 28 October 2002) and turned into the Convention Européenne, Presidium, Secretariat, *Project de Constitution*, CONV 848/03, Brussels, 9 July 2003. The IGC and the Treaty confirm this crucial decision.
46. As regards this controversial and difficult issue, which was affected by the internal implications of the Iraqi crisis, during the Convention, V. Giscard d'Estaing presented the Presidium's project on 23 April 2003 entitled *The Institution of the Unions, Draft Articles on Title IV of Part I of the Constitution*, CONV 691/03.
47. This question was dealt in a controversial way at the Convention. See Convention Européenne, Secretariat, Rapport final du Groupe de Travail VII, *Défense*, CONV 461/02, chaired by J.L. Dehaene, Brussels, 16 December 2002.
48. This comment has nothing to do with the trivial opposition of the EU to NATO, as argued by J.L. Cinbalo, 'Saving NATO from Europe', *Foreign Affairs*, 83, 6, 2004, pp. 111–20.

49. Eight CEEC countries (Slovenia, Hungary, Czech Republic, Slovakia, Poland, Estonia, Latvia and Lithuania) and two Mediterranean micro-states (Cyprus and Malta) joined the EU on 1 May 2004. The 'decreasing proportionality' criterion, which, although modified, was maintained by the Nice Treaty, raises the prospect of an unwieldy situation for both the Commission (each member state is entitled to a commissioner) and the Council: while the population of the CEEC countries that joined in 2004 accounted for 15.3 per cent of the EU of 25, these countries make up slightly less than one-third of all the 25 EU member states; in the European Parliament, the CEEC countries account for 20.63 per cent of the seats and in the Council of Ministers they control 24 per cent of the votes. Therefore the Convention proposes strengthening the role played by population by reforming the notion of the qualified majority vote according to two criteria: 60 per cent of the population plus the majority of member states; this proposal was rejected by Spain and Poland, and the December 2003 European Council did not reach an agreement on it. The compromise eventually signed in June 2004 at the end of a difficult IGC (and as a consequence of the change of government in Spain) revises QMV, setting the threshold at 65 per cent of the population and 15 member states out of 25 (art. I, 25).
50. G. Majone (ed.), *Regulating Europe*, Routledge, London, 1998.
51. J.-L. Quermonne, *La question du gouvernement européen*, Rapport Notre Europe, Groupment d'études et de recherches, Paris, 2002.
52. The solution proposed by the Convention was controversial, albeit counterbalanced by the parallel strengthening of the Commission. The Treaty signed in 2004 (art. I, 21 and I, 22) confirms the balanced compromise proposed by the Convention (see European Convention, *Draft Treaty Establishing a Constitution for Europe* (submitted to the European Council in Thessaloniki on 20 June 2003), European Communities, Luxembourg 2003 (including parts 1 and 2)). The European Council could no longer be maintained in its ambiguous position: on the one hand it has a kind of primacy over the institutions of the EU (see art. 3 and 4 of TEU regarding the European Council leadership and the EU 'single institutional framework'), on the other, it is a 'special Council' (art. 121 and 122 of TEC read 'the Council, meeting in the composition of the Heads of State or Government'). In practice very often, the pyramid tends to be reversed and the European Council is reduced to being nothing more than a sort of court of appeal of the Council. The final version of the Constitutional Treaty confirms both the transformation of the European Council into an institution of the EU (art. I, 21) and the 'external representation' role of its President (art. I, 22). For a more detailed comment, see J.V. Louis and M. Dony (eds), *Commentaire J. Megret. Relations extérieures*, no. 12, Editions de l'Université de Bruxelles, 2005.
53. On that point the IGC provided an important amendment of the Convention draft, namely by the Protocol adopted at the Naples Council in 2003 regarding the 'permanent structured cooperation' (art. I, 40.6 and III, 213). On the Convention proposal, see European Convention, Presidium, Secretariat, *Enhanced Co-operations*, CONV 723/03, Brussels, 14 May 2003.
54. An excellent analysis is provided by Quermonne, *La question*, op. cit.
55. See section 3.1 on the social side of the Convention.
56. J. Habermas, *Der gespaltene Westen*, Suhrkamp Verlag, Frankfurt a.M., 2004.

Index

References to notes are in *italic* type.

ABM Treaty, *94*
ACP (Convention between EU and
    African–Caribbean–Pacific
    countries), 55, *102, 105, 141,
    143,* 199, *243*
Afghanistan, 17, 26, 27, 35–6, 57, *92,
    101,* 204
Africa, 31, 35, 55, 60, 67, 70, 108,
    115, 138–41, 164
    Great Lakes, 35, *101,* 139, 202, 204
African Union, 138, 141, 145
Aids, 31
Albert, M., *191, 192*
Al-Qaeda, 4, 17
Amato, G., *92, 276*
Americanism, 19, 21, *96*
Amin, S., 12, *86*
Andean Community, 114, 122,
    129, 131
Annan, K., 5, 7, 65, 68, 70, *99*
anti-Americanism, 23, 58, 220
APEC, 27, 59, 120, 123, 136–7, 218
Arab countries, 24, 70, 114
Archibugi, D., *275*
arms export, *249*
Aron, R., 12, *85, 87,* 125
ASEAN, 28, 36, 55, 114, 118, 122,
    123, 125, 127, 135–8, *147, 150*
ASEM (Asia–Europe Meeting), 29, 56,
    137–8, 143
asylum, 52, 264
Aznar, C.M., *84,* 173, 187, *194*

Baldwin, R., *148*
Balkans, 33, 35, 52, 56, 64, *103,* 203,
    236, *247,* 254
'Barcelona Process', 52, 55, 56,
    127, 143
Barroso, M., *84*
Begg, I., *245*
Belgium, 158, 159, 161, 170, 224, *247*
Bergsten, F., *85*

Bernstein, E., 154, 156
Bhagwati, J., *148, 248*
bilateralism, 60
Blair, T., 32, 36, 71, *84, 93,* 173,
    194, 205, *247,* 260
Bobbio, N., 71, 72, 78, *100, 103,
    248,* 256, 274, 275
Bosnia, 203, 204, *247*
Brandt, W., 38, 202
Brazil, 29, 31, *98,* 115, 116, 126, 131,
    132, 221, 229, 241, 265
    example of de-proliferation, 38
Breslin, S., 147
'Bretton Woods' institutions, 21,
    48, *103,* 111
    link to the UN system, 66–7
Bull, H., *86, 94, 95,* 207, 210, 231,
    246, 256, 274
Bush, G.W., *83, 84, 85, 91, 97,* 120,
    129, 130, 217, 238
    long-term impact on international
    relations, 8, *250*
Buzan, B., *92, 94*

Canada, 24, 51, 241, *244,* 265
capitalism, 109, 241
Caporaso, J., *275*
Carlnaes, W., *246*
Castells, M., *275*
Central Eastern European countries
    (CEEC), 48
    EU enlargement, 35, 52, 59, 213,
    244, 247, 277
    multilateral framework, 35
Cerutti, F., *83, 190, 196, 274*
China, 24, 27–30, 69, 115, 131,
    223, 238
    arms embargo, 27
    conflict with Soviet Union, 18
    economic strength, 34
    as international power, 27, 77
    and Korean crisis, 28, 38

multilateral external relations,
  28–9, 135
nationalism, 27–8, 221
relationship with EU, 29, *92*,
  184, 203, 241, *244*
US oscillations between cooperation
  and containment, 28–9
Chirac, J., 24, 29, *84*, 205
Chomsky, N., *84, 90*
Christianity, 153, 159, 160, 163,
  170, *190–1*, 235, 254, 261
Christian democracy, 124, 157,
  159, 162, 164
'clash of civilizations', 32
  critique, 35, 124–5
Clinton, W., 10, 37, *85*, 129, 262
cold war, 46
  see also world order, bipolar
Community method, 126, 168,
  175, 181, 187, *243*
conflict prevention, 38, 142,
  227, 244–5
Congo, 57, 204, *245*
Constitution, 252, 253, 254
constructivism, 40, 50, 81, 82,
  94, 127, 222, 228, 257
  ideational factors, 40, 47, 82,
    122–3, 222
  and institutionalism, 43–5
  and realism, 41–2
'continental trading state',
  213–18, 233, 240
Cooper, R., *93, 100*
cosmopolitanism, 49, 69, 81,
  242, 261–6, 272, *275*
Council of Europe, 202, 214,
  225, *243*
Cox, R.W., 18, *90*, 119,
  148, 248
Crouch, C., *148, 190*
CSCE/OSCE, 67, 113, 127, 145, 202,
  214, 225, 227, *243, 247*
Czempiel, E.O., *85, 86, 94, 97,
  99, 102, 147*, 264

Dahl, R.A., 64, *98, 192*, 256
Dahrendorf, R., 64, 78, *104*
Dante Alighieri, 216
Deblock, Ch., *244*

defence budgets, *85, 91–2, 103*,
  152, *190*, 208, 220,
  224, 238–9
De Gaulle, Gaullism, 30, 112,
  157, 206, 259
De Giovanni, B., *98, 173, 275*
Deighton, A., *246*
Delors, J., 67, *100, 103, 160*, 174,
  193, 195, 264
democracy
  global multi-level, 108
  liberal, 236
  national, 64
  and neoregionalism, 108, 143–6
  theory, 51, 108, 125
  social, 161
  supranational, 179–81
  various models, 108
  Western, 73
democratic international
  intervention, 73
democratization, 52, 73, 130,
  142, 143–4, *250*, 261
deregulation, 114, 152, 163, 165–7,
  174, 176, 177, 178, 189, 226
Derrida, J., *83*
Deutsch, K., *96*, 127, *149, 243, 273*
developing countries, 53, 81, 121,
  138–41, *150*, 218, 221
diplomacy, 59–60
Dony, M., *277*
Dos Santos, T., 12, *90*
Duchêne, F., 81, 208–9, *246*,
  255, 264, *274*

East Asia, 60
  East Asian security complex,
    28, *92*
economic crisis
  of 1929, 124, 158
  of 1997/99, 124, 135
ECOWAS/CEDEAO, 55, 116,
  138, 140–1, *150*
EFTA, 44, *98*, 112, 135, *247*
embedded capitalism, 21
empire
  Austro-Hungarian, 14
  British, 14, 109
  conception and its critique, 12–18

empire – *continued*
  other (Dutch, Portuguese,
    Spanish . . .), 109
  postmodern, 15–18
  Roman, 14–15, 17–18, 59, 185
environmental issues, 175, 176,
    232, 238, 261, 263
Europe, 27
  continental stability, 35
  memory of past tragedies, 222–4,
    236, 255, 273
  'old and new', 8
  secularized region of the world, 125
European Community (EC), 48, 112,
    123, 126, 198, 208–9, 254, 255
  EEC, 21, 44, 112
  Founding Fathers' Epistemic
    Community, 111–13, 255
European Concert, 25, *96*, 261
European Convention for the
    Protection of Human Rights (and
    'Strasbourg Court'), 52, 225
Europeanization, 212, 227, 259,
    260, 265
European project, 153, 189–90,
    192, 217
European thought, 153, 159, 160
European treaties, 227, 253, 259
  Constitutional Treaty (2004), 32,
    61, 76, 80, *98, 100, 104,* 155,
    168, 179, 184, 186, 205, 211,
    213, 227, 234, 236, *249,* 252
  European Coal and Steel
    Community (1950), 111
  European Defence Community
    (1952), 112, 202, 212
  Single European Act (1986), 80,
    114, 199, 202
  Schengen Treaty, *104,* 205
  Treaty of Amsterdam (1997), 57, 80,
    98, 103, 168, 175, 203, 204,
    212, 243, *245, 246,* 259
  Treaty of the European Community
    (TEC), 53, 187, 189, 243
  Treaty of the European Union
    (TEU), 53, *99, 104, 192,* 204,
    227, *244*
  Treaty of Maastricht (1992), 80,
    168, 170, 174, 177, 199, 201,
    203, 205, 209, 255

Treaty of Nice (2000), 32, *103,*
    205, 211, *245,* 259
Treaty of Rome (1957), 80, 112,
    167, 172, *192,* 199, *243*
Western European Organization
    (WEO, UEO) Treaty, 267
European Union (EU)
  acquis communautaire, 216, 217,
    234, 270
  Broad Economic Policy Guidelines,
    175, 176, 178, 188
  budget, *103,* 141, 167, 182, 183,
    192, 204, 215, 235
  Charter of Fundamental Rights
    of the Union (or 'Charter of
    Nice'), 80, *98,* 168, 186, 267
  Common Agricultural Policy, 21,
    44, 112, 167
  common external political action,
    64, 203
  Common Foreign and Security
    Policy (CFSP), 32, 53, 56, 76,
    80, *99, 103–4,* 201–7, 209, 211,
    215, 228, 231, 236, *245,* 255,
    267–72
  Common Security and Defence
    Policy (CSDP), 204–5, 215,
    267–8
  competencies, 172, 187, 188,
    212, 269
  competition policy, 199, *243*
  conditionality, 52, 53, 81,
    200, 230
  continental stabilizer, 35, 53, 232
  Convention (2002–3), 3, 79, *104,*
    177, 186, 187, 217, 231, 259,
    266, 270, *276, 277*
  convergence policies and national
    diversities, 153–4, 168, 169–74,
    177, 184, 189
  Council of Ministers, 5, 32, 63, 112,
    175–6, 177, 178, 179, 184, *196,*
    211, 212, 270
  crisis of 2005, 30, 186, 189
  democracy, 108, 144, 145, 270–2
  democracy stabilizer, 233–5
  democratic deficit, 165, 171,
    179–80
  development policy, 53, 56,
    140–1, 199

Directory of the Big Three, 60
discourse, 80, 82, 222
economic entity, 33, 53, 198–9, *243*
employment policy, 173, 174, 175,
    176, 178, *194*
'enhanced cooperation', 'closer
    cooperation' (EU), 76, *103–4*,
    205, 239, *245*, 260, 268, 277
enlargement, 60, 210, 219, *244*,
    269, 272, *277*: central-eastern
    enlargement, 52, *100*, 168,
    205–6, *247*; Copenhagen
    Criteria, 234; various trade-offs
    between widening and
    deepening, 210–12, 214, 220,
    232–7
euro, single currency, 32, 48, 53,
    59, *98*, 113, 173, 189, 199,
    216, 269: political implications,
    53, 201, 226
European Armaments, Research and
    Military Capabilities Agency, 268
European Central Bank, 117,
    195, 216
European Charter of Fundamental
    Rights, 52
European Commission, 5, 56, 63,
    76, *92*, 176, 177, 178, 179, 181,
    188, *191, 192, 195*, 204, 233,
    268–9, 270, 276
European Council, 5, 36, 56, 57, 63,
    76, *83, 84, 100*, 168, 171–2, 174,
    175, 176, 178, 179, 180, 181,
    188, *192, 193, 194, 195*, 204,
    217, 244, 268–9, 270, *277*
European Monetary Union, 170,
    172, 174, 177, 189, 213,
    239, 255
European Parliament, 5, 76, 80,
    82, 179, 180, 188, 202, 266,
    269, 270
European Political Cooperation
    (EPC), 80, 113, 202, *244*
European Social Dialogue, 168, 178
external relations, 81, 235, *243*:
    citizens' expectations and EU
    legitimacy, 78, 209, 272; first
    pillar, 213, 228, *243*; horizontal
    and vertical coherence and
    consistency, 63, 79, 200, 208,

211–13, 227, *246*, 267, 270–2;
    political implications, 200–1;
    role of states, 199, 211–13
humanitarian aid policy, 53, 199
influence on near abroad, 52
institutional system, 51, 82, 270
Inter-Governmental Conference
    (IGC), 186, 187, 231
intergovernmentalism, 219
'internal foreign policy', 51, 198,
    229, 235, 253
internal governance, 62, 80, 82,
    174, 178, 185, 211–12, *247*, 269
internal market, 53, 59, 173, 178,
    184, 199
internal multilateralism, 35, 51
international (global) actor, 29, 53,
    61, 143, 198, 201, 209, 215,
    236, 240, 252: critical
    assessment, 206
international political identity, 53,
    54, 67, 75, 80, 82, 162, 185,
    189–90, 206, 209, 214, 223–6,
    231–2, 236, *244*, 254, 267, 273
Justice and Home Affairs
    Cooperation (JHA), 52, *98*
'Laeken Declaration', *83, 186*,
    253, 266
law, 173, 225, 262
leadership, 178, 181, 189
legal personality, 267
legitimacy, 236: through democratic
    participation, 79–80, 179–81,
    231–2; double, 269; through
    increased efficiency, 79;
    substantive, 82, 171, 231
multi-level diplomatic corps, 56, 213
neighbourhood policy, 52, 234, *250*
new methods of policy coordination
    and cooperation, 76
non-state kind of polity, 60, 211,
    213, 252–4, 268–9
peacekeeping missions, 57
'Petersberg tasks', 57, 76, 184, 204,
    212, 239, 259
Political Union, 234, 235, 237, 239,
    257, 260, 261, 262, 263, 270
public sphere, 231–2, 272
Rapid Reaction Force, 57, 75,
    239, *245*

European Union – *continued*
  research policy, 176, 182–5, 188,
    193, 196, 197
  role in reforming global
    governance, 71–4, *99*, 198,
    206–7, 224, 239
  second global actor, 53, 206,
    213, 254
  socio-economic model (models),
    2, 52, 59, 113, 152, 161,
    166, 167–8, 170, 172, 186,
    215, 216, 225, 272
  'Solana paper' ('A Secure Europe in
    a Better World'), 36, 63, *84, 94,
    97, 100, 103*, 236, 239
  'solidarity clause', 267
  space research, 54, 98, 184, 217
  'strategic partnerships', 29, 52, 235,
    241, *244*
  'strategy against proliferation', 36,
    38, 39
  structural foreign policy, 58, 79,
    81, 227–32, 242: definition
    and theoretical dimension,
    228–9
  Structural Funds, 167
  'structured cooperation', 76, 268
  supporting regional cooperation in
    the world, 55, 143, 198, 200
  trade power, 53, 199, *243*
  treaty-making power, 199–200
  unlikely as military power, 30–1,
    33, 54, 75, 77, 152, 204, 207–8,
    220, 231
  values, 153, 155, 172, 174, 183,
    186, 224, 225, 255–6, 263
  weighted voting (Council), 187,
    268, 270, 277
  workshop of regulation and
    regional and global gover-
    nance, 52, 62, 66, 72, 73, 80,
    82, 143, 146, 168, 198, 233,
    259, 262–3: limits and
    discrepancies, 81, 146
  'world's Scandinavia'
    ('Scandinavian Europe'), 58,
    60, 169, 222, 225, 226–7
  see also 'Lisbon Strategy', 'Galileo
    Project', European treaties

Fascism, 155, 223, 224, 238
Fawcett, L., *150*
federalism, 110, 153, 168, 187, 213,
    220, 256–7, 261, 262, 263, 268–70
Ferguson, N., 14–15, *87, 91*
Fischer, J., 24, 76, *84*
foreign policy, *148*, 209–12, 224,
    227–8, *244*
'fortress Europe', 114, 166, 218–22,
    235, 240
France, 19, 24, 30–2, 51, 53, 63, *92,
    98*, 155, 158, 159, 161, 170, 182,
    189, 202, 219, 224, 239
  anti-EC waves and their limits, 112
  Franco-German axis, 30, 60, 76,
    104, 112–13, 132, 173, 209,
    235, 239, 259, 271
  Franco-German reconciliation, 223
free market economics, 166
Free Trade Area of the
    Americas (FTAA), 17, 56, 59, 120,
    123, 129–30, 218
free trade zones (FTZ), 44, 59, 130,
    166, 214, 216
Fukuyama, F., 10, *85, 88*, 262
functionalism and neo-functionalism,
    41–2, *95*, 213

G7 and G8, 67, 79, 139, 199
  British Presidency, 31, 139
  French Presidency, 31
  reform, *92*
G20, *98*, 131
Gadamer, G., 182, 185
'Galileo project', 54, *99*, 176,
    184, *196*, 217
Galtung, J., *274*
Gamble, A., *89, 93*
GATT, 21, 54
  art. XIX, 44
  art. XXIV, 44, 112, 123, 200, 240
  Tokyo Round, 44
  Uruguay Round, 44
Germany, 3, 25, 29, 30–2, 116, 158,
    159, 161, 170, 182, 202, 252
  axis with France, 30–2, 203
  Bonner Republik, 60, 216–17, 238
  civilian Power, 51, 222–4, 239,
    254, 259, *275*

misleading interpretation as 'fourth Reich', 31
Nazi Germany external relations, 46: imperial regionalism, 109, 110
Ostpolitik, 202
peace-oriented public opinion, 30–1, 202
Giddens, A., *94*, 156, *192*
Gill, S., 19, *90*
Gilpin, R., 16, 18–19, 20, 54, *85, 88, 89, 99*, 119, *147*, 201, *244, 248*
Giscard d'Estaing, V., 214, 266, *276*
globalization, 40, 106, 109, 240, 261
  civil society, 68
  competition, 216
  critical theory, *85*
  definitions, 10, *85*, 115, 119, 165
  discourse of a globalization beneficial to all, 10, 32, 115
  emergencies, 69, 79, 258, 261
  'fragmegration', 106, 218
  globalism, 67, 119, 120, 166, 218
  global markets, 218, 225
  interplay with regionalism, 114, 119, 120–1, *148*, 153, 169, 221
  interplay with states, 108, 115, 116, 120, *147*, 153, 258
  limits, 11, 23, 115, 164
  social impact, 153, 170
Gnesotto, N., *100, 246, 250*
Goetschy, J., *193, 195*
Gold Standard, 21, 45, *96*, 110
Gorbachev, M., 202
governance, global, 10, 258, 264
  accountability, 64, 145, 262: mixed multi-level system of control, 78
  agenda, *101*, 224
  authority, 40, 42, 43, 117, 165, 170
  Clinton era as cradle of global governance research, 10
  concept, 10–11, *86, 101*
  democratization, 66, 78, 81, *101*, 143–4, 273
  dilemma, 64
  effectiveness, 64: implementation deficit, 12, 65–6
  functional logic versus territorial logic, 115–17, 240

imbalances, asymmetries, 218, 240
informal networks on global issues, 65
interaction with regional governance, 66, 145, *148*
legitimacy, 59, 64, 78
multi-level, 12, 77, 106, 108, 165, 240, 262
policies, 65: policy coordination, 48
polity, architecture, 66–7
securization, 56, 207, 265
subnational entities, 115, 117
theories, 10–12, *101*
government, 11
  EU, 256–7, 268–70
  mixed, 76, 80, 182, 188, 211
  national, 126, 177, 178, 181
Gowan, P., *248, 274, 275*
Gramsci, A., 12, 19–20, *87, 89, 90*, 156
Gulf War, 5, 18, 71, 78, *103*, 206

Haas, E., *95, 146, 243*
Habermas, J., 25, 71, 72, 81, *83, 91, 94, 98, 103*, 152, *190, 196*, 217, *248, 251*, 263, 273, 276, 277
Hardt, M., 15–16, *87*
Hassner, P., *83, 87, 91, 97, 103*
Hegel, G.W.F., 7, 12, 18, 19, 20, 57, 63, 72, 73, *94, 100*, 117, *148*, 154, 155, 252, 257, 273, *275*
hegemonic stability theory, 18–24
hegemony
  definitions, *19, 97*
  Gramscian conception of hegemony as dominance plus consensus, 19–20
  liberal and realist conception, 20
  post-hegemonic era, 48, 112–14, 124, 129, 229
  see also US, empire, unipolarism
Held, D., *86, 104, 275*
Hettne, B., *99*, 125, *146, 149, 248*
Higgott, R., *99, 148, 150*
Hill, C., *244, 246, 247, 276*
Hinsley, E.H., 256, *275*
Hirst, P., *85*
Hobbes, Th., 20, *93*, 154, 257
Hobsbawm, E., 22, *87, 91, 93*

Hobson, J., 11–12, *86*
Hoffmann, S., *83, 85, 91,*
    92, 244
Holland, M., *246*
Holocaust, 68, 255
Hu Jintao, 28, 29
human rights, 27, 48, 78, *104–5,*
    155, 158, 241, 242
  EU policy, *104*, 232, *255*
  Universal Declaration, 68
humanitarian intervention, 62,
    68, 78, 241
Huntington, S., *87, 93*, 124, *149*
hyperglobalizers, 11

identity, 115, 122, 152, 162, 165,
    166, 182, 189
immigration, 52, 166, 167, 169,
    219, 234, 264
imperialism, 46
  economic and political theories,
    12–13
India, 27, 34, 37, 51, 69, 115, 131,
    184, 203, 221, 241, *244*
individualism, 154
Indonesia, 35, 69, 221, 228, 265
information and communication
    technologies (ICT), 29, 116, 164,
    165, 173, 183, 184
institutionalism (liberal
    institutionalism), 117–20, 213
  definition, 41
  overcoming the limits of realism,
    17, 40–1, 81, 228–9, 257–9
  supporting research on
    multilateralism, 40–50
international arms trade, 10, *85*
international competitiveness, 52
International Criminal Court (ICC),
    4, 54, 65, *94, 99*
international institutionalization,
    42, 118, 119
International Labour Office (ILO),
    65, 169
  Geneva Strategy, 66
international law, 62, 80
  violations of, *103*
International Monetary Fund (IMF),
    47, 124, 165, 169

international political economy, 19,
    53–4, 228
international public goods, 14, 18–21,
    72, *89*, 225
  and regional public goods, 62
international regimes theory, 40, *95*,
    118, 228, 257
inter-regionalism, 129
  EU-centred, 48, 55–6, 60, 63, 128,
    129, 137–8, 140, 142–3, 144,
    150–1, 200, 220–1, 240–1, *244*:
    difficulties, 56, 133
  South–South, 29, 131
  US-centred, 56, 123, 128, 129–30,
    132–3, 137–8, 218, 221
international system, 9, 39
  see world order
Iran, 36, 64, 232
  nuclear programme, 37, 39, 238
Iraq, 232
  regime change, 8, 73
  post-war reconstruction, 24–6, 73
  war, 7, 24, 26, 38, 70, 73, 201,
    207, 217, 254
Islam, 233
  Islamic fundamentalism, 7
  Islamic world, 36, *84*, 234
Israeli–Palestinian conflict, 7, 26, 27,
    56, 67, *101*, 114, 202, 238
Italy, 28, 31, 51, 216, 223, 224, 238
  Constitution, 254, 259

Japan, 27, 38, 51, 70, 77, *98*, 109, 136,
    138, 178, 183, 203, 223, *248*, 265
  bilateral relationship with US, 21, 44
  Constitution, 223, 255
  imperial regionalism between the
    two world wars, 109
  and neighbours, 28, 109, 255
  strategic partnership with EU,
    241, *244*
Joffé, G.H., *94*
'just war', 71, *103*

Kagan, R., 23, 57, *84, 87, 245,*
    246, 276
Kant, I., 19, 58, 72, 154, 223,
    251, 263, 264
Kaplan, M., 37, *92, 94*

Katzenstein, P.J., *94*, 239, *275*
Kelsen, H., 72, 81, *88*
Kennedy, J.F., 23, 75
Kennedy, P., 22, 54, *99*
Keohane, R.O., 17, 40–3, 62, 64,
    83, 84, 89, 91, 95, 100, 104, 105,
    177, *244, 250, 274*
  complex interdependence theory,
    19, 41, 53, 111, *243, 249, 275*
  institutionalism, 40, 43, *148*, 258
  regime theory, 40–1
  theory of hegemonic stability,
    18–19, *90, 147, 276*
Keynes, J.M., 12, 44, 112, 160, 162,
    163, 165, *191*, 264
Kindleberger, Ch., 18–19, *89, 91, 147*
Kissinger, H., 24, 76, 114
knowledge economy, 54, 122, 167,
    172, 176, 182–3, 189, *192–3,*
    225, 230, 231
Kohl, H., 203
Kojève, A., 81, 264
Korea, 27, 35, 137, 223
  North Korea, 4, 27, 37, 38, 238
  six-parties talks, 28, 38
  South Korea, 38
Kosovo War, 6, 71, 102, 207
Krasner, D.S., 47, *95, 148*
Krugman, P., *91, 148*
Kupchan, Ch., *85, 91, 94, 103*
Kyoto Protocol on the Environment,
    4, 54

Lamy, P., *84, 98, 99, 150, 276*
Latin America, 24, 55, 56, 60, 70, 108,
    115, 124, 129, 144, 202
  regional cooperation, 131–5, *244*
  South American Community of
    States, 134
Laursen, F., *149, 150*
legitimacy, 61
  democratic, 180
  global governance, 41
  input (by participation), 179, *195*
  output, 25, 171, 231
  regional governance, 132
  social, 179–80
liberalism, 109, 153, 157, 163,
    170, 254

liberalization
  economic, 60, 65, 165
  trade, 56
'Lisbon Strategy' (EU, 2000–10)
  aims and objectives, 171–4, *192–3,*
    225, 260
  democratic deficit, 179–81, 187
  implementation, 177–9, *193–4*, 231
  failure, 220
  international implications, 183–4
  methods of governance, 66, 176–7,
    181, 187
  research policy, 177, 182–5
  treaty reform, 186–9, 272
  see also Open Method of
    Coordination
Louis, J.-V., *277*
Lowy, T., *87*, 211, *247*

Macedonia, 204, *247*
Machiavelli, N., 110, 154, 224, 256
Magnette, P., *93, 190, 193, 195, 245,*
    249, 274
Majone, G., *148, 195, 277*
Manners, J., *246*
'Marshall Plan', 44, *96*, 229, 261
Marx, K., 155, 228
Maull, H.W., *275*
Mearsheimer, J.J., 35, *93*
Mediterranean
  Partnership, 52, 200
  region, 48, 60, 109, 200, 203, *244*
MERCOSUR, 55, 114, 119, 123,
    126, 129, 131–5, *147, 149*
Meyer, Th., *93, 149, 192*
Middle East, 25, 35, 36, 59,
    109, 202, 203, 206, 233, 236, 254
military and political intervention
  ad hoc coalitions, 5
  as asymmetric war, 7
  distinction between different
    cases, 5
  legitimacy, 5
Milner, H.V., *148, 149, 249*
Milward, A.S., *146, 192*
Mitterrand, F., 203
Monar, J., *98*
Monnet, J., 30, 47, 51, 110, 112,
    126, *195*, 229

Montesquieu, Ch. S. de, 53, 78, *87*, 125, 128, 188
Moravcsik, A., *103, 104, 146, 147, 148, 151*, 179, *195, 276*
Morgenthau, H., 20
most favoured nation clause (MFN), 44, 46, *96*, 111, 221
Multilateral Agreement on Investments, 217
multilateral organizations, 118, 221, 222
multilateralism, 258
  'ad hoc', 48
  authority and power, 43
  constitutional, cosmopolitan, 81
  definition and history, 43, 50, *96*
  economic, 21
  effective, 63, *100*
  EU, 39, 45–8, 54, 60, 62, 77
  European internal, 47, 52
  and hegemonic stability, 21
  limits and durability of, 46
  new, 10, 143, 237: as a potential world order, 39–42, 50, 58, 77, 240, 263, 273; as 'subsidiary government of world order', 71–2
  political, 46
  regional, 48
  US-centred, 22, 40, 43–6, 110
  values and interests of promoting powers, 40, 48
multipolarism, 10
  definition, 24–5
  limits of, 25, 27, 31
Myrdal, G., 154, 182, 264

NAFTA, 24, 114, 123, 125, 129–30
national economic policies, 44
nationalism, 35, 124, 125, 142, 218, 226
  economic, 221
NATO, 25, 46, 74, 97, 127, 145, 184, 204, 213, 221, *246*, 260, 268, *276*
  art. 5, 46, 47
  reform, 76, 237
Negri, A., 15–16, *87–8*
neo-conservative revolution, 162–9, 189

neo-corporatism, 159, 161, 171
neo-liberalism, 113, 152, 153, 265
neo-marxism, 13, 15–16, 19, 90, *96*
neo-medievalism, 11, 65, 116–17, 120, 146, 265
neo-mercantilism, 54, 166, 220–1
neo-regionalism, new regionalism, 55–6, 82, *90, 99*, 120–7, 129, 221
  benevolent and malevolent, 221
  bottom-up process, 108, 110, 114, 131–2, 136, 143, 229
  cultural factors, 122, 124
  definition, 110
  domestic democratization, 144–5
  domino effect, 123
  economic factors, 121
  endogenous factors, 121, 123, 131, 137
  'EU model', 108, 110, 125, 131, 142, 213–14
  exogenous factors, 114, 123, 137
  impact on global governance, 49–50, 56, *102*, 124, 240
  interaction with globalization, 121, 139, 141, 169, 214, 221
  internal impact, 124
  interplay with cosmopolitanism, 262
  interplay with multilateralism, 64, 240
  multidimensional and structural phenomenon, 55, 106, 114, 123–4, 143
  political factors and dimension, 121, 131–2, 135, 136, 139, 141, 142, 218: and democracy, 108, 131–2, 142, 143–5; establishing peace between previous enemies, 229
  resistance to crisis and unipolarism, 55, 124, 142
  socio-economic factors, 122
  systemic factors, 122, 123, 128
  variations, 55, 135, 229
NEPAD, *102*, 139
networks, 42, 47, 52, 139, 165, 217, 237
new economy, 122, 170, 172
Nicolaydis, K., *83, 276*

non-governmental organizations
(NGOs), 69, 78, 80, *86*
normative issues, 51, 58, 60, 61,
222, 261
Non-Proliferation Treaty (NPT),
37, 45, *94*
Nye, J.S., 2, 50, 54, *83, 87, 97, 99,*
222, 231, *244, 249*

OAS, 131, 145
OECD, *190*
OEEC, 22, 111–12
Open Method of Coordination
(OMC), 66, 171–5, 176, 177,
181, 184, *192–3*

Padoan, P., *148*
Padoa-Schioppa, T., *83,* 216
Pakistan, 37
Patten, Ch., *244–5, 246*
Payne, A., *150*
peacekeeping missions, 78
regional dimension, 67
Peterson, J., *245, 247, 276*
Polanyi, K., *91, 191*
poliarchy, 12, 211–12, 257
political parties, 164, 165, 188
politics, 60, 61
declaration of war and state of
exception as negation of, 61
postmodernism, 11, 17, 49, 63, 242
Powell, C., *97*
power, international, 210, 256
and 'absolute right', 20, 63, *100,* 119
American, 12–14, 61, 207, 231
civilian, 2, 29, 43, 48, 50, 57, 58,
60, 62, 73, 75, 77, 80, 82, *100,*
134–5, 152–3, 169, 183, 185,
207–10, 222–34, 239, 254–61:
efficiency assessment, 74, 206;
legitimacy, 231–2; mixed
government, 268–71; realistic
definition, 51, 199
civilizing, 2, 70, 81, 208, 261
collective, 50, 55, 56, 58, 274
critique of governance theories,
10–12
critique of postmodernism,
16–18, 49

critique of realism, 209, 223, 224
distinction from influence, 216,
219, 222–3, 225
French model, *Europe puissance,* 30,
207–8, 210, 219, *246*
hard, 2, 14, 57, 231
hegemonic, 58
interrelation between pre-political
and political dimensions, 53–4
neo-mercantilist, 218, 221
normative, 222
politics, 51, 54, 58, 115, 207, 221
socio-economic dimension,
152–4
soft, 2, 28, 48, 54, 222
shifts of power, 29, 77
structural, 54, 230–1, 258
Preferential Trade Agreement (PTA),
44, 121, 220–1, 230
preventive war, 23, 25, 31, 38, 66,
68, 130
opposed to preventive policies,
64, 66
Prodi, R., *84, 99,* 183, 184, 189,
196, 246
protectionism, 16, 67, 123, 133,
142, 166, 216, 219, 226, 240
public opinion, 25, 66, 79, 80,
82, *83*
European, 30, 31, 165, 180, 189,
223, 231, 237, 238

Quermonne, J.L., *151, 196, 277*

Rasmussen, P.N., *84, 101*
rational choice theory, 40, 118
Rawls, J., *98*
realism and neo-realism, 24–9, 37,
81, 116, 146, 228, 256
challenging the concept of
civilian power, 51, 223,
256, 264
challenging institutionalism, 120
interpreting multilateralism, 40
interpreting the second half of
twentieth-century Europe,
30–3, 201
limits, 258
reformism, 163

regional cooperation and integration
  convergence rate, 121, 140, 141
  deeper integration, 124, 129, 135,
    142, 144
  'EU model', 125, 128, 141
  institutionalization, 119, 128, 132,
    135–6, 141, 213, 262
  intraregional trade, 138
  positive and negative integration,
    126, 153, 166, 168, 174,
    178, 189
  security cooperation, 127, 132,
    135, 141
  spillover dynamics, 119, 135
  theories and comparative analysis,
    125–8, 141–2
regionalism, 66, 106, 108–10,
  113, 138
  see also neo-regionalism
regionalization, 109, 115
regional organizations, 55, 60, 62, 66,
  102, 115, 117, 119, 129–46, 218,
  221, 229, 231, 240, 273
regionness, 109, 125
regulation, 44, 117, 163, 166–7
religion, 233
Remacle, E., *193, 245, 249*
republicanism, 116, 223, 224,
  226, 259, 272
research agenda, 64
Rice, C., 4, 36, 75, *84*, 238, *250*
'Rio de Janeiro Interregional Process',
  55, 129–30, 143
Rischard, F.J., 65, *101*
Rodrigues, J.M., *192–3, 195, 196*
Roosevelt, F.D., 22, 23, 40, 45, 211
Rorty, R., *87*
Rosenau, J., 10–11, 43, 49, *86, 87*,
  106, *146, 147, 148, 190, 247*,
  264, *275*
Rosencrance, R.N., 217, *247*
Rousseau, J.J., 223
Ruggie, J.G., 40, 42, 44, 45, *89*,
  94, 95, 248, 275
Rumsfeld, D., *93, 250*
Russia, 24, 26, 27, 52, 59, 124, 203
  Chechnya, 27, 35
  military strength and economic
    weakness, 34

relations with EU and US, 27, 234,
  235, 241, *247*
relationship with China, 28

SAARC, 55, 114, 132, *147*
SADC, 55, 114, 138–41, *147*
Santander, S., *249*
Sapir, A., *192, 248*
Sassoon, D., 190
Scandinavia, 58, 60, 109, 155, 158,
  161, 169, 170, 183, 224, 226, 259
Scharpf, F.W., 126, 179, *192, 195,
  196, 247*
Schlesinger, A., 12, *87*, 211
Schmidt, V.A., *192*
Schmitt, C., 212, 256, 257, 273
Schmitter, Ph., 145, *149, 151, 190,
  191, 192, 195*, 215, *247*
Schumpeter, J., 11–12, *86*
Second World War, 44, *99*, 109,
  158, 161, 201
security, 49, 66, 67, 118, 208, 213
  collective, 46, 127
  community, *96*, 127, *149*, 253
  comprehensive, 236
  distinct national and regional
    needs, 67, 72
  different threat perception,
    237, 238
  dilemmas, 57, *93*
  global, 77, 227
  internal and external, 219
  regional, 127, 132, *149*
Seidelmann, R., *93*
September 11th 2001 attacks, 2, 4,
  6, 10, 47, *83, 84*, 253, 256
Smith, H., *242, 249*
Smith, K.E., *99, 100, 242*
Smith, M., *242*
social democracy, 153, 155, 158–9,
  162, 163, 170
socialism, 154, 254
social market economy, 159
Söderbaum, F., *99, 150*
Solana, J., 36, *84, 94, 100*, 204, *246*
solidarity, 154–7, 159, 162, 166, 167,
  168, 169, 170, 172, *190*, 222,
  225, 226
Sorensen, G., *146, 147*

South Africa, 29, 31, 116, 131, 138–9, 202, 204, 221, 229
South-East Asia, 27–8, 109, 124
sovereignty, 60, 77, 106–7, 118, 126, 213, 219, 235–6
  classical, 17, 51, *89*, 137, 138, 165, 212, 229, 240, 242, 252, 255, 256, 269–70
  and global governance, 42, 68
  ironies of, 17
  shared, 1, 62, 72, 254, 256–7
  see also power, state
Soviet Union, 18, 22, 33, 45, 59, 68, 202, 213, 270
Spinelli, A., 202
state, 164, 221
  competitor state, 107, 165, 166, 173, *191–2*
  core functions, 12, 212
  decline, 258
  failed, 8, 35–9, 63, *101*
  hegemonic, 19, 47
  internal governance, 107, 258
  and international cooperation, 42, 45, 49, 106–7, 122, 172, 222
  national variations, 106, 116, 141, 146, 165, 220
  open, 111–12, *151*
  'rogue states', 4, 17
  role in the economy, 44, 164–5, *191*
  state-centred paradigm, 106, 115–16, 199, 254, 256
  transformation and adaptation, 41, 107
Stavridis, S., *100*
Stein, A., *89*
Strange, S., 54, 119, *147*, 230, *249, 275*
Strauss, L., 264, *276*
Streeck, W., *148, 190, 192, 247*
struggle against poverty, 31, 48, 65, 68, *102*, 238
subsidiarity, 71–2, 181, 212
Summers, L., *148*
supranationalism
  EU, 52, 80, 165–6, 170–2, 179–81, 200, 215, 259, 266, 267, 272
  functionalist theory, 41
  global, 68, 72, 78

institutions, 42, 165–6
  regional, 107, 117, 132, 146
Sweden, 51, 183, 222, 226

Tanaka, A., *86*
Taylor, P., *88, 149*
technology, 37, 163, 164, 169, 170, 172, 174, 175, *196*, 218, 231, 261
territoriality, 16–17, 116–17, 146, 240
terrorism, new, informal, 7–8, 37, 59, 209, 218, 264
  definition, 4, 6, *84–85*
  fight against, 6, 27, 63, 66, 73, 75, *83, 84*, 137, 204, 238, 263, 268
  link to failed states, 36
  sense of insecurity, 6, 218–19
  see also September 11th 2001
Therborn, G., *100, 149, 192, 248*
Toqueville, A. de, 12, 53, 78, 160, 199, 223
trade unions, 44, 157–9, 164, 165, 179, *194*
transatlantic relations, 4, 58, 204, 217, 221, 237–42
  alliance, 49, 112, 208, 255
  conflicting economic and geopolitical interests, 238
  different security threat perception, 237, 238
  partnership, 7, 63, 74–7
  rift, 45, 72
  triangle, 130, 132–3
transgovernmentalists, 11
transnational corporations (TNCs), 116, 117, 164
transnational relations, 41, 52, 55, 82, 116–17, 122–3, 125
transregionalism, 129, 144
Tsoukalis, L., *246, 274*
Turkey, 124, 204, 219, 232–7, *250*

Ukraine, 52, 59, 64, 203, 232, 234–5, 237, *247*
unilateralism, 9, 25, 119, 242
United Kingdom (UK), 155, 158, 163, 217
  and EU, 31–2, 51, 112, 187, 212, 239, 260

United Kingdom – *continued*
  international hegemony, 21, 40,
    110, *191*
  and war on terrorism, 32
United Nations (UN), 62, 221, 239
  Atomic Agency, AIEA, 37, 39
  'Brahimi Report', 70–1, *101, 102*
  CEPAL, *87*
  civil society, 69
  conferences, 54, 65, *101*
  corruption scandals, 69
  Economic Security Council
    proposal, 31, 67
  General Assembly, 69
  human security, *102*
  inertia and failures, 71
  link to Bretton Woods
    institutions, 66
  'Millennium Report', 5, 65, 68
  peacekeeping, 45, 70
  principles and values, 227
  reform, 64, 66, 68–71, *101*, 262:
    democratic intervention and
    multilateral use of force, 73–4;
    obstacles, 69–70; potential
    role of regional groupings
    and rotation, 70
  representation of regional
    organizations, 66, 72, 144
  'San Francisco Charter', 46, 62, 68,
    259, 267: Chapter VII, 68, 70
  Security Council, 5, 24–5, 55,
    68, 70, 76, *103*, 259, 265:
    Resolutions, 3, 24, 25, 26,
    91, 92
  UNDP, 134
  war on terrorism, 24–5
  Wise Men Report, 2004, *102*
United States
  as archetypal federal republic, 12
  decision-making process, 211
  declining hegemony, 22–3, 216, *244*
  defence budget, 33–4, *91–2*, 152,
    190, 207, 238
  domestic democratic system, 12,
    17, *89*, 120, 238, 257
  economic power, 33–4, 178
  empire ideology, 14, *87–8*
  globalism, 113, 119, 218, 221, 240

  international hegemony, 21–2, 44,
    46, 109–13, 216, 241
  isolationism and neo-isolationism,
    38, 46, 238
  limits of power, 24, 63, 119, 184
  'long war against terrorism', 8, 25,
    36, 38, 71
  military power, 13–14, 25, 33–4, 73,
    77, *85, 88, 91*, 202, 207
  multilateralism, 26, 110–11,
    129, 240
  neo-conservatives, 5, 9, 12–14, 31,
    57, *87–8*
  new security strategy, 4, 59, 75, *83,
    84, 97*, 238, 241, *250*
  'Pax Americana', 8, *88*, 201
  public opinion, 60, *89*
  strategy of emerging markets, 218
  supremacy, 22–3, 73, 119, 130, 205,
    207, 237, 265
  trade and current payment deficits,
    12, 27
  UN, 46: Security Council, 24–5
  see also unipolarism, empire and
    hegemony

Van Langenhove, L., *99, 147, 150*

Wallace, H., *192, 195, 275*
Wallace, W., *82, 147, 244, 275*
Wallerstein, I., *90*
Waltz, K., 20, 36, *90, 91–2, 93, 94,
    95*, 228, *249, 275*
Waltzer, M., *103*
'Washington consensus', 47, 153,
    165, 241
weapons of mass destruction (WMD)
  multilateral anti-proliferation
    regimes and organizations
    (HCOC, MTCR, AIEA), 39
  proliferation, 4, 35, 36, 59, 73,
    204, 209, 241–2
Weber, M., 11, *96*, 117, 128, 256
Weiler, J.H.H., *83, 105, 151, 192,
    195, 274, 276*
Welfare State, 152, 163, *192*, 225
  chauvinism, 226
  national, 40, 52, 153, 154, 157–62,
    167, 169, 173, 187, *191*, 264

single European system as
  unrealistic, 171
Wessels, W., *148, 195, 247*
Weyemberg, A., *98*
Whitman, R.G., *83, 246*
Wilson, W., *83*
World Bank, 67, 169
world order, international system,
  9, 39, 50, 58, 218
  anarchy, 35–9, 47, 60, 80, 242
  balance of power, 20, 27,
    33–4, 222
  'bifurcated', 49, *86*
  bipolar, 24, 44–5, 96, 122, 199,
    201, 207, 222, 241, 255
  change of 1971, 44, 113
  change of 1989–91, 2, 206, 207,
    210, 224, 255
  change of 2001, 6, 10, 207, 253
  disorder, 34, 264
  fragmented, 10, 60, 218
  heterogeneous, 10, 33–4, 39, 241
  hierarchical, 49, *94*, 218
  legitimate, 82
  multilateral, 108, 115: new multi-
    lateral, 39, 50, 61, 71–4, 240–2

multipolar, 10, 24, 26, 33–4, 45,
  60, 221, 273
post-cold war, 206, 214, 218, 264
transition, 4, 7, 10–13, 35, 39, 49
unipolar, 4, 9, 39, 60, 142, 222
unit veto, 37
universalistic, 26
Westphalian, 1, 41, 58, 68, 117,
  142, 228, 231, 242, 252, 272
see also empire
world politics, 41
World Trade Organization (WTO)
  Cancún, 29, 53, *98, 99*
  China, 27–29, 53
  constitutionalization, 65, *104*,
    262–3
  dispute settlement mechanism,
    44, 65
  Doha agenda, 53, 65, *98*, 200
  EU role, 200, 262
  intellectual property rights, 29
  Millennium Round, Seattle, 12, *98*
  original objectives, 65
  uncertainties, 122, 144

Yugoslavia, 35, 78, 115, 203, 206, *245*